WITHDRAWN

DEMOCRACY IN THE UNDEMOCRATIC STATE: THE GERMAN REICHSTAG ELECTIONS OF 1898 AND 1903

In *Democracy in the Undemocratic State* Brett Fairbairn offers a probing analysis of the pivotal Reichstag campaigns of 1898 and 1903. At the turn of the century the German party system showed signs of stress as the elites who directed the older, more established parties were confronted by the new populist appeals of both left and right. It was in this volatile political climate that the German Social Democratic Party experienced explosive growth. The elections of 1898 and 1903 were the turning points, as nationalists and governments tried to use Germany's new battle-fleet and protectionist tariff to rally patriotic voters. However, as Fairbairn demonstrates, it was the opposition of the Social Democratic Party that scuttled the reigning parties' strategies, climaxing in its three-million-vote victory in 1903. Fairbairn challenges the popular misconception of Imperial Germany as a purely authoritarian state, and raises intriguing questions about how a modern, participatory democratic culture evolved under the undemocratic *Kaiserreich*.

Based on original archival research, this study makes a significant contribution to historiographical debates and our understanding of turn-of-the-century electoral democracy.

BRETT FAIRBAIRN is Professor of History at the University of Saskatchewan.

BRETT FAIRBAIRN

Democracy in the Undemocratic State: The German Reichstag Elections of 1898 and 1903

UNIVERSITY OF TORONTO PRESS
Toronto Buffalo London

© University of Toronto Press Incorporated 1997
Toronto Buffalo London
Printed in Canada

ISBN 0-8020-0795-3 (cloth)
ISBN 0-8020-7154-6 (paper)

Printed on acid-free paper

Canadian Cataloguing in Publication Data

Fairbairn, Brett, 1959–
    Democracy in the undemocratic state : the German
    Reichstag elections of 1898 and 1903

    Includes bibliographical references and index.
    ISBN 0-8020-0795-3 (bound)   ISBN 0-8020-7154-6 (pbk.)

    1. Germany. Reichstag – Elections, 1898.   2. Germany.
    Reichstag – Elections, 1903.   3. Germany – Politics
    and government – 1871–1918.   I. Title.

    JN3838.F35 1997   324.943'084   C96-931688-7

University of Toronto Press acknowledges the financial assistance to its publishing
program of the Canada Council and the Ontario Arts Council.

This book has been published with the help of a grant from the Humanities
and Social Sciences Federation of Canada, using funds provided by the Social
Sciences and Humanities Research Council of Canada.

Contents

Figures and Tables

Figures

Tables

viii   Figures and Tables

Preface

No one can pretend that Imperial Germany – the *Kaiserreich*, 1871–1918 – was a democratic place. And yet its elections illuminate a complex society in which much more was going on than simple authoritarian manipulation. The subtle (and sometimes unsubtle) interplay of democratic and anti-democratic tendencies becomes only more fascinating the deeper one probes.

This book examines democratic participation and culture, parties and election campaigning, under the authoritarian regime of Imperial Germany. Much historiography (often as part of a legitimate search for explanations of twentieth-century National Socialism) has emphasized the ways in which democratic institutions and values were deformed in Germany. But there was another side to the coin: a substantially positive culture of democratic participation was emerging in turn-of-the-century Germany, despite attempts by the state and certain elites to oppose this development. In these respects, the German experience was rather 'normal' for a world in which a larger number of twentieth-century regimes have been authoritarian, or only partially democratic, than have been full democracies along the pattern of the Western industrialized nations.

When I began doing research more than a decade ago into turn-of-the-century German elections, it seemed more than likely that voting results under such a regime would only illuminate a system of static political and social structures. After all, election results did not vary wildly from one election to the next (or, at least, not as much as in some modern democracies); and it seemed clear from the literature that 'the story' of German politics consisted of the repeated successes of reactionary elites. But three factors led me further and further astray from this orthodoxy. The first was the influence of a group of Anglo-American scholars, especially David

Blackbourn and Geoff Eley, who were arguing energetically for a revised view of the *Kaiserreich* in which more stress was laid on elements of instability and change. While I do not view the present book as a contribution to a school of thought, there is no doubt that contemporary historiographical debates provided me with an opening into a relatively little-touched field of research. The second factor was my own, undoubtedly also Anglo-(North) American bias towards viewing elections as dynamic contests between ideas, organizations, and people – and not only as sociological institutions reflecting underlying structures. There is a certain drama to elections, when they are not a sham. And finally, there was the research itself. As I read the documents, it seemed clearer and clearer that German elites did not control these elections – in fact, they hardly seem to have understood them.

The right to vote in national elections was granted to the great majority of adult German males in the 1867/1871 constitutions, giving Germany a broader suffrage than most other countries at that time. The establishment of a legal entitlement, however, did not immediately produce a culture in which great numbers made effective use of the right to vote. Instead, participation was initially low, and increased where elites sought to mobilize voters to create coherent communities of support – as in the *Kulturkampf* or 'cultural struggle' of the 1870s, or later election campaigns on nationalist issues. A generation after the introduction of the broad suffrage – by the 1890s – participation was increasingly coming to be driven by considerations of class, economic interest, and questions of the equity or 'fairness' of fiscal and social-economic policy. These issues gave new meaning and content to electoral participation. The rise of newer parties, movements, and populist styles of campaigning was driven by candidates and elites who appealed self-consciously to the social-economic concerns of voters.

Contemporaries – especially officials in the established liberal and conservative parties and in the government – perceived these changes as signs of 'fragmentation' of the political nation under the impact of competing 'interests.' One such sign they saw was the rise of the Social Democratic Party of Germany (SPD), an oppositional and ostensibly revolutionary party which they abhorred. Such officials also generally criticized economic interest groups like the Agrarian League (Bund der Landwirte, BdL) using the same language they used against Social Democracy, and the same went for right-wing populists like Germany's anti-Semites. Party and state officials attempted to resist such trends by appealing to a culture of nationalism, patriotism, and hierarchy. In some cases, they resorted to coercion and intimidation of voters, harassment of opposition candidates, or manipulation of the election process or its results. The striking thing about turn-of-the-century Germany is not that reactionary elites attempted these things, but rather that they largely failed. The parties that 'won' in popular support were not, at the turn of the century, the ones favoured by the regime.

Nowhere was this more apparent than in the elections of 1898 and 1903, which illustrated the abject failure of the strategies of *Sammlungspolitik* (the 'politics of rallying together') and social imperialism favoured by some in the government and in the older parties. *Sammlungspolitik*, as articulated by Prussian finance minister Johannes von Miquel, was an electoral strategy of rallying patriotic forces behind a platform of protectionist tariffs for agriculture and industry. This did not succeed, for several reasons. First, tariffs were not a unifying issue for the governmental parties, but a divisive one. The tariff issue generated a great deal of the 'heat' that occurred in these two elections, contributing to tensions in the governmental camp, to breakaway agrarian candidacies on the pro-tariff side, and to breakaway liberal candidacies on the anti-tariff side. Nor was the pro-tariff position electorally helpful: the tariff issue helped the opposition Social Democrats score large electoral breakthroughs. And, in any case, rallying the governmental camp was not enough, because the governmental parties were declining in overall popular support. To stop the Social Democrats, the government needed the support of free-trading left liberals, a strategy that later proved its effectiveness in 1907 – but left liberals were not part of *Sammlungspolitik*.

Germany's high-seas battle-fleet, about which a great deal has been written, was also an issue. The battle-fleet was approved in the spring of 1898, just weeks before the Reichstag voting. Some hoped that the fleet would become a means to divert the attention of voters away from German domestic politics, and to rally support for the regime's dynamic foreign-policy stance. This social imperialism was even less effective than was *Sammlungspolitik*. The 1898 and 1903 campaigns show that the parties supporting the battle-fleet were handicapped by that stance among the wider electorate; that the government avoided the issue as disadvantageous in the elections; and that the parties opposing the battle-fleet made their opposition noisy and enthusiastic, and scored victories doing so. German voters were *not* aroused by social-imperialistic nationalism in these elections. The parties they supported were the anti-militarist SPD and the sometimes-populist Catholic Centre Party, which posed as an honest broker and a moderator of government policies.

The failure of appeals to nationalism, patriotism, and social imperialism reinforced the impression by established politicians that the electorate was fragmenting. However, what some contemporaries saw as the fragmentation of Germany's political culture was in fact the building of a new one – and the building of a more democratic culture than what had preceded it. In retrospect, the rise of 'interest' politics was not a threat to German democratization, but the driving force behind it. Voters were increasingly concerned with the equity of taxation policies, the fairness of the treatment of Catholics or workers or other subordinate populations, and with the preservation of the democratic Reichstag suffrage and the civil liberty it implied. At least, the parties that were rewarded by voters' ballot were the ones that touched these kinds of sectional, popular, or populist issues.

This is an appropriate place to acknowledge another intellectual debt. A decade ago Stanley Suval pointed out that 'affirming' patterns of participation, such as can be discerned in Imperial Germany, are important to the development of democratic culture. Whereas Suval examined a generation of Reichstag elections in a single sweep, using multiple regressions covering the entire Wilhelmine period (1890–1918) and all its elections, this book builds on Suval's ideas with an intensive examination of the dynamics of two specific and fairly similar election campaigns. The detailed analysis of campaigns provides a context within which to illuminate the interplay of issues, party platforms, and strategy – factors that are difficult to analyse over a lengthy series of elections. While these campaigns reveal many tensions, stresses, and contradictions, they verify that voters were affirming choices that were uncomfortable for the regime. Despite attempts at manipulation, a culture of democratic participation was emerging even under the undemocratic state.

Of course, the story was not all positive. It boded ill for the future that the losers in this contest for popular legitimacy did not accept the verdict of democracy, and that the different elites – those who appealed to the older political culture and those who appealed to the newer – were so little inclined to compromise. There is in the history of German electoral politics a story that can be read two ways: the resilience of participatory values and culture even in hostile environments; but also the danger inherent in the persistence of unreconciled opposition to democratic practice.

The research and writing of this book made a somewhat tortuous odyssey. It involved the insides of most of Germany's federal and state archives over a period of nearly ten years. These included the cramped former

Merseburg archive of the former GDR, where folders often arrived coated in black soot from the nearby railway-yard; and at the other extreme, the moody eighteenth-century Kalkum Palace outside Düsseldorf, where I was almost the only researcher on long, dim autumn days. Writing was done initially in a damp north Oxford basement flat, but mostly in an office overlooking John Diefenbaker's grave above the South Saskatchewan River. Parts were finished in a cabin beside Wakaw Lake, with geese and loons calling from the water and rabbits rustling in the bushes. It is sobering to realize that the first chapter drafts were typed with my newborn daughter Catherine sleeping on a pillow on my lap – the same daughter who is ten years old as this is being written, and who now has Elena and David to keep her company.

In the course of writing this book, a revolution occurred in personal computers. The earliest drafts were typed, and the first numbers crunched, on a desktop computer possessing a full 64K of memory and using software I wrote myself in a compiler BASIC. Final revisions were done on a Macintosh PowerBook Duo with roughly 250 times as much memory. Whereas the former machine had to be left on overnight to perform relatively simple statistical calculations using the large data sets employed in this study, the latter machine did complex multiple regressions using the same data in minutes. The power of desktop computers, along with the excellent SHAZAM statistical software developed by researchers at the University of British Columbia, made possible the multiple regressions that worked their way into this book.

Many colleagues have influenced me along the way. I have already acknowledged some of my intellectual debts of gratitude above. In a direct and personal way, this book was inspired by Hartmut Pogge von Strandmann, who supervised the original D.Phil. thesis and whose suggestion it was that I might want to look at the 1898 or 1903 elections. I owe a considerable amount to him for piloting me through to completion. Tony Nicholls and Volker Berghahn carefully read and scrutinized the original version, catching many errors and infelicities. Regrettably many more have probably crept in through the extensive changes and revisions since they did so. James Retallack read and shared many papers and drafts, and urged that this should become a book. Perhaps it never would have if not for his persistent advice; he has been the truest of colleagues. Peter Steinbach and Karl Rohe gave important encouragement and inspiration at key stages. So too did Jürgen Falter, Roger Chickering, and many of the participants in a 1990 conference at the University of Toronto on German elections and mass politics, sponsored by the German

History Society, the Goethe Institute, and the German Historical Institute. Funding for my study was provided in the initial stages by the Rhodes Trust, by an Imperial Oil of Canada Graduate Research Fellowship, and by a doctoral fellowship from the Social Sciences and Humanities Research Council of Canada. My current employer, the Centre for the Study of Co-operatives at the University of Saskatchewan, and my colleagues there, have been supportive of my continuing work on German elections and provided key cross-disciplinary help: Murray Fulton's expertise in statistics is awesome, and David Laycock gave me important pointers in democratic theory. That this book has appeared at all is to be attributed in large measure to these far-flung communities of scholars and institutions, whose influence only improved what would otherwise have been.

Throughout it all, Norma was more than understanding and encouraging. She endured stoically the stress and absences (real or virtual) involved in living with someone who takes more than a decade, off and on, to research and write a book. The least I can do is to dedicate this to her.

Abbreviations

The following abbreviations are used in the main text. For a complete guide to the abbreviations used in the Appendices, Notes, and Bibliography as well as the main text, see Appendix E.

BdI   Bund der Industriellen (League of Industrialists)

BdL   Bund der Landwirte (Agrarian League)

CDI   Centralverband Deutscher Industrieller (Central Association of German Industrialists)

DVP   Deutsche Volkspartei ([South] German People's Party)

FVg   Freisinnige Vereinigung (Left Liberal Union)

FVP   Freisinnige Volkspartei (Left Liberal People's Party)

HVV   Handelsvertragsverein (Trade Treaty Association)

RgS   Reichsverband gegen die Sozialdemokratie (Imperial League against Social Democracy)

SPD   Sozialdemokratische Partei Deutschlands (Social Democratic Party of Germany)

VkD   Volksverein für das katholische Deutschland (People's Association for Catholic Germany)

DEMOCRACY IN THE UNDEMOCRATIC STATE

1

Democratic Participation in an Undemocratic State

Imperial Germany is widely understood to have been an authoritarian society – and yet from its origin in 1871 it contained one of Europe's and the world's most democratic national suffrages.[1] This central paradox of democratic institutions within an undemocratic state is examined in this book through two Reichstag campaigns that bracketed the turn of the century, the general elections of 1898 and 1903. By the time of these elections, it had become clear that the 'universal' and equal ballot for the German Reichstag, introduced at the time of German unification during 1867–71, had released a dynamic of party and electoral development.[2] In the 1890s popular and populist mobilization facilitated by the democratic suffrage was remaking the German party system. These developments are of conceptual as well as historical significance, because German parties at the turn of the century provided basic models for European theorists who were trying to define how political parties develop. Those who analysed power relationships in mass organizations, and those who developed theories of how social-economic cleavages become expressed in politics, looked to elections like the German elections of 1898 and 1903 to understand what was modern in twentieth-century parties – and what they saw was a party system in transition to a new kind of mass politics. Social Democracy and new populist styles were advancing. Liberalism and, to a lesser extent, conservatism were declining. The government was seeking to compensate, unsuccessfully, by supporting its partisan allies, by pursuing *Sammlungspolitik* or the politics of rallying, and by considering social-imperialist appeals to patriotic voters. Try as it might, the government could not nullify the effects of growing democratic participation.

The Significance of Elections

If Imperial Germany (1871–1918) was not democratic, why study elections such as those of 1898 and 1903? The assumption behind this kind of question – that elections do not matter in regimes that are not formally or fully democratic – may explain why too little attention has been paid, generally speaking, to pre-1914 German electoral history. It is true that Imperial Germany was not a democratic place, in the specific sense, first of all, that it was administered by men who were not elected. The executive of government was not formally responsible to the elected, law-making Reichstag. Ministers were appointed by the German kaiser (who was king of Prussia) and could be retained, in theory, no matter how unpopular they became. In practice, failure to achieve in elections and in the Reichstag the results desired by the kaiser – specifically Kaiser Wilhelm II (1888–1918) – contributed to the dismissal of a number of chancellors, beginning in 1890 with the dismissal of Otto von Bismarck. But while resistance from the electorate or from the chamber could help cause the fall of ministers, the government of Imperial Germany was not, in an official sense, democratically responsible. Beyond this, some writers have claimed that Imperial German society was permeated with undemocratic attitudes and values, whose effect was to make democratic or party politics meaningless.[3] These observations, however, point to the need to consider carefully and define appropriately what we mean by democracy.

In the context of rational-choice theories of democracy, German elections in this period indeed make little sense. Joseph Schumpeter, and related 'economic' theorists of democracy, have argued that elections are largely a device to limit and constrain governments, much as markets constrain firms.[4] In brief, by subjecting parties to electoral competition, and governments to periodic change, the political process is made more efficient and avoids stagnation. This view does not presuppose any issue content to elections or any policy preference on behalf of voters – the important thing about elections is the simple fact of competition for office. This concept is not easily applicable to Imperial Germany, because elections were not directly tied to changes in governments. Parties were competing for something, influence perhaps, or legitimacy for their ideas, but not for ministerial office.[5] The degree of connection between the election result and the composition of the government was too weak to explain the interest that these elections aroused among German voters. Presumably when, after the turn of the century, more than 80 per cent of eligible voters took the time to cast ballots, they were not motivated by a Schumpeterian vision of democracy. Other theorists have argued for a broader social or cultural concept of democracy, including not only techniques of selecting government or shaping particular policies, but also ideas of participation and citizenship.[6]

Alan Ware has identified three aspects of democracy that have commonly been defined by political theorists: interest optimalization – policy results that are optimal for the interests of the largest number of people; the exercise of control over governments (Schumpeter's thesis); and, the development of a civic orientation in which people, through participation, come to appreciate larger issues and shared interests.[7] Democracy in its various senses is not achieved simply when everyone is given the vote. 'The idea that there can be more and less democracy in a process, an institution, or a regime is important, and it is misleading to believe that a process must either be democratic or undemocratic.'[8] Evaluating just how democratic a certain process may be depends on the relative weight assigned to the three aspects of democracy.

Political parties typically play a key role in all the various democratic processes. Parties articulate and aggregate interests, so that politics may take account of them; alternate in government (where there is partisan government and ministerial responsibility); and foster symbolic and actual participation of the mass public in political affairs.[9] It may not immediately be clear how a party helps aggregate interests or provide meaningful mass participation in a situation where it is shut out of exercise of actual power. It may lobby, of course, or use votes in a legislative chamber to influence bills, but a more powerful concept may be Antonio Gramsci's idea of 'hegemony.' In a Gramscian perception of politics, ideologies aim to dominate not the state but first and foremost civil society – the social space in which consent, persuasion, and values are created. An ideology has hegemony when its values and assumptions are unquestioned, when its claims to speak on behalf of classes, regions, and communities are unchallenged. This hegemony is created by organization, penetration, debate, competition, and many social and political processes. It is clear, however, that parties could fight for (or against) a Gramscian kind of hegemony, using both parliamentary and extra-parliamentary activity, whether or not they gain power in the short term. Indeed, they would have to fight over hegemony before they could gain power at all.[10]

In contrast to the idea of controlling governments, the articulation of interests and their aggregation into coherent groupings, as well as increasing participation by citizens, were aspects of democracy clearly visible in Wilhelmine elections. Agriculture, industry, workers, Catholics, regions, and ethnic minorities were all represented in elections by parties and candidates attempting to define and voice their distinct identities. Participation rates were rising and a culture of voting was emerging. A decade ago this increasing coherence between social groupings and politics convinced Stanley Suval that German mass politics was healthy and revealed broad groups of the population 'operating according to their most profound beliefs.' Suval's *Electoral Politics in Wilhelmine Germany* – 'Wilhelmine' denoting the period of Wilhelm II's reign, 1888–1918 – turned the established interpretation of Imperial Germany's backwardness on its head by arguing that the 'affirming' voting behaviour of Catholics, working-class Social Democrats, and agrarian Conservatives was in fact modern.[11] Suval's book was a welcome antidote to generations of functionalism, reductionism, and sweeping generalizations that diminished the significance of elections. Along with current research by specialists such as Peter Steinbach and Karl Rohe, Suval opened up Imperial German elections as a subject for more study.[12] Perhaps German society was not as patently undemocratic as historians sometimes assumed.

This idea of multiple aspects and degrees of democracy hints at additional answers to the question Why study elections? A few years ago, Martin Harrop and William Miller answered this question by pointing out that only by studying elections can one conclude whether they do make a difference, whether they are 'instruments of popular control' as democratic enthusiasts have argued, 'or the tools of government' as pessimists claim:

Another good reason for studying elections is to find out about society and politics in general. Elections provide a major test of the political system: '... with argument at its height and parties at their most active much of the essential nature of a country's politics can be revealed.' A close look at a nation's electoral system and electoral behaviour reveals the extent to which elites dominate society and whether they do it by coercion or manipulation, by intention or by default. It reveals how open that society is to new people and new ideas, how far it is willing to tolerate disagreement and dissent. Electoral patterns show how different social groups interact with each other, how individuals interact with their families and friends, how they respond to the actions of political elites or the content of the mass media.[13]

Elections illuminate political attitudes and ideologies, the 'mass political psychology' of the people, and 'provide valuable indicators of social and political change' such as class conflicts or changes in class structure, or regional and ethnic divisions.[14] If a society were indeed imbued with undemocratic ideas and values, one would expect to see this reflected in electoral behaviour.

Not only do elections illuminate a political nation – its classes and divisions, its ideals and its regions – but they also produce results which in and of themselves are political events that carry weight in shaping perceptions and expectations. As long as the results of the election are perceived to represent some actual political force, are perceived to have a particular meaning, then they actually acquire this meaning and make a real impact on consciousness. An election result is constructed, not just tabulated.[15] It is in this sense that the legitimacy of regimes and governments is at stake when elections are held, even in cases like Imperial Germany's where the governments were not elected. The steady advances of the Social Democratic Party (SPD) in German elections in the 1890s and early 1900s were more than an embarassment for the government: they undermined its legitimacy and helped create an impression of a dark future for supporters of the German state. This perception affected the behaviour of government elites as well as those in business, non-socialist parties, interest groups, and cultural associations. All of this illustrates the point that a key role of elections is to confer legitimacy on ideas and institutions. And above all, 'the unique achievement of genuinely competitive elections is to legitimise *opposition.*'[16]

Democracy is not only a mechanism for selecting leaders: it is a complex social and political process of participation, representation, mobilization, and legitimation. This process conditions the exercise of power even when the powerful are not elected – so that democratic elections make a practical difference, even in the undemocratic state. But elections in Imperial Germany are of interest for another reason as well. The situation of incomplete democracy evidenced in Imperial Germany has proven in the twentieth century to be much more common than full democracy.

Analysis of political developments in Germany has been limited by a certain tendency to contrast German constitutional developments against those in Britain, the United States, and France.[17] These three countries are sometimes taken as a standard of democratic development, from which Germany is then considered to have deviated. This general approach has produced analyses of why the revolutions of 1848 failed, why liberalism was supposedly so weak, or how anachronistic premodern or feudal elites maintained influence in a world that should have passed them by.[18] Insightful as many of these studies have been, the comparison to a few ideal-type democracies looks increasingly artificial in a world now seen to be filled with diverse, contradictory, and incomplete kinds of democratization and modernization. Imperial Germany's democratic incompleteness is more the rule than the exception and contains instructive lessons if studied on its own merits – as part of a range of possibilities and parallels, and not as a deviation from a single ideal type.

Elections are focal points for those aspects of a system that are democratic. One international survey of elections asserted that 'the electoral process lies at the heart of democratic government, and the critical difference between democratic and nondemocratic regimes is to be found in whether or not they hold elections and, if they do, what kind.'[19] The authors of the same study concluded that a 'democratic general election' is one which largely or wholly satisfies six conditions: substantially the entire adult population has the right to vote among candidates; elections take place regularly within prescribed time limits; no substantial group is prevented from forming a party and putting up candidates; all the seats in the major legislative chamber can be contested and usually are; campaigns are conducted with reasonable fairness – law, violence, or intimidation do not bar the candidates from presenting their views; and, last, votes are cast freely and secretly, are counted and reported honestly, and the winning candidates take office and serve out their terms.[20] This set of standards, though framed for modern elections, determines that national elections in Imperial Germany were democratic (always with the exception that at that time all women were excluded from the suffrage) and must have been the central institutions 'at the heart' of whatever degree of democracy existed.

How democratic was Imperial Germany as a whole? One political scientist recently devised a numerical 'index of democracy' for use in comparing the relative degrees of democracy in various countries.[21] Applying this contemporary framework of evaluation to German national elections, the result would apparently be that Imperial Germany was about as democratic a place as Bangladesh or Nepal in the 1980s, less democratic than India or Argentina but more so than China, Nigeria, or Tanzania. In fact, in Imperial Germany political freedoms were much greater than in many of these countries, but it rates lower than some of them because its governments were non-elected and women did not have the vote.[22] While such a numerical rating is surely superficial and based on numerous assumptions over which scholars will disagree, the exercise is enough to suggest that the historical experience of partly democratized regimes is a topic of legitimate interest. The marginal cases of democracy may in some respects be the most interesting ones.

The comparison with developing countries is relevant in one other respect: in Imperial Germany a century ago, as in developing countries today, the political nation was only a generation or two removed from its formative and unifying political experiences. Parties, ideologies, and elections first became important elements in German politics in the revolutions of 1848, and the country was unified as a federal nation-state only in 1871. Germany at the turn of the century was a new or emerging constitutional monarchy incorporating substantial elements of democracy. One of the challenges the country faced, in common with other emerging modern nations, was to develop a political culture supportive of democratic participation. This process proceeded from an elite-dominated system, through mobilization by the elites of mass followings, to development of more intense, more genuine, or more committed popular participation. Mass electoral parties and new styles and techniques of campaigning played a central role in political development.

Political Parties, Cleavages, and Electoral Mobilization

In Germany, as in many countries, the formative era of mass politics came in the wake of state modernization and alongside industrialization. In Germany's case, the abrupt introduction of universal male suffrage simultaneous with the creation of a unified, modernized state was a shock to the political system. Industrialization took off at the same time, contributing to urbanization, regional movements of people, changing occupational structures, new ways of life, and new conflicts. Cleavages were multiple and deep, and had profound impacts on the party system and on electoral politics. The exact connection between political institutions and social cleavages has been a topic of long-standing debate, with late nineteenth- and early twentieth-century Germany often used as a basic case in the development of models.

The idea that political parties owe their origins to the extension of the suffrage and the mobilization of mass electorates goes back to the work half a century ago of Maurice Duverger. Duverger observed that in 1850 no country except the United States had political parties 'in the modern sense of the word,' while by 1950 parties existed in most countries.[23] The general scheme of party development sketched by Duverger was that, as representative legislatures were created, caucuses of deputies formed the nuclei for political groups. Electoral requirements caused deputies to

form local electoral committees, which began to create an extra-parliamentary structure for parties. At first this structure was decentralized and
relatively informal: committees had no lasting existence from election to
election, and parties had no actual membership base or decision-making
structure. With the extension of the suffrage, the electoral machines
became larger, more permanent, more structurally integrated, and more
institutionalized – modern political parties, in Duverger's sense.[24]

Duverger's model was constructed with European historical examples
clearly in mind and applies to turn-of-the-century Germany. By the late
nineteenth century, all German national parties were under pressure to
adopt what Duverger called the 'modern' form of institutionalized structure. There were still some parties that had only the loosest of connections between local committees and central parliamentary delegations,
only the merest wisp of an organizational existence in constituencies
between elections, and that had no formal party membership whatsoever.
These were precisely the parties that were in electoral trouble. Another
feature of Duverger's model is also applicable. He noted that when the
suffrage is extended, traditional elites can continue to make do for some
time with fairly conventional, relatively less formal channels of influence
– it is their opponents who are driven to adopt 'modern' party structures.
Thus Duverger explained the fact that it was left-wing parties like the German Social Democratic Party (SPD) that best exemplified his bureaucratic model of a 'modern' party. The mass organizational structure of
the SPD appeared new and perhaps intimidating to contemporaries,
above all because the new-style party was so successful in elections: it surpassed all other parties in popular vote in the 1890s, and in seat totals by
the First World War. The Social Democratic breakthrough in Germany in
the 1890s was part of what Duverger called the first 'revolution' in the
development of modern parties.[25] Between 1890 and 1900, observed
Duverger, socialist parties substituted for the old system of informal committees a new system of popular sections, open to participation by all supporters and solidly articulated into an integrated system.[26]

It was not only Duverger who saw the German Social Democratic Party
as a characteristic organization of the twentieth century: before him, both
Robert Michels and Moisei Ostrogorski used the German party as an
example in their well-known arguments about the bureaucratization of
parties, the development of oligarchies in organizations, and the pessimistic prospects for participatory democracy.[27] Duverger, in viewing parties such as the SPD in essentially a favourable light, was turning the
evaluations of these earlier writers on their head. It could be said,

though, that the so-called oligarchy identified by Michels was the beginning of the analysis of the internal power structure of parties. Even (or especially) highly institutionalized parties are dominated by some kind of core leadership group, or what in the more recent literature has been called the 'dominant coalition' within the party.[28] Michels's and Ostrogorski's fears that party organization would mean the 'end of free representation' can be taken as symptomatic anxieties of an age when one pattern of politics was visibly being replaced by another that, to these observers, seemed unpalatable.[29] Like them, but less negatively, political theorists have continued to regard the German Social Democratic Party as 'the first mass party in Europe.'[30]

Others have seen the emergence of the SPD and other parties of the age not only as the expression of a principle of organization, but as an expression of underlying social cleavages related to modernization and industrialization. The most systematic and useful formulation of these ideas was the political sociology presented in the mid-1960s by Seymour Martin Lipset and Stein Rokkan.[31] Lipset and Rokkan argued that 'two revolutions: the national and the industrial' had produced four cleavages critical to modern politics. The process of nation-building and unification produced cleavages of centre and periphery, and of church and state – cleavages expressed in party systems through the development of minority and confessional parties opposed to nationalist and liberal ones. Industrialization, on the other hand, produced labour-market conflicts between workers and employers, and commodity-market conflicts between primary producers in the countryside and industrial interests in the cities. To varying degrees in varying countries, these cleavages were expressed in the development of working-class and agrarian parties opposing other more business-oriented or urban parties. While Lipset and Rokkan framed this as a general explanation or hypothesis, they clearly had Germany in mind when doing so.

In Germany's case, the 'national revolution' and the 'industrial revolution' overlapped chronologically. The unification of Germany in 1871 led to a variety of particularisms, expressed politically in regional and minority parties representing Polish, Danish, and Alsatian populations, and the dynastic separatism of the province of Hanover. Unification was followed by the *Kulturkampf* or 'struggle for civilization' between the secular, liberal-allied government of the new nation and the Catholic community, which became organized politically in the Catholic Centre Party. Thus by the 1870s both the national-periphery and the secular-confessional cleavages were clearly expressed in the party system – and reinforced each other, since Catholics were a minority mostly located on the geographical fringes of the east, south, and west; and allied frequently with the Poles and other particularist parties. The 'industrial' cleavages were expressed above all in the development of the Social Democratic Party, a self-styled working-class socialist party, after its formation in 1875 and especially in the 1890s, when its size swelled enormously. Agrarian-industrial cleavages also came to the fore in the 1890s through new agrarian interest groups and political parties and in the bitter debates leading up to Germany's new tariff law in 1902. While both sets of cleavages can be seen to date from the 1860s and 1870s, it could be said that the cleavages related to industrialization became more severe later, particularly in the 1890s. As for the older liberal and conservative parties, which had developed before either 'revolution,' these were not unaffected by the later cleavages. The controversies of Bismarck's unification split the liberals and conservatives each into two parties, divided initially by their orientation towards nationalism, and later divided between and within themselves by divergent economic interests. The result of all these partisan expressions of structural cleavages, as shown in table 1, was a system of four party groupings and over a dozen parties.[32]

Clearly the 'two-revolution' cleavage theory has some considerable explanatory power for turn-of-the-century Germany, but it has also come under criticism for a variety of reasons. One difficulty is that Lipset and Rokkan wanted to use their theory to show that Europe's *present* party systems – as of the 1960s – had been shaped by the cleavages existing in the 1920s, and that these party systems had changed little since that time. This proposition seemed more plausible to political scientists in the 1960s than it does in the 1990s. Theorists looking back on the last generation of protest movements, new social movements, ecology parties, the crisis of the welfare state, and the collapse of communism are not sure that European party systems are frozen.[33] But while new studies of European and Western political parties tend to reject Lipset and Rokkan's stability hypothesis, it is noteworthy that few of these studies have revisited or attempted to make deeper assessments of the earlier history of parties. Most recent comparative studies of parties and party systems deal exclusively with the post–Second World War era.[34] The cleavage theory, inasmuch as it applies to the pre–Second World War period, has not been reexamined in detail; but researchers are with time coming to suspect that it is too functionalist and too deterministic to be a good analytical tool. While cleavages exist, the theory does not sufficiently allow for the variety of ways in which those cleavages can be exaggerated or muted, even dis-

TABLE 1
Parties in Wilhelmine Germany

Right-Wing

German Conservative Party (DKP)	Right-wing, monarchical, agrarian
Imperial Party (RP)	Also called Free Conservatives in Prussia, right-wing, patriotic
Anti-Semitic parties	Radical right-wing, nationalist, incorporating democratic or 'populist' elements
Agrarian parties	Agrarian League (BdL) , Bavarian Peasants' League

Liberal

National Liberal Party	Right-wing liberals, nationalistic, generally willing to ally with government and conservatives
Left-liberal parties*	Free-trade and civil-rights liberals, generally opposed to government, differing in degrees of nationalism and democratic commitment

Particularist

Catholic Centre Party	Confessional base, defender of minority interests and constitutionalism, generally right-wing on economic and social questions
Small particularist parties	Poles, Danes, Alsatians; Guelph Party in Hanover

Left-Wing

Social Democratic Party (SPD)	The classic mass-bureaucratic, working-class socialist party

*Freisinnige Volkspartei, Freisinnige Vereinigung, and Deutsche Volkspartei ([South] German People's Party). While the term *freisinnig* has been rendered as 'free-thinking,' 'independent,' and 'Radical' (this last after the French equivalent), it will be translated throughout this work as 'left-liberal.' For a qualification of this usage, see Peter Pulzer, *The Rise of Political Anti-Semitism in Germany and Austria*, p. 95, second footnote.

torted, by political institutions. Supporters of the cleavage concept have recently attempted to salvage it by emphasizing that it was not as deterministic as it sometimes appeared, and by separating the cleavage idea from the hypothesis of the freezing of party systems.[35]

When all is said and done, the analysis of cleavages only explains a certain amount about parties and elections. Whatever caused the cleavages, the ways in which they were articulated into the political culture mattered in and of themselves. More recently, party theory is moving away from the sociological/functionalist approach towards a renewed emphasis on institutions as factors in and of themselves. In reaction against sociological generalizations, theorists now increasingly emphasize how 'the formative phase of an organization ... continue[s] in many ways to condition the life of the organization even decades afterwards ... [T]he crucial political choices made by its founding fathers, the first struggles for organizational control, and the way in which the organization was formed, will leave an indelible mark.'[36] In other words, history – the actual pattern, sequence, context, and conjunction of events – really does matter. And as part of this, consideration of the role and history of parties and elections is more important than ever.

The Constitution and the Party System

Apart from cleavages in society, party development may in addition be affected by the rules surrounding the electoral system. The literature on party systems is divided on the question of whether and in what ways electoral laws influence the long-term development of political parties. One of the best-known ideas in this vein is the notion that simple-plurality systems (the 'first past the post' in each constituency wins the seat, regardless of percentages) tend towards two-party alternation, while proportional representation tends towards multi-party systems – 'Duverger's Law,' as this idea has been called.[37] Some recent works argue that electoral rules can make or break a party, 'or even a country,' because electoral systems are one of the most easily designed or manipulated aspects of a political system.[38] Others have disagreed, arguing that in the long run the electoral system itself is shaped to fit the party system and the underlying social cleavages, not vice-versa.[39] With the return to a new institutionalism in political science, the safest conclusion may be that international generalizations either way, about the effect of electoral systems on parties and cleavages or vice-versa, are difficult.[40] Seen in this context, Imperial Germany provides some evidence for the effect of constitutions and electoral laws on party systems and structures – and offers a case study of a number of unusual legal-constitutional features. These include universal suffrage introduced at an early date and alongside restricted and unequal state suffrages; the two-ballot absolute majority system of election; the constitutional limitations on the elected assembly; the lack of redistribution of constituencies; and the federal nature of the empire, especially the powerful position of the state of Prussia.

The suffrage for the national Reichstag was, by the standard slogan of the times, 'universal, equal, free, secret, and direct.' Such a suffrage was 'a revolutionary innovation,' as one historian has called it, in the context of

Germany's generally restricted or unequal state suffrages.[41] Universal and equal in this case meant that each male German twenty-five or over who was not a member of the armed forces, a criminal deprived of civic rights, or a recipient of poor relief was eligible to cast one vote. The important restrictions were the first three – gender, nationality, and age – for the others excluded only a few.[42] In Württemberg during 1907–12 an estimated 96 per cent of males over twenty-four listed in the census were eligible to vote; the remainder were mostly foreigners or soldiers.[43] Given the demographic profile of the nation, this broad suffrage among adult men resulted in about 22 per cent of the total population having the vote.[44] This broad suffrage was an important precondition of the development of mass politics and of mass parties in Germany, though this was hardly Chancellor Bismarck's intention when he introduced it in the constitution of the North German Confederation in 1867. Rather, Bismarck had hoped to undercut the electoral support of liberals, which, he believed, was derived mainly from middle-class and wealthier voters. Enfranchising the common people, particularly the peasantry, was to create an electorate more loyal to its conservative social superiors.[45] In the longer term, it was socialists, not conservatives, who benefited from the Reichstag suffrage. Despite the plots of some arch-conservatives, it did not prove possible to reverse the egalitarian enfranchisement of the masses.

The broadness of the Reichstag suffrage became a powerful political symbol, because it existed alongside restricted state suffrages. In Saxony (before 1896) and Bavaria, as many as one-third of adult males were excluded from the suffrage by property and tax requirements.[46] The Prussian suffrage, on the other hand, was only a little less broad than the Reichstag suffrage, but it was unequal, not secret, and indirect. Voters were placed into three classes in such a way that, within their district, each class paid a similar amount of taxes and elected a similar number of members of an electoral college. The first class often contained only a handful of voters, who however elected as many delegates as did the massive assemblies of the third class. Votes were cast by voice in public meetings, leaving economically dependent workers or labourers vulnerable to pressure or reprisal.[47] While this system strongly favoured the conservatives, it is interesting that the Prussian liberal parties did not do badly. It was the socialists and other mass-oriented political newcomers who were really handicapped by the Prussian three-class system, and, correspondingly, it was they who most strongly defended and advocated the Reichstag suffrage. 'Universal, equal, secret, and direct,' in the context of the times and alongside patently undemocratic state and municipal suffrages, was no empty slogan. By its very existence, the Reichstag suffrage became a symbol for democratically inclined parties and people.[48]

The exercise of any broad suffrage depends on the methods of registering voters and casting ballots. In Imperial Germany it was up to local officials to make a new list for each election of all eligible voters resident in each polling area, and post this list twenty-eight days before the voting. The list had to remain posted for eight days, and individuals could file written objections up to six days before the election. The ballot papers were not issued by the polling officials, but by the parties, each of which distributed papers preprinted with its candidate's name. Voters carried these slips to the polls, inserted the one of their choice into an envelope (from 1903 on they did this in a private side-room or behind a screen), and gave the envelope to the officials at the ballot box. Any piece of paper was a valid vote, even if it was hand-scrawled or had the printed name crossed out and another written in, as long as it met the size requirements for ballot papers and unambiguously contained the name of an identifiable person who was eligible to be elected.[49] This system had two advantages: preprinted ballots allowed voters who were illiterate or barely literate to vote; and the practice of write-in candidates was in its way an extra guarantee of secrecy. Even if a ballot paper for a given candidate was pressed upon a voter, he could strike out the name on it and substitute his choice. By the standards of the times, these methods were generally fair and maintained the integrity of the suffrage.

The two-ballot election system was, like the suffrage, carried over from the 1867 constitution of the North German Confederation. If no candidate achieved an absolute majority on the first ballot in a constituency (that is, more than 50 per cent of all valid votes cast), a deciding ballot was held about ten days later between the candidates who had come first and second. This system had a variety of implications. Like all majority or plurality systems (in contrast to proportional representation), it gave an important advantage to parties whose vote was regionally somewhat concentrated, rather than spread too thinly or concentrated too thickly. Parties received, as it were, wasted votes if these were insufficient within a given constituency to carry that party's candidate to victory, or if the votes were in surfeit of what was required. Insofar as the effect on the number of parties is concerned – Duverger's Law – the impact of the system is hard to judge. One statistical study of various countries concluded that the norm, when graphing the 'advantage ratios' for parties of various sizes in a given electoral system (the percentage of seats won divided by the percentage of votes won), should be a smooth curve from poor advantage ratios for small parties through to beneficial ratios (in effect, a bonus of seats) for large parties. The difference between plurality and proportional-representation systems can be seen as a difference in the steepness or flatness of this curve – in other words, just how advantaged large parties are relative to small ones. When the authors of the study in question did this graph for Imperial Germany, however, the result was not a curve at all, but a 'wide scatter' graph.[50] In other words, there was no clear pattern in Imperial Germany as to whether large parties or small parties were disadvantaged. Some parties were more advantaged than others, but size was not the distinguishing criterion.

One feature of the electoral system that decisively affected the lives and fates of parties was the institution of run-off elections. From 1893 onward close to one-half of all election contests required a second ballot. These second ballots automatically eliminated parties that had won small proportions of the first-ballot vote, so that in this respect they favoured the larger groupings within each constituency. However, the run-off campaigns penalized some large parties, notably the SPD, when the other parties 'ganged up' on them; and rewarded some small parties like the left liberals, most of whose seats came in run-off victories with the help of supporters of other parties who considered a left liberal their second choice.[51] In general this run-off system provided little incentive for politicians to combine into two or three broad major parties. In most circumstances, every party could run its own separate candidate on the first ballot, testing the waters, gaining what support it could, perhaps jockeying for position to gain concessions from larger parties needing its votes. Then, on the second ballot, the parties could combine according to their most urgent interests. If they strove for their maximum program on the first ballot, they had the opportunity on the second to be satisfied with their minimum. The second ballot therefore became the focus for the construction of party blocs. Perhaps one could propose that the two-ballot system tolerated a moderate tendency towards a multi-party system: small parties had more chances than under a straight one-ballot plurality system, but it was by no means as wide open as proportional representation would have made it.

The constitutional limitations on the Reichstag had important effects on the parties and also reinforced their 'fragmentation.' Just as elections provided only a relatively weak incentive to form big, centralized parties, the lack of ministerial responsibility did the same. It is true that, in practice, there was a degree of ambiguity about the Reichstag's power. Ministers needed to obtain majorities in the Reichstag in order to have legislation or budgets passed. Chancellors spent time assembling majorities for important measures and could be politically crippled if they failed. The Reichstag clearly had a considerable role in the legislative and political process. While it could not name or unseat a government, could not even initiate bills, it constrained and in some cases influenced the government.[52] Still, there was in this no strong reason for parties to merge in a permanent way in order to obtain or protect power. The lack of party government also meant a lack of practical promises: since no party could enact any specific measure, elections tended to deal with fairly general ideological programs. Parties maintained quite distinct, some would say rigid, ideological identities.[53] Ever since Max Weber, this lack of 'responsibility' has been seen by some as having warped German political parties. Truly responsible leaders did not bother entering parties, the argument goes, and those who did made building the organization and defending its ideology their sole goals, producing a system in which there could be no compromise.[54] Weber's views reflect a turn-of-the-century disillusionment with modern parties, but they also reflect a preoccupation with only one definition of democracy: responsible government.

The multiplicity of parties did not necessarily interfere with their performing the interest-aggregation or participatory functions of democracy assigned by modern theory. Their number and ideological character may even have helped. In any case, one ought not to exaggerate the degree of 'fragmentation.' Parties that would have been united in a one-ballot, plurality system were in Imperial Germany separate on the first ballot, united on the second. What in another system might have been a tendency within a larger party was a party within a larger (second-ballot) coalition. Moreover, they did, in electoral politics, regularly reach compromises with each other. It also makes the party system look less chaotic when one notes that, although the Reichstag contained more than a dozen parties, many states and provinces were developing regional three-party systems.[55] The multiplicity of parties created a perception of fragmentation and some problems for governments in finding Reichstag majorities; but it is not clear to what extent all this reflected a greater fragmentation of politics or society than in other countries.

The failure to revise constituency boundaries also led to a progressive distortion in the way the electorate was reflected in the legislature. Constituencies were not redistributed at all between 1871 and 1918, even though massive urbanization and industrialization occurred. Initially, the system was a fair one, with one seat for roughly every 20,000 eligible voters, and a minimum of one seat per federal state.[56] The differential impact of urbanization meant that by 1912 the tiny principality of Schaumburg-Lippe still had only 10,709 eligible voters, while Charlotten-burg, into which Berlin had overflowed, had 339,256. Both elected a single deputy to the Reichstag.[57] This pattern of inequity benefited parties based in relatively stable, rural areas, notably the Centre, the German Conservatives, agrarians, and the right wing of the National Liberals.[58] On the other hand, historians have been prone to overemphasize the importance of lack of redistribution, compared to other factors in the party and electoral system. It is true that the SPD, which was especially strong in the cities, was disadvantaged. At the most unequal point in 1887, the SPD needed 3.5 times as many votes to elect a single candidate as was average for all parties; and needed over five times as many votes as the Conservatives to elect a deputy.[59] But the disparity, measured in this way, was generally declining over time – even though the effects of the lack of redistribution were ever more extreme. Calculated as a ratio of average votes needed to elect one deputy, the disparity was greatest in 1887 and 1907, when party alliances were especially unfavourable to the SPD, and least during 1881–4 and 1898–1903, and above all in 1912 – when the SPD was hardly disadvantaged at all.[60] In other words, the patterns of alliances between parties – which have been largely neglected by historians – made a greater difference to the outcome than the unfairness of the constituency boundaries. Strategies really do matter in elections.

Elections and parties in Imperial Germany were also influenced in a variety of ways by the fact that the Reich was a federal state. Federalism reflected, and perhaps preserved or reinforced, regional cultural and historical identities. The coexistence of state legislatures beside the federal Reichstag created a two-tier party and election system, with inevitable interweaving of issues and organizations. Influences occurred in both directions, and perhaps most notably concerning suffrage questions: the Reichstag ballot made the perfect protest vote against privilege-bound state electoral systems. There is evidence of growing integration between voter behaviour in state and national campaigns, especially in southern Germany, suggesting that both levels of elections were coming to revolve around similar issues and party ideologies.[61] The federal system also forced parties to build autonomous organizations in different states, and to run, in many cases, autonomous campaigns. The Prussian association law of 1850, which was emulated in Bavaria, Saxony, Hesse, Oldenburg, and Brunswick, forbade federations of political clubs (the *Verbindungsverbot*). Each political organization in each locality or region had to be independent, which weakened central control and strategy and accentuated localized campaigning.[62] Restrictive association laws of this type were overridden by a Reichstag law of 1899 (the *lex Hohenlohe*), but the effects on some of the parties, notably the National Liberals, were long-lasting.[63] State laws on the press and political meetings also indirectly affected Reichstag campaigns: while Reich law guaranteed free campaigning during Reichstag elections, this only applied to the period between the issuing of the writ and the final day of voting. Between elections, party organizations were subject to state law. In addition, since the states administered the Reichstag elections, there were small regional differences in how the elections were conducted – such as the degree to which Social Democratic campaign workers were harassed.

But the federal structure of the Reich had one other aspect of overriding importance: the curious interdependency it created between the Reich government and that of the largest component state, Prussia. Prussia dominated the empire with two-thirds of its territory and 60 per cent of its population. Under Bismarck's constitution of 1871, the crown, ministries, and bureaucracies of Prussia and of the Reich were intertwined. The king of Prussia was *ex officio* the German emperor; the minister-president of Prussia was normally also the chancellor of Germany; and the Reich government had only the skimpiest of bureaucratic apparatus. The real centres of power lay in the Prussian ministries. In relation to Reichstag elections, it was the Prussian Ministry of State (cabinet), not the federal Bundesrat (ostensibly the executive in the federal constitution), that decided on government strategy for national elections. It was the Prussian Ministry of the Interior that served as the 'Ministry for Elections,' as one diplomat called it.[64] And it was Prussian local officials who implemented the government's Reichstag strategy. While officialdom in states like Bavaria had a liberal character, a broad recruitment base, and little involvement in election campaigns, the Prussian civil service was the last bastion of the values of the conservative Prussian aristocracy.[65] Its conservatism was not ostensibly party-political, instead emphasizing the duty of officials to the crown and the state, and the *Überparteilichkeit* – the character 'above the parties' – of these obligations.[66] Ministers considered it legitimate to discipline the political bureaucracy by purging it, and to use it to represent state policy in elections.[67]

The effectiveness of any system depends on the respect shown by the state for the process of voting, yet there has been little research on this topic for Imperial Germany.[68] Briefly, while some scholars have found evidence of deliberate 'fixing' of elections by Prussian officials in the 1840s and 1850s, gross violations appear to have been eliminated by the turn of the century.[69] The key factors in safeguarding the franchise despite the power and influence of officials were, first, the respect for the concept of a *Rechtsstaat* or state ruled by law, even among many conservative officials; second, Germany's lively opposition press (left-liberal, Social Democratic, and Catholic), which delighted in exposing scandal and ridiculing pompous officials; and, third, the Reichstag's control of its own elections through its Election Verification Committee.[70] This committee had the power to investigate complaints, make recommendations to authorities, and invalidate elections it found to have been compromised – a power used fairly frequently, especially in the 1890s. In the period 1893–8, when some crucial interpretations of electoral law were worked out and enforced (including the rules for what officials could and could not do), this resulted in one-seventh of all protests leading to invalidated elections, representing one election in thirty overturned. Invalidation represented only the most extreme of the tools available to the Reichstag, and was used only where abuses were of such a scale that they might have decided the overall outcome of the voting. In many other cases, the Reichstag used the threat or warning of possible invalidation to force the discontinuation of dubious practices.[71] The key to the committee's effectiveness in the Wilhelmine period was its membership, which reflected the strength of the different parties in the Reichstag. This ensured, effectively, that the parties that most strongly defended the Reichstag suffrage and opposed repressive measures (the Centre, the SPD, and the left liberals) had a lasting majority on the committee.[72]

The government's internal documents show that it was most concerned that its officials avoid activities that could damage its credibility. In March 1903 the minister of the interior in Berlin wrote a circular for distribution to every *Landrat* (the senior local official) in Prussia, in which he carefully drew the distinction between the right of officials to be involved in politics as citizens and the need to avoid any situations in which 'misunderstandings' might arise as to whether officials were using their official title or public influence to favour a certain candidate. Murky as the distinction might be in practice, the effect was that officials had to show greater restraint.[73] Such warnings were echoed by the governmental parties themselves, who had no interest in seeing both themselves and the bureaucracy discredited in scandals over election laws. In 1897, in the aftermath of the spate of invalidated elections of the mid-1890s, the Conservative Party published a reference manual entitled *Die Ungiltigkeit von Reichstagsmandaten und deren Verhütung* (The invalidation of Reichstag mandates and its prevention). The manual warned that the Reichstag jealously guarded the rights of free assembly and freedom from official influence during election campaigns. The Conservatives called on all state officials 'to take special care that in exercise of their official capacities they [not] take any steps which could arouse the appearance of an influence on the elections.'[74]

While officials could not use their formal authority, officials in Prussia – the only large bureaucracy under the direct control of the leaders of the Reich government – were thought nevertheless to have a duty to 'represent the policy of the government' in elections. This they did, by the 1890s, not by manipulating the count or coercing voters, but by placing articles in the press, harassing Social Democratic workers where possible, and primarily in backroom activities in which they sought to influence the parties friendly to the government in such a way as to increase their commitment to government policy and their effectiveness in winning votes, as will be examined in chapter 3. This activity was not, as defined by the Reichstag, illegal, and neither did it compromise the fairness of the act of voting as such. What it did mean was that Prussian officialdom participated actively in the cadre-level politics of the governmental parties. Perhaps this legally constrained, political civil service is a transitional form between authoritarianism and democracy, and it may be peculiar to a system where there is no ministerial responsibility. But in any case, to judge it by its effectiveness during 1898–1903, it is a system that had little to commend it. The obvious unfairness of a state bureaucracy taking sides in national elections, bending rules and being caught, only exposed the government to humiliation when its allies were defeated despite its support. At the turn of the century, this is precisely what was happening. While officials could intervene in certain ways and in certain kinds of politics, increasingly electoral politics was beyond their control, and possibly beyond their understanding.

Populism

Party systems are not shaped only by underlying, long-term social forces, nor only by external rules and constitutional power-relationships. Parties are made and remade as part of a dynamic and sometimes turbulent process. Among German parties in the 1890s, especially, there were signs of stress and change. In this decade, Social Democracy made its explosive growth to become Germany's largest party; electoral anti-Semitism reached its peak; mass agrarian movements were launched; and pro-

tracted mass-political agitation developed around divisive issues like protective tariffs for agriculture or suffrage reform. As one would expect,
these changes were not sudden – their roots went back in many cases to
the 1870s and 1880s – but they reached a new height in popular awareness in the 1890s.[75] Theorists of political parties have generally referred
to the organizational aspects of these changes, especially the development of bureaucratic mass parties; but there were other signs of change.
Analysis of issues and language in turn-of-the-century elections shows that
new styles of campaigning were gradually gaining the upper hand, new
concepts of representation were being forcefully pressed, and new sorts
of issues centring on social-economic questions and popular rights were
forced onto the political agenda by mass parties and interest groups. In
general, what these styles and issues involved was an increasing critique of
the elite-based politics perceived to be dominant in the older parties, and
the advocacy of issues, language, symbols, and approaches that were
believed to be closer to the people.[76] It is profitable – admittedly in part
for lack of a better term – to refer to this complex of ideas, styles, and
kinds of issues as 'populism.'

'"Populism,"' to concur with Ernesto Laclau, 'is a concept both elusive
and recurrent. Few terms have been so widely used in contemporary
political analysis, although few have been defined with less precision.'[77]
Intuitively, the term is irresistible, particularly when trying to capture the
dynamism and spontaneity of political phenomena that do not easily
remain contained within established categories. In practice, the word is
used in a variety of ways in different disciplines and subdisciplines. In
American history, populism refers to the People's Party of the 1890s and
associated political and cooperative movements of farmers. While one
group of writers see this populism as having been backward-looking, nostalgic, and a dead end, others are passionate that this was one of the
strongest democratic alternatives in American history, presenting a radical critique of society and a program of reforms verging on the social-
democratic.[78] Two historians have written about what they see as parallels
between American populism and German agrarian movements in the
1890s.[79] In wider European history, populism refers to certain socialist-
radical, peasant-oriented movements in eastern Europe in the late nineteenth century, and later – in the interwar period – to the successor movements in the independent East European states. Interwar East European
populists were still peasant-oriented, but not so clearly socialist.[80] In twentieth-century German history, the word has been used to characterize the
campaign style and approach of the Nazis in Weimar Germany.[81] In Latin

American history, meanwhile, populism is more urban than rural, and is used to characterize movements based around charismatic leaders who seek to mobilize interclass electoral alliances against domestic oligarchies and foreign imperialists, with varying degrees of sincerity and with disputed degrees of success.[82] For the developing world generally, 'populism' has been used to denote attempts at alternative paths to development, based often on combinations of nationalism, socialism, and agrarianism.[83] Finally – quite distinct from all of the above meanings – there is the derogatory use of the term in commentaries on American politics in the 1980s and 1990s to refer to right-wing, anti-government demagogy. To give the other side its due, one of Ronald Reagan's former advisers has provided a simple, positive definition: populism is the alternative to elitism.[84]

It is possible to sort out a set of concepts of populism that is indeed quite useful for analysing the dynamism and instabilities of turn-of-the-century German party politics, but first it is important to make clear what populism is not. Populism was not an ideology – not an alternative 'ism' to others that existed – but a syndrome, a phenomenon that existed within various ideological forms, left and right as well as urban and rural. In its broad meaning, populism generally refers to movements that emphasize the virtue of the ordinary citizen and attack elitism; while a narrower and more sociological meaning applies particularly to agrarian protest movements rebelling against or seeking alternatives to the effects of industrialism. Most historians and political scientists do not seem liable to fall into the trap of assuming that populism is inherently and always good. To assume that populism is inherently and always bad may be more common, but no more valid: this implies the most pessimistic possible view about the character of the population, and the most optimistic possible view of government by elites. Populism, like a style of speech or a symbol – both of which are indeed the kinds of things of which populism is made – can be employed in causes good or bad, left or right. To return to Laclau, populism 'is that "something in common" which is perceived as a component of movements whose social bases are totally divergent. Even if it were a pure illusion or appearance, we would.still have to explain the "illusion" or "appearance" as such.'[85]

Germans at the turn of the century were perceiving 'something in common' between very different parties when they referred to the Social Democratic Party and the Catholic Centre Party as the parties of the 'masses,' or when governmental politicians decried 'radicalism' and 'demagogy' and 'agitation' among not only Social Democrats but also anti-Semites and agrarian Conservatives and the oppositional left liberals.[86] These parties and movements all broke in various ways and degrees from *Honoratiorenpolitik* – the politics of notables, in which parties were only weakly institutionalized, lacked a permanent base of support or enduring local presence between elections, appealed to the electorate in a manner typically based on deference rather than issues, and offered voters mostly only superficial and symbolic participation. *Honoratiorenpolitik* has been described and analysed by a variety of scholars, and corresponds in many respects to the early stages of party evolution in the models of Duverger and others.[87]

The new style of politics differed in four significant respects. First, populism worked from a democratic framework of political activity: it consciously promoted the use of mass suffrage for the heightened political involvement of broad groups of society. In Laclau's definition, populism is present whenever the discourse of popular-democratic ideas is used against the dominant ideology, no matter from what direction.[88] Second, its agitational style attempted to mobilize and integrate the 'masses' in emotional and symbolic ways that were more intense than what previous styles of politics had attempted. To do this, it used techniques like mass propaganda and meetings, a more permanent and more systematic organization, and mass-membership parallel organizations like trade unions, farm cooperatives, or cultural groups. Hand-in-hand with this organizational integration, third, populists accepted the social and economic issues of the time and formed them into binding programs suited to mass agitation, programs that appealed to the material and status interests of ordinary voters. Finally, populism appealed to the 'common man' and was against 'privilege,' however defined. Populists tried to embody a new idea of representation based on their legitimacy as 'men of the people,' not as notables or social superiors to the voters. Let us consider these four points in turn.

The first point is that populists advocated greater and more intense political involvement by the masses, and specifically defended the institution of the Reichstag suffrage. The SPD made a point of being its leading advocate; the party's strategic decision to emphasize the suffrage issue contributed greatly to its electoral success in 1898 and 1903. The Centre and the more agitational left liberals also defended the suffrage. To these parties, voting was by no means just a tool for choosing legislators. All of these parties revealed their attitude towards the suffrage through their practice of running candidates in every remotely possible seat, using multiple candidacies (*Zählkandidaturen*) if necessary. Their aim was not only to win seats, but also to bolster the abstract representative claims of their movement by giving every citizen an opportunity to provide support. Even the anti-Semites were advocates of egalitarian mass participation. They made their position clear when they tried to petition the chancellor in the Reichstag to extend the universal right to vote into a universal *duty* to vote.[89]

The appeal to 'the people,' the invitation to voters to see themselves reflected in the party, was the second characteristic of populists noted above. It contrasted with the old-fashioned campaigns of *Honoratioren-politik* in which candidates appealed to the trust and loyalty of members of the local community. Parties that were effective in the new style developed a mass membership base and a dense network of auxiliary organizations in which members could participate, like the SPD did; or, like the Catholic Centre, they worked through a network of closely affiliated cultural-political and economic organizations to gain an organized mass base of support (chapter 6). In urban centres, especially, mass meetings and leafleting tried to make a closer connection between voters and the party. The style of speech was part of the populist appeal as well: to invite the voter as an equal, to lay out concrete commitments in plain language, to arouse the voters against elites and privileged interests. One anti-Semite complained that old-fashioned politicians dismissed 'everything ... which moves the people' as 'demagogic.' Eduard Ulrich-Chemnitz implored 'our honourable deputies' to become 'more accustomed to striking the tone of the people.'[90]

'Striking the tone of the people' included talking about questions of immediate relevance to them. One premise of populism may indeed be 'that government should be as responsive as possible to the wants of the citizens,' as Alan Ware has put it – not only to their 'interests' as defined and interpreted by elites.[91] Old-fashioned politicians de-emphasized conflict within the local community, and often avoided divisive social-economic issues. The Social Democrats, in this respect as in others, broke the political rules, above all by choosing social-economic issues that exploited the material and status cleavages within industrial society. They were not the first to do so: the more popular-democratic among the left liberals had blazed the trail already with successful campaigns in the 1880s against unfair and regressive taxes and against militarism. Social Democrats emphasized much the same issues in the 1890s, with greater effectiveness, while tying them together into a system of issues (see chapters 2 and 7). This use of language and issues to exploit cleavages was believed by governmental politicians to be 'subversive' in and of itself, for it seemed to undermine authority; and they liked it no better when it occurred in parties other than the SPD. The most scathing criticisms the National Liberals could make of anti-Semitism were that its anti-militarism and boundless social-reform demands were indistinguishable from the SPD's style. Governmentalists decried that even within the Conservative Party 'separatist sectarian formations' were emerging 'that cultivate a single thought in a radical and one-sided fashion.'[92] This was how social-economic cleavage politics looked to outsiders.

The new popular-democratic activism also increasingly asserted that voters could only be represented by someone of similar social-economic status to themselves. The SPD claimed only a 'workers' party' could represent workers. To quote Aneurin Bevan of the British Labour Party, 'a representative person is one who will act in a given situation in much the same way as those he represents would act in that same situation. In short he must be of their kind.'[93] The idea that voters should choose deputies 'of their kind' is a distinctive populist notion, and an implicit critique of elites and of elite-based politics. Agrarians argued in an exactly parallel fashion that farmers must elect deputies who were also farmers in order to further their interests. As the Bavarian Peasants' League put it, 'simple peasants must get in – they must be the excellencies.'[94]

These four characteristics, considered separately, were not unique to populists, and did not appear suddenly. In combination, and in the strength in which these patterns of politics had developed by the turn of the century, they were formidable. During 1898–1903 all parties, especially in the face of the growing SPD challenge, had to fight to keep and extend their bases of popular support, and all parties faced some populist challenge or alternative. Within the conservative grouping, radical agrarians and anti-Semites fought governmentalist moderates over party style, leadership, and policy. The Centre Party had to compromise with agrarian populism to meet internal agrarian revolt in the Rhineland and Westphalia, as well as to deal with the external challenge of the Bavarian Peasants' League; and in southwest Germany the Centre adopted 'demagogic,' anti-socialist, rural populism to mobilize voters.[95] Among liberals, Eugen Richter's Left Liberal People's Party (FVP) was noted for mass agitation resembling that of the SPD, and for its committed attacks on privilege and *Reaktion*. Even among the small particularist parties there were populist episodes. A confrontation developed in 1898 between a self-styled 'Polish People's Party' and what was thereafter called the 'Polish Court Party' (*Hofpartei*); this was resolved in 1903 when the former achieved the 'deselection' of most of the latter's Reichstag candidates.[96]

Even the miniscule Hessian Rights Party faced an internal split as younger party activists pressed for a more radical economic program and agitational style.[97] Nor, one might add, was this kind of polarization between traditional politicians and populists limited to political parties: one can also find evidence of it in pressure groups, where 'radicals' fought against governmentalists to carry the agitation to 'the people.'[98]

All of this activity can be interpreted as a symptom of stress and adaptation in the party system as it moved from a nineteenth-century pattern to one more typical of the twentieth century, and as a national political culture – begun in 1871 with the introduction of mass suffrage – developed and began to mature. The change was not wholesale, and may indeed reflect fundamental ambiguities in modern electoral politics. In some ways and in some places, the politics of notables still survives today and is still challenged now and then by populisms. But one hundred years ago, German parties were changing to reflect more effectively the cleavages in society that resulted from state modernization and industrialization – or, more precisely, those parties that strove to articulate cleavages were enjoying success. Voters had been given the suffrage and mobilized in the elections of the 1870s, but a generation later there was visible pressure for a more intense identification between the electorate, on the one hand, and candidates, parties, and programs, on the other. The parties did not all adapt equally or fast enough to social and political change, and one of the results was that populist impulses could not be channelled within the bounds of existing political institutions.

Political History and Political Culture

Recently, a collection of scholars heralded the 'return' of the concept of 'political culture,' now that the economic reductionisms of left and right have supposedly been discredited.[99] A review of the literature on developing countries suggests that the main contribution of political-culture theory since the 1960s has been in relation to the roles of elites, intellectuals, and political leaders in framing and fostering what might be considered democratic norms or values. Various political-culture theories show how relatively small numbers of agents set the tone for a wider social and political system in its early stages. 'We observe during democratic consolidation the emergence of an elite political culture featuring moderation, accommodation, restrained partisanship, system loyalty, and trust. These norms enhance the predictability and mitigate the intensity of political conflict.'[100] Political culture, then, is about the relationship between elites and mass mobilization of voters. Viewed in these terms, Imperial Germany was a place where a democratic political culture had not yet been shaped. Indeed, some of its elites, far from moderation, accommodation, and system loyalty, promoted radicalism and exclusion.

Parties, in the new analysis that has succeeded political sociology, are crucial 'intervening variables' between the state and society. They express and mobilize cleavages, serve as vehicles for social movements, and participate in policy formation.[101] Recent theories emphasize 'the active role of political parties in determining their agenda,' suggesting that not only social forces but also issues and strategies affect the outcome of elections. 'Social problems cannot crop into political decision-making unless [they are] being politicized by the major political actors, i.e. mainly the political parties. The politicization of cleavages in society is a necessary condition' for those cleavages to be reflected in society, 'and the process of politicization needs to be understood on its own terms. Issues provide the missing link between the structure of society with its cleavage bases and government institutions and their properties.'[102] To understand the development of parties or of an electoral system means delving deeply into the context, and intensively examining campaigns, strategies, and tactical manoeuvres. This is a type of study that has not often been done for German elections in this period.

German election campaigns have not been the subject of a great deal of research. Some commentators have even suggested there may be decreasing historical activity in this area.[103] Indeed, while there are monograph studies of the major parties before 1914, there are few studies of election campaigns.[104] This is a deficiency in the literature to the extent that an election is an interactive process in which different parties react to each other's issues and strategies. It is precisely these interrelationships that are difficult to capture in single-party and longitudinal studies. Only an issue- and institution-oriented study of the context of campaigning and voting can illuminate the ways in which parties, strategies, and events interacted in campaigns. Gerhard A. Ritter twenty years ago called this a 'completely neglected theme' in historical research and called for study of such interconnections, of 'how the government tried to influence party-internal arguments and the construction of coalitions, how the administration intervened in election campaigns,' and how the construction of second-ballot coalitions affected the relationships among the parties.[105] A few years later, Otto Büsch issued a similar call for integrative studies and suggested 'supra-regional, "cross-sectional" monographs of individual Reichstag elections.'[106]

FIGURE 1
Popular (%) Vote by Party, Reichstag Elections, 1890–1912

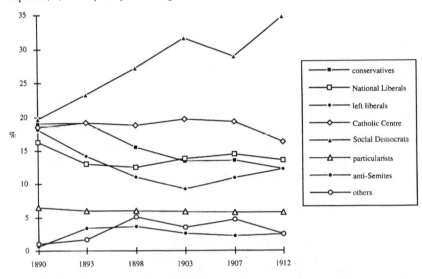

Note: Here and in the following graphs, 'conservatives' combines the German Conservatives (DKP) and the Imperial Party (Reichspartei); 'left liberals' includes the Freisinnige Volkspartei (FVP), Freisinnige Vereinigung (FVg), and Deutsche Volkspartei (DVP, [South] German People's Party); 'particularists' includes Poles, Alsatians, Guelphs, Danes, etc.; and 'other' consists mainly of agrarian candidates, chiefly Bund der Landwirte and Peasants' Leagues.

This book looks particularly at two elections in Imperial Germany, the general elections of 1898 and 1903, and aims to produce a variation on the kind of monograph called for by Büsch – a study, not of a single campaign, but of two consecutive and closely related ones, situated in the politics of their time. This is 'election analysis in historical context,' to use the formulation of Karl Rohe.[107] The goal is not to isolate the elections, but to relate them closely to the history of the parties, of the state, and of the era. Such an approach differs from other approaches such as national-level trend studies of series of elections.[108] Both of these methodologies, election monographs and trend studies, examine the national level; they are complemented by regional or micro-studies.[109]

One place to begin establishing the context for these elections is by reviewing the wider electoral trends of the era. Figure 1 shows the percentage vote across all of Germany won by eight major parties and party groupings in the six elections of the Wilhelmine era (1890–1912).[110] The

FIGURE 2
Popular (%) Vote, *Kartell* and Other Groupings, Reichstag Elections, 1890–1912

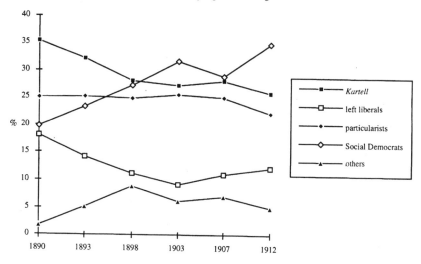

main story is the steady advance of the Social Democratic Party among the electorate, interrupted only once, by the effective anti-socialist coalitions in the 1907 elections. In a growing electorate, the Social Democrats attracted proportionately more voters, and by 1898 were clearly substantially larger than any other party in the electorate – reinforcing the impression that they were the characteristic mass party of the new age. The Centre and the ethnic and regional particularists were stable, in percentage terms, at least until 1912 – which suggests they just held their own in attracting new voters among the expanding electorate. The liberal and conservative parties were the ones that showed a decline, especially in the early to middle years of the Wilhelmine period. They dipped in support, then recovered or stabilized, while the anti-Semites and 'other' candidates, mostly agrarians, did the inverse – peaking, then declining somewhat. As would be expected given the nature of the parties and the Reichstag – never governing, focused on long-term programs rather than short-term issues or promises – there were no wild fluctuations in support from one election to the next.

The same information looks a little different when presented in terms of the *Kartell* group of governmental parties, and other party groupings. The fate of the *Kartell* parties as illustrated in figure 2 was one of decline (apart from 1907) but not as sharp a decline, or as much of a recovery, as

FIGURE 3
Seats Won by Party, Reichstag Elections, 1890–1912 (Total 397)

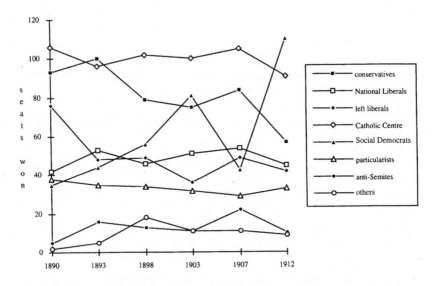

experienced by the left liberals. The *Kartell's* decline as an electoral bloc
is significant because (as will be discussed in chapter 3) government intervention in the elections was aimed to help the *Kartell* parties. The decline
represents the steady and repeated failure of the government's electoral
strategy, a symptom of the ways in which mass electoral politics was escap-
ing the control of the government. Contrasted to the *Kartell's* decline in
the 1890s, the combination of agrarians and independents under the
rubric 'other' swelled to a peak in 1898. Seen in terms of these blocs of
parties, it appears that the SPD did not achieve pre-eminent status among
the party groupings, in popular vote, until 1903 or 1912.

Of course, winning votes is not the only object of an election; the seat
totals are also significant (fig. 3). Predictably, given the system of representation, the seat totals did not perfectly mirror the steady movements of
popular vote and overrepresented rurally based parties. Despite the vast
margin in the votes it won, it was not until 1912 that the SPD became the
largest party in the Reichstag. The success of the Centre Party's electoral
strategy is even more apparent when one observes that it was the largest
party in four of the six Wilhelmine Reichstags (and second-largest in the
other two), giving the party its 'key position' to influence imperial politics
(chapter 6). The particularist parties were similarly successful, winning

nearly 10 per cent of the seats with only a little over 5 per cent of the votes. The conservative parties were greatly overrepresented, and to a lesser extent the liberals. And yet, as far as the elections of 1898 and 1903 are concerned, the seat totals do not qualitatively distort the trends in the electorate: advance of Social Democracy, stability of the Centre, decline of conservatives and liberals, and the peak of agrarianism. In these elections the inequities of the representative system muted but did not change the trends.

In the context of these trends, the elections of 1898 and 1903 represented a significant moment in the development of the political system: the electoral breakthrough of Social Democracy, the bottoming-out of liberal decline, and the ebbing of the populist tide of agrarians, anti-Semites, and other breakaway candidates. There is also some significance in what did *not* occur, as detailed analysis of issues and programs (chapter 2) will show. A variety of works on Wilhelmine politics have suggested that in these years battleship-building and aggressive foreign policy served a 'social-imperialist' function in generating support for the regime.[111] But even though 1898 and 1903 were the first elections of the era of *Weltpolitik*, they were breakthroughs for the SPD, which vociferously opposed these measures, and were the worst-ever elections for the National Liberals, the only party that strongly and publicly supported the battlefleet. Overall, the government's interests as represented by the *Kartell* parties lost ground. The elections of 1898 and 1903 disprove assertions by historians that 'mass political action' produced 'a groundswell of support for the development of the German navy,' that the popularity of the fleet 'was the culmination of Wilhelm II's symbolic leadership of the Germans,' and that his 'vision of naval and world policy was greeted with widespread and intense popular enthusiasm.'[112] Overlapping the fleet / social imperialism debate is the historical concept of *Sammlungspolitik*, the 'politics of rallying together,' which is held by some historians to have been a basic strategy of German regimes from 1897 to 1933. In *Sammlungspolitik*, agrarians are supposed to have been placated by protectionist tariffs, and industrialists by battleship-building, in order to hold together an anti-socialist, agrarian-industrial constellation that dominated the empire and resisted change.[113] But the term *Sammlungspolitik* was coined precisely in 1898, as a term for an electoral strategy in the Reichstag campaign that year (see chapter 2); and the Reichstag elections do not reveal what one would expect. The first elections for *Sammlungspolitik* saw the tariff issue and agrarianism, like the fleet, complicate and undermine the government's task (chapter 3), so that far from greater unity the opposite was the result.[114] These pieces of the electoral puzzle become clear only when the issues and campaigns are examined intensively and in context.

The elections of 1898 and 1903 show a mid-Wilhelmine period of transition. These elections witnessed major breakthroughs in the advance of Social Democracy, the decline of liberalism and the slower decline of conservatism, the relative stability of particularist and Catholic parties, and the eruption of breakaway populisms. Unpalatable as these changes were to the German government, the government's policies of supporting the *Kartell* parties, *Sammlungspolitik*, and social imperialism proved to be failures. What was emerging in these elections was a new kind of politics, perhaps a new political nation, that was not driven by the government or mainly by the older, established conservative and liberal parties. This new mass politics brought with it new structures and new issues, and created an environment to which the parties were compelled to respond, with varying degrees of adaptation and success. These elections did not decide who would form the government, or what the policies of the state would be, though they did condition those choices. They were battles for the empire, however, in a symbolic sense. Who was the majority in the nation? What were the key concerns and values of the political nation? Was democracy legitimate? Was the state legitimate? Germans looked at the popular vote and wondered about the balance of social forces and the direction of political change. As the campaign literature, press commentary, and party strategies reveal, these elections were fought not just for numerical ascendancy in the Reichstag, but for moral ascendancy in the nation.

2

The Context of Campaigns: Structures and Issues

On Thursday 16 June 1898, and again five years later to the day, voters in every corner of the German Empire made their way to the polls. Party workers might well have been about early: in one large Berlin constituency in 1898, the Social Democrats distributed 110,000 pamphlets at 6 a.m. on election day to counter a propaganda effort by their opponents the day before.[1] As polls opened at 10 a.m., attention centred on local inns and restaurants, where balloting typically took place.[2] Workers from all parties lined up at the doors to offer ballot papers printed with their candidates' names. Other party workers raced about on foot or on bicycle carrying news of the progress of voting. In an impressive exercise of participation, more than two-thirds of German men twenty-five years of age or older anonymously declared their political choices; in 1903 it was more than three-quarters. In nine hours of balloting, ten million Germans expressed their preferences from among the many candidates and parties courting their support. The purpose of this chapter, in line with the institutionalist approach to politics described in chapter 1, is to place these campaigns into the context of their times, beginning by looking at the elections themselves and then at the surrounding structures and issues.

Disciplined Conflict: The Practice and Language of Elections

The 1898 and 1903 elections were orderly and regular. Armies of polling officers and ballot-counters efficiently marked their tallies in carefully prescribed fashion on forms distributed by central governments.[3] Results were telegraphed to the Reich Office of the Interior in Berlin within hours. Newspapers carried the local results the morning after the election and within two or three days had the entire national outcome. In 1898 the official results from the polls, which closed at 7 p.m. on Thursday, June 16, were posted by 10 a.m. on Monday the 20th; and the second ballot, where required, was held before the end of the week. In an electoral system in which most procedures were regulated and aggrieved candidates could appeal to the Reichstag, few cases of meddling, corruption, or incompetence surfaced. Civic disturbances were also few. There were crowds of excited people on the streets, especially Social Democratic supporters after the elections celebrating their party's victories. The occasional crowd became unruly with an excess of enthusiasm.[4] Such disturbances reveal a degree of underlying tension but were not the typical form in which Germans' political enthusiasm was expressed. In their quarterly reports to the kaiser, district governors emphasized that the elections had 'run completely peacefully.'[5]

The process was orderly and regular in other ways as well. In both 1898 and 1903, the Reichstag's mandate expired naturally. Unlike the elections before and after (those of 1893 and 1907), the two elections that bracketed the turn of the century were not the result of parliamentary crises or sudden dissolutions. They were not dominated by any single immediate issue of the government's choice. Instead, the issues were defined by Germany's parties and interest groups. Participation in elections was high and increasing. In cities such as Bremen and Lübeck, which saw turnouts of 89–90 per cent in 1898 and 90–1 per cent in 1903, a large majority of those eligible clearly voted in both elections; a habitual voting culture was emerging. Voting behaviour often reflected consistent long-term allegiances or attitudes rather than short-term issues.[6]

This regularity, and the corresponding steadiness and gradualism of German electoral trends, made the elections in some respects unexciting. But those who commented negatively on the elections had their own political reasons for doing so. Bernhard von Bülow, foreign secretary in 1898 and chancellor from 1900 to 1909, commented in his memoirs merely that the 1898 elections 'brought fresh progress for the Social Democrats,' and reported the seat totals. He apparently considered the aged Prince Bismarck's last public statement to be a greater political event.[7] The kaiser was perhaps the most dismissive of all. In 1898, at the exact moment when the polls were opening throughout Germany, he began reviewing his guard regiments at Potsdam as part of the ten-year anniversary celebration of his reign – undoubtedly in his opinion a superior aspect of the life of the state, and likely intended to inspire the voters to patriotic behaviour – which it did not.[8]

Privately, however, a senior minister described the six-week Reichstag campaigns as a 'turmoil in the whole country.'[9] All areas of the country were penetrated by leaflets, meetings, speeches, and discussions, and the campaigns were reported in detail in Germany's lively and partisan press, so that none could doubt that the elections were the number one political event in Germany.[10] Interestingly, this was less apparent in the government press than in that of the opposition. Opposition papers devoted long columns to campaign reports from around the country, published regular editorials and exhortations to their sympathizers, and chose national election items as their lead front-page stories. 'Respectable' periodicals consigned such material more to the back pages, declining to indulge in continuous agitation or prolonged propaganda duels with their competitors.[11]

In Wilhelmine Germany, the most popular analogy for voting was warfare. 'Even the vote is a rifle, and ballots are also bullets,' the *Volkszeitung* had said in 1867, and this might well have set the tone for at least a half-century thereafter.[12] The casting of the ballot was the act of a soldier – a bullet fired at an enemy and in support of a glorious cause. Terms like *Kampf* (struggle) and *Schlacht* (battle) were commonplace in newspapers and pamphlets. Parties appealed to the loyalty of followers to defend a *Hochburg* (fortress, an especially strong seat) or tried to rally their class comrades in a second-ballot coalition against a traitorous enemy. Such language was supplemented by aggressive rhetoric about victory and defeat, winners and vanquished, historic moments, and decisive confrontations with the enemy. And with the German electorate divided among dozens of parties, and with the rules, procedures, and legitimacy of democracy still in some dispute, perhaps elections did, indeed, resemble warfare. Like warfare, the purpose was patriotic: the fate of the country (or the confession, or the nationality, or the class) was seen to be at stake.

Elections were military actions within patriotic causes, but were not only patriotic – they were also patriarchal. These competitions for the future of Germany were only for adult men (twenty-five years of age and older). Women, children, and those under age twenty-five whom we would not today call children were systematically excluded by law not only from running for office or voting but, in many cases, even from attending political meetings. Until the federal associations law of 1908, women were not allowed to join political parties, and in most states neither were men younger than twenty-five. From the local pub (where many political meetings were held, in the cozy atmosphere of a male drinking circle) up to the podium at the front of the Reichstag chamber, visible politics was almost exclusively male. This raises an important issue, because a study like this one is based on the visible phenomena of electoral politics. 'Is it possible,' one historian asks, 'to construct a general account of German politics in this crucial period that does not systematically and obtusely exclude women?'[13] And, in a vein relevant to the present study, she continues, 'it may be that the best we can hope for from political history is an account that regretfully and self-consciously excludes women ... This would constitute an acknowledgement that the historical study of politics ... is as much a special field as the history of medicine, military history, or indeed women's history.'

We do know, however, that despite their systematic and explicit exclusion, women influenced the political environment and culture of Germany, and directly or indirectly they influenced male voting patterns. This was demonstrably true on certain issues and in certain social groupings. The debate on the 1896 Civil Code was one of the issues in which women, organized as lobby and pressure groups, affected political debate.[14] Women were especially present within the Social Democratic grouping (the SPD, free trade unions, and affiliated clubs and cooperatives), which found ways to involve women in meetings, where they could certainly influence their male colleagues. Women contributed both between and during elections to strengthening and mobilizing Social Democratic support. A few Social Democratic women are famous, including Clara Zetkin and Rosa Luxemburg; but there were also many less well known women whose activism at the local level helped build the labour movement: women like Ottilie Baader, a seamstress in Berlin who rebelled against the sweatshop owners and, through doing so, discovered Social Democracy; or Adelheid Popp and Aurelia Roth, self-made women of the Austrian Social Democratic movement.[15] The party itself consciously cultivated female support, and its leader, August Bebel, wrote a book on the situation of women that went through fifty reprints before the First World War, and, in the 1890s, a tract outlining the party's support for electoral reform, including proportional representation and the vote for women.[16] The strength of the Social Democrats in mobilizing a strong social grouping (as outlined in chapter 7) was partly a result, then, of their inclusion of women activists and women's issues, bearing out Eve Rosenhaft's comment that 'the entry of women into politics marks the beginning of mass politics.'[17] It would be interesting to know whether women (having a traditional interest in family and religion) played any role in generating support for the Catholic Centre, the other recognized mass party based on a coherent social grouping. Perhaps they did, though Suval noted that through to 1912 he could find 'no instances of a woman ever attending a Centrist political rally although some had crowds greater than one thousand.'[18] Social and institutional processes ensured that only men were on the stage during election campaigns.

The elections of 1898 and 1903 fully exhibited the male, warlike rhetoric of the times, which perhaps reflects the fact that these were the first elections of Germany's era of aggressive *Weltpolitik* and battleship-building. Then again – as will be shown later in this chapter – analysis of these elections does not support far-reaching hypotheses that battleships were popular or that social imperialism stabilized domestic politics. Martial words were popular, but martial causes and the taxes to support them were not. Warlike rhetoric reflected not so much an actual militarization of society in terms of policy, but rather a degree of commitment to politics that could only be expressed in the most dramatic symbols of striving and comradeship available to the male gender: the symbols of warfare. 'Military symbols,' says Suval, 'were used because they were not trivial, because they demanded the most intense loyalties and the hardest efforts.'[19] By the late nineteenth century these symbols were being employed to raise mass participation, mobilize social-economic cleavages, and especially to reorient the electorate around new patterns of politics.

The transition to a new form of politics in Germany in the 1890s can be viewed in two interrelated dimensions: a change in *structures* and a change in *issues*. Behind these changes lay multiple causes: the legalization of the SPD and its explosive growth beginning in 1890, the gradually developing patterns of electoral participation during the generation since universal suffrage, urbanization and industrialization, and also the increasing articulation into politics of the status-related cleavages of industrial society. Viewed in organizational terms, the older, looser varieties of parties based on cliques of local notables were being superseded by more bureaucratic and participatory forms of organization, either agitational mass parties like the Social Democratic Party or specialized interest and pressure groups. These more highly organized groups were more centralized and more permanent, remaining active between elections. Their style was suited to mass leafleting, large or rowdy public meetings, appeals for the personal or symbolic participation of large groups of people, and other forms of 'agitation' frowned upon by old-fashioned politicians. At the same time, there were new issues in German politics, including the issue of democracy itself – the Reichstag suffrage defended and advocated by the mass-based parties – as well as issues which tended to be economic in focus such as tariffs or the cost of military armaments. This complex of issues associated with the new mass agitation might be characterized as 'fairness' issues, insofar as they revolved around protecting or enhancing the rights, power, and economic welfare of broad classes of the population. Both of these dimensions of change – in structures and in issues – were evident in the 1898 and 1903 elections.

The Changing Basis of Politics

The system by which self-appointed, largely upper-middle-class leaders spoke in the name of the general interest was known to contemporaries and historians of political parties as *Honoratiorenpolitik* – the 'politics of notables.'[20] In essence this resembles an early stage in Duverger's model of party development, when the party is weakly institutionalized, depends mostly on informal personal connections, and has little in the way of permanent structure or identity. Within each locality, small groups of influential citizens joined in selecting a candidate, and organized support for him using their contacts. Frequently clubs and associations provided the framework within which notables could extend their influence to wider groups, or from towns out into the surrounding countryside.[21] While the traditional small-town liberal organizations were the epitome of *Honoratiorenpolitik*, it was not unique to them: in many respects, Conservative organizations were similar in their use of aristocratic, bureaucratic, and patriotic connections as a basis for local political candidacies, and Catholic organizations also relied on notables and non-political associations.[22] The liberal mode of *Honoratiorenpolitik* was the purest form in that it lacked the official and aristocratic ties of the one, and the confessional ties of the other. Instead, the hegemony of liberal notables was purely a *civic* phenomenon, with connotations of public-mindedness, enlightenment, and community improvement – all commendable and enduring democratic ideals, except to the extent that it was only notable citizens who were believed capable of exhibiting such qualities. It was the largely unspoken elitism in the politics of notables that came increasingly under attack a century ago.

The informal mechanisms of *Honoratiorenpolitik* were increasingly unsuited to the growing requirements for mass fund-raising, extended speaking tours, agitation, and long campaigns. As a result, the structures of *Honoratiorenpolitik* were gradually adapted in a piecemeal way. The informal clique became an explicitly political club with a network of contact people (*Vertrauensmänner*), and became more involved in agitation between elections and in staging public events. In urban centres, the full-blown structure of a constituency association with mass membership and regular public meetings developed. Before 1900 these were not coordinated into national party structures, yet with the removal of the *Verbindungsverbot* and similar restrictive legislation, even the National Liberals created central organs and a regular hierarchy in the years following the turn of the century.[23] In other words, the politics of notables found some ways to adapt structurally and live on in the age of mass politics – and some will argue it lives on, in places, even today. But while the mechanisms of *Honoratiorenpolitik* adapted somewhat according to necessity, the thinking of those involved was slower to change.

One of the chief claims by notables in campaigns of the old-fashioned variety was that they possessed, by virtue of their status in local society, exceptional competence to represent the interests of the whole community. Voters were to judge, not the stands of candidates on individual issues, but their general qualifications and trust the candidate to do the rest. Correspondingly, candidates in such campaigns were reluctant to issue manifestos and commit themselves to particular points of view. Indeed, they sometimes preferred to campaign on the basis of their endorsements and sponsors rather than their pledges. A graphic illustration was when candidates of the *bürgerliche Parteien* (roughly, middle-class parties) put up posters consisting almost entirely of the names of the local citizens endorsing them.[24] The message conveyed by such a communication is that voters should not be concerned with policies or platforms, but only with personages.

It was not just a good reputation that counted in *Honoratiorenpolitik*, but also the nature of the candidate's wealth and livelihood. Liberals in Bremen, for example, rejoiced in 1893 after the defeat of an SPD incumbent that they would finally have 'worthy representation in the Reichstag' because 'Bremen, as a trading city, can naturally only be represented by a businessman.'[25] Leadership by notables was elevated to the status of a right or a special mission of the propertied and educated classes. As one of the country's leading nationalist daily newspapers put it, 'the cautious and inhibitory influence of property owners' was essential in politics if the collapse of society into revolution and anarchy was to be avoided.[26] Such commentators believed collapse was already beginning, and they saw signs of it in the victories of the SPD and the Catholic Centre Party, and in the rise of divisive class-oriented economic issues in elections, all of which had 'nearly destroyed the honour and reputation of parliamentarism.'[27]

The concept of political leadership as a social responsibility of male upper-middle-class notables lent a certain dignity to political office, a dignity which the middle-class parties tried very hard to preserve. Again and again the liberal press contrasted the 'peaceful and matter-of-fact' speeches of their candidates with the (alleged) confessional fanaticism of the Centre Party, the disruptive tactics of the SPD, and the one-sided extremism of agrarians. Middle-class candidates, according to the ideals of *Honoratiorenpolitik,* were always reasonable and well-behaved, and stood above fanaticism and sectionalism for the national good.[28] Conservative and liberal meetings were *polite,* almost ceremonial, with candidates and party leaders expressing their thanks and admiration to each other on stage, addressing the audience placidly, and winding up, not with a general question or discussion period, but with patriotic mottos. The difference in styles was evident in countless cases such as that in Witten (near Bochum) in 1903, when a National Liberal meeting was invaded by rowdy Social Democrats. The Social Democrats were granted five minutes to speak, but when the chair attempted to cut them off after that time, the intruders refused to be silenced. They were finally drowned out by the National Liberals' singing 'Deutschland, Deutschland, über Alles,' and walked out.[29]

The presumption of the established parties was that respectability ought to earn the support of the electorate. The defeat of a candidate with good reputation and local standing was, in light of this assumption, nearly inexplicable. In 1903 the National Liberal deputy Dr Paasche was challenged on his home ground by dedicated and radical Agrarian League agitation. Paasche was compelled to campaign furiously in a run-off, touring his constituency to make speeches and meet voters. The nationalist press was perplexed by how, in modern politics, 'this so hard-working and exceptional people's representative' could be forced to campaign bitterly against a 'fully unknown opponent.'[30] The crisis of *Honoratiorenpolitik* in the 1890s was that votes were no longer won by simple right of status.

The deficiencies of organization in the older parties were apparent during 1898–1903, above all in the moderate and right-wing liberal camp. In October 1897, the National Liberal chairman in Bavaria complained of 'the deplorable apathy which dominates the widest circles,' and of the need to improve the organization of the party and make it more active in an agitational sense. 'It is not sufficient, when in the last instant before the elections a number of self-sacrificing supporters of the party take on election business without sufficient preparation,' he reproached his colleagues. 'The necessary apparatus of election committees, chairmen, and agents must be appointed promptly and instructed in its functions.'[31] Both poor structure and low morale lay behind these problems. Those more eager to adopt mass agitation – the SPD, some of the left liberals, the Centre, the anti-Semites, the Agrarian League – almost invariably beat the governmental parties to the punch in nominating candidates, as in the Rhine province where the 'agitational' parties often nominated their candidates before Christmas, while the other parties had not yet decided on theirs in May. The weakness of the less formal structures of *Honoratiorenpolitik* was that it depended a great deal, first of all, on the vagaries of individual capabilities and morale; and second, on protracted negotiations among cliques of notables that had to be conducted prior to each and every election.[32]

Nothing shows the difficulties of the older, less formal, and more decentralized party structures better than the fluid and complex negotiations that preceded every election in many constituencies across Germany. Nomination committees strove for the agreement of the local liberal and conservative camps, sometimes extending the negotiations to include agrarians, anti-Semites, Catholics, and left liberals – and in doing so, they were often urged on by government officials anxious to avoid fragmentation of the 'German,' 'national,' or anti-socialist camp.[33] As late as 24 May 1898, just three weeks before the voting, one such common front in Breslau collapsed when the Conservatives insisted on nominating a separate candidate. In Kassel a joint National and left-liberal candidate was proclaimed on 12 May, yet only on 24 May was the official agreement of the left liberals reported, and on 5 June (with only ten days remaining) the left-liberal press reported that 'the election campaign tide is rising only slowly.' As late as 3 June the National Liberals in Hagen were still courting the support of the Conservative Party, offering the latter a state Landtag seat if they would withdraw their Reichstag candidate. In 1903 a deal was reported on 23 May whereby the liberals were to drop their candidates in two Reichstag seats in exchange for a Conservative Landtag seat. On 12 June 1903 the dismissed *Regierungspräsident* (district governor) von Arnstedt, campaigning in Wanzleben, announced that he was not, after all, a National Liberal and was really campaigning for the Conservatives. All of this meant that voters in the liberal and conservative camps, especially, could not be sure until the last few weeks or days who their candidates would be, or even what parties they would run for.[34]

This fluidity in nominations and party allegiances among (mainly) the liberals and conservatives led locally to large blocs of votes switching back and forth from one party to another between elections – though sometimes the candidate was the same, merely claiming a different party affiliation. In effect, the German Conservatives, the Imperial Party, and the National Liberals (the three *Kartell* parties of 1887) functioned as a single electoral unit in many cases in which socialists or particularists posed a threat. In constituencies such as Westhavelland-Brandenburg, a steady 27–35 per cent of the vote went to a single *Kartell* party candidate in every election from 1890 to 1907, but in 1890 this candidate was German Conservative, in 1893 National Liberal, in 1898 again German Conservative, in 1903 Imperial Party, and in 1907 again National Liberal.[35]

The 'modern' style of politics, in opposition to all this, was clearly stated and embodied in the SPD and in the Centre, left-liberal, agrarian, and anti-Semitic parties: a permanent, centralized organization with formal decision-making structures and a dedication to agitation, and with clear boundaries against all other parties. This was an alternative, and in retrospect one would say more modern, vision of what a 'party' was and how it related to society. The political terminology of turn-of-the-century Germany was laced with value-laden terms like *Demokratie* and *Demagogie*, *Volkspartei* and *Volkstümlichkeit* ('popularity'), *Radikalismus* and *Agitation*. To traditional politicians and government leaders, all of these words had universally negative connotations; but the populists who opposed them were rather less disturbed by them, even proud to be associated with them. Furthermore, the firm organization of the 'agitational' parties represented a firmer set of integrating principles: sectional economic interest, class, minority religion or ethnicity, and so on – not merely community loyalty to benevolent social superiors. The debates about the working class and the state, about agriculture and the national interest, and more generally about 'moderation' and 'extremism,' the debates that dominated the popular politics of the day, were permeated by this subtle, pervasive opposition of political style and content. The campaign against the 'subversion' represented by the SPD involved at the same time the reassertion *within* the anti-socialist camp of moderate, governmentalist politics, against centrifugal pressures that tended to pull apart the older, established parties.[36]

These pressures on *Honoratiorenpolitik* were interconnected with the development of nationwide 'superstructure *milieux*' or social groupings, typically oriented around and articulating the cleavage structures of industrializing society. Nationally oriented patterns of behaviour were penetrating local and regional communities.

From 'National' Campaigns to 'Fairness' Issues

If parties are conceived as 'intervening variables' between society and government, as argued in chapter 1, then there are a number of different ways to conceive of their ties with society at large. The sociological concept of *milieu* has been introduced to represent the local roots of some later nineteenth-century parties. The *milieu* is taken to have been a strict, closed local environment in which membership was by birth and which was organized politically into a single party bound up with all the institutions of local society. Typically, this is considered a transitional structure, as the 'nationalization' of politics broke down local *milieux* and introduced national issues and competitive politics.[37] Yet by the late 1890s few areas were so isolated from the whole as to constitute closed *milieux*. Competitiveness and interpenetration of *milieux*, evidenced by growing numbers of run-off elections (required where no candidate could win an absolute majority on one ballot), as well as growing standardization of issues and trends between regions, are evidence that 'nationalization' was well advanced. The change noted by one historian, from 'foundation *milieux*' determined by birthplace to 'superstructure *milieux*' shaped by lifestyle and socialization, was evident by the beginning of the twentieth century.[38] In a key book on Wilhelmine elections, Stanley Suval chose the even more vague 'social grouping,' a term that says the least possible about the internal structure of the thing described. In this way, the role of Catholicism in cementing the Centre Party's support, of class in mobilizing socialist workers, and of sectional agrarian interests in organizing Conservative support can all be subsumed under one model, with the implication that different mechanisms serve integrating functions in different 'groupings.'[39]

In the early years of the Reich, shortly after unification, patterns of electoral behaviour varied starkly from one region to another. Figure 4 illustrates the range between the highest and lowest average turnout in Germany's states and *Regierungsbezirke* (administrative districts of larger states). Two main patterns are of interest: first, electoral participation was increasing; and second, turnout in different regions was converging, as the bottom of the range of turnouts rose faster than the top. There was a vast difference in behaviour between Swabian voters in 1871, more than 70 per cent of whom turned out to vote, and those in Lübeck, fewer than 30 per cent of whom did so. By 1912 turnout was between 60 and 90 per cent in almost all regions of the country. It was in the 1880s and 1890s that the distance between top and bottom narrowed, albeit fitfully (about

FIGURE 4
Highest and Lowest Turnout in Reichstag Elections, 1871–1912,
by *Regierungsbezirk* or State

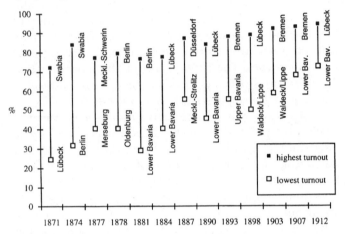

Source: Prepared from data in G.A. Ritter and M. Niehuss, *Wahlgeschichtliches Arbeitsbuch*,
pp. 67–96.

which more will be said below). After 1878 urban areas (above all, the
northern Hansa cities) became the most highly mobilized, while rural
areas remained the least mobilized. A statistical test shows that in the Wilhelmine period, the standard deviation of constituency turnout rates –
the amount by which rates in each constituency deviated from the average for all constituencies – decreased steadily in every election but 1898.[40]

The differences in regional behaviour can also be analysed by contrast-
ing the confessional structure of different regions (fig. 5). During the
Kulturkampf, the struggle between Catholics and the government of the
new empire (up to 1878), areas that were largely Catholic had higher
turnout than those that were largely Protestant; afterward, this relationship was reversed. This confirms the conclusion that the *Kulturkampf* provided an impetus for Catholics to mobilize politically in the young Reich.
However, constituencies of mixed confession almost always had higher
turnout than those that were dominated by one or the other. This suggests that the division or polarization strengthened political interest and
organization. As in figure 4, the lines converge in the later Wilhelmine
era, but it is noticeable that in 1878, (especially) 1887, 1893, and 1907 they
'pinch' closer together, indicating more homogeneous electoral behaviour between constituencies and regions. These were so-called 'national'

FIGURE 5
Turnout by Confessional Structure of Region, 1871–1912

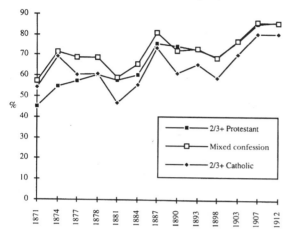

Source: Prepared from *Regierungsbezirk-* and state-level data in G.A. Ritter and M. Niehuss, *Wahlgeschichtliches Arbeitsbuch*, pp. 67–96. Particularist areas (where confession was secondary to Polish, Alsatian, etc. nationalism or regionalism as a factor in polarization) are left out.

elections, in which the government employed patriotic issues in a bid to arouse the electorate.

There were two distinctly different kinds of Reichstag elections in Imperial Germany: 'national' campaigns, and all the rest. The 'national' elections stand out as those in which the government set the tone of the campaign with a rousing patriotic or nationalistic cause; in almost every case, the Reichstag was dissolved over the failure of a piece of legislation considered essential by the government, which then took the initiative in a campaign against the Reichstag majority. These were one-issue, government-led campaigns. In this category belong the election of 1878, based on the government's proposed anti-socialist legislation; those of 1887 and 1893, both concerned with failed military bills; and that of 1907, which resulted from a dispute concerning colonial policy (table 2).[41] In each case there was increased turnout from the preceding election and increased percentage votes and significantly increased seat totals for the governmental parties, a result mainly of firmer tactical alliances among them. The losers in such campaigns, before 1907, were generally the left liberals.

Each of these dramatic, polarized campaigns reinforced certain perennial issues and party alignments in German politics. The first such cam-

TABLE 2
'National' Elections, 1871–1912

	1871	1874	1877	1878	1881	1884	1887	1890	1893	1898	1903	1907	1912
Dissolutions		D		D			D		D			D	D
% Turnout	51.0	61.2	60.6	**63.4**	56.3	60.6	**77.5**	71.6	**72.5**	68.1	76.1	**84.7**	84.9
Change		+10.2	-0.6	**+2.8**	-7.1	+4.3	**+16.9**	-5.9	**+0.9**	-4.4	+8.0	**+8.6**	+0.2
Kartell seats	219	210	206	**215**	125	157	**220**	135	**153**	125	126	**138**	100
Change		-9	-4	**+9**	-90	+32	**+63**	-85	**+18**	-28	+1	**+13**	-38
% Vote for Kartell	52.9	43.7	44.7	**49.6**	38.2	39.7	**47.2**	35.2	**32.1**	27.9	27.2	**28.0**	25.7
Change		-9.2	+1.0	**+4.9**	-11.4	+1.3	**+7.5**	-11.8	**-3.1**	-4.2	-0.7	**+0.8**	-2.3

Source: Calculated from figures given in G.A. Ritter and M. Niehuss, *Wahlgeschichtliches Arbeitsbuch*, pp. 38–42. Different versions of this table appeared in Brett Fairbairn, 'The Limits of Nationalist Politics: Electoral Culture and Mobilization in Germany, 1890–1903,' *Journal of the Canadian Historical Association* N.S. 1. 1 (1990): 147; and in 'Interpreting Wilhelmine Elections: National Issues, Fairness Issues, and Electoral Mobilization,' in Larry E. Jones and James Retallack, eds., *Elections, Mass Politics, and Social Change in Modern Germany*, p. 24.

Comments: All four elections of 1878, 1887, 1893, and 1907 resulted from dissolutions, involved some kind of patriotic issue promoted by the government, saw an increase in turnout followed by a decrease in the subsequent elections (except 1907), and saw an increase in the number of seats won by the right-wing (*Kartell*) parties. Note that the dissolution of 1874, following the beginning of the *Kulturkampf*, went together with a similar increase in voter turnout.

paign, in 1878, had seen Bismarck exploit the shock value of two assassination attempts on the kaiser to conduct an anti-socialist and anti-liberal campaign that rallied support to the conservative parties. This election brought the newly reorganized German Conservative Party firmly into the governmental camp for the first time since the founding of the Reich. The new right-wing grouping also introduced another recurrent theme: protectionism. The new government policy was higher tariffs to protect both industry and agriculture, which some historians have seen as the embodiment of an anti-revolutionary alliance of big business and aristocratic landowners.[42] The National Liberals were compelled to choose between associating with the left liberals in opposition or with the conservatives in government, and their gravitation to the latter strategy was indicated in the 1884 Heidelberg Declaration.[43] The cooperation among the Conservative and National Liberal parties was formalized in the *Kartell* elections of 1887, which were the definitive 'national' elections in Imperial Germany. In these elections, Bismarck achieved the combination of conservatives and right-wing liberals in a systematic first-ballot alliance, cemented in this case by a military bill and a war scare against France, and he created thereby a configuration which persisted in electoral politics until 1912, long after the *Kartell* as a coalition within the Reichstag itself was dead. The *Kartell* parties saw their combined share of the vote increase from 39.7 per cent in 1884 (already a good performance) to 47.2 per cent, and their seat total from 157 to a firm Reichstag majority of 220. The 1887 elections were the only ones between 1878 and 1918 in which the government's allies won a majority, and this success provided an inspiration and a hope (as it turned out, a forlorn one) for those parties in subsequent elections. For twenty years after 1887, government electoral strategy, to the extent there was any unified strategy, consisted of attempts to recreate the ideal coalition of that year.[44]

The 'national' strategy perfected in 1887 never worked well again, however, partly because election campaigns themselves were changing. The government found no adequate response to the advance of the Social Democratic Party following the lapsing of the anti-socialist law in 1890.[45] At the same time, the coalition of 1887, based on a nationalistic-ideal cause, was undermined by economic issues. Under Chancellor Leo von Caprivi (1890–4), a policy of freer trade was pursued. Agrarians, especially, made a return to protectionism a major issue in the 1890s, and while they eventually worked out a rough compromise with heavy-industrial interest groups, in terms of popular electoral politics the issue fragmented the governmental camp and set liberals against conservatives.

Finally, 1887 saw the first significant inroads of political anti-Semitism into electoral politics, and this added a further, disruptive element to the 'national' camp in the 1890s.[46] For these and perhaps other reasons, the 1893 campaign (based again on an army bill) did not work as well for the government as in 1887; the *Kartell* parties increased their seat total only from 135 to 153. The last 'national' elections of the imperial era, in 1907, had to follow an entirely different pattern, which included the left liberals as allies instead of enemies of the government.

No doubt these 'national' elections played a fundamental role in the formation of German electoral culture. They ensured that great, abstract national-interest questions were reintroduced to the electorate periodically, and this decisively affected the style of argument of the parties and the way in which they defined their causes. Elections were seen as battles between absolute and opposing systems, so that casting a vote took on an idealized character of loyalty to a historic cause. Such campaigns built in this respect on the formative battles of the *Kulturkampf* era in the 1870s, when in Catholic parts of the Reich, elections revolved around the conflict between church and state, religion and patriotism, freedom of conscience and secularization. The *Kulturkampf*, combined with the campaigns against particularists in eastern Prussia, Hanover, Schleswig, and Alsace-Lorraine, and reinforced by the 'national' campaigns and anti-socialism, created a systematic opposition of 'German' and 'anti-German' causes, of *Reichsfreunde* and *Reichsfeinde*. These various polarizations enhanced the sense of identity of the groups that were attacked (Catholics, Poles, socialist workers), while also enhancing the unity of the governmental parties.[47]

In some respects, however, the great *Kartell* victory of 1887, and all the 'national' campaigns by the government, carried within them the seeds of their own negation, for they whipped voter participation up to record levels. The 1887 election saw turnout leap to 78 per cent, compared with the previous high of 64 per cent in 1878. Turnout did not dip back below 70 per cent except in 1898. New voters first mobilized by 'national' issues remained mobilized even when the issues were different, which likely helped provide the fertile ground for recruitment by Social Democrats, agrarians, and anti-Semites in the 1890s. As Theodore Hamerow has commented with respect to the suffrage question, 'by initiating the age of mass politics in Germany, Bismarck unwittingly strengthened those civic forces which in time undermined the system of authority he had spent his lifetime defending.'[48]

In spite of the importance of 'national' elections, only four or five general elections of the thirteen that occurred in Imperial Germany fit this pattern. Most of the elections in Imperial Germany came about through the natural expiry of a Reichstag, with the important issues of the legislative session already resolved. The relative calm of these elections was generally reflected in lower voter participation, although this still increased from one normal election to the next. Given the lack of one specific issue set by the government to dominate the campaign, the parties were freer to choose their own issues and concentrate on the sort of campaigns that were advantageous in their respective regional and social environments. Each competed with the others to define what the election was about. Normal elections gave them the opportunity to stress their programmatic goals. These elections, too, were abstract and ideological, but without a simple polarization, and certainly without the polarization desired by the government.

The elections of 1898 and 1903 were of the non-'national' variety. They occurred as the result of natural expiration of the respective Reichstags. The government did not mount strong campaigns, nor appeal to the voters against the Reichstag majority. There was no sharp increase in participation, no boost to the vote ratios of the governmental parties, no increase in their seat totals. This in itself is significant, for these elections were the first two elections of Germany's era of imperialist *Weltpolitik*, of aggressive fleet-building, and of *Sammlungspolitik*; elections in which one would expect signs of 'social imperialism.' Yet there is little evidence of this. The election campaigns did reflect issues and interests raised both inside and outside the Reichstag, but on the whole these reflect the development of social-economic and political 'fairness' issues among the mass electorate. In most places, nationalism failed as a political tool in the face of new issues and organizations oriented around social-economic cleavages associated with industrialization.

Economic Interests and Pressure Groups

Apart from the advance of Social Democracy, what struck contemporaries most about politics in the 1890s was the extent to which it was increasingly shaped by economic debates, such as conflicts over economic and trade policy between agriculture and industry. This is an example of the Lipset-Rokkan cleavage theory (chapter 1), in which social-economic cleavages caused by industrialization became articulated into the political system through the activity of parties and, in this case, interest groups. The conflict between agriculture and industry in industrialization is unavoidable insofar as industrialization, conventionally, is defined as a process of the reduction in importance of agriculture, carried out with economic surpluses extracted from agriculture.[49]

Following Bismarck's fall in 1890, Chancellor Caprivi's government signed a series of trade treaties intended to reduce tariffs and promote trade. Agrarians reacted with a hostility that is only understandable in the context of the massive development of industialization and urbanization in the preceding generation, which gave a clear impression that the economic and political balance was tipping away from agriculture and rural Germany, towards industry and the cities.[50] The unprecedented degree of mass agrarian mobilization was most clearly expressed in the formation in 1893 of the Agrarian League (Bund der Landwirte, or BdL). The 1893 Reichstag elections caught the league hardly prepared, so that 1898 was the agrarians' first chance at a systematic political campaign. And, indeed, the BdL's efforts in 1898 were among the best-organized propaganda and pressure campaigns it or any other German interest group ever conducted. Its members and leaders began discussing election issues and formulating their platform nearly two years early, a process resembling the workings of the SPD machine. The exact election program was announced six months ahead of the anticipated date of the elections, well before the conservatives and liberals, the parties the BdL most wanted to pressure, had chosen their candidates or agreed on their own programs. Then, in the last two to three months before the voting, the BdL went into high gear with a propaganda campaign led by its agitational organs and its speakers.[51] While most of the league's effort went into influencing the right-wing parties, persuading them to nominate agrarians, or pressuring their candidates to endorse the league's program, the league itself also acted as a political party and ran its own candidates in some areas.[52]

The Agrarian League was not, however, the only agrarian phenomenon in Germany. There were the anti-Semites, the most successful of whom had rural populist movements supporting their bids for Reichstag mandates. There were agrarian movements within other political groupings, such as the agrarian wing of the Centre Party in the Rhineland and Westphalia, and left-liberal peasant associations. There were also independent peasant leagues, of which the most vociferous was the Bavarian Peasants' League, which challenged the Centre Party in some of its southern strongholds. These movements had their own agitation, propaganda, and electoral activities, as well as affiliated cooperatives and other organizations. Together they illustrate the emergence of an agrarian mass politics that was broader than any one organization. To see these populist eruptions as an adaptation to modern conditions of mass politics and new economic issues is to stand some entrenched assumptions on their heads. The rural peasantry has long and excessively been associated with traditionalism and backwardness.[53] In appropriating popular-democratic language to attack the established parties, and in articulating social-economic cleavages related to the industrial policy of the state, these agrarian movements were in tune with the 'modern' dynamism and innovation of the 1890s.

On the other side of the debate from the Agrarian League, there was no equivalent industrial interest group that waded into mass politics or adopted a populist stance. The Central Association of German Industrialists (Centralverband Deutscher Industrieller, CDI) was much more an elite lobbying organization, intertwined mainly with the Imperial Party and, after 1901, with the National Liberals. It did not strive, as the BdL did, for mass membership, nor to seat its own deputies in the Reichstag. It did, however, provide support and funding to partisan campaigns and to the governmental cause. In early 1893, for example, the CDI subsidized the distribution of anti-socialist literature, and did so again in mid-decade when anti-socialist measures were being discussed by the Reichstag. In 1907 (another 'national' election campaign) there was substantial funding through the CDI and related regional business organizations for the campaigns of the governmental parties.[54] Its members also helped support some of the nationalist pressure groups, notably the Colonial Society and the Pan-German League. While the CDI was generally representative of heavy industry, and was protectionist, the processing, banking, and export-oriented industries broke away and developed their own organizations. In 1895 they played a role in founding the Industrialists' League (Bund der Industriellen, BdI), which conceived of itself as a free-trade counterweight to the BdL.[55] When in 1897 a pro-tariff committee was founded with governmental sponsorship (Prussian Finance Minister Johannes von Miquel's Wirtschaftlicher Ausschuß), the BdI and related industrial associations established a counter-organization dedicated to promoting trade treaties, formalized in 1900 as the Trade Treaty Association (Handelsvertragsverein, HVV). The HVV was more tightly organized and more political than the BdI, managing to boost left-liberal funding and organization, and figuring in the 1903 Reichstag elections in some Baltic areas, in the Hansa cities, and in a few other urban centres where left liberalism was comparatively strong. Its effectiveness in party politics was limited, however, by the fact that its unity extended only to the tariff issue.[56]

Not only agriculture and industry but also the industrial working class had distinct economic-interest organizations, and these too were growing in the 1890s. They included the Free Trade Unions (Social Democratic), Christian Trade Unions (Catholic), and Hirsch-Duncker Trade Unions (left-liberal). Unions played little overt role in elections, probably because each major trade-union movement already had a political party with which it was associated. Even in the case of the most politicized movement, the Free Trade Unions, there was a rigid division of functions between the party (the SPD) and the trade unions. Indeed, the Social Democratic unions were becoming less and less political in this period. Following the legalization of socialist unions and associations in 1890, and in conjunction with their massive growth in membership and the reform-ist tendencies apparent at the turn of the century, the unions entered a 'period of neutrality' in which they concentrated on organizational tasks. With these developments came the 'two pillars' theory, that the unions were the economic representatives of the movement, the party the politi-cal organ. When radicals like Rosa Luxemburg advocated that the unions intervene in politics through the use of general strikes, this was resisted by the union leaders.[57] The current of pragmatic economic-interest mobi-lization in the 1890s was paralleled within Social Democracy itself by the bureaucratization of the trade unions.

The last years of the nineteenth century and the first years of the twen-tieth also saw the emergence of the so-called *Mittelstand* movement, which claimed to represent the interests of the lower-middle classes. Beginning at the end of the 1890s, a series of loose and mainly short-lived associa-tions appeared, different in breadth and politicization from earlier and more strictly occupation-related artisans' organizations. These *Mittelstand* interest groups demanded a combination of anti-socialist policies with government intervention to protect artisans, shopkeepers, and lower-level white-collar workers from economic decline. The shopkeepers' organizations, for example, were specifically concerned with the 'unfair' competition of innovative forms of retailing, including department stores, door-to-door salesmen, and consumer cooperatives. Like the BdL, these groups were radical, politicized, aimed at a mass audience, and will-ing to oppose the government in spite of their conservatism.[58] In num-bers, they were not an electoral factor, nor did they have the funds or organization to help or hurt major parties significantly, but their rhetoric became a part of right-wing political culture and of Germany's semi-per-manent anti-socialist crusade. *Mittelstandspolitik* was taken up by the con-servative and right-wing liberal groupings in their search for votes and legitimacy.

If one were to generalize about the importance of all of these interest groups in regard to *electoral* politics, it would seem that their main role was not in the campaign itself (the BdL is the exception), but in formulating and structuring the general environment of political ideas and discussion. To be sure, certain interest groups had a role in 'stiffening' the organization or financial basis of their favoured parties. The German Conservatives benefited, overall, from the BdL, the National Liberals from the CDI, left liberals from the free-trade interest groups and the Hirsch-Duncker unions, the Centre and the SPD from their trade unions. But more generally their effect was to raise the profile of their sectional interests and compel the parties to respond. The activities of the BdL, CDI, working-class organizations, and *Mittelstand* agitators meant that all parties had to take positions concerning the needs of agriculture, industry, labour, and small property owners. It was partly through the effects of interest organizations that the cleavages of the new industrial society were articulated into politics.

While economic-interest politics permeated the political culture, Germany's nationalist pressure groups were of marginal significance in these elections. The Colonial Society, the Pan-Germans, the Society for the Eastern Marches, the Evangelical League, and their companion societies promoted 'national' causes and had a role in providing institutional backbone and party workers for certain parties, generally the National Liberals.[59] But most of them played no significant role in the non-'national' elections of 1898 and 1903.[60] Of the Colonial Society nothing appears to have been heard, and that in spite of the fact that the seizure of Kiaochow, the Spanish-American War, and imperialist and naval matters in general were widely discussed in the press in the run-up to the 1898 elections. Even the more extreme and agitational Pan-German League, in spite of its occasional aspirations to compete with or replace political parties and to agitate against the government, declined to publicize its views in these campaigns. In its meetings in the midst of both the 1898 and 1903 Reichstag campaigns, it appears to have ignored the elections entirely.[61] All of these groups were, in any case, small; the Navy League was the only nationalist group to attain a 'mass' membership in these years, swelling from its founding in April 1898 to attain a membership of two hundred thousand within eighteen months, under the official patronage of heads of states. The success of this semi-official organization has been interpreted as 'a response to the patent inflexibility of the existing political parties, a striking testimony to their inability to accommodate the needs and aspirations of wide sections of the populace.'[62] But while this may have been true in a social-psychological sense for the minority of activists who found the prime outlet for their political energies within the Navy League, it was not true in terms of electoral campaigning. The Navy League made no attempt to challenge or supplant parties, or to compete with them for votes. The invisibility of even the Navy League in mass electoral politics reinforces the impression that nationalist activists belonged to a separate cultural community of their own making, and had little taste for partisan politics.[63]

However, the elections of 1898 and 1903 were not all economics. Nationalistic causes did enter in, especially in certain regions. There were two particular nationalist movements that were significantly involved in electoral politics. Unlike such groups as the CDI or the Navy League, which exerted their influence at the centre – on party deputies and leaders – these two were particularly capable of conducting grass-roots level agitation to affect local election campaigns in certain areas of the Reich. The first of these were the veterans' associations (*Kriegervereine*), which, where they were active, conducted anti-socialist campaigning and promoted the unity of the non-socialist, patriotic parties.[64] The second was the anti-Polish crusade widely supported by German nationalists and led nationally by the Society for the Eastern Marches. The 'H-K-T Society,' as it was also known after the initials of three of its leaders, had a receptive audience among the governmental parties and enjoyed official patronage from the Prussian government and bureaucracy. From about 1899 onward, the Reich government strengthened its existing anti-Polish stance through heightened anti-Polish propaganda and through subsidies to German settlers in Polish eastern territories. The fanaticism of the national conflict within the Polish regions spilled over inevitably into election campaigns. Regardless of legislative issues, much of the so-called 'German' population and most of the Polish population treated the election battle as a crusade for national identity. This prompted the increasingly strict unity of non-Polish and non-socialist parties in a single coalition in these provinces, including even Centrists and left liberals. The campaigns of the 'German party' were supported by the patronage and funds of the Prussian provincial and district governments, and by the related local 'societies for the defence of Germandom' and the like. In this nationalist battle, the H-K-T Society 'appointed itself as a "get-out-the-German-vote" committee.' In spite of these efforts, the society's campaign has been judged only 'moderately successful.'[65]

The activity of German interest and pressure groups has been interpreted as anti-democratic in nature and as a parallel system of mass organization weakening the party system. One historian calls these groups 'a secondary system of social powers'; another refers to their *Ersatzfunktion* in compensating for the weakness of parties; a third describes them as agents of governmental bureaucratization of society. They have, further, been charged with creating a deviant form of 'direct, plebiscitarily articulated democracy' or facilitating 'manipulative, bonapartist Caesarism.'[66] All of this is overstated and perhaps based on fuzzy thinking about the actual functions of parties and interest groups in modern democracies. As debates in the theoretical literature suggest, it is never easy, in any country, to draw a sharp line between the activities of parties and those of interest groups.[67] There may indeed be nothing unique in the German situation – nothing to explain why German democracy should have been more compromised by all this than was democracy anywhere else.[68] Certainly interest groups competed with parties to *articulate* interests, as they do in all countries. They did not so much compete with parties in *aggregating* interests into coherent social-political groupings, which is a distinctive function of parties; nor did they put up candidates and mount campaigns during elections, which is arguably the only unique function of a political party – always with the exception of the BdL, which by the standard definitions became a political party as it did these things. To speak of an *Ersatzfunktion* for groups other than the BdL is misleading. It is true that interest groups affected parties and that some of them provided homes for agitators whose values were not democratic. But if it is taken as modern for parties in industrialized societies to reflect industrial cleavages – urban or rural, worker or employer, agriculture or industry – then the economic interest groups in Wilhelmine Germany, in particular, were agents for the modernization of party politics.

The accentuation of economic issues provided special problems for those parties whose electoral support was not united on an economic basis. This included most of the major non-socialist parties, especially the liberals and conservatives – the government's chief allies. Parties that represented diverse economic bases could respond only by repudiating interest politics, by opposing all exclusive demands or the favouring of one interest over another.[69] They were driven to claim a role as bargainers or brokers above the interests. In this vein the National Liberals advocated, 'Fatherland above party, the general good above special interests, independence from left and right as with respect to the government ...'[70] The Left Liberal People's Party emphasized that it was indeed 'a people's party; it does not want to represent individual occupations or estates or confessions, but rather the whole people.' In this context, it criticized the way 'special interests are pushing themselves forward and are seeking with misleading slogans of *Sammelpolitik* ... to exploit the collectivity.'[71] In somewhat similar terms, the Westphalian Centre Party proclaimed that its goal was 'to serve the entire people, to further the just compromise of all interests.'[72] In all of these claims, we can see the efforts of these parties to keep their heads above water in the tide of interest politics of the 1890s. The problem was that the choice of issues was in this respect beyond their control.

The Parties and the Issues, 1893–1903

The issues discussed in Reichstag campaigns reflected the major debates and legislative initiatives in the Reichstag itself. In the decade from 1893 to 1903, the agenda of the parliament and the political nation was dominated by the questions of the reaction to Social Democracy; the defeat of politically repressive measures; tariffs; taxation policy; and military and naval spending.

The 1893–8 Reichstag began with 'national' issues and ended in the primacy of questions of economics, fair taxation, and popular rights. In these ways, perhaps, it summed up the Wilhelmine era as a whole. The 1893 Reichstag had been elected in the midst of Chancellor Caprivi's efforts to pass a controversial new military bill that increased the basic strength of the army. As in previous cases in imperial history, military budgets and parliamentary control became points of contention between government and opposition.[73] While the controversy around the military bill weakened Caprivi, the issue that provoked his downfall was the question of how to deal with Social Democracy. The middle years of the 1890s were dubbed the 'Stumm Era' after one of the most vocal proponents of repression, the Imperial Party deputy Baron Carl von Stumm-Halberg. With the 'Subversion Bill' (*Umsturzvorlage*) of 1894–5, conservatives proposed legislative measures to stem the alarming advance of the SPD. Compared with Bismarck's law of 1878, the new proposals were mild, yet they occasioned determined opposition from the Reichstag majority, and ultimately a governmental crisis. Late in 1894, Caprivi and Prussian Minister-President Count Botho zu Eulenburg, the sponsor of the bill, were dismissed simultaneously. The bill was lamed by the controversy and virtually abandoned by the new chancellor, Chlodwig Prince zu Hohenlohe-Schillingsfürst. Eventually it failed, after a long, drawn-out debate which damaged the government's prestige and crystallized the opposition to the reactionaries. Thereafter the campaign against *Reaktion* provided a useful battle-cry for the non-governmental parties.[74]

Useful as the spectre of *Reaktion* was in opposition propaganda, it was even more effective when linked to rumours that conservatives wanted to change the Reichstag suffrage. Indeed, some conservatives now believed that only changing the suffrage could remove Social Democracy from the Reichstag and produce a more compliant legislature. At the height of the 1894 crisis, the kaiser, Miquel, and Botho zu Eulenburg had proposed a *coup d'état* to change the suffrage, but had been blocked by Caprivi. Hohenlohe and others also warned of the dangers of such a step, arguing that the Reichstag's cooperation was essential to the regime, and that an unconstitutional action could dissolve the federal union and lead to revolution and war. No initiative was taken; indeed, there does not appear to have been a concrete plan for a suffrage revision at any point by any group capable of implementing such a plan.[75] Yet rumours persisted, and vocal reactionaries repeatedly made suggestive speeches critical of universal suffrage. As a result, Hohenlohe's chancellorship has been referred to as 'political life under the threat of a *coup d'état*.'[76] Whether the threat was real or not, the 'constitutional' opposition to the government (the SPD, the left liberals, and the Centre, which consistently opposed political repression) took the threat at face value and made defence of the Reichstag suffrage a focal point of their election declarations. It was to these parties' advantage in Reichstag elections to claim that 'the suffrage is in danger,' to adopt the stance of defenders of popular rights, and thereby to enhance their images as 'people's parties.' In 1898 the SPD national election platform listed defence of the Reichstag suffrage and of trade union rights as its first and second priorities, ahead of tariffs and of military-naval questions.[77] The Centre deputy Richard Müller-Fulda, who favoured a stronger alliance to the left in these elections, issued a statement during the campaign claiming a plan existed to restrict the suffrage, and that a decree to this effect had already been drafted. Both the left liberals and the SPD picked up this story and publicized it widely. The predictable denials from the conservative press did nothing to detract from the story's usefulness to the opponents of *Reaktion*.[78]

The suffrage issue neatly symbolized the claims of the parties of the constitutional opposition that they were the true defenders of popular interests, and that the elections revolved around the conflict between popular rights and privileged interests. Tariffs, regressive mass consumption taxes, spending on the military and navy out of the pockets of the poor, and political repression were all neatly tied together into one bundle of policies, in the propaganda these parties distributed to voters. But the suffrage issue was especially important for one additional reason. It not only helped tie this popular rights platform together but also permitted the dovetailing of state and federal politics. For the SPD and the Centre, in particular, the reform of state suffrages was a first priority in many of the federal states. Campaigns for suffrage reform were under way throughout southern Germany, while in Saxony, in 1896, a conservative and National Liberal majority had actually introduced a more restricted suffrage on the lines of the Prussian three-class system. Advocacy of the Reichstag suffrage was congruent with the state suffrage reform campaigns and lent greater cohesion to the opposition's efforts at different levels. The dynamics of state suffrage controversies meant that this issue continued to increase in importance through to 1903 and beyond – even though at the national level the threat of a coup declined.[79]

The 1893–8 term was also when the vocal demands of *Mittelstandspolitik* – protective measures to help the lower-middle class – became part of national debate. The law of 1895 on artisanal chambers was an explicit initiative to help traditional manufacture, as was the 1897 revision of the *Reichsgewerbeordnung* (Reich trades regulations), which increased the powers of guilds. Such measures were paralleled by legislation to limit 'unfair competition' by restricting special sales and advertising (1896) and by demands to restrict department stores and consumer cooperatives, offer favouritism to small contractors in government tendering, and provide greater security for small building contractors when tenderers went bankrupt. More so than in previous Reichstags, these sorts of concerns were stridently raised and earned responses from the government, the conservative parties, and the Catholic Centre.[80] Even the new legal code passed in 1896, the final national codification of civil law and one of the 1893–8 Reichstag's most important achievements, became controversial in the light of *Mittelstandspolitik*. Agrarian, anti-Semitic, and *Mittelstand* activists attacked the code for its liberal 'impartiality' in economic matters, alleging that the law should, for policy reasons, instead give preferential treatment to certain economic groups, rather than uphold the right of contract and 'unfair' competition.[81]

These background issues – military spending, anti-socialist repression, *Mittelstandspolitik* – were supplemented in the last year before the 1898 elections by new issues, and yet another governmental crisis. The chancellor had announced his intention, without gaining the kaiser's full approval, to reform courts-martial, a cause that was popular with south German anti-militarists.[82] This occasioned not only an internal govern-

mental crisis between the chancellor and the kaiser but also a federal conflict among the states of the Reich, and it absorbed immense amounts of
official energy throughout 1897 and 1898.[83] Meanwhile Admiral Alfred
von Tirpitz, appointed secretary of the navy in one of a series of top-level
personnel changes during 1896–7, introduced in December 1897 a bill to
increase the size of the German navy. Tirpitz encountered opposition
from the Bavarian Centre Party deputies, agrarians, anti-Semites, and, of
course, the SPD. In both issues, the kaiser's personal prestige was deeply
engaged: it was the kaiser who blocked the military reform, who had dismissed Tirpitz's predecessor for failing to obtain satisfactory fleet funding
from the Reichstag, and who had called the Social Democrats 'vaterlands-
lose Gesellen' – 'louts without a fatherland' – for their role in obstructing
his wishes. Both issues came to a head in the last six months before the
1898 Reichstag elections.[84] There were those on both sides who desired a
confrontation, especially on the fleet issue. Those sharing the kaiser's
attitude would have been happy to teach the Reichstag a lesson, while
National Liberal and Centre leaders (for different reasons) were itching
for a 'national' campaign on the fleet issue.[85] But the fleet question
(unlike the courts-martial question – Wilhelm would not sign the code
passed by the Reichstag until December) was definitively resolved *before*
the elections. This was possible because of the willingness of the government and the Centre Party to reach an important practical and symbolic
compromise.

Ernst Lieber, leader of the Centre Party, wanted badly for his party to
become the government's legislative partner and saw the fleet bill as an
opportunity to prove his party's usefulness. In order to minimize the electoral damage, however, of being linked to naval spending, he needed to
be able to argue that his party had stood up effectively for popular interests. Specifically, Lieber wanted a commitment that no new indirect taxes
would be levied to cover the cost of the fleet, and he wanted a reduction
in the multi-year budgeting period, in order to increase somewhat the
Reichstag's control. Lieber obtained his concessions, critical to the Centre's ability to portray itself as a 'people's party' that had defended the
financial intersts of the public. In spite of the fleet's unpopularity, the
Centre's middle-class leadership was able to pass the bill and make itself
indispensable to the Reich government.[86] None of this would have been
possible if the government had desired a confrontation. Presumably, the
government was not willing to launch a 'national' election on the fleet
issue.

One newspaper of the time commented that 'increased expenditures for the armaments of the Reich on water and on land are never popular and cannot be so.'[87] The elections of 1898 and 1903 bear this out, for in each case the fleet's opponents attacked it with devastating effectiveness on the basis of its cost and the unfair tax base of Reich finances, while parties that had voted for the fleet tried to apologize and shift the blame. 'What will all the millions from tariffs and taxes be applied to?' asked the Social Democrats rhetorically in a 1903 pamphlet. 'Are they perhaps to the benefit of the people? On, no! They serve primarily to *cover the costs* which the *army and fleet require* ...'[88] The Centre, for its part, took pains to show itself, not as the party instrumental in approving the fleet, but rather as the party that had forced the government to scale down its excessive projects. As the national election platform put it, the Centre stood for 'prudent thrift in all areas of the Reich budget, particularly with the army and navy.' Among its achievements, it listed the prevention of 'new taxes, namely those which would have been a further burden to the broad masses of the people.' The 'important principle' in relation to the fleet was that new taxes not rest 'on the consumption of the broad masses ... on the shoulders of the weak.'[89] As for the conservatives, they avoided mentioning the fleet, or treated it as a patriotic if unpleasant duty for the good of the Fatherland. 'As burdensome as [the level of] armament is that the German people has to bear,' the small Imperial Party consoled its voters after declaring its support for the fleet, 'it is nevertheless the precondition for the power, the influence, the health of the German empire.'[90] Of the major parties, only the National Liberals exhibited unreserved enthusiasm for the fleet, declaring in their 1898 national platform that they were filled with 'joyous pride' at Germany's fleet and colonial policies. They accepted the distinction of being 'the first party which recognized unanimously and without reservation that the fleet law was a necessity for ... the health and power position of Germany.'[91] This solitary distinction brought the party no perceptible gains among the electorate: the National Liberals' share of the popular vote in 1898, at 12.5 per cent, was their lowest in the history of the *Kaiserreich*.[92]

In light of the campaign platforms and relative fates of the parties, one has seriously to question whether 'social imperialism' exerted a perceptible effect on the electorate.[93] The widest claims for the fleet argue that it won 'mass loyalty,' 'widespread and intense popular enthusiasm,' or 'a groundswell of popular support' for the government.[94] This is clearly not the case. The fleet was controversial and fitted too well into the opposition parties' critiques of the regime's military spending and regressive tax base. 'The masses' were won in these elections by the SPD, which opposed the fleet uniformly, and the Centre, whose deputies approved the fleet bill but whose propaganda tried very hard to dissociate the party from it. Those historians whose concentration is specifically on the fleet in the German domestic politics of these years have been careful in their claims: while they note that Bülow and to some extent Tirpitz *claimed* the fleet would win mass support, they note that it was really the middle classes to which it appealed, not to the broad masses of the electorate.[95]

Like the fleet – and distinct from it – *Sammlungspolitik* or 'the politics of rallying together' became a catch phrase in 1897. Finance Minister Miquel had selected an 'Economic Committee' (*Wirtschaftlicher Ausschuß*) representing big industry and agriculture, together with members of, mainly, the conservative parties. Shortly before the 1898 elections, the committee issued an 'Economic Declaration' intended to rally the governmental parties to unite on the basis of tariff protectionism and anti-socialism. As envisioned by Miquel, this was to be an active governmental campaign to reconcile the divisions among the governmental parties. The government, however, was itself divided, for Hohenlohe counselled caution lest the government put its prestige on the line and suffer defeat. Many liberals refused to accept *Sammlungspolitik*, which they saw simply as conceding to the agrarians on the tariff issue; while to the Centre the *Sammlung* was indistinguishable from the restoration of the *Kartell.* In the end there was no formal governmental sponsorship of *Sammlungspolitik.*[96]

The 1898 *Handbook for Social Democratic Voters* listed the development of the agrarian movement as the most prominent new development since the last elections, more important than attempted repression, more important than the fleet. This was echoed in local campaigns that opened by mentioning the tariff as the main issue.[97] Rather than treating the tariff issue in a narrow fashion, the SPD linked the agrarian movement to the government's turn to the right in the 1890s, to 'reactionary anti-worker and anti-popular endeavours.' The left-liberal press broadened the issue in the same way, launching a prolonged campaign in May-June 1898 featuring 'the struggle against Junkers and reactionaries' as the number-one election issue. All liberals were to unite to fight the Junker, the 'enemy of the peasant, the bourgeois, and the worker.' Left-liberal slogans were 'Down with the Junkers' and 'Rise up in the struggle against Junkerdom and reaction.' Clearly, the opposition was happy to take the agricultural issue and convert it into an attack on privilege and regressive taxation.[98] The opposition's criticisms were only one of the ways in which the new agrarian stridency created problems for the government. Separate BdL candidacies, and candidacies by anti-Semitic agrarians, challenged moderate conservative and liberal candidates in many widely separated parts of the Reich. Under such circumstances, *Sammlungspolitik* represented a desired, not a real, unity of interests, a damage limitation policy to control agrarian defections from the government cause. And in electoral terms it was neither consistent nor effective.

To sum up: the issues of 1893–8 were successfully woven together by the opposition, and especially by the SPD, into a platform of opposing tariffs and regressive taxes, opposing military and naval expenditures, and defending popular rights against oppression and *Reaktion*. This amounted to advocating social-equity or 'fairness' issues – fair taxation, popular democracy – in opposition to privilege. Not only the SPD but the left liberals and even the Centre (despite its role in cooperating with the government) staked out this kind of ground in their platforms. On the other side, governmental parties were left with the anti-socialist, pro-tariff, and pro-fleet positions, the last two of which, however, tended to divide governmental liberals and conservatives from each other. To put it another way, the opposition parties' campaigns worked with economic, class, and status cleavages. The governmental parties tried to form coalitions across those boundaries, for example under the banner of national unity, and had less success.

The course of the 1898–1903 Reichstag accentuated these issues and divisions. Once again, the new legislature opened with an army bill, which was followed by a new and greater fleet bill. The Centre Party, having supported the bills, continued to defend itself by emphasizing its role in 'frugality' and 'lightening the military burden' (it claimed to have cut 7,006 soldiers and five million marks), while the SPD again fit its opposition to armament spending into its campaign against taxes.[99] The advocates of legislative repression of socialism tried two new tactics: the *Zuchthausvorlage* (hard labour bill) demanded personally by the kaiser in 1899, which tried to strike at the trade union base of Social Democracy; and the so-called *lex Heinze* of the same year, a measure designed to protect public morality. The first was defeated humiliatingly (the rejection of its key provisions was one of the Reichstag's only unanimous acts in its history); the second passed, but stripped of all provisions that could be applied to the press, literature, or the arts. By 1899 it was clear that the path of legislative repression was firmly blocked by the Reichstag.

The suffrage question remained in the foreground of politics. Voters in Saxony had by now all experienced the extreme inequality of the 1896 system, and a powerful protest movement was growing there that could only effectively express its dissatisfaction using the Reichstag suffrage.[100] In

Prussia, the conservatives and National Liberals were stubbornly resisting all reform, and the SPD decided to contest Prussian Landtag elections for the first time (starting with the autumn elections of 1903) as a means to express protest. In southern Germany, the suffrage reform movements were gathering momentum, and here the SPD and the Centre joined forces at several crucial junctures in using the suffrage issue to attack entrenched liberal regimes. The Bavarian state election in 1899 saw the SPD and Centre conclude a coalition and gain seats; at the next election in 1905, the two parties together gained the two-thirds majority of deputies needed to revise the constitution. In neighbouring Württemberg, the state elections of 1895 had brought a powerful Centre presence to the legislature, and from 1900 the SPD began to overtake the left-liberal People's Party. As a result of the advance of the SPD and the Centre, Baden, Bavaria, and Württemberg saw suffrage reform enacted during 1905–6.[101]

Long-standing regional, particularist, and confessional divisions had also been inflamed since 1898, not only by the accelerated campaign against the Poles, but now by a renewed crystallization of anti-Catholic nationalism. Events during 1900–1 exacerbated the resentment that Protestant nationalists already felt as a result of the 'hegemony' won by the Centre Party in the Reichstag in 1898. The Centre Party used its new-found influence to push its campaign for 'parity,' the removal of civil disabilities on Catholics, and introduced a Toleration Bill in the Reichstag in 1900. This was the latest in a series of attempts to override discriminatory state civil codes, taxes, and church and school regulations. The following year, controversy arose over Strassburg University, starting with the government's plans to establish a Catholic theological faculty. The proposal aroused the ire of Protestant extremists, but not as much as did the appointment of a Catholic, Martin Spahn, son of a well-known Centre deputy, to a history chair at the university. Friedrich Meinecke – the historian – commented, 'Catholic history professors are and remain a monstrosity.' Shortly before the 1903 elections the Centre obtained a concession on its most important single demand: a commitment from Bülow (chancellor since 1900) to remove article two of the Jesuit Law, which banned the order from Germany.[102] Bülow's concession scandalized both the Bundesrat and nationalists, the former because it had not been consulted (this verged on a breach of the constitution and represented, in any event, a derogation of the federal council's status in comparison with that of the Reichstag), and the latter because it was seen as proof of the extent of 'clerical influence' on German politics. Left-wing National Liberals, and their close cousins in the Left Liberal Union (Freisinnige Vereinigung), now claimed that the 'confessional domination' of German culture and politics posed an equal or greater danger than the 'interest politics' of the agrarians. Everyone perceived that the concession was a tactical announcement for the electoral benefit of the Centre, a 'reward for the adoption of the tariff' as the Württemberg envoy put it.[103]

Of all of the issues that had been carried over from the previous Reichstag, the tariff was the most contested. The tariff law debates of 1901–2 dominated the session, consuming huge amounts of the Reichstag's time and provoking acrimonious disagreements both among and within the parties. The basic party positions and alignments had not altered greatly since 1898, but the level of tension was greater. The SPD conducted a filibuster to prevent the measure for as long as possible, and as a result the tariff law could not be passed until December 1902. This left the government barely six months before the constitutional expiry of the Reichstag in which to pass its other essential measures, including the financial estimates. Given the bitter tariff debate, the lateness of the decision, and the housekeeping nature of the remaining business, the parties could be in no doubt about the basis on which the election would be fought. The campaigns of the SPD and the BdL, opposing the tariff as too much and not enough respectively, ensured that the tariff would remain the top issue even after the law was passed. But the BdL's exceptionally well prepared campaigns of 1898 and 1903 did not result in widespread electoral success.[104] Instead, the SPD and the left liberals were more than willing to make the Agrarian League itself a central issue in the campaign, and lashed out at the 'boundless demands' of the 'East Elbian Junkers.'[105]

The even greater prominence of economic issues in the 1903 campaign as compared with 1898 was probably reinforced by the short, sharp downturn experienced by the German economy between 1900 and 1902, overlapping the tariff debates. This recession visibly hurt the wage levels and employment prospects of industrial workers, weakening the socialist labour movement and providing abrupt setbacks in membership growth and strike success rates among the SPD unions.[106] The party programs and the press coverage of the 1903 campaign indicate that the anxiety among farmers about their livelihoods was now complemented by an increased concern among workers and consumers for their interests. The backlash against agrarian demands and the opposition campaigns against privilege and unfair taxation now had a sharper edge.

The Social Democratic filibuster in the Reichstag also helped change the complexion of the issue. The Reichstag majority was forced to overpower the opposition of the SPD by enforcing a form of closure, but by their disruptive tactics the Social Democratic deputies had advanced their claim to be the most determined opponents of the tariff bill. When closure was invoked, the SPD was able to claim not only that it was the sole party to fight the tariff effectively, but that the Reichstag majority had violated freedom of speech and the rights of the socialist deputies in forcing the measure through. 'This new tariff is in our eyes a product of illegality and barbarism,' claimed the *Schwäbische Tageszeitung*.[107] In this way the SPD tightened the association between tariffs and privilege, opposition to tariffs and defence of popular rights. Meanwhile the stridency of the SPD repelled the other major parties. In the case of the left liberals, it also robbed them of their traditional championship of the free-trade issue. Relations between the SPD and the Catholic Centre Party were seriously damaged, for the latter remained committed to 'responsible' conduct in parliament and what it referred to as 'positive legislative accomplishment.' The conflict between the two parties came to a head in January 1903, when Franz Count von Ballestrem of the Centre Party resigned as president (speaker) of the Reichstag in the aftermath of the SPD's and the BdL's criticism.[108] The other parties therefore attempted to convert the issue from that of the tariff itself to the *Obstruktion* of the SPD, accusing the socialists of terrorizing parliament and sabotaging the nation's business. The 1903 National Liberal platform attacked the SPD as 'a reckless minority' who 'undertook the attempt to tyrannize the majority, to make any parliamentary business whatsoever impossible.'[109] The SPD's behaviour in the tariff debate epitomized what governmentalists most feared and loathed about the party and its effect on German public life: it accentuated the cleavages in German society.

More than ever, the question for the other parties was how to fight Social Democracy. By 1903 their approach to this question was beginning to exhibit tinges both of fanaticism and despair. The elections of 1898 had shown that the SPD could not be defeated in normal competition with other parties, and the government's hesitation in 1898 to undertake an aggressive campaign, either on the basis of the fleet or on the basis of the economic issues of *Sammlungspolitik*, showed that anti-socialists could not rely on governmental leadership to defeat the SPD in elections. Letters and pamphlet and newspaper literature show that by 1903 more and more of the activists in the other parties were coming to believe that the time for a showdown had come, that the unity of the non-socialist parties to halt the SPD advance was the most important strategic consideration in the campaign. The conservatives, in particular, made the fight against Social Democracy the centrepiece of their campaign across Germany,

proclaiming 'a clear unambiguous slogan: Against Social Democracy!'
They ridiculed other parties for not making this 'struggle' their 'chief
task ... in the election campaign.'[110] Government support behind the
scenes for such efforts was greater than ever. Bülow instructed one of his
governors that SPD victories 'must under all circumstances be prevented'
and that this consideration should guide all tactical decisions.[111] Yet the
hoped-for unity remained difficult to achieve. The BdL and agrarian conservatives argued that further protectionist measures for agriculture were
the highest priority, that the 1902 tariff law was not enough, and they
broke ranks with the government over this issue. Anti-clericals believed
the influence of the Centre Party was more dangerous than that of the
SPD. Liberals in general continued to emphasize that, now the tariff law
had been passed for agriculture, industry had to have its interests protected by ensuring long-term trade treaties and stable foreign markets.
And the Centre, while generally joining the campaign against the SPD,
simultaneously continued its opposition to *Reaktion* and 'one-sided interest politics,' its defence of the Reichstag suffrage and trade union rights,
and its battles in favour of 'parity' and against nationalist *Kulturkämpfer.*
While the desire to fight the SPD had increased generally among all the
parties, the ability to do so had not.

The issues in 1898 and 1903 were endemic issues of Wilhelmine politics: tariff, suffrage, army, navy, taxes, confession, socialism, and particularism. But something had changed; the old party structures, the old-
fashioned campaigns, and the old 'national' issues that once roused the
electorate were not working nearly so well. Issues and elections had been
cast in a new light. Now they were more successfully bound together into
a polarized system of issues, pitting either 'fairness' against privilege or,
in the terms used by the other side, loyalty against subversion. There was
a sense of transition to a new system, one that revolved around mass agitation and mass-membership parties, populist appeals to voters instead of
the comfortable presumption of *Honoratiorenpolitik*, and, of course, economic and sectional issues that clearly articulated the cleavages of the
newly industrialized nation.

3

The Official Machine and
the Failure of *Sammlungspolitik*

Germany's government was not democratically responsible to the elector-ate, and yet it did campaign in elections. This was one aspect of the para-dox of democracy in an undemocratic state. It is a curious circumstance by comparison to modern Western democracies, but perhaps is not unheard of in relation to developing countries – what it reflected was the incompleteness of democracy in turn-of-the-century Germany. The nature of the government's campaigns in 1898 and 1903, and their results, also illuminate the multiple meanings and functions of democ-racy. For although according to the government's plan the influence should all have been in one direction – by the government and its offi-cials on the elections – this was not what happened in practice. In these key elections, the government's overall campaigns failed, by any electoral measure. Officials did not understand and could not much influence mass politics. The government fought precisely those parties that were attempting to mobilize the cultural and social-economic cleavages of modern Germany. In combating them, it only deepened the cleavages, strengthened its opponents, and retarded the modernization of its allied parties. In the process, the credibility of the government and perhaps even the legitimacy of the regime were significantly undermined. In other words, while democracy was not permitted to perform the function of determining the composition of government, it did perform its legiti-mizing function – in particular, legitimizing of the opposition.

The curious federal nature of Imperial Germany meant that the Reich government in Berlin did not possess an extensive network of officials throughout Germany. Instead, it worked to a great extent through inter-mediary state bureaucracies. Through the overlap and blending of the Reich and Prussian governments, the state apparatus of Prussia stood at the disposal of the same men, more or less, who directed the policy of the Reich. Prussian officials – and Prussia covered two-thirds of the empire – were the sole direct means for the leaders of the Reich government to intervene locally in electoral politics.[1] And Prussian officials were not neutral in elections. Prussian political officials, mainly the *Landräte* in rural districts, formed a kind of governmental machine which supplied Germany's leaders with information on the prospects of election campaigns and (with varying degrees of discipline and effectiveness) attempted to implement electoral strategies emanating from the central government. Mostly, they tried to help the parties friendly to the government, the right-wing parties that had made up the *Kartell* of 1887–90: Conservatives, Imperial Party, and National Liberals. Agrarian and anti-Semitic candidates complicated the unity of the German right and were sometimes a factor in official calculations. But during 1898–1903 the official machine, for all its size, was remarkably ineffective. The tactical help of officials was not enough to help the governmental parties with their strategic difficulties, above all those created by the rise of Social Democracy and the economic-interest politics of the late nineteenth and early twentieth century.

The Government's Message

On 28 January 1898 the minister of the interior wrote to the provincial governors to give them the 'guidelines' (*Leitsätze*) for the political role of officials in the Reichstag and Landtag elections that were both due that year. Most official correspondence concerning electoral politics was confidential; this document was extremely so. The governors were instructed to pass on the ministry's guidelines to their subordinates only verbally, and without reference to the existence of the document of 28 January.[2] The secrecy is itself significant: the government issued no public program, only a covert one. The secret guidelines covered two general themes: the parties that were to be considered friendly to the government, therefore deserving of help; and the treatment of issues.

Regarding party preferences, officials were put in no doubt as to the general rule: 'the government bases itself preferentially on the Conservatives, Free Conservatives [Imperial Party], and National Liberals' – the *Kartell* parties of 1887–90. But that general strategy was complicated by local conditions, which could lead to candidates from other parties being favoured by government officials. 'The government supports the Centre only against the Social Democrats and the radical anti-Semites, as well as against Richter's party [the left-liberal FVP]' – although the guidelines also exhorted officials to treat the Centre in all cases 'in the most friendly possible way' in consideration of its important role in the Reichstag. As for agrarian candidates, a member of the BdL was acceptable 'if another candidate cannot be brought through and the individual offers some assurance of a moderate position,' which was hardly a wholehearted endorsement. Finally, the directives emphasized that 'the cooperation of the state-supporting elements is everywhere to be strongly encouraged.'[3] Perhaps this set of instructions seems complicated, but reality was more so. As will be shown below, officials responsible for representing the government's strategy and policy were caught in complex local politics, in some cases even supporting left liberals ('Richter's party'). The only constants were the opposition to Social Democracy, and to particularist parties in various regions of Germany.

The same guidelines went into exhaustive detail on issues. First, the ministry outlined dangerous issues that were to be avoided at all costs: above all, any rumours of tampering with the Reichstag suffrage were to be denied. 'Never should any doubt be left about the determination of the government to govern absolutely in accordance with the constitution.' The government's positive program, on the other hand, mostly emphasized agriculture, protectionism, and social policy: 'protection of national labour,' 'resistance to pure free trade and one-sided commercial interests ... [but] resistance also to *excessive* protectionism, *compromise* between the opposing interests of trade and agriculture...'[4] The 'great measures' demanded by the extreme agrarians, policies like bimetallism and a state grain-marketing monopoly (known as the Kanitz bill), were to be rejected as impossible. The government's program, then, involved concessions to agriculture while stressing moderation, compromise, and exclusion of agrarian extremists. These guidelines were drafted with both the Reichstag and state Landtag elections in mind. Many of the issues (though not tariffs) were in the jurisdiction of the state legislatures; but some issues the government wished to avoid, like the suffrage issue, inevitably found better expression under the equal, secret, and direct Reichstag suffrage. From the outset, the government's plans were better suited to the more controlled Landtag campaigns than to the wide-open free-for-all of the Reichstag elections.

The officials throughout Prussia who received these instructions verbally, were, first of all, observers and analysts, the government's local eyes and ears. They reported on the candidacies, campaigns, and likely outcome in each district to the 'Ministry for Elections' in Berlin, as the Interior Ministry was facetiously known.[5] The ministerial central office then compiled charts of all the constituencies in Prussia, with notes on the nominations and likely outcome in each. The information came, usually, from the *Landrat*, the senior local political official, or from mayors and police officials in large cities, and was passed on to the ministry by these officials' superiors (the district administrators or *Regierungspräsidenten* and provincial governors or *Oberpräsidenten*). In both 1898 and 1903 there were at least two internal canvasses of officials, one during February or March preceding the June elections, and another in April or May.[6]

Officials were also the government's press agents, distributing information in the other direction; but the difficulty here was that the government had difficulty agreeing on a coordinated message. Under Bismarck an 'official' press had been created and used to bring items reflecting the government's interest to the attention of the public, a system that came to be understood by all of Germany, but his use of this system was sporadic and its direction emanated from him personally. In the 1890s the Reich Office of the Interior and the Prussian Ministry of State attempted to extend, develop, and systematize the government's influence over the press. In 1894 it was decided to provide 'unified leadership' for the governmental press, to ensure that 'all news whose distribution is desired by the government can be published.' This was to be an interministerial effort feeding information to all friendly papers in the country, and eventually took form as the *Berliner Korrespondenz*, a kind of central news service from which local publications could take articles for reproduction. This effort proved unsatisfactory, however, and the ministers reviewed their press arrangements again in 1896, 1898, 1899, and 1904, evidently displeased with their efforts to shape public opinion.[7] The difficulties are illustrated by the case of the *Süddeutsche Reichskorrespondenz*, launched in February 1898 with the backing of Krupp. Finance Minister Miquel and other individual ministers supported the project, but Chancellor Hohenlohe and Bülow at the Foreign Office declined to participate.[8] Hohenlohe's circle expressed the fear that the paper would 'develop in a one-sided Miquelian direction' – that is, would espouse Miquel's *Sammlungspolitik* and the gratification of agrarian demands. In short, the ministers had trouble agreeing on a unified press representation in the run-up to the 1898 elections because they disagreed on policy and were suspicious of each other's projects.

Given the importance of 1898 as a Reichstag as well as Prussian election year, the Prussian Ministry of State made a renewed attempt to coordinate the government's public relations. On 1 April 1898 the minister of the interior presented a proposal which was designed to go much further than Krupp's news service, and give the government a centrally coordinated, three-tier press strategy with a clear framework of goals and methods. As he explained, the government's main means of communicating its policies was through its spokesmen in parliamentary sittings, but between sittings this was not possible. Since the parties were not strong enough in representing the government's interest, the government itself would have to take on the task of presenting Germany with a unified direction. Elections were the most important time to do so:

Especially in election campaigns, which ... render party relations even more confused, it is indispensable that the government take the leadership and give the election battle its direction. In order to satisfy this duty, the government needs above all a press that stands unhesitatingly at its disposal. Only by such means is it possible to make the broad masses aware of the intentions of the government and to exercise an influence on them.[9]

The interior minister's proposal, eventually adopted by the other ministers, organized government management of information on three distinct levels. First, the 'direct representation' of government interests in the press had to be maintained by distributing articles on policy questions by leading figures in the government. Articles 'which in short, clear, calm and moderate style ... present the questions of the day in the sense of the government's viewpoint' were to be distributed through the *Berliner Korrespondenz*, as before. But a single publication, perceived as an official organ, did not reach enough people. Second, therefore, the ministers agreed that it was essential to increase the government's *indirect* influence through independent (but friendly) papers. This was to be accomplished through personal contacts of senior officials with the larger regional papers, providing informal support and material, and through friendly but formally independent press networks that reached smaller provincial papers. Finally, public opinions in elections was also to be guided through the mass distribution of leaflets representing the government's point of view, and this, too, would be through the channels of local officialdom.

More so even than under Bismarck, the *Landrat* was now to be a covert press agent for the government. One month after the above proposal was discussed in Berlin, the governor of the Rhine province wrote to his officials on the express instructions of the minister of the interior to emphasize that they were to 'use the press in an exhaustive fashion to represent the policy of the government.' To these ends the *Landräte* were charged with seeing that local papers picked up articles concerning the elections from the approved networks. To make their job easier, they were provided with a list of the friendly papers in the region.[10] This semi-official network supervised by the *Landräte* was used to give signals to the government's sympathizers about its desires concerning the election campaign, and particularly was deployed in the battle to discredit Social Democracy and to unite the governmental parties against that threat. Articles of this sort were widely recognized by the opposition press and parties as official in origin, substituting for formal governmental statements.[11]

The mass distribution of leaflets was the second task assigned in the Ministry of State's strategy to Prussian local officialdom. The central office of the Ministry of the Interior contacted the nationalist publishing firm of Mittler and Son in Berlin, and in conjunction with that firm worked out a selection of pamphlets and a national ordering and distribution system overseen by Prussian officials. For 1898 the exact mechanism is only scantily documented in the central files, but for 1903 there is evidence of a full-fledged propaganda machine operating out of the central office. By mid-April the deputy in charge of that office had one thousand copies each of seven pamphlets, designed for free and secret circulation within the Prussian civil service. At the local level, *Landräte* were to show the pamphlets to the campaign committees of the governmental parties and get the latter to place orders directly with Mittler and Son. In addition, managers of state industries were informed that the leaflets were available and were suited for mass distribution to their workers.[12]

This propaganda machine was supported by significant financial resources. The arrangements described above, for example, required that the publishers keep the minister of the interior personally informed of all orders placed, so that he could identify certain orders to be paid for out of his discretionary budget and delivered free of charge – presumably to subsidize candidates who enjoyed special favour or whose ridings were especially sensitive. Governors of Prussian provinces also had discretionary funds, and these, too, helped to subsidize the costs of governmental candidates' pamphlets and other campaign expenses.[13] There is also evidence of larger sums collected 'for election agitation.' In the files of the central office of the Ministry of the Interior is a tally sheet for a collection, apparently all in one effort, of 154,300 marks for the 1898 elections, in contributions ranging from 1,500 to 36,000 marks and received from the provincial governors. This might be something similar to the CDI's fund for anti-socialist propaganda in the 1890s, or the 1907 election fund raised from private industry – or perhaps it represents only the application to the elections of discretionary funds already at the officials' disposal.[14]

As for the contents of the propaganda, the pamphlets during 1898–1903 covered a range of subjects and were intended for a variety of target constituencies. The intention appears to have been to provide a different pamphlet for every type of local election contest; thus, some criticized the Social Democrats from a conservative point of view, as underminers of monarchy and religion, while others attacked from a liberal point of view, emphasizing the danger socialism posed to middle-class property and society. Others, aimed at workers themselves, lauded the government's social legislation and contrasted it favourably with that in other countries. Still others were directed against left liberals. Only some of these pamphlets emphasized the 'Miquelian' issues of *Sammlungspolitik* – pro-tariff economic policy as a basis for rallying the government's allies – while others presented the traditional nationalist issues of fleet, army, and patriotic duty. There was no one common program or viewpoint. Whether the approved candidate was an agrarian conservative or a National Liberal, or even a left liberal or a Catholic running against a socialist, at least one of the range of pamphlets would be usable. The government was able to sponsor the distribution of such varied pamphlets because they would be perceived to come from the parties, and its own prestige would not be on the line.

Among the approved pamphlets there were several that explicitly promoted *Sammlungspolitik*. As one of these explained, 'The election policy that we must follow today, which is called *Sammlungspolitik*, is like a medallion with two sides. On the one side is written, "Protection of National Labour!"; on the other, "Struggle against the inner enemy, Social Democracy!"' But the main emphasis of the pamphlets was the patriotic duty of state-supporting voters to vote for a governmental candidate:

Above all it will be a question of *electing honourable, independent men*, of whom one can be convinced that they will, with devotion and loyalty, champion the *general good of the nation*, the *interests of the fatherland*, and the *foundations of our state existence*.

In its call for 'honourable independent men' representing the 'general good of the nation,' the government harkened back to representation conceived of as *Honoratiorenpolitik* and to nationalist causes, rather than to the mass-oriented economic agitation of the 1890s. Similarly, the leaflet

Wen wählen wir? (For whom do we vote?) outlined the criteria for 'nation-ally' minded voters to apply to candidates: 'in the first place must stand for every German the defence and preservation of the Fatherland ... For that, the first requirement is a strong army and a strong fleet.' In other words, the 'national' issues of the old *Kartell* were given top billing.[15]

By 1903 the leaflet campaign had shifted still further towards the broadest possible anti-socialism. To be sure, Mittler and Son still offered titles with the ring of *Sammlungspolitik* about them, like *Wahlparole: Schutz der Arbeit in Stadt und Land!* (Election slogan: Protection of labour in town and country!). But the manner of treatment was more reserved. Other leaflets, meanwhile, were now aimed at moderating extreme agrarianism and convincing agrarians of the need for trade treaties, high seas fleets, and so on. *Wozu brauchen wir Handelsverträge?* (Why do we need trade trea-ties?) and *Wie stützt unsere Flotte Deutschlands Wohlfahrt?* (How does our fleet support Germany's well-being?) represented much more of what National Liberals could agree with. If the protectionist and economic aspects had been de-emphasized following the bitter tariff debates and the wider breach between the government and the radical agrarians, the anti-socialist aspects were now accordingly accentuated more strongly. The SPD was now the sole enemy; the attacks on 'left liberals' and 'free traders' had receded into the background. *Aufruf zur Reichstagswahl Gegen die Sozialdemokratie* (Reichstag election declaration against Social Democ-racy) was evidently intended for use in rallying liberal voters, with its call to unite against the party which

has boasted with brazen arrogance that Social Democratic election Candidates have good prospects in *well over a hundred* constituencies to defeat all other candi-dates. *This must never be!* It would be a *disgraceful defeat of the entire German middle class (Bürgertum).*

Listing Social Democratic subversion of the state, of the economy, and of the Reichstag (a reference to the *Obstruktion* issue in the tariff debates), the pamphlet concluded, 'Voters of the middle class, be united!' The complementary pamphlet *Nieder mit der Sozialdemokratie!* (Down with Social Democracy!) was more hard-line and politically conservative in its approach. 'Social Democracy is a sworn enemy of monarchy,' argued the pamphlet; 'it wants to topple the Hohenzollern throne.' If this was not horrifying enough, the SPD also wanted (said the leaflet) to abolish prop-erty, the family, religion, and all authority and personal freedom through armed revolution.[16]

The 'shotgun' approach evidenced by the varied pamphlets hints at the government's true goal: not to issue a real platform on the issues of the day, but simply to oppose Social Democrats as well as Poles and other particularists wherever possible. At the end of January 1898, the governor of the province of Hanover outlined in a confidential letter to his officials the broader purposes of their electoral involvement. He stated that he wanted his officials to 'be in contact with each other' because

given the character that the election campaign in this province ... threatens to assume, I must point out that it is the first priority of the Royal State Administration to keep elements hostile to the state – as such only the Social Democrats and Guelphs really come under consideration in this province – out of parliamentary bodies, and that therefore every fragmentation or mutual conflict among the state-supporting parties is extremely undesirable.[17]

In short, the rationale for the bureaucracy's involvement was that the (governmental) parties were too fragmented and were doing an inadequate job of fighting the enemies of the state. The governor went on to warn officials away from any public activity, as usual, since this would jeopardize the elections. Instead, their work was to be behind the scenes. In the second ballot in 1903, the governor of the Rhine province was even more emphatic and more explicit. In a top-secret letter he told his *Landräte* to work 'with all energy ... within legal limits' to ensure

that everywhere in the run-offs those candidates be supported who stand in opposition to the parties that undermine the existing state order, such as Social Democrats and Poles. As for the more specific party of the opponents of these ... parties, in particular whether they belong to a conservative, middle, or left liberal tendency, that is not relevant.

I expect that all political officials under me will be active in this sense of the cooperation of all state-supporting parties ...

The means of influence to achieve these goals was to be 'personal influence through party contacts.'

Tactical Problems: Local Officials and Party Alliances

Like the government's press and pamphlet policy, the 'personal influence' of officials was a *decentralized* effort in the individual constituencies. Political officials, primarily the *Landräte*, were called upon to use moral suasion to bring about the unity of the governmental parties (primarily the *Kartell* parties but, as the January 1898 directives indicated, potentially also others) against the Social Democrats, the Guelphs, the Poles, and so on. Their role was conceived to be part of the patriotic duty of officials to defend the existing constitution of the state, and more specifically to represent the policy of the government, rather than as an explicit partisan strategy. In the process, however, officials became involved in political judgments about the effectiveness of the governmental parties' campaigns and their relative prospects for success, about which party affiliation and which candidate was most likely to promote the unity of 'state-supporting elements.'

Sensitive political judgments were often required of local officials in their role as organizers of governmental party unity, and some examples might help indicate why they found the German party system hard to manage. One confusing question in 1898 and 1903 was the relationship of the Catholic Centre Party to the government: traditionally an enemy, was it now to be included in the governmental camp? The January 1898 directive indicated it could be considered an ally where a Centre candidate stood against a Social Democrat, a Pole, or one of Richter's left liberals. In 1903 the governor of the Rhine province wrote to his district administrators requesting that where 'candidates friendly to the government's policy' were competing and had 'good prospects, the *Landräte* were to draw up lists of 'dependable and foreseeably hardworking contact people' [zuverlässige und voraussichtlich arbeitsfreudige Vertrauensmänner]. The district administrator for Aachen replied, however, that there were no such candidates in his region: 'In this district only Centre Party candidates seriously come into consideration. For this reason the naming of *Vertrauensmänner* does not come into the question.' He explained that the orders would only become relevant if, in the future, 'national' candidates opposing the Centre majority were named; and even then, any official furthering of their campaign would probably *hurt* their election prospects. The official on the spot was continuing to interpret the Centre Party as oppositional. His superior overruled him and obtained the required list. The incident shows that as late as 1903 the government was having difficulty getting its officials in the provinces, especially in the Rhineland, where interconfessional tensions were high, to accept the Centre as friendly.[18]

In other parts of the same province, circumstances were different and far more complex. Lennep-Mettmann-Remscheid was endangered by the SPD in 1903, but, as the *Oberbürgermeister* noted, 'the result of the main ballot depends on the participation of the non-socialist parties [bürgerliche Parteien]. If these do their duty and vote, then it is not to be expected that the Social Democrat will win on the main ballot.' Positioning a friendly candidate for the second ballot, though, was not easy for the local officials. The governmental parties were split among National Liberal, Imperial Party, and German Conservative tendencies, with the Conservatives subject to Agrarian League influence. The exact choice of candidate was essential to maintain a union among these parties. Moreover, there was a question of trying to attract Centre supporters: in 1898 the Centre had supported the left liberals on the first ballot; but it would not announce its intentions until the last minute. While the National Liberals and Imperial Party had a candidate in mind, the individual in question would repel the Centre, causing the Catholics to support the left liberal again; and would also fail to attract the votes of the agrarian-minded Conservatives. One of the *Landräte* identified a candidate who might attract enough Centre and Conservative votes to win the seat; but could not convince the other governmental parties to nominate him. In the end, the National Liberals and Imperial Party nominated a candidate unacceptable to the agrarians, a separate Agrarian League candidate ran, and as a result *none* of these candidates made it to the second ballot. The Centre–left-liberal coalition faced the SPD in the run-off and failed because of confessional divisions to attract sufficient support to win.[19] In nearby Elberfeld-Barmen, the worry of government officials was to attract, not agrarian votes, but left-liberal ones. Here the Centre, the left liberals, and the united conservatives had all decided on separate candidates for the first ballot, while the National Liberals were still debating what to do. The conservative had a chance to make it into the run-off against the SPD but would not attract the left-liberal votes nor all of the Centre support, 'so that the election of the Social Democrat would unfortunately be impossible to prevent.' Here, a right-wing candidate meant certain defeat; only a liberal candidate, able to draw left liberals into the anti-socialist cause, suited the government's interests.[20] From one seat to another, and from one election to another, government officials were drawn into contradictory alliances depending on the shifting balance among the parties.

The bureaucracy that styled itself, as well as the national purpose it represented, to be 'above the parties' was therefore deeply entangled in the parties, and particularly in the personality politics of the old-fashioned kind. The social world of Prussian officialdom overlapped that of the professionals and businessmen and landowners who formed the local liberal and conservative committees, and it was within that environment that government officials were active. With Catholic organizations and trade unions, and with agitational left-liberal, anti-Semitic, or Social Democratic associations, they had next to no contact – the information in their reports on these groupings was usually little more than could be gleaned from the press. Germany's two 'mass' parties, the Catholic Centre and the SPD, were beyond their ken, as was the bulk of the voters at large. The bureaucracy's narrowness of experience, combined with its doctrine of loyalty to the state 'above the parties,' on one hand provided the opportunity and rationale for its intervention in electoral politics and, on the other, severely restricted what could practically be achieved with the seemingly formidable electoral apparatus of the Ministry of the Interior. Because more than one party was recognized as 'state-supporting,' and because local situations varied so widely, the government's strategic options were limited for any centralized campaign. It could not, for instance, support the National Liberals against the conservatives in one place and vice-versa in another; this would have discredited the government with its allies and damaged its prestige. Officials faced difficult decisions about whether they could support clericals or left liberals, about whether liberals or conservatives would be better for the government, about how to reconcile moderates and extremists, nationalists and agrarians, within the governmental camp. In dealing with these divisions, they were following, not formulating, the realities of popular politics.

Agrarianism, especially the Agrarian League, was the biggest headache for officials during 1898–1903. As one official commented, the 'bitter opposition' between the National Liberals and the Agrarian League meant that 'unification on the presentation of common candidates, [which was] to be strived for with all energy, [would] probably not succeed everywhere.'[21] While generally careful not to oppose agrarian conservatives publicly, the government opposed them in many other ways when they threatened to provoke disunity. Where an existing strain of moderate, governmental conservatism was challenged by a more radical agrarian strain, the government and its officials generally tried to bring about the victory of the former, in line with the directives of January 1898. In March 1898 the *Landrat* in Kolmar (Bromberg), hearing of the funds available to support governmental candidates, proposed that a governmental conservative campaign be funded to oppose the campaign of the Agrarian League. He reasoned that the League appealed only to the 'larger peasant producers,' and failed to mobilize small peasants or urban voters. 'In order not to lose these numerous elements, it is worthwhile if the combating of the Polish and left-liberal candidates can also be taken up from the non-agrarian side.' The cleavages associated with economic issues cut across the kind of broad, patriotic bloc desired by the government.[22]

The duty of officials to work for the unity and effectiveness of the governmental parties led them, sometimes as a last resort, to stand as candidates on behalf of the parties concerned, even though this was officially discouraged.[23] This was nearly invariably linked to the broadest possible program of compromise, particularly on the divisive economic issues of the day. For example, in 1898 the governmental supporters in the rural district surrounding Cologne, traditionally National Liberals, had difficulty finding a candidate willing to fight what amounted to a hopeless battle against the Centre Party. The *Landrat* Dr von Dreyse, agreed at a late date to stand as a liberal candidate on behalf of the governmental forces and fight both the Centre and the SPD. Outlining his platform barely ten days before the voting, he claimed to stand for 'an even further development of the inner consolidation of the Reich' (a euphemism for renewed fighting of socialism and particularism, probably also political Catholicism), but within the constitution. He went on to say he approved in principle of social legislation, but workers' insurance was a burden to the economy; that he supported the extension of the guild system for artisans and that, on tariffs for agriculture, 'one will eventually have to see whether it is not necessary – naturally under consideration of the interests of the other branches of the economy – to increase them.' In fact, the only issue on which the *Landrat* took a firm liberal line was in favour of freedom of movement for workers – hardly a controversial issue anywhere outside of the labour-scarce estates of the northeast, and certainly not in the Rhineland, where many villagers supplemented the family income with wage-paying jobs. Dreyse sat on the fence, campaigning as a liberal while expressing moderate and qualified support for illiberal policies. He carefully avoided associating himself with exclusive interests, or even with a firm policy on the single most important question of the day, the tariff. In all this, he was following the letter of the 28 January 1898 guidelines. The only electoral package a dutiful official could support was a conglomeration of compromises cemented together with appeals to loyalty and professions of service to the state.[24]

Officials sometimes stood for election to forestall divisions between the conservative and National Liberal camps. In Bromberg in 1903, the German Conservative Party, the strongest 'national' party in the constituency, proposed three different candidates and could not convince the National

Liberals to support any of them. The problem was that the Agrarian League had vetoed the incumbent deputy, the district administrator von Tiedemann, and demanded a more right-wing one, which however was unacceptable to the National Liberals. A split seemed inevitable until Tiedemann caught the vacillating Conservatives out by announcing unilaterally that he would stand under the banner of the small, conservative Imperial Party – a favoured choice for officials in his position. The Agrarian League and the anti-Semites eventually felt obliged to support him, in spite of grave reservations, while the support of the left liberals was bought in a deal in which the Conservatives agreed to give them an extra seat in the Prussian Landtag. The National Liberals held out longest, demanding a seat in the state legislature for themselves, too, but ultimately they felt compelled to side with the governmental cause for no reward at all. An uneasy combination of bluff, deals, and moral pressure allowed the high-ranking official to keep the governmental coalition together.[25]

But where electoral calculations led to officials standing as candidates, they frequently proved themselves the most inexperienced of politicians, bound as much as any old-fashioned notable to traditional ideas of what campaigning involved. The rough and tumble of electoral politics in the 1890s and 1900s was not for the Tiedemanns of the world. As a high official with a prestigious career, he was incensed when the local Social Democrats dubbed him 'Tiedemann in the wooden clogs,' alleging that he had said workers did not need boots, clogs were good enough for them. The SPD went on to organize a public meeting whose published agenda included a 'report by Reichstag deputy von Tiedemann.' The latter of course would not attend such a meeting, and as a result was ridiculed mercilessly by his opponents. Social Democratic agitators circled the hall shouting his name, until the chairman announced that Tiedemann had not turned up, 'apparently out of laziness.' When Tiedemann saw the press reports of this, he was furious, and his first reaction was to demand of the police chief why the meeting had not been dissolved. The latter explained carefully that no offence had been committed – except (he did not add) to Tiedemann's pride. The meeting had been properly convened. It was not disorderly. No incitement to criminal violence occurred; even the statement 'if he had appeared, pieces of him would have flown in all directions' was not grounds for dissolution, because statements of hypothetical events were not the same as incitements to commit them, nor were statements by individuals grounds for acting against a whole meeting. Finally, it was not a crime to publish an agenda featuring a speech by someone who was not coming.[26]

If an illustrious figure like the administrator of Bromberg could, with difficulty, hold together the governmental forces, this was not everywhere the case. In other regions, the divisions among the government's allies extended into the ranks of the bureaucracy itself, and in such cases the discipline of the political machine proved insufficient to enforce one uniform behaviour. The desire of local officials to support the Agrarian League caused major problems where the governmental party was the National Liberals, notably in the province of Hanover. Provincial and district administrators sent letters to *Landräte* insisting that support for Agrarian League candidates against other governmental candidates was out of the question. Nevertheless, some local officials persisted and, in cases like that of the 'three Hildesheim *Landräte*' in 1898, flaunted election rules and instructions from their superiors alike in their public endorsement of agrarian candidates. The matter was taken all the way to the Ministry of State, where Prussia's ministers decided to remind the *Landräte* firmly of election rules, and to 'instruct the district administrators on their conduct and on the policy of the government,' with the intention that the governors give better instruction to their *Landräte*. Once again, the government, given the agrarians among its allies, did not want to commit itself openly and especially not on paper, but the kind of conduct to be expected from the officials is clear from another letter, this one from the district administrator in Hanover to the *Landrat* in Linden in 1903:

[A]ccording to the issued instructions the furthering of the election of the candidate put forward by the Agrarian League ... is not feasible.

I propose, however, for discussion, whether it is still possible to proclaim Rehren [the Agrarian League candidate] as some kind of Free Conservative candidate, who is only supported by the Agrarian League. In this case a certain official furthering of his candidacy would at least be made easier.

The administrator went on to suggest that the incumbent National Liberal deputy, Hische, was the ideal governmental candidate and that 'it would be on this candidacy that official interest should be directed in the first place.' The current National Liberal and Agrarian League candidates ought *both* to be withdrawn in his favour, for 'in this way a candidate loyal to the Reich could most easily be brought into the run-off and save the heavily endangered constituency from loss to the Social Democrats.'

While the government desired Agrarian League support, then, every tactic was to be used to prevent it from fielding its own agrarian candidates.[27]

These kinds of examples are important because they show how fluid the boundaries among the governmental parties were, and how the government's officials made this fluidity worse through their efforts to promote broad governmental coalitions. In the literature on political party development, this speaks to the question of the relative degree of *institutionalization* of the governmental parties. Institutionalization is a normal characteristic of modern political parties and amounts to the party having an enduring existence 'in the public mind.'[28] In the above examples, the different governmental parties had no enduring separate existences in the constituencies in quesion, but instead were in various ways interchangeable and overlapping. Parties institutionalize as members develop interests in the organization and its continued success, and develop enduring loyalties: these are qualities that allow the organization to maintain a collective identity and function as a coherent unity. According to Panebianco, institutionalization has two dimensions: autonomy with respect to its environment, and 'systemness' or interdependence of parts. The above examples show governmental parties that were only weakly institutionalized in both dimensions. From one election to the next, the local committee or candidate might change from liberal to conservative, according to external pressures from officials and other governmental parties; and would do so according entirely to local circumstances, independent of any nationwide party organization.[29] Precisely when the governmental parties were under pressure to adapt to mass politics, the coalition-building efforts of officials were holding them back from establishing their separate identities in the minds of the voters. Officials were actively hindering the government's allies from following a normal path of party modernization and development.

Even though the government had at its disposal a relatively disciplined network of political officials, officials whose press and party contacts helped give backbone to the governmental electoral coalition, it had difficulty enforcing a single strategy upon its own officials, and even more difficulty getting the governmental parties to accept that strategy. Lacking a single, unified governmental party, officials were themselves drawn into the network of associations and institutions, of notables and influence, that still comprised a substantial part of the loose structure of the liberal and conservative parties. No amount of official suasion could entirely heal the breaches that existed in certain localities between

National Liberals and radical agrarians, or between moderate conservatives and anti-Semites. No amount of talk (for this was in the last resort
the main weapon of the Prussian official) could necessarily convince committees still relying on notables and on old-fashioned ideas of representation and of campaigning to change their style of politics and build a more
effective party machine – even presuming that the officials themselves
understood what was necessary. It is questionable how much, in the long
term, the governmental parties were really helped by the Prussian
bureaucracy. Promotion of cooperation rather than competition among
the *Kartell* parties blurred their identities and encouraged them not to
contest each other's seats, rather than to crusade for their points of view.
Help of this kind was perhaps not what the liberal and conservative parties most needed in a new age of mass politics.

Strategic Questions: Electoral *Sammlung*

The difficulties faced by officials throughout Prussia in putting together
effective party alliances reflected the lack of a single, clear, overarching
national strategy. As was clear from the government's secret election
guidelines of 1898, the three *Kartell* parties – German Conservatives,
Imperial Party, and National Liberals – were to remain the main focal
points of government favour; but under certain circumstances, other parties could be supported. The governmental coalition was therefore not
precisely defined. It was also not solid, for agrarian issues set many of the
German Conservatives against many of the National Liberals. And, most
problematic of all for the government, it was not a *big* enough coalition to
secure a reliable majority in the Reichstag. Given the legislative inadequacy of the *Kartell* formula and the 'fragmentation' of the Protestant
non-socialist parties, the government was under pressure to define an
electoral coalition on a new basis. In a period when economic issues dominated the political agenda, it could do so either by changing the agenda
(for example, by re-emphasizing a patriotic 'national' cause) or by defining an economic coalition. The latter idea was the basis of the *Sammlungspolitik* proposed by Miquel and his 'Economic Committee' during 1897–8.
    Miquel saw his *Sammlungspolitik* as 'an economic election program'
intended to make the pro-tariff policy into a 'political factor' on the government's side. Talk of 'blocs,' 'cartels,' and 'rallying' was endemic to German politics; the novelty of Miquel's idea was that tariffs should be the
basis of a broad rallying, when traditionally they were a divisive issue that
split liberals from conservatives. Miquel's 'economic election program,'

the founding public statement of *Sammlungspolitik*, was issued on 5 March 1898, just over three months before the balloting for the Reichstag, and was titled an 'Economic Declaration.'[30] The signatories numbered some fifteen hundred in all, notably most of the agriculturalists from the Agrarian League (BdL), the German Agriculture Council (Deutscher Landwirtschaftsrat), and the Catholic regional peasant leagues, plus representatives of the CDI on behalf of heavy industry, accompanied by Miquel and Posadowsky from the government and by ex-Chancellor Bismarck. The statement advocated that parties should make the tariff question paramount in their internal politics and selection of candidates:

Representatives of industry, agriculture, trade and commerce must unite to support only those candidates inside the individual parties who stand firmly on the long-standing program of protection of national labour and equitable consideration of all branches of economic life.

This passage attempted to put the policy into the context of non-partisan loyalty to a 'long-standing' program, but contemporaries were fully capable of reading between the lines to understand the implications of making tariff protection the number one issue in the campaign. Agrarian demands were to be gratified, at least in part; that was what the 'economic election program' was about.

Sammlungspolitik was a minority proposal. No leading ministers other than Miquel and Reich interior secretary Arthur Count von Posadowsky-Wehner would lend their names to the document. The Reich and Prussian caucuses of the National Liberal and, initially, the conservative parties refused to sign, as did many prominent National Liberal heavy industrialists. Within ten days the chemical, machine, electro-technical, trading, and banking communities (including many of those involved in the BdI) had issued a counter-declaration calling for a 'liberal *Kartell*' to oppose agrarian demands. The logic of their response is evident in the decision by most of the same groups to join in the founding of the Trade Treaty Association (HVV) in 1900, which aimed at making itself an explicit counterweight to the BdL in German politics. *Sammlungspolitik* was widely seen as identical with concessions to the agitation of the BdL. Social Democrats, particularists, the Centre, free-trading left liberals, and left-wing National Liberals criticized the proposed coalition, while moderate government leaders and governmental politicians held themselves aloof.[31]

Miquel took his proposal to the Ministry of State on 19 April 1898, describing what would be required to make *Sammlungspolitik* a reality:

In connection with the question of the elections [Miquel] described it as desirable that before the Reichstag elections the general position of the government on the great economic questions be presented by His Majesty in the Reichstag or in the [Prussian] House of Lords. A short indication that the government desired the cooperation of the state-supporting elements against subversion, unity of the productive classes, protection of national work, in particular of agriculture and of the *Mittelstand*, would make a favourable impression. With such a statement one could best pull the rug out from under the charges by enemies that the government wants to dispense with universal suffrage, and the like.

However, conscious of the objections other ministers were about to raise, Miquel admitted the danger 'that with such a governmental program one would say too much for the one (Agarian League) and too little for the others (liberals),' and that this 'would be turned into ... agitational material for the parties.' These reservations were strongly echoed by the remainder of the ministers.[32] Miquel argued that in spite of all difficulties he still thought it possible to phrase a short appeal broad enough to rally all 'the parties of order, including the Centre.'[33] The rest of the cabinet, however, progressively diluted his proposal.

Chancellor Hohenlohe emphasized the risk to the government: 'If the government intervened decisively for the conservative party, it would take its possible defeat upon itself, and equally with a National Liberal program; in intervening for trade treaties it would awaken a storm among the agrarians.' Any conceivable government statement 'could therefore only be completely colourless.' Hohenlohe's view of the government's problems was tinged with pessimism, although in the event the pessimism was justified. 'The next Reichstag,' he said, 'will probably ... remain under the bondage of the suffrage of the masses: the parties that rule the masses (Centre and Social Democrats) will take the victory ... Fighting subversive tendencies will have the result that the propertied classes certainly will be defeated ...' 'A formal program could only be presented by the government,' the chancellor summed up the predicament, 'if it based itself on *one* party, which, however, does not work with our party fragmentation.'[34] The alternative was what one critic in 1903 called a policy of 'satisfaction,' of avoiding provocative measures, preserving the regime's prestige 'above the parties,' and permitting the SPD its activities – in the hope that it really was just the scandal of *Reaktion* that drove voters to support the opposition.[35]

Posadowsky supported Miquel with faint praise, saying a few 'general phrases' could do no harm because they had already been uttered.[36] He conceded that on the day 'when His Majesty gave such a general program, some would take a fierce stand against the government, while others would declare that such general phrases were insufficient.' For that reason the government should *not* make a spectacle of the statement (Miquel had argued for a prominent speech by the kaiser, supported by a statement from the chancellor), but instead should slip the 'general phrases' unobtrusively into the campaign. The ministers of the interior and of agriculture chimed in that 'there could be no talk of a formal government program,' but 'a few short phrases' would not hurt. Revealingly, the latter added that the advantage of such short phrases was that 'they would not be regarded as a gauntlet' thrown down 'against the Agrarian League.' In other words, the minister of agriculture feared that any formal statement the government could make would amount to a challenge to the League.[37]

Every political party, every newspaper, and virtually every politician talked about *Sammlungspolitik* in the 1898 campaign, and again in 1903, but there was no common understanding of what it meant. Most understood that it meant a 'rallying-together' of governmental forces, but to some it was no more than this, a new catchword for the old patriotic cause of the *Kartell.* Moderate conservatives effectively treated it as such. The general perception that the *Sammlung* was simply a 'national' electoral combination of the older type was shared by the Badenese envoy to Berlin, who referred to 'this Miquelian *Sammlungs-Politik,* by which the Centre is regarded as the excluded and fought-against part.'[38] The Centre Party, which supported tariffs and therefore ought to have been in the *Sammlung* if it was really about protectionism, chose consistently to interpret *Sammlungspolitik* as directed against itself – 'the new *Kartell*' whose purpose was to drive the Centre from its 'decisive position' in German politics.[39] Others insisted the protectionist aspect was the real meaning, and that the coalition was directed, not against Catholics, but against free traders. Agrarians insisted that *Sammlungspolitik* involved defending the traditional sectors of the economy, 'the *Mittelstand* [lower middle class] in city and country,' who were also the bulwarks of the religious and monarchical state; while anti-agrarians (who included many liberals as well as Social Democrats) argued this really amounted to gratification of extreme, sectional interests of agriculturalists. Whatever it was, it automatically excluded the irreconcilable enemies of the state, Social Democrats, Poles, and the rest; it automatically included the old *Kartell* parties; and it left the status of the extreme agrarian right, the Centre, and even in some cases the left liberals in doubt.[40]

In electoral strategy as actually pursued by the government, it was the purely political, anti-socialist aspect of *Sammlung* that was dominant, rather than the agrarianism, economic policy, and tariff compromises associated with Miquel's original proposal. The dynamics of electoral politics strictly conditioned what the government could do in electoral alliances as well as what it was beneficial for it to do. Wherever one of the *Kartell* parties could win, that party was supported and defections to other parties, including to other, smaller governmental parties, were discouraged by officials. The German Conservatives were supported in eastern Prussia, the National Liberals in Hanover and provincial Saxony and Hesse, and the Imperial Party where it fielded candidates, often as a compromise between the other two.[41] The Centre Party cooperated with the government in the Reichstag in 1898 and could have been considered governmental, but by and large it did not figure in the government's strategy simply because its base was limited to Catholic Germany, where the *Kartell* parties were weak, socialism was weak, and Prussian officialdom had little influence in any case. Where the Centre and the National Liberals clashed, as in the Rhineland and the mixed-confession regions of southern Germany (parts of the Palatinate, Franconia, Baden, Württemberg, and southern Hesse), politics were on confessional lines: officials could do little to heal the breach, while in any case there was little need since socialism was relatively weak.[42] Only in certain seats threatened by Social Democracy or by the Poles and where the Catholic electorate held the balance of power was there a realizable benefit to electoral coalition with the Centre, and by 1898 this was frequently achieved on an *ad hoc* basis.

But while electoral dynamics limited the usefulness of alliance with the Centre, they enhanced the importance of the left liberals, and this was the true litmus test of *Sammlungspolitik* – if free-trade left liberals were part of the government's coalition, then that coalition was not based on economic policy. The degree to which their electoral base overlapped that of the *Kartell* parties made the left liberals, in the 1880s, the primary electoral enemies of the governmental forces, but the advance of Social Democracy made them by the later 1890s the most useful potential allies. There were two main situations in which left liberals were indispensable to the government if it was to achieve its electoral goals. The first was in cities in the Polish regions of Prussia, where a left liberal frequently attracted wider support than any other possible 'German' candidate. The second, increasingly frequent, situation was in Germany's Protestant cities, where as time went on *Kartell* candidates were less and less able to compete with the SPD. By 1898 the left liberals in important centres like Berlin were the sole alternative to socialism. In both of these types of cases, the government already relied by 1898 on 'German' or 'middle-class' (*bürgerlich*) coalitions that included the left liberals. At the same time, the overall decline in liberal electoral support in the 1890s, and its virtual collapse in most agricultural areas, made the left liberals less serious competitors to the *Kartell*. Election trends were taking them out of governmental strongholds and into socialist ones. It was after 1903 that Chancellor Bülow became the first to follow through on the logical implications of these facts. Assisted by left-liberal votes in key marginal seats, the Bülow Bloc of 1907 inflicted a loss of thirty-eight seats on the SPD and increased the representation of every liberal and conservative party. The potential for such a combination was already emerging during 1898–1903, and as a result any official government strategy that attacked the left liberals (for example, Miquel's protectionism) was essentially misguided. 'The policy of *Sammlung* proved its worth brilliantly here,' declared a long-time conservative party official in Berlin in 1898, 'if we had not supported a left liberal the Social Democrats ... would have won.' Electing a free trader instead of a Social Democrat was hailed in the liberal press as 'a triumph' of '*Sammelpolitik*.'[43]

Tactical considerations also dominated the government's attitude towards agrarian and anti-Semitic splinter candidates. While these were opposed where they splintered the governmental vote, there were certain regions – notably the towns of the Kingdom of Saxony and certain rural areas of Schleswig-Holstein and middle Germany – where anti-Semites or agrarian radicals did better against the SPD than did moderate governmental candidates.[44] In such situations, the government could not voice displeasure. Overall, the fight against the few totally proscribed parties, the SPD and the particularists, was increasingly overpowering all other electoral considerations, even the government's dislike of left liberals and of agrarian radicals.

Opposition to the particularist parties was a constant, no matter what hair-splitting there was over the meaning of *Sammlungspolitik*. A consensus existed among most of the other non-socialist parties that lesser differences were to be put aside in the face of Polish, Danish, Guelph, or Alsatian candidates; and of these, the Poles were the largest, the most radical, and the most worrisome to nationalists because the Polish areas of eastern Prussia were becoming depopulated rather than Germanized, while surplus Polish labour was forming ethnic Polish colonies in the Ruhr. While the Centre, the left liberals, and the SPD had cooperated with the

Poles in the past, the radical trend that triumphed in the Polish movement at the turn of the century insisted on separate Polish candidates.
The left liberals and the Centre, as a result, became more deeply involved
in the 'German' coalition fighting the 'Polish danger.' Between elections
there was, by 1900, a nearly continuous pro-German and anti-Polish campaign in place in eastern Prussia. German cultural and political associations were led and funded by state officials, while Polish ones were
harassed over language regulations; communal self-government was
denied to Polish regions; and large 'Settlement Funds' were approved by
the Prussian diet to subsidize German farmers and settle them or keep
them on the land. The implication of all this for Reichstag elections,
which Germans usually thought of in any case as battles between ideal
causes, was predictable. Ethnic Germans who did not turn out to vote
(*how* they would vote could be assumed) were subject to administrative
sanctions, from expulsion from patriotic organizations up to withdrawal
of credit.

The central government encouraged this kind of political mobilization
as part of its electoral strategy. A few months before the 1898 elections the
Ministry of State approved a 'Decree ... to Civil Servants in the Provinces
of Mixed-Language Population' – that is, of Polish-speaking population.
Miquel, one of the leading advocates of sharper anti-Polish causes in the
central government, proposed the measure to remind Prussian officials
of their duty ('officials should not proceed aggressively against the Poles,'
he reassured more moderate ministers, 'but positively strengthen Germandom') and rally support to the government by establishing an image
of decisiveness in 'national' causes. The minister of religion argued
against making the decree public, saying that greater *resources* should be
devoted to the problem, basing the government's reputation on solid
achievement rather than rabble-rousing. The discussion showed, however, that the agitational effect was precisely what Miquel and the majority of the ministers wanted in the run-up to the Reichstag elections.
Chancellor Hohenlohe and the minister for religion contented themselves with moderating the language, changing the decree from an
appeal to 'German national feeling' to refer instead to 'Prussian state
consciousness,' from a response to the 'artificially aroused' antagonisms
of the 'Polish' population to a means of dealing with 'existing' antagonisms of the 'foreign-speaking' population. On 12 April 1898 (when the
crisis of the naval bill was safely past), the Ministry of State ordered the
decree's publication.[45]

In the spring of 1898, then, there were several different ways in which the government might rally loyal forces, ranging from economic *Samm-lungspolitik* to nationalistic crusades. While there was no firm agreement on any one of these approaches, there was a clear understanding of who was absolutely excluded from any local, governmental coalition: from the government's point of view, these were campaigns against particularists, especially Poles, and, above all, against Social Democrats. These were the parties that deliberately attempted to mobilize the centre-periphery and social-class cleavages of modern Germany, which was unforgiveable as far as the government was concerned because the articulation of cleavages appeared to threaten national strength and unity. Ironically, of course, in taking the field against parties that were exploiting national and class cleavages, the government could only succeed in deepening the cleavages against which it was fighting. Though this was a strategic dead-end, the government tried every conceivable exclusionary and manipulative tactic, short of gross violations of law.

Anti-Socialist Tactics and Constitutional Propriety

The complex, nationwide battle against the SPD was quite different from the localized campaign against the Poles, confined to a few remote regions of Germany. Anti-socialism was the government's primary preoccupation in turn-of-the-century electoral politics, a consideration that influenced all aspects of government strategy. Yet fighting an election on socialist/anti-socialist lines proved to be a difficult task. This was partly because there was no easy answer to thwarting the party's growth; partly because of the government's own hesitation and narrow range of options; and partly because the government could not persuade the other parties that socialism was the only issue.

The calculations of the Ministry of State began with the most elementary of considerations: when did the elections *have* to be held, and when *ought* they to be held to minimize the Social Democratic vote? The ministerial debate reveals that the government's control of the elections was narrowly restricted by external technical and political realities (even more so by its narrow perception of those realities), within which it used what latitude it thought it possessed to create unfavourable circumstances for the SPD. During 1897–8 the ministers grappled repeatedly with the question of whether to hold the Prussian Landtag elections or the Reichstag elections first, as both were due in 1898. The debate began in July 1897, when the Landtag was considering (and about to reject) a more restrictive Prussian association law. There was talk of dissolving the Landtag over the issue; but the ministers agreed it was a disadvantageous cause. As Miquel explained, the issue of repressive association laws would play into the opposition's hands. The government would be better off (this was Miquel's *idée fixe*) to leave aside such fiery political issues and concentrate on an economic program. The other ministers concurred at least that the association law was the wrong issue to provoke an election. Nevertheless (again it was Miquel who voiced the thought), the Landtag elections had to be held as soon as possible; they 'must precede the Reichstag ones in order that the elections to the Landtag not be impaired by the turmoil in the whole country during the Reichstag elections.'[46]

In spite of this, the matter was still unresolved seven months later when the government's time for such manoeuvres was virtually exhausted. On 4 March 1898 Hohenlohe again put the question 'whether it would be more correct to proceed with the elections to the Reichstag before or after the elections to the House of Deputies.' The minister of the interior explained the political calculation involved: 'It is to be feared that, if the Reichstag is elected first, a bad outcome of the Reichstag elections would also unfavourably influence the elections to the House of Deputies.' To this was now added the argument that early Landtag elections, conversely, would exert a positive influence on the Reichstag ones. The restricted Prussian suffrage could be relied upon to produce results favourable to the government and encourage its allies for the subsequent Reichstag campaign. The *sooner* the elections are held the better (explained the minister) since the SPD would have less time to campaign. A snap Landtag election early in the year would 'turn out better ... than later.'

Had the ministers agreed to such a strategy, it would have been an interesting exploitation of the constitutional system of the empire: the deliberate use of state elections and state suffrage to influence freer Reichstag elections. The arguments used also implied a certain Prusso-centrism on the part of Germany's leaders, for part of the purpose was to keep the Prussian diet 'pure' from the effects of Reichstag agitation. It was better, the minister of the interior had claimed in 1897, 'in opposition to the unfavourably constituted Reichstag ... to preserve for as long as possible the well-constituted Landtag' by keeping the elections to the latter untainted by the democracy of the Reichstag campaigning. Despairing of winning a majority in the Reichstag, the government could have resorted to relying on the Landtag as a counterweight in the constitutional system. The option to do so existed and was discussed, but was not attempted.

The argument that in fact swayed all the ministers (as the interior minister summed it up at the March 1898 meeting) was that an earlier election of the Landtag was to be avoided as 'an exception from the natural course, since the Reichstag in fact comes to its end sooner than the Landtag.' In order to justify altering the 'natural' order of the elections, the government would have to offer some kind of explanation to the public; and the prospect of merely obtaining better results was not enough. In other words, according to the minister of the interior, it *would* be tactically advantageous to hold the Landtag elections first, but the government could not depart from convention without a pressing reason. This reveals the extraordinary degree to which the government was governed in its electoral strategy by considerations of legality and public perceptions. The desire to abide by and to be seen to abide by the normal legal and constitutional course of action was uppermost in the government's thought.[47] It is a telling commentary on the government's situation that it would do everything privately, but nothing publicly, to hinder Social Democracy.

While the general timing of the elections was determined by routine, the exact date involved some more explicitly anti-socialist calculation, though it, too, was heavily influenced by legal considerations. Hohenlohe told the ministers on 19 April that the elections ought to be held in the last half of June – as he described it, between the end of the hay harvest and the beginning of the grain harvest. This would maximize the turnout in rural areas, which were (from the government's viewpoint) more reliable. Posadowsky agreed, and further suggested that the day of the week be taken into account, since Social Democratic agitation was most effective on weekends. The minister of the interior concurred that 'main elections and run-offs must in the view of all experienced' campaigners be held 'in the second half of the week.' The ministers' assumption, that Social Democratic propaganda was a kind of influence that wore off by the end of the week, speaks volumes about their view of politics. But together these two considerations (to hold the elections between the two harvests, with both ballots late in the week) determined the timing of the elections virtually to the day.[48]

The 1903 discussions reflect similar considerations, and even more clearly. The new minister of the interior, Baron Hans von Hammerstein-Loxten, presented a memorandum on 10 March 1903 stating that the Reichstag elections that year should be held 'as early as possible' in order to avoid interfering with the Landtag elections or with the busy summer of the rural population. 'In addition,' he argued, 'it seems to me to be of great interest to arrange the elections such that the days of the Whitsuntide holiday cannot be used for agitation, in that such an agitation on these work-free days could really only benefit Social Democracy.' This would mean holding the elections before the May 31 holiday, which left little time to organize the electoral apparatus. Hammerstein outlined the aggressive schedule that would be required: a secret order from the chancellor in barely a week's time ordering the preparation of the voters' lists; public announcement of the elections on 14 April; first ballot on 14 May; and final ballot on 25 May.[49] Four days later, on 14 March, the Ministry of State met to consider Hammerstein's proposal, but the majority, as in 1898, were unsure about so active and irregular an approach. Posadowsky put the counter-argument, which was, once again, that the government must put precedent before politics. It was 'strongly' recommended, he said, 'to avoid with extreme caution every disrespect or departure from constitutional stipulations and in relation to the judging of legal questions not to make oneself dependent on the views of individual party leaders ...' The ministers noted that Reichstag elections 'had already taken place several times in the middle of June,' and that early elections would mean shortening the term and impeding necessary legislative work in both the state and national parliaments. The new Reichstag, moreover, if elected so early, would have to be convened during the summer, which was most inconvenient for everyone concerned. There was little support for Hammerstein's idea. The debate was postponed until 18 March, the last day the plan could be put into motion, 'and until then to gather confidential information on the provisional stances of the parties to the political and legal questions' just discussed.[50]

When the ministers reconvened, Chancellor Bülow had marshalled new arguments about what he saw as the unconstitutionality of the Hammerstein proposal. The old Reichstag expired only on 15 June; to elect a new one before that date without a formal dissolution would result in two legally constituted Reichstags existing simultaneously. 'No precedent is found in the history of the Reich for the election of a Reichstag so long before the end of the legislative period,' he stated; 'no party was willing to accept with the government the responsibility for a legally questionable action of that sort.' Furthermore, he added in subsequent discussion, if the elections were called early the SPD could filibuster in the budget debates and cause the estimates to fall when the Reichstag expired. If, on the other hand, elections were held *later* than 16 June, *no* legally constituted Reichstag would exist in the interim, and this, too, could be unconstitutional. Posadowsky concurred. Only a dissolution could solve the constitutional conundrum, but the government had no good reason to dissolve the Reichstag, lose the pending legislation, and rush the complex preparation of voters' lists and polling arrangements. The ministers of the interior, of trade, and of public works insisted early elections were legal and desirable, but Bülow and Posadowsky (after resorting once more to consultations with politicians and state ambassadors) decided on the now-customary date of 16 June.[51]

It is revealing that the Ministry of State should, in its majority view, have felt so strictly bound by constitutionality and propriety, and furthermore consult with party leaders and state governments in formulating its interpretations – the implication being that it would not proceed if opinion was against it. The Bavarian envoy, for one, favoured Hammerstein's aggressively anti-socialist approach, and was instructed by his government that Munich agreed with him in this.[52] The advocates of an aggressive approach quoted primarily right-wing National Liberal and Conservative deputies, while Posadowsky quoted the Centre deputy Peter Spahn as his authority on constitutional correctness. There is an element in this of a common stand by the leading administrators of the Reich and by the Centre Party in defence of normal constitutional procedure, against right-wing politicians, some federal states, and purely Prussian officials who advocated less restraint. In any case, the debate was so widespread that it could not be kept secret; *Vorwärts* (SPD) got wind of the rumour that voters' lists were to be prepared in secret and published a report guessing that the elections would be in May. In spite of misinformation published by the governmental *Nordeutscher Allgemeine Zeitung* – the paper denied the Reich administrators had ever made any such decision, when in fact it was the Prussian ministries who were involved – the SPD stuck to its guns, although the liberal press criticized the party for alarmism.[53]

Precedent, in the end, was followed in both elections, and disagreements within the government were concealed as much as was possible and with only a whiff of scandal. The government's concern in both 1898 and 1903 was to present an image of business as usual, of responsible administration and constitutional rectitude, and deliberately to avoid stirring up the electorate with failed pieces of legislation or parliamentary dissolutions. Anti-socialist policy was pursued quietly, rather than by provocative political manoeuvres. Germany's leaders, it appears, wanted to defeat the threat represented by the SPD by cooling down electoral politics, not heating it up further. In 1898 the government wanted to conduct elections under the 'favourable impression' to be created by the resolution of the fleet and military court controversies of that spring, while in

1903 it was anxious to avoid dissolution and pass both its budget as well as its measures to improve electoral secrecy – the latter a demonstration of its good faith. Positive measures and the capability to govern were to be emphasized at the national level; anti-socialism was a matter for the local electoral level, to be conducted through the partnership of Prussian officials and the governmental parties.[54]

This should lay to rest one possible interpretation of the government's inactivity in elections, namely that it was the fault of feeble leadership. John Röhl has emphasized the weak position of Bismarck's successors until 'personal rule' was achieved by ministers reflecting the kaiser's confidence during 1897–1900; he has particularly emphasized Hohenlohe's age and tiredness, observations supported by contemporaries. 'Government by procrastination' is the verdict of another student of Hohenlohe's chancellorship. This may all be true, but Bülow and Posadowsky exhibited a similar passivity in 1903. The government surrendered the initiative, not because of tired or uninspired individuals, but because of a systemic problem. No higher German official could find any viable way out of the political quandary of 1898–1903. The domestic political constellation was unsupportive of an activist central government campaign no matter who led it.[55]

Still, the growing urgency of the Social Democratic problem led to a growing desperation for the government to do something. Barely ten days before the vote in 1898, with the chancellor in Paris on a state visit, Posadowsky telegraphed to him requesting permission to leak a letter to the press that would provide a rallying point for the governmental forces. 'It is urgently necessary,' stated Posadowsky, 'that from the side of the Reich government a specific directive be issued for the Reichstag elections, for which the prospects are very doubtful.' The leak occurred in the form of a letter from Posadowsky to an anonymous 'notable politician,' which was published in the *Berliner Neueste Nachrichten*. The rest of the press instantly recognized it for what it was: the National Liberal *Nationalzeitung* called it 'an openly political statement intended from the beginning for publication as a governmental announcement.'[56]

Posadowsky's statement was a vigorous call to unity in the fight against Social Democracy. It specifically did *not* mention the words '*Sammlung*' or '*tariff*,' nor indeed anything about economic policy other than the standard phrases about 'the positive furthering of the great common interests of our economic estates' with special consideration of 'the most endangered' sectors, agriculture and the *Mittelstand*. Even this was moderated by express support for working-class social reform. The key to the statement was not economic policy, which was brushed aside with vague phrases, but Posadowsky's statement 'that in my opinion the non-socialist parties cannot be in doubt about their stance in the coming elections. The Social Democratic party has not only *declared* itself publicly to be a revolutionary party, but is also *in fact* just that.' Any non-socialist politician who did not acknowledge this fact was suffering from 'theoretical misunderstanding ... political short-sightedness ... or lack of courage.' The state-supporting parties must forego all conflicts among themselves; every supporter of the fatherland 'must subordinate his personal inclinations and disinclinations to the *one* political duty, the *common struggle against subversion!*' Those who insisted instead on their separate party claims 'run the danger of effectively supporting the Social Democratic movement' by weakening the patriotic cause. With this statement, Posadowsky tried to substitute anti-socialism for economic issues as the focal point of the campaign.[57]

The attention of the press turned immediately to several key features of the leak. Why had Posadowsky made it, rather than the chancellor? Did this imply the chancellor was of a different opinion? Almost every paper noted how little support the letter gave to economic *Sammlungspolitik*. The Centre-affiliated *Kölnische Volkszeitung* commented that 'the economic passage in [Posadowsky's] letter is overshadowed by his fear of Social Democracy. The word "*Sammlung*" was not even used by him.' The governmental *Norddeutsche Allgemeine Zeitung* called the letter 'self-explanatory but very necessary' as a call for the parties divided by the tariff issue to unite themselves. The pro-*Sammlung*, Conservative *Kreuzzeitung* tried rather weakly to dismiss these interpretations by scoffing at them, but offered no substantial response. Since *all* non-socialists (including free traders) were to unite to fight socialism ahead of *all* other issues, Posadowsky's statement was recognized at the time as an implicit rejection of economic-interest politics.[58] This made Posadowsky's letter more significant for what it left out than for what it said, for the letter's positive message had long been known to every politician in Wilhelmine Germany. There was never any doubt that the government thought the fight against the SPD to be the highest electoral priority; the disagreements were over *how* this was to be done, which was not discussed in the leak. *Vorwärts* had cause to write dismissively that 'what Count Posadowsky has said there has long been known by all the world.' The left-liberal *Vossische Zeitung* commented that the letter was redundant, because the parties agreeing with it needed no reminders, and dangerous (echoing Hohenlohe's comments in the 19 April Ministry of State strategy discussion) 'because it must still further increase the gravity of an eventual victory of Social Democracy.' And the *Nationalzeitung* disagreed with the emphasis, since the fight against the SPD was the same as it always had been, whereas the new threat of 'reactionary agrarianism' needed urgently to be dealt with.[59]

The break with *Sammlungspolitik* was made still more explicit when Posadowsky's leaked letter was compared to another, initially less spectacular, leak, this one by the chancellor himself. Hohenlohe wrote a supportive letter during the campaign to Prince von Schönaich-Carolath, a liberal candidate in Guben-Lübben in Brandenburg. Schönaich-Carolath, dubbed the 'red prince' by his conservative opponents for his support for the Caprivi trade treaties and other liberal causes, was opposed by an agrarian conservative and by the local *Landräte* in his district. Hohenlohe's encouragement of the prince was considered a public rebuke both to the agrarians and the officials, or, as one paper put it, 'in governmental circles [people are] ... most distressingly surprised ... this telegram [is] ... well-suited to letting the chancellor appear to be standing in harsh opposition to his lower officials.' While Posadowsky's letter at least tolerated the idea of an economic *Sammlung*, merely de-emphasizing it, Hohenlohe appeared to repudiate the whole idea. The press took this letter as evidence of the chancellor's genuine opposition to the agrarians and economic *Sammlungspolitik*.[60]

In 1903, instead of leaking further letters, Posadowsky resorted to personal intervention. He called together the Centre deputy Karl Bachem and the National Liberal Paasche for a private meeting, in which he suggested that they work out a Reich-wide deal for the run-offs covering exchanges of support to defeat SPD candidates. Bachem then acted to obtain his party's compliance to the deal.[61] Yet, while this is another reflection of Posadowsky's consistently anti-socialist position, and of the major non-socialist parties' general agreement with it, it was an unambitious tactic. The arrangement in 1903 was only for the second ballot, where anti-socialist cooperation was in any case a tradition, and not (like his leaked letter in 1898) intended to encourage first-ballot coalitions. It was also secret, committing the government to nothing and putting no prestige on the line.

Official leaks were problematic, but the government did still have its press and pamphlet networks through which it could distribute semi-official statements directly to the local press and voters, avoiding the spotlights of the national stage. These reinforced Posadowsky's message of anti-socialist unity, without much committing the government's prestige. Consider the tactical advice of the *Süddeutsche Reichskorrespondenz* in 1903:

Everywhere where the unification of non-socialist elements against Social Democratic votes opens the prospect of victory, the alliance must already be ready in the main ballot and not pushed off to the run-off ... No 'luxury candidacies' and, wherever a federation of several parties is possible, alliance already before the main ballot! Those are principles whose observance will save the non-socialist parties from the danger of self-inflicted defeats and which can make seats insecure for the Social Democrats contestable ...

The increased stridency of such calls to unity also involved criticism of all who undermined the unity of the governmental camp, including those who pursued confessional politics (anti-clerical liberals) and, even more, agrarian extremists:

... a healthy electoral movement that will further the common good of the nation finds its slogan not in confessional struggles, but in struggle against the economic Ultras. The Ultras are the Social Democrats and the Agricultural Leaguers.

The *Reichskorrespondenz* allowed the government to say here what it could not plainly say elsewhere: the extreme agrarians were the greatest barrier to the anti-socialist coalition it wished to construct.[62]

Government Election Strategy: Reactions and Results

In the chaotic environment of a multi-party system heated up by contentious issues and presided over by a silent government, *Sammlungspolitik* had little practical meaning. What the government wanted to do was to lower the temperature of mass politics, but it was unable to do so – the best it could have done was to avoid itself heating things up further. Cleavages of national integration, class cleavages, agrarian-industrial cleavages, and uncontrollable populist styles frustrated the government's desired coalition-building, and in fact the actions taken by the government and its officials made things worse. In fighting the proscribed parties, it made them stronger; in trying to help its allies, it impaired their development. In a fully democratized state, this kind of impasse might reach clear resolution with a change of government, and indeed the administration as such might be kept neutral by the prospect of such change. But in the partly democratized state, officials and government leaders felt it was their duty to guide the parties and the electorate, and at the same time were handcuffed by their very isolation from mass politics.

The passive policy of respectability and mostly quiet anti-socialism, which the government followed both in 1898 and in 1903, was a deliberate choice which involved the rejection of specific suggestions as to how the government could have been more active. The government's behaviour reflected the decision not to pursue a 'national' campaign on a military issue, not to pursue Miquel's electoral *Sammlung* openly or aggressively, and not to seek an open confrontation with Social Democracy. Politicians in the governmental parties were variously dissatisfied with the rejection of these options. Some advocated an energetic governmental campaign, in 1898 even hoping for the defeat of the fleet bill to give the government a pretext for dissolution and a 'national' campaign. The National Liberals were positively anxious that this happen, since none of the other issues of the later 1890s was beneficial to their party's campaign. As the National Liberal deputy Dr Paasche put it in May 1898, 'I hold it for undesirable that divisive economic questions stand in the foreground of the political movement; it would be much better for the development of our people if great ideal political questions, like we once pursued, were decisive in our elections.' The passage of the fleet bill and the 'favourable impression' the government hoped to create by resolving the issue were therefore a disappointment to nationalists, as the *Krefelder Zeitung* made clear in its yearning for simpler, more idealistic issues:

... the fleet law has been passed 'by the grace of the Centre [Party],' and instead of great popular tasks economic things with their thousandfold encumbrances push themselves more and more into the foreground.

But the Conservatives and the Centre disagreed, considering the fleet an actual liability for the elections, and the government de-emphasized the issue.[63]

Apart from the fleet issue and a possible dissolution on that basis, other, mostly right-wing, politicians favoured an energetic official campaign on the economic issues of *Sammlungspolitik*, as Miquel had proposed within the Ministry of State. As several agrarian anti-Semites commented in the Reichstag in the spring of 1898, they were *glad* the fleet issue had been dispensed with. Not only was it unpopular with their consituents, but 'patriotic election campaigns ... lead very easily to completely unnatural economic groupings in the elections.' Now, as they saw it, the path was clear for the government to take up the reins and ride to victory on the protectionist cause.[64] The government, as has already been described, was not willing to 'take upon itself the defeat' that would result

TABLE 3
Index of Right-Wing Unity, 1890–1912, by Region

	Germany	Prussia	Bavaria	Saxony	Württemberg	Baden	Hesse
1890 H^*	.942	.948	.929	.976	.951	.998	.902
1893 H	.876	.885	.889	.761	.995	.831	.684
1898 H	.876	.878	.954	.819	.974	.840	.658
1903 H	.879	.871	.902	.966	.820	.898	.833
1907 H	.921	.928	.908	.829	1.00	.926	.814
1912 H	.836	.820	.890	.784	.873	.914	.865

*Herfindahl's index; the closer the index is to 1, the more unified the parties. To give examples of how the index works, if three of the parties won votes in a ratio of 60 per cent to 25 per cent to 15 per cent in a single seat, the H for that seat would be .44. Two parties splitting their votes 55 per cent to 45 per cent would produce an H of .506; 67 per cent to 33 per cent, .56; 80 per cent to 20 per cent, .68; and a split of 95 per cent to 5 per cent would produce an H of .91. Parties not present do not figure in the calculation.

from challenging 'the parties that rule the masses.' Following the agrarian road would lead to the government's disgrace.

The bitter division between agrarians and liberals, together with the success of the 'parties that ruled the masses,' led to widespread perception of 'fragmentation' among the Protestant non-socialist parties. As one district administrator commented in 1902 following a fiercely contested Hanoverian by-election, 'the prospects for the [Reichstag] election in the coming year ... appear doubtful. Differences over economic policy are bringing the state-supporting parties ever further from one another.' In the by-election in question, agrarians had defected from the National Liberal incumbent and abstained, or even voted for the Guelph particularist, nearly causing the loss of the seat to the government. Officials concluded 'that the cooperation of the national parties will be impeded to the extreme next time' and that 'scorn and malice' now characterized relations between National Liberals and conservatives.[65] Conservative extremists lashed out at the 'party egoism' of the National Liberals and called in some regions, like Bavaria, for alliance with the Centre instead, whose votes would be more useful in some of the marginal seats there.[66]

Analysis of the election results confirms the deleterious effects of agrarianism on the unity of the right-wing parties, and among these the *Kartell* parties. Table 3 shows an index of the unity of all the parties of the right (ranging from the National Liberals through conservatives to the Agrarian League and anti-Semites): the closer this index is to a value of one, the more united were the parties concerned.[67] As the chart indicates, the unity of the right-wing parties was high in 1890, and declined in the three elections during 1893–1903, the elections that saw the eruption of political anti-Semitism and agrarianism as independent electoral forces (see chapter 4). The index declined because rebel anti-Semites fought established conservatives or National Liberals, and because agrarian conservatives or Agrarian League candidates fought National Liberals where, earlier, the governmental parties had been more united. Really both of these divisions, splinter anti-Semitic and splinter agrarian candidacies, were rural phenomena, different aspects of the same agrarian mobilization, since most of the serious challenges by anti-Semites were in rural seats where the electorate consisted of the small and middling peasantry.[68] Table 3 also shows regional variations in the unity of the political right. Noteworthy are the extreme fragmentation of right-wing forces in Hesse during 1893–8 (a National Liberal stronghold where anti-Semitism and agrarianism took hold in several seats) and in Saxony in 1893. But perhaps equally remarkable, in 1903 the largest state in the empire, Prussia, despite all the efforts of Prussian officials to rally the 'national' and anti-socialist parties, showed a degree of right-wing unity that was marginally *less* than the Reich average.

Case by case examination of Prussian constituencies shows that from 1893 to 1903 the number of significant conflicts among the parties of the right increased despite all the efforts to promote unity. In those seats in Prussia where the parties of the right had some chance of winning, serious conflicts were more numerous than before.[69] In 1893 and 1898 the government's broadest possible coalition (from agrarians and anti-Semites across to National Liberals) broke down at least partially in 29–30 per cent of winnable seats in Prussia; in 1903, in 34 per cent.[70] In 1898 the increase in conflicts in western and northern Prussia (mainly between National Liberals and agrarians) was balanced numerically by the elimination of some former rivalries in the east. In 1893 significant National Liberal candidates opposed significant conservative or agrarian candidates in 19 seats in Prussia; in 1898 the figure was 18. Finally in 1903 the number of such conflicts in Prussia doubled to 37 constituencies. These National Liberal–agrarian battles represented about 20 per cent of all Prussian seats in which governmental candidates stood any chance of victory. The degree of division in 1903 was the lowest ebb of right-wing unity in Prussia in the entire Wilhelmine period, save 1912.[71]

The preceding comments apply to the unity of right-wing forces in general; but though broad coalitions including agrarians and anti-Semites were pursued by government officials where necessary to stop socialists, it was, in a practical sense, the *Kartell* that remained the focus of government attention. As ministers' comments indicated, other parties carried varying degrees of suspicion: if the government said anything about agrarians, it would only be to 'throw down the gauntlet.' This left the two conservative parties and the National Liberals as the government's clearest allies. The mixed success of the government in fostering the unity and success of the *Kartell* parties is illustrated in table 4.

Table 4 shows an index of the unity of the three *Kartell* parties alone, and reveals both the tactical success and strategic failure of the government's efforts to promote unity. Tactically, the index remained extremely high, well above 0.9, even above 0.95 for much of the Wilhelmine period. This indicates a remarkable success by governmental officials and politicians in forestalling direct conflicts among National Liberals, Imperial Party candidates, and German Conservatives. It is true that *Kartell* unity in Prussia was lower than the Reich average in 1903, reflecting a number of National Liberal–Conservative contests. This was in contrast to Saxony, which in 1903 showed an exemplary degree of governmental unity.[72] But in spite of such variations, the practical unity of the *Kartell* parties was so great that, electorally, they acted very much like a Reich-wide coalition. The degree of coalition unity evidenced in table 4 should give pause for thought about how independent these parties really were from one another – how low their individual degree of institutionalization really was. However, there is a second story, apparent in the number of seats contested by all the *Kartell* parties put together. The number of seats contested by the coalition never, across Germany or across Prussia, regained the levels of 1890. The *Kartell* remained electorally united until after 1907, but it was diminished.

The contraction of the *Kartell* parties, evidenced by their running fewer candidates, is also apparent in their vote totals and proportions. Figure 6 shows the vote totals won by the three *Kartell* parties in the general elections of the Wilhelmine era. The 1898 and 1903 elections stand out as a particular low point: the National Liberals' and Conservatives' (DKP) lowest points in pre–First World War history came in 1898, the Imperial Party's (RP) in 1903. This in spite of the fact that the electorate and the turnout were increasing, so that the largely stagnant vote totals of the two conservative parties meant a decline in percentage terms. Bearing out the comments of ministers, politicians, and journalists, the 1898–1903 elections were not good for the moderate parties of the right. The fate of these parties was a barometer of the government's success.

All observers of German politics noted the 'silence' of the government

TABLE 4

Index of *Kartell* Unity, 1890–1912, by Region (Together with Number of Seats Contested by *Kartell* Candidates)

	Germany	Prussia	Bavaria	Saxony	Württemberg	Baden	Hesse
1890 H*	.956	.964	.929	1.00	.951	.998	.969
seats contested/total seats	386/397	233/236	48/48	23/23	17/17	14/14	9/9
1893 H	.940	.942	.905	.967	1.00	.911	.998
seats contested/total seats	345/397	202/236	42/48	23/23	15/17	13/14	8/9
1898 H	.969	.970	.970	.954	.956	.956	1.00
seats contested/total seats	327/397	203/236	29/48	20/23	15/17	13/14	7/9
1903 H	.963	.952	.988	1.00	.956	.975	1.00
seats contested/total seats	351/397	219/236	39/48	17/23	16/17	14/14	9/9
1907 H	.961	.966	.955	.866	1.00	.963	1.00
seats contested/total seats	309/397	205/236	31/48	19/23	6/17	13/14	7/9
1912 H	.874	.857	.937	.765	.931	.914	1.00
seats contested/total seats	326/397	210/236	30/48	20/23	14/17	13/14	8/9

*Herfindahl's index; the closer the index to 1, the more unified the parties.

Note: All seats are counted where the recorded votes for *Kartell* candidates were greater than zero. It is relevant that officials did not attribute votes to any party unless at least twenty-five votes in a constituency were cast for a single candidate. Thus, the figures here are really equivalent to seats where a *Kartell* candidate won at least twenty-five valid votes.

FIGURE 6
Votes Won by the *Kartell* Parties, 1890–1912

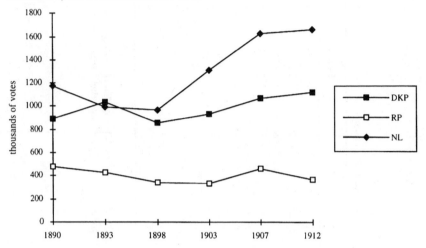

and speculated on its significance. One left-liberal columnist commented in 1898,

The Reich government has by and large exhibited a noteworthy reserve in the midst of these efforts by the parties. It almost seems as though individual members of the Reich agencies are not quite comfortable with the thought that an even more extremely agrarian Reichstag majority than previously might emerge from the elections.

If opposition parties noted with some irony and satisfaction that the government was failing to support agrarian radicalism, more right-wing analysts exhibited simple frustration. A prominent 'national' paper complained at the end of February 1903, 'New elections stand at the threshold, new elections of special, far-reaching importance. If the government really wants to "govern" and not just "administer," then it must make the attempt to create and to represent some kind of election program ...' The government's allies were eager that it commit itself, and they were largely disappointed.[73]

The two indirect signals by the government in 1898 – Posadowsky's leaked letter and Hohenlohe's – comprised the sole active public role it played in the elections, and both leaks involved a careful non-association with *Sammlungspolitik* and agrarianism. The National Liberals and conservatives were both unhappy with this state of affairs, but for opposite reasons. Prominent National Liberals like Friedrich Hammacher feared the 'breakup' of their party in the turmoil of the 1898 campaign:

The precarious state of the party is substantially contributed to by the unclear position of the government in the Reich, which apart from proclamations against Social Democracy has no solid program and declines to intervene against agrarian excesses, anti-Semitism, and other tumours.

The Miquelian call 'to *Sammlung*' is extraordinarily unclear and in spite of many attempts there has been no success in bringing the finance minister to a clear pronouncement on what we are actually supposed to understand by it, particularly in relation to the Centre Party.

On this point, party leader Ernst Bassermann added that the only program proposed from within government circles was one 'which in fact has its sources more in conservative circles, namely the call for higher protective tariffs.'[74]

Conservatives were only a little less dissatisfied, for, while they had Miquel's speeches and a few phrases from the kaiser to quote in their support, the agrarian wing expressed bitter disillusionment with the government for failing to champion agricultural interests more than it had. By 1903 Miquel was dead, the tariff law was passed, and the breach between the government and the Agrarian League was clear. The BdL commented during the election campaign, 'This posture of the government [on the tariff question] will have finally opened the eyes of those who until now always believed in the honesty of the promises of the government and in its real intention to grant agriculture the protection it deserves.' The *Kreuzzeitung* wrote that Germany had 'an exceptionally taciturn government,' and whereas this had some advantages in terms of facilitating the passage of legislation, the need in the current campaign was urgent: 'We stand now in an election campaign. The whole world would gladly like to know which course the government intends to take, on which parties in the new Reichstag it will support itself. The government shrouds itself in the deepest silence.' The left-liberal press had only ironic amusement for the agrarians' predicament:

Count Bülow has, in the face of the pleading and pressure of the Conservatives to free them from their precarious situation with a powerful election slogan, shown himself [to be] reluctant ...

The reason for this passive behaviour of the government lies close at hand.

Cooperation with the left is today out of the question; but equally forbidden for a government that wants to bring about any trade treaties is cooperation with the agrarian right ... So the government is silent.

It was rare for the conservative and left-liberal press to agree on anything much, but they both read the same message into the government's silence – the one group with frustration, the other with amusement. The government's hands were tied; it was not going to provide any great help to its allies.[75]

The government clearly perceived election campaigns to be fights against the proscribed parties. It clearly committed its entire apparatus and did everything it perceived to be possible to unite its allies and defeat those enemies. It considered a variety of 'national' policies and strategies to assist in these efforts. And it failed, judging by both the voting trends and the seat totals during 1898–1903, either to stop the decline in popular support for the governmental parties or to increase their effectiveness in winning seats. At the end of June 1903, the leading Social Democratic paper, *Vorwärts*, crowed with jubilation:

The officials have worked against two parties in these elections, including through official influence. Two parties were excluded from the brotherhood of all parties: the Social Democrats and the Poles. And these parties are the sole ones to conclude the election battle with successes ... No bourgeois party ... is capable of living on its own strength, in its own right. They exist only out of mutual declarations for the lesser evil [electoral pacts] and receipt of electoral help ...[76]

The lesson was not lost on others. Officials despaired privately that 'the tendency of general suffrage inclines ever more to the left.'[77] Liberals blamed economic-interest politics. As one leading left-liberal paper opined, 'the apple of discord that Prince Bismarck threw to the masses with his support for economic-interest representation has had its effect. More and more the great national and cultural questions fall back before all manner of particular desires and particular causes.'[78] Others, however, said the exact opposite – what Germany needed was precisely another Bismarck. 'The New Course steers right and steers left and stops then in the middle ... What should the people get excited about?' asked one governmental paper.[79] 'In earlier times,' lamented another, 'at least the powerful figure at the head of the Reich provided a solid pivot in the general turning and aimless swaying. When meek hands took the imperial rudder, the ship began to list more strongly. The firm will from below pushed itself into the general confusion above.'[80] The 'firm will from below' was represented before all else by Social Democracy, whose support the government had done everything it could think of to reduce, and without effect. But this challenge was not purely external: Social Democracy was one kind of mass-democratic challenge, employing popular-democratic language and techniques to mobilize against the government. But there were also populists within the other parties. Each party had to confront in its own way the external challenge of Social Democracy, and the internal challenge of the new mass politics, without any great help from the government.

4

Mass Politics and the Right

Nowhere does the concept of populism outlined in chapter 1 apply better than to the breakaway movements that thrived in the 1890s and early 1900s on the right wing of the German political spectrum. Not only does the broad definition of populism apply, concerning movements that employ popular-democratic ideas to attack establishment elites, but also the narrow definition of agrarian-based attacks against the effects of industrialization. These movements erupted, surely not coincidentally, at a time when the structures of the old parties were under great strain from the pressures of mass politics. The classic definition of an old-fashioned political party, 'the individualist and decentralized cadre parties of the nineteenth century,' fits Germany's conservative parties better than most, and it was precisely this unmodernized party structure that left them vulnerable to attack by populists.[1] These 'radical' and 'demagogic' agitators also pressed for a closer connection between parties and material interests such as those of agriculture and peasants. Social-economic cleavages, becoming more and more manifest in party politics, eventually forced Germany's largest conservative party, the German Conservatives, almost against their will to become an agrarian regional party. While this contradicted many conservatives' and government leaders' ideas of what parties were for, it also ultimately gave the German Conservatives the most coherent, one might even say 'modern,' basis and structure of any government party.

With the failure of *Sammlungspolitik* and the ineffectiveness of the government to promote anything other than the vaguest sort of anti-socialist and anti-particularist unity (see previous chapter), the governmental parties were left largely on their own to deal with the multiple challenges of the new mass politics. These challenges included the need for more effec-

tive organization to cope with a growing and increasingly politicized electorate; the need to cope with the politics of economic and class interests,
with the ascendancy of 'fairness' questions and the relative decline of
'national' appeals; and the need to compete with those quicker to adopt
the 'agitational' methods. The problems posed by changes in electoral
politics were potentially greatest for Germany's two conservative parties,
the German Conservatives and the Imperial Party.

Since the late 1870s, the 'dominant coalition' in each conservative
party was defined by patriotic loyalty and moderate governmentalism.[2]
Conservatives were closely intertwined with officialdom in most parts of
Prussia, and usually professed (like the bureaucracy) to put loyalty to the
crown ahead of all partisan and sectional considerations. They were also
the parties with the most rudimentary institutional structures, least able
to fight expensive and agitational campaigns of the type gradually becoming more common. Thus they were the parties most in need of change
and adaptation. The German Conservatives had their greatest concentration of strength in rural Protestant Germany, where the anti-Semitic and
agrarian 'Ultras' reached their peak in the 1890s. The dominant formulation of conservatism therefore faced a challenge from within the con-
servative-agrarian grouping, which took shape as a direct challenge to
the leaders' cherished governmental principles. The struggle to defeat
or accommodate the new tendencies, to digest right-wing populism,
brought conservatives to a historic low in voter support during 1898–1903.

The Conservative Electoral Base

The two conservative parties in Wilhelmine Germany were *the* parties of
loyalty to established authority, of monarchism and statist patriotism. In
addition, the German Conservatives, with their close ties to agriculture
and its interest groups, on the one hand, and to the Protestant churches
and the Evangelical League, on the other, represented traditional values
in social and moral questions. The Tivoli program of the German Conservatives, adopted in 1892, listed as its first three elements the 'strengthening of the Christian view of life,' the strengthening of national unity, and
the maintenance of the monarchy against parliamentary assertiveness.[3]
The Conservatives were also known as the party of agriculture. By and
large, between the later 1870s and the early 1890s, there was little conflict
among the party's roles as a party of agriculture, a party of government
and officialdom, and a party of traditional values.

In their core regions of electoral support, Conservatives fought mainly against the constitutional opponents of the government, especially left liberals. In these kinds of electoral battles, patriotism and the community solidarity of rural Protestant Germany were mobilized against the oppositional liberals. Conservative candidates rarely led the Protestant field in confessional battles against the Catholic Centre, nor did they generally face the SPD in its strongholds in Germany's large cities. Governmental conservatives, strongest in the countryside, especially where there were large estates, fought oppositional left liberals, whose support was stronger from the peasantry and from towns and cities. This pattern of two-party politics through broad stretches of eastern Prussia persisted in many cases up to 1903, complicated by the steady emergence of the SPD.[4] In 1890 the left liberals came second in forty-four of the seventy-three seats won by the German Conservatives. The general polarization in many parts of Prussia between left liberals and conservatives reinforced the definition of conservatism as loyalty to the crown and social order, opposing the 'progressive' and 'democratic' tendencies of left liberals. Parliamentarism, free trade, and liberal ideas of free speech stood on one side; loyalty to the status quo of constitutional monarchy, protectionism, army, and bureaucracy, on the other.

By 1898 the SPD had replaced left liberalism as the main alternative to conservatism; in that year, Social Democrats came second to German Conservatives in twenty-eight of the Conservatives' fifty-six seats, and fought run-offs in thirteen of those, compared to only eleven seats in which left liberals came second. But this electoral evolution did not substantially change matters for the Conservatives. In fact, their stance as defenders of the social, economic, and political status quo was even better suited to fighting Social Democracy than to fighting liberalism. By the turn of the century, Conservatives considered themselves the *real* antisocialist party and blasted the SPD in their campaign literature for its anti-monarchical, anti-property, feminist, and 'atheistic' views.

Although it was clear that Conservatism opposed left liberalism and, later, socialism, it was not entirely clear what Conservatives supported in terms of social policy. Probably in most of their strongholds it was sufficient for them to emphasize agriculture, monarchism, religion, the family, anti-liberalism, and anti-socialism, but in more marginal seats the party was driven to an explicit attempt to justify itself as a social-reform party. In 1903 the central association of German Conservatives made five titles available for mass distribution in the elections. The very fact that these were intended for mass distribution suggests they were for seats and campaigns that were not typical of Conservatism. By far the longest was a

FIGURE 7
German Conservative (DKP) Popular Vote, by Constituency Type, 1890–1912

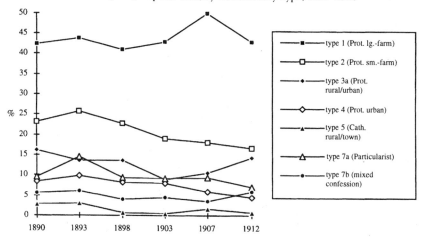

Comments: The DKP did consistently best in types 1 and 2 (Protestant rural) seats, worst in types 5 and 6 (Catholic, latter not shown).

Note: For clarity of presentation, type 3b and type 6 seats are not shown.

pamphlet about 'Workers' Assistance and the *Mittelstand,*' which tried to portray the DKP as a social-reform party favourable to the needs of industrial workers, peasants, and artisans alike. Another leaflet, *Wähler! Arbeiter!* (Voters! Workers!), was 'directed exclusively against Social Democracy and enlightens workers about the true nature of this party.' Another promoted the '*Sammlung* of the electorate against Social Democracy.'[5] Given these leaflets' anti-socialist, social-reform tendencies and the fact that the party office did not distribute any others specifically on agriculture or protectionism, it appears that its concern was to help party organizations where they were weakest, in towns and cities threatened by the SPD. Where the Conservatives fought against anti-Semites, they also found it important to emphasize their social program. In Marburg in 1903, they argued that the well-being of agriculture and protection from foreign competition was the priority for the new Reichstag, while 'preservation and strengthening of the German Reich' came second, and *Mittelstand-spolitik* and further social reform for workers, third and fourth.[6]

Despite local strains of social-reform Conservatism, the German Conservatives were regularly caricatured as the party of the so-called 'Junkers,' the east-Elbian aristocracy. A brief look at their electoral base (fig. 7) gives some support to the stereotype. When analysed according to their performance in various types of constituency, it turns out that the German Conservatives did by far the best in Protestant agricultural constituencies dominated by large landholdings (type 1 seats; on the typology, see Appendix A). While these seats were, indeed, east of the Elbe River, one could also describe the region they covered as 'Baltic,' for they stretched in a broad band south of the Baltic Sea from Schleswig-Holstein to East Prussia. A couple of seats in northern Saxony were also of the large-land-ownership type. Over the six elections of the Wilhelmine era, the German Conservative share of the votes in the large-landholding seats increased to a peak in 1907. This performance was cut only in 1912, when the National Liberals started putting up opposition to the Conservatives in these seats.

Outside the large-landownership regions, the German Conservative share of the vote was generally falling throughout the Wilhelmine period. They did second-best in Protestant rural seats that were not dominated by large holdings (type 2), but here their share of the vote went steadily downward after 1893. The third-best electoral environment for the German Conservatives were those seats that were Protestant and largely rural, but which contained a large town of over ten thousand people (type 3a). The Conservatives also did reasonably well in seats where 'national' polarization played a role, whether the enemy was particularist (7a) or confessional (7b) in nature. They did worst of all in Catholic and in urban seats. The seat totals reflected these patterns of support. In 1890, before anti-Semitism had much electoral success outside of Hesse, and before the emergence of agrarian radicalism, the German Conservatives won 73 seats. Of these 23 were in the 'German,' Protestant, large-landownership agricultural districts of north-eastern Germany, and, together with Imperial Party candidates, conservatives had a near-monopoly of such seats. Another 13 Conservative seats were from rural Protestant seats outside the area of large landownership (type 2), while 17 were from Protestant 'mixed' seats that were largely rural but also contained a city (type 3a). Together, 73 per cent of Conservative Reichstag deputies came from these Protestant majority-rural environments, which comprised only 32 per cent of the Reichstag's seats. In short, the picture of the German Conservatives as a party with an overwhelmingly Protestant and largely rural base is borne out by where its candidates got elected. There are two ways to interpret this: that the Conservatives had a strong, well-defined constituency; and, that they were confined to a certain electorate and were vulnerable to tensions and disruptions within it. Conservatism, by virtue of its electoral base alone, had to be intimately involved with any Protestant agrarian movement, particularly in northeastern Germany.

The Imperial Party (Reichspartei) was a small conservative grouping distinct from the German Conservatives. Imperial Party members were often referred to as the Free Conservatives, a term used in the Prussian state legislature to designate a grouping that had been loyal to Bismarck and his new Reich since 1871, whereas the German Conservatives had taken until 1876–9 to become reconciled to his revolutionary handiwork. In a sense, this Bismarckian loyalty still characterized the party in the 1890s: to the extent that the Imperial Party had a clear electoral identity, it was as the party of loyalty to the regime, irrespective of social and economic interests. The Imperial Party hardly had a formal program and made few election commitments beyond its patriotic statements; the duty 'to defend religion, monarchy, family, property against all attacks' was as true a summation in 1898 as when it was stated in 1882.[7] The 1898 campaign declaration mentioned four points: that armament, however expensive and heavy a burden, was essential to the health of Germany; that 'equal furthering of interests' must be observed in new trade treaties; that there should be continued legislation to protect workers; and that there should be a *Sammlung* of patriotic men from right and left.'[8] Again, the emphasis is compromise within an overarching patriotism, with agrarians and industrialists and workers, left and right, united behind a strong state.

In general, governmental candidates stood as Imperial Party candidates when, in widely scattered constituencies, this purely patriotic appeal best captured what was required to hold the governmental parties together. A good example is the district of Marienwerder in West Prussia, where governmental candidates fought against a strong Polish minority. Here the Imperial Party elected between two and four deputies in every Wilhelmine election, making the eight-seat administrative district one of the Imperial Party's strongholds. Elsewhere, Imperial Party candidacies often appeared in one election, disappeared in the next, according to the internal calculations and negotiations among circles of governmental politicians. It was typical that officials campaigned under the Imperial Party banner in order to unite quarreling National Liberals and German Conservatives, traders and farmers, town and country, against opponents of the regime.[9] In widely scattered constituencies where firm patriotic unity was required, the Imperial Party served as the governmental compromise party.

The Imperial Party's thin and fluctuating electoral base is reflected in figure 8. Imperial Party candidates did not do particularly well in any single category of constituency. Up to 1898 they did best in Protestant agrar-

FIGURE 8
Imperial Party (RP) Popular Vote, by Constituency Type, 1890–1912

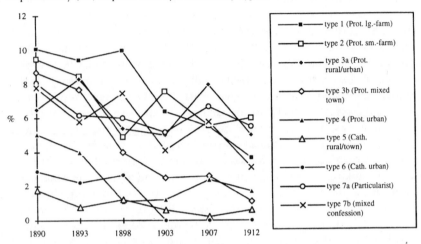

Comments: Support for the RP was scattered and inconsistent, but in general the party did better in Protestant rural seats and in confessional or nationalistic conflicts.

ian seats (types 1 and 2), but their support was scattered roughly evenly across five different types of constituency. Not much had changed by 1912 except that support in all kinds of constituency had declined; but it is noteworthy that the Imperial Party's performance held up relatively well in seats where there was conflict with particularists (7a) and in seats split on rural/urban lines (3a). Both of these were types of environments where the Imperial Party could survive as a compromise party of the patriotic right, bridging divisions such as those between right-wing liberals and agrarians. This characteristic of being a patriotic compromise party ('national,' non-liberal, and non-agrarian) gave the Imperial Party a variable and shallow electoral base: of 126 seats where the party won at least 5 per cent of the vote at some time between 1890 and 1903, there were only 13 where it won that much in *all* of the four elections. In a sense, the Imperial Party was not, within the electorate, a free-standing party at all, but rather an option exercised at local discretion within the loose governmental coalition.

This brief overview of electoral trends and environments for the two conservative parties suggests a contrast: the small and marginal Imperial Party became smaller and more marginal, while the German Conservatives retained their hold on their Baltic-region strongholds. In the electoral environment of the late nineteenth and early twentieth centuries, the decline of the Imperial Party is what might be expected. It lacked a solid organization either centrally or in the regions, had only a vague program, and appealed to no clear cultural or social-economic constituency. These were not accidental omissions, but reflected a concept of politics in which structure, program, and social-economic mobilization were distasteful. The Imperial Party was increasingly just a flag of convenience for governmental candidates. On its own it was one of the most weakly institutionalized of all parties, and its decline in the face of more modern competitors is to be expected. The relative stability of the German Conservatives, on the other hand, belies stress and adaptation, above all adaptation to the storm of agrarian protest in the German countryside. The contrast between the old and new conservatism is epitomized by the difference between seats won by deference or even manipulation, and the growing number where 'agitation,' perhaps with agrarian or anti-Semitic assistance, was a necessity.

Deference and Authority

Conservative aristocrats and notables saw themselves as natural leaders of their communities, and had through the civil service a dense network of official contacts – so that it is no surprise that complaints about electoral abuse by officials typically centred on election of conservatives. There is evidence, for earlier periods, of what has been called a conservative system of election manipulation centred on the Prussian *Landrat* (the senior official in Prussian rural districts),the 'master of ceremonies' for elections, who, in the 1850s, ensured the victory of conservative candidates.[10] Again in the early 1880s, the *Landrat* appears in the key role as the monitor of local campaigns, the planter of articles representing the government's interests in the local press, and the coalition-builder among the government's allies, reducing friction among them and helping to choose their candidates.[11] These kinds of general political activities continued through the Wilhelmine period, as described in chapter 3, and often benefited conservative candidates. Ultimately activities through which officials exerted *influence* were tolerated; but pressure or coercion were forbidden with increasing effectiveness. The state's own legalism ultimately prevailed, reinforced by a watchful partisan press and a Reichstag majority, who shared an interest in ensuring the validity of voting, as has been described in chapter 1.

The complaints brought to the Reichstag's election verification committee show that aristocrats, employers, and officials continued to try to influence their social subordinates, though their ability actually to coerce them was increasingly limited. There were frequent charges of improper use of authority. Opposition voters remained uneasy about the possibility of some kind of violation of the Reichstag suffrage's secrecy, especially since there was no tradition of maintaining secrecy for Prussian state elections. On occasion the governmental parties catered to such fears by implying that individuals' voting behaviour *could* be found out. One device (before the 1903 regulations that closed this loophole) was to print ballot papers of a slightly different size or quality of paper than that used by other parties and hand these out in the polling station, where it would be difficult to substitute another ballot or write in a different name. The conservative parties in Potsdam-Spandau-Osthavelland refused in 1898 to adopt a standard ballot size, theoretically leaving the ten thousand workers in the Spandau munitions industries vulnerable to dismissal if they were observed to vote with one of the SPD candidate's ballot papers.[12] However, if any such device really did lead to large-scale intimidation or reprisals, a complaint could be brought to the Reichstag's committee, which was prepared to step in and invalidate elections in such cases. By the 1890s, such attempts walked a fine line and risked invalidation of the result.

Where the state was the employer, the possibilities to exert influence were greater – but were also subject to more intense political scrutiny. In 1898 the director of the Royal Artillery Works in Danzig issued an 'order of the day' to his workers, attacking the SPD. When the complaint was reviewed, the Reichstag electoral committee at first judged it 'not relevant' because, first of all, it did not tell the workers for whom to vote (it only made a general statement about Social Democracy), and, second, only sixteen hundred workers were involved, whose votes could not (in the committee's opinion) have affected the overall result. The matter did not end there. The government was attacked in the Reichstag and Admiral Tirpitz, speaking in the government's defence, was forced to concede 'that the works should not have come forward in the elections in so questionable a fashion.' For taking this stand, he was bitterly attacked by the right-wing and nationalist press, who charged him with 'too lax a stance.' The controversy shows, again, that the government's approach emphasized the maintenance of legality and propriety, rather than the *Reaktion* of Baron Stumm and others who criticized Tirpitz over the affair. Second, the ultimate safeguard of the ballot was not legal, but political.[13]

In 1903 in Saxe-Weimar, a speech to forest workers was condemned by the Reichstag committee because it contained threats of dismissals if

Social Democratic votes were cast. In the three villages, forest workers were assembled to hear anti-SPD harangues from Oberförster Kallenbach and the incumbent Reichstag deputy, Oberförster Fries. The Reichstag committee concluded this was 'an unacceptable official influence of elections.'[14] Also in Saxe-Weimar in 1903, a large landowner was said to have led two of his workers forcefully to the poll and to have put ballots for the 'national' candidate into their hands. The Reichstag election committee's response was that the landowner's action 'would only become significant if the allegation were supported through the further accusation of some supervision of the voting ... Since, however, no such supervision ... is even alleged, the committee does not regard this protest as substantial.' The landowner was free to hand out ballot papers like any citizen could, even to his own workers, as long as they were free inside the poll (and especially in 1903 in a private voting cubicle) to substitute another ballot paper or to write in a different name on the one they had been given. This was a legalistic, but clear, definition of free voting. When in Kalau-Lücke in 1898 an aristocratic landowner served as chief polling officer on his own lands, *and* personally distributed conservative ballots at the door, *and* looked in the ballot envelopes to see how his labourers had voted, this was recognized as 'of substantial significance, influencing the validity of the entire voting result.'[15]

The fear expressed most commonly in newspaper articles and letters to the editor was that ballots would fall, or be placed, in the ballot container in such a way that they lay flat directly on top of each other in the exact order in which they were dropped in. This would allow a vengeful official, employer, or landlord to compare the stack with a list of the order in which people had voted and arrange some punishment for those who had voted the wrong way. This, almost alone among the possible ways of violating electoral secrecy, would be difficult for the Reichstag to detect, at least as long as the reprisals were not massive. Professor R. Siegfried of Königsberg published a study of this in 1906, concluding that the main problem was that all kinds of containers were used for ballot boxes which, as he put it, 'did not correspond to the worth and importance of Reichstag elections.' The most common were soup cauldrons and cigar boxes, but also employed were drawers, suitcases, hat boxes, cooking pots, earthen bowls, beer mugs, plates, and wash tubs. By 1903, however, this kind of improvisation was becoming a quaint anachronism of the backwaters of eastern Prussia. The government was actively encouraging large, slit-topped ballot boxes, and manufacturers of such products were plying the country with catalogues advertising their range of styles for every taste and pocketbook – some emphasizing formality and ceremony, with ornate handles, others more solid-looking to emphasize security.[16] This was not enough for some, but given the spread of purpose-designed ballot boxes, plus the 1903 secrecy regulations, and the scrutiny of the Reichstag majority overseeing the whole system, it is not likely that overt, large-scale violations of secrecy occurred, even in eastern Prussia.[17] As a last resort, one might, like Willy Brandt's grandfather, just tip the ballot box over 'accidentally' to mix up the contents. 'When Grandfather approached the table he overturned it, as if by accident,' Brandt recalled the story, 'the ballots scattered, the overseer fumed and cursed, but there was nothing he could do: he could not find out which ballot belonged to which worker.'[18]

The Reichstag gradually worked out what amounted to a code of conduct for officials that restricted not only their use of official channels, but the way they were to behave in public. In 1898 it was alleged that *Landrat* von Puttkamer in Kolberg, Pomerania, had supported the conservative candidate in numerous public meetings. This was considered to be within his civil rights; the Reichstag committee noted 'that officials, especially a *Landrat*, must be at liberty to make their political opinions count and to put them into action, otherwise they would possess fewer political rights than other voting citizens.' The majority of the committee, with dissension, decided it was all right for Puttkamer to speak in public meetings, as long as he did not make a point of his rank and status. But the committee was concerned about whether, in the process, the *Landrat*'s official authority became even indirectly involved. It was alleged that Puttkamer had addressed a meeting that included some of his subordinate officials, and 'in a commanding tone energetically called upon all people ... to prepare themselves, so that they participate in the election.' On the surface, this was merely a call to participate; Puttkamer did not make the obvious mistake of mentioning any particular party or candidate. But the committee was suspicious of the 'commanding' and 'energetic' tone, when used in the presence of subordinates, and decided that it was possible to infer from Puttkamer's *other* speeches whom he favoured. Therefore, considering the unspoken circumstances and the tone of Puttkamer's address, he was held to have 'asserted his official authority as a state official, and an election influence of this sort is not allowable.' In this kind of judgment, the Reichstag committee was narrowing the opportunities for conservatives to exploit authority and deference for political success.[19]

Similar suspicion was extended to all public activities in which officials made their status recognizable. Complaints that leaflets for governmental candidates were distributed from the *Landrat*'s office were scrutinized carefully by the Reichstag, as were cases in which civic employees handed out leaflets. A key consideration was whether officials wore their uniforms as they campaigned, in which case the activity was singled out as reproachable or illegal. Law enforcement procedures – for example, regulation of SPD leafleting – were also carefully examined. In one hotly contested 1898 election in eastern Prussia, a *Landrat* sent a circular to various communal officials warning them of a planned SPD leafleting effort:

In notifying you of this planned distribution, I expect that you, without transgressing against legal provisions, will agree to exert influence in an appropriate way against this and in this way to intervene for state-supporting elements in the next Reichstag elections.

The vague and convoluted wording, as well as the qualifying phrases about legal provisions and appropriate methods, did not satisfy the parliamentarians. The circular was 'unallowable' in spite of its careful wording because, as the committee tactfully put it, it 'could very likely have given cause to misunderstandings' – that is, officials would have felt they were ordered to harass SPD leafleters.[20]

In Wilhelm von Kardorff's election in Groß Wartenburg-Oels in 1903, the committee received a flurry of protests. Most can be explained simply on the basis of how close the election was (Kardorff won by five votes above an absolute majority), which encouraged the losing parties to file every possible complaint. Even the tiny anti-Semitic party complained of official influence because the local *Landrat* had vetoed the publication of its program in his newspaper on the grounds that it 'incited class hatred' (the commission merely noted that private papers were not obliged to publish party programs). Of all the complaints, the committee treated with seriousness only the complaints that conservative ballot papers had been displayed on a polling table, and that a priest who had served as a polling officer had handled ballot envelopes in such a way that he could read them against the light. While this 'base compromising of electoral secrecy' could have led to the 'cashiering of the entire election,' the commission noted that the poll in question had not contributed to Kardorff's victory. They suggested the chancellor publicize such cases and warn that they would result in invalidation wherever they had any effect. This left would-be manipulators knowing that their actions would be tolerated only as long as they made no difference.[21]

Clearly conservatives at the turn of the century continued to try to use position and authority to influence voters, but with decreasing effectiveness. The alternative to the politics of deference was to accept, at least in part, the new rules of politics and appeal to 'the people' for a less contrived if not wholly democratic kind of support. Populism was a general phenomenon associated with the increasing political involvement of the German public through mass politics. Even the German Conservative Party, the party of the 'Junkers,' flirted, almost against its will, with populism: anti-Semitism and agrarian radicalism. In electoral terms, both of these reached their limits during 1898–1903.

The Anti-Semitic Option for a Conservative Populism

In the 1880s and early 1890s the '*Kreuzzeitung*-faction' of the Conservatives proposed a radical alternative agenda for the party. This group consisted of those associated with the Prussian Conservative newspaper, the *Kreuzzeitung*, most notably its chief editor after 1881, Baron Wilhelm von Hammerstein, and Court Preacher Adolf Stöcker, one of Germany's most prominent anti-Semitic campaigners. While their bases of support were separate, the two elements of the *Kreuzzeitung* group were united in their opposition to the Conservative Party leadership, and most notably its national chairman at the time, Otto von Helldorff-Bedra. The high point of the group's power came in 1892, when it succeeded in removing Helldorff from office and, at the Tivoli party congress, achieved the inclusion of *Mittelstandspolitik* and some anti-Semitic phrases in the official Conservative program.[22] The Tivoli triumph occurred just three days after an anti-Semite defeated a German Conservative and a left liberal in a by-election in Arnswalde-Friedeberg, demonstrating graphically the waxing power of populist anti-Semitism.[23]

The anti-Semitism of the *Kreuzzeitung* group presented the party with an option to transform itself into a 'people's party' rather than a government party. Supported by the party's activists in the provinces, the revolt against Helldorff was simultaneously a revolt against governmentalism, against domination by well-connected notables, and against alliance with liberalism in the *Kartell*. Anti-Semitic radicals and populist reformers wanted a stronger partisan conservative line, sharper hostility to liberalism, more independence from government, and a stronger social-reform emphasis (attacks on big business and finance) to win mass appeal. They were the advocates on the right of mass meetings, local organization, and personal contact with voters as a means to arouse the electorate.[24] Exploiting controversy within the Conservative Party over relations with

Chancellor Caprivi's administration and over the failure of the Prussian School Bill of 1891, the advocates of a populist approach gained a temporary victory at Tivoli. Their success in pressing for a conservative *Volkspartei*, however, discredited the Conservatives with the government and with their allies, and laid the basis for a governmentalist backlash. Helldorff rallied the governmentalist cause by denouncing anti-Semitism as 'the ... seed of Social Democracy' because it incited the masses against their social superiors.[25]

The anti-Semites' appeal to 'the people' contrasted with the old-fashioned campaigns of notables and aristocrats, in which candidates appealed to the trust and loyalty of members of the local community, and to historic traditions of hierarchical solidarity. One anti-Semite, in criticizing *Honoratiorenpolitik*, noted that governmentalists dismissed 'everything ... which moves the people' as 'demagogic.' Eduard Ulrich-Chemnitz implored 'our honourable deputies to become a little more "demagogic"' in the good sense of the word, 'more accustomed to striking the tone of the people.'[26] To governmentalists, this style and language was akin to Social Democracy. It was 'subversive' in and of itself, for it appeared to undermine authority, morality, and property. Governmentalists decried the way outgrowths of conservatism like 'anti-Semites ... and extreme Agrarians' now attacked the Conservative Party. These were 'separatist sectarian formations that cultivate a single thought in a radical and one-sided fashion.'[27] For all of these reasons, it was not easy for anti-Semitism to flow in the channels of the established parties, and it developed simultaneously both within them and outside.

Independent political anti-Semitism achieved electoral breakthroughs mainly from 1893 to 1903. The groundwork was laid by the election of the first anti-Semitic deputy to the Reichstag, Otto Böckel, in 1887, as a result of the stormy mobilization of the peasants of provincial Hesse. Böckel's seat, Marburg, had been a safe Conservative stronghold with low electoral participation for most of two decades. He changed both.[28] By 1890 his new Central German Peasants' Union had fifteen thousand members, and five anti-Semites reached the Reichstag, all from Prussian Hesse and the adjacent Grand Duchy of Hesse. The real breakthrough for electoral anti-Semitism came in 1893, when sixteen deputies were elected, mainly from Protestant, rural regions of the Reich. Ten of these were former Conservative seats.[29] In 1898 and 1903 fewer seats were won, as the anti-Semitic protest ran its course. The potential of their movement to grow had clearly reached its limits, and contemporaries already perceived that the movement had lost its drive. The period around 1900 is seen as a turning point in the development of anti-Semitism, marking its absorption into the broader right and its reduction to a subservient tactical role.[30]

Böckel's campaigns in Marburg demonstrated both what a conservative populism could be, and why the German Conservatives could not fully adopt it.[31] The battles over that seat between anti-Semites and governmental Conservatives continued bitterly into 1898 and 1903. The anti-Semites considered themselves to be conservative in the sense of supporting the state as well as traditional elements of society like the peasantry, and so were incensed when the Conservatives turned their invective against *them* instead of against the common enemy, the Social Democrats. The resulting acrimony between Conservatives and anti-Semites resembled a civil war. In one, not wholly atypical case, the anti-Semitic propaganda ridiculed the 'high-noble lord and great landowner,' opposing those who, it said, talked down to voters and understood 'nothing of the common people's burdens and need.' The image cultivated by Böckel, on the other hand, was that of 'a simple man of the people; no "high position in life" hinders him from being approachable by the little man.'[32] Perhaps it testifies to the effectiveness of this image that Böckel's opponents attacked him, not for having the wrong ideal in trying to represent 'the little man,' but for betraying his own rhetoric. 'He has wholly changed his opinions,' claimed opponents' leaflets, 'since he became a paid official of the Agrarian League.' In 1903 a rival anti-Semitic faction published a leaflet entitled 'The Old and the New Böckel,' charging once again that the populist had sold out to established conservative interests. Böckel had to devote a leaflet of his own to proving that '*my program is the old one.*' Even the man who, as much as any other in Germany, invented the rural populist image, could not prevent it being turned against him.[33]

One of the reasons that traditional conservatives had difficulty assimilating anti-Semitism was that the latter was not a traditional conservative philosophy. Böckel and regional populists like him drew explicitly on the liberal-populist traditions of 1848, borrowing republican symbols like the black-red-gold colours used by his party and intentionally democratic rhetoric. In attacking privilege and titles and exploiting local particularism, they were continuing in the channel cut previously (and with successful results) by German liberals of an earlier era – and the privileged and titled elites they attacked were normally associated with Prussian Conservative aristocrats. Two of its analysts note that anti-Semitism 'contained substantial democratic-revolutionary elements' and cannot strictly be classified as a form of conservatism in spite of its anti-liberalism.[34] In substance, anti-Semitism shared more with conservatism than with any other creed, and in many cases shared similar electoral environments, voters, and activists. Both anti-Semites and Conservatives were elected mainly in Protestant rural areas, and they shared beliefs ranging from anti-socialism to defence of farmers and the *Mittelstand*. Where they differed was in their attitudes towards what anti-Semites called 'reform,' meaning attacks on privilege and support of the underprivileged, especially the lower middle class, and for democratic politics. The recurrent use of the word 'social' by anti-Semitic groups (Christian-Social, German-Social Reform, National-Social) is another clue. Prior to anti-Semitism, the word 'social' referred, more or less, to the program and style of Social Democracy – meaning, agitation aimed at the masses and promoting the idea of social change. Anti-Semites (and others) wanted to win for the 'national' cause the same 'social' basis that the SPD was clearly gaining among the electorate.

Given the tragedy of anti-Semitism in German history, it is important to note that there were reasons, not logical or well grounded, but arising from circumstance, for the appeal of anti-Semitic imagery. These circumstances were not unique to Germany. Anti-Semitic propaganda used 'the Jew' to symbolize the alien, outside elements that traditionalists saw embodied in the growth of cities, of industry, of capital and finance, and also of the socialist working classes. Campaigning against Jews meant reasserting the traditional, 'German' values associated with what were understood to be the common folk, the bedrock of the German people. And anti-Semitism provided a simplistic, mono-causal explanation for all of Germany's woes: capitalism, socialism, economic problems, interest conflicts, and social tensions were not the result of real divisions or flaws in the 'German' nation; the 'red and gold internationals' caused it all.[35] There is also a broader populist pattern in the need to have a caricature of an enemy. Social Democrats inveighed against capitalists; agrarians and peasant populists condemned 'big financial capital'; Richter's left liberals presented voters with a demonology of 'Junkers'; Catholic propagandists talked about ruthless *Kulturkämpfer* on the opposing side. The anti-elitism inherent in populist appeals almost demanded a symbolic representation of the enemy, and for populists of the right, this was often the Jews.

The National-Social movement of the 1890s and early 1900s illustrates the ambiguity of anti-Semitism. Out of anti-Semitic roots, it grew into a left-liberal movement, with the ideas of mass agitation, social reform, and social synthesis providing the bridge between the two seemingly opposite affiliations. Under Friedrich Naumann, a former member of Stöcker's

Christian-Social movement, the National-Socials became the leading sponsors of the idea of a reform coalition of the left, including all liberals and stretching out towards the socialist working class – a coalition 'from Bebel to Bassermann' as Naumann called it at the 1901 National-Social congress. As their name implied (and this was a characteristically anti-Semitic idea), they hoped to combine nationalism with social reform, in particular with the democratic ideas of universal suffrage and income taxes. Given the predominant 'national'/anti-national and anti-socialist/socialist battle lines along which many Reichstag campaigns were fought, however, the synthesis was difficult to achieve. After crushing electoral failures in 1898 and 1903, Naumann dissolved his group and joined Theodor Barth, a leading advocate of liberal reunification, in the Left Liberal Union.[36]

Almost alone among the major anti-Semitic groups, Stöcker's Christian-Socials tried to retain an explicitly Conservative affiliation, splitting from the party proper only in 1896. Stöcker's movement attempted to emphasize what it had in common with traditional Conservatism in one of its draft programs:

... the Christian-Social Party strives on the basis of the Christian idea of the state, of monarchical loyalty and patriotism, for the rallying (*Sammlung*) of all popular circles penetrated with Christian-Social spirit in all strata and professions.

This patriotic, religious, and monarchical orientation represented the movement's claim to legitimacy within Conservative circles, but it was not sufficient. Other versions of the party program emphasized more explicitly a dedication to radical *Mittelstandspolitik*, demanding reforms to help artisans and farmers and in general to promote 'the elevation of the labouring classes.' This social radicalism and activism, expressed also in the movement's attempt to appeal to urban workers, were too extreme for the party hierarchy and did not sit easily beside the party's greater commitment to governmental loyalty.[37] Between 1892 and 1896, parallel to the development of the BdL as an alternative compromise with populism, Stöcker was gradually frozen out of the Conservative Party. He left in disgust in 1896, calling it un-Christian and controlled from above, while spokesmen of *Reaktion* like Baron von Stumm commented that 'I hold Christian-Social agitation to be much more dangerous than Social Democratic [agitation],' because unlike socialism it subverted monarchical and conservative elements.[38]

Anti-Semitism was a complex, fractured, highly regionalized movement. Stöcker's Christian-Social Party was prominent at the national level

TABLE 5
Multiple Regression for the Anti-Semitic Popular Vote, 1890–1912

	Var. type	1890	1893	1898	1903	1907	1912
% Catholic	C	−0.0235	−0.0535	−0.08733	−0.0687	−0.0514	−0.0110
		−2.79	−4.06	−6.26	−5.26	−3.80	−1.36
% Rural	C	0.0985	0.109	0.0694	0.145	0.0837	0.0583
		3.62	2.44	1.48	3.20	1.81	2.26
% City	C	0.0689	0.101	0.0506	0.0952	0.0104	0.0315
		2.82	2.53	1.22	2.38	0.250	1.37
% Turnout	C	−0.0142	−0.122	−0.176	−0.138	−0.100	0.0322
		−0.524	−2.15	−3.62	−2.44	−1.21	0.619
Prov. of E. Prussia	D	−1.71	−5.00	−5.82	−5.82	−3.50	−1.10
		−1.26	−2.25	−2.56	−2.66	−1.55	−0.875
Westphalia	D	0.908	−0.0535	3.75	5.42	5.15	1.36
		0.693	−0.0251	1.69	2.56	2.35	1.12
Hesse-Nassau	D	11.2	15.0	15.2	15.9	18.2	4.65
		7.82	6.43	6.22	6.85	7.59	3.50
Kingdom of Saxony	D	1.17	13.2	9.32	8.82	9.87	4.01
		0.951	6.59	4.52	4.44	4.77	3.53
Hesse	D	9.56	18.6	11.5	6.04	3.18	−0.432
		5.41	6.38	3.83	2.11	1.08	−0.263
Adjusted R^2		.211	.278	.262	.227	.215	.062
$F(11/385\ DF)$		10.6	14.8	13.8	11.6	10.9	3.40

Source: Multiple regression based on the author's constituency-level Reichstag election data; see Appendix C. Independent variables which did not show significant t-ratios at the 5 per cent level in at least two elections are not shown.

Note: The dependent variable is the percentage of the vote for the anti-Semitic parties (including the Deutsch-Soziale Reformpartei, the Christlich-Soziale Partei, and others). In the body of the table, the regression coefficient is on the top, and the t-ratio beneath (385 DF); significant coefficients are shown in bold, and the insignificant ones in italics. (See Appendix D for explanations of terms and abbreviations.)

and did win some votes in cities (which few anti-Semitic groups were able to do), but rarely enough to be a serious contender for seats. Other anti-Semitic parties lacked a national figure of Stöcker's prominence and behaved more like regional or local federations than organized parties; but in certain rural regions, they were strong enough to dominate. This scattered support is reflected in table 5, which shows a multiple regression trying to explain the anti-Semitic vote.

The most important feature of table 5 is the *weak* correlation it shows between social and demographic characteristics, on the one hand, and anti-Semitic voting patterns, on the other (i.e., the low value of the adjusted R^2). In other words, social statistics do not explain anti-Semitic behaviour very well; the anti-Semitic vote may have depended heavily on unquantified local and regional factors.[39] The table shows a negative correlation with Catholicism – electoral anti-Semitism was largely a Protestant phenomenon. There are a couple of possible reasons for this. Anti-Semitism was conditioned (as indicated above) both by long-standing Christian prejudices as well as by modern nationalist ones, and by anxiety about social change. Perhaps the nationalistic element in anti-Semitism explains why, electorally, it was almost exclusively a Protestant phenomenon. Protestant Germans were accustomed to 'national' causes, while Catholics were not. But there is another way to see this issue: Protestant areas of Germany were most affected by industrialization, and most fragmented among many political parties. The Catholic Centre was much more successful at representing and integrating a coherent social grouping (see chapter 6). It was the Protestant areas, or some of them, that left an organizational vacuum that a new populism could fill.

The table also reflects the two different varieties of anti-Semitism, urban and rural, in that anti-Semitic votes were positively associated both with cities of over ten thousand people (where the Christian-Socials won votes) and with rural communities of under two thousand (the typical base for the German-Social Reformers). The cities of Saxony are an example of an urban environment where anti-Semites succeeded; rural Hessen illustrates the opposite case. In three elections, 1893–1903, there is a significant negative correlation between anti-Semitic voting and low turnout, implying that it was particularly in undermobilized Protestant seats that anti-Semites made inroads.

In considering regional variations, the anti-Semites did worse than usual in East Prussia, where the Conservatives retained their hold, and better than normal in Hesse-Nassau, Hesse, the Kingdom of Saxony, and Westphalia. The success in Saxony is mainly a result of the coalition support of non-socialist voters for anti-Semites as the leading competitors to Social Democrats in a number of seats. Where governmental parties had to support an anti-Semite to defeat a Social Democrat, they often did so, if reluctantly. The other three areas of unusually strong support indicate that electoral anti-Semitism clustered in Protestant, west-central Germany – an area of strong peasants' movements.

Turning from votes cast to seats won, there is a clearer pattern. It was in the most politically divided areas of Germany, namely Protestant seats outside of the Social Democratic strongholds in the cities and the Conservative ones in the countryside, where peasants predominated or rural-urban divisions within the seat were sharp, that anti-Semitism was most successful. Almost 90 per cent of anti-Semitic victories during 1898–1903 were in Protestant, 'German,' rural seats dominated by the peasantry rather than by large landowners, or in other seats that were similar but divided on rural-urban lines.[40] The degree of 'fragmentation' in these categories of seats (2 and 3a) is represented in the fact that so many of them required run-off elections during 1898–1903, often against the SPD. No single party won more than a third of such seats, and even all the *Kartell* parties together (whose strength was concentrated in such Protestant rural areas) won only 48 per cent of them. The anti-Semites and the (noticeably anti-Semitic) BdL, though they did not contest every seat in these categories, still won 14 per cent of them. It was mainly in the seats that were economically less industrialized and undermobilized, too much characterized by small farms to be Conservative strongholds, that separate anti-Semitic and BdL candidacies succeeded.[41] Anti-Semitism, where it was strong enough to elect candidates, was a populist movement of poorly integrated, mostly rural Protestant, voters. Anti-Semites (led by Stöcker's Christian-Socials) did try also to campaign in cities; a large proportion of anti-Semitic candidacies were in urban centres. But except in urban Saxony, where anti-socialist coalitions reinforced their cause, anti-Semites could usually only win or come close in seats with a rural majority.[42]

It is frequently impossible to distinguish local anti-Semitic movements from agrarian ones, or the Conservative electorate from either. Agrarians and anti-Semites shared not only populism and the rural Protestant environment, but in addition voting support shifted among them where they overlapped. The Pomeranian constituency of Pyritz-Saatzig gave 14 per cent of its votes in 1893 to an anti-Semite opposing the official Conservative (who received 57 per cent); in 1898, when a BdL candidate ran, the anti-Semitic vote collapsed and the Conservative vote dropped sharply, giving the agrarian victory on the first ballot. This implies that the BdL candidate was able to draw votes from both anti-Semites and Conservatives. In 1903 the seat returned to the anti-Semite versus official Conservative pattern, though this time the anti-Semite won in the run-off. In all three elections, the 'right' received some 70–80 per cent of the vote, but in each case a different group won the election.[43] Examples like this one support the view that, on the spectrum from respectable governmentalism to radicalism, the BdL could be a hybrid between the Conservatives and the anti-Semites, sharing enough in common with each to attract both their votes. In any case, it shows the potential fluidity of support among the parties of the right.[44] And it was not only at the level of the electorate, but also at the level of activists and their ideology, that the Protestant agrarian movement and Protestant anti-Semitism blended together.[45]

In the course of the 1890s, the anti-Semitic cause became subsumed in the broader agrarian cause, which was more far-reaching in influence and even more problematic for the governmental parties. The power of governmentalists in the Conservative Party was such as to make the 1892 victory of the anti-Semitic faction at Tivoli a transitory one; at subsequent congresses, they were better prepared.[46] In the 1893 elections, Conservatism and anti-Semitism diverged, and by 1896 anti-Semitic 'demagogy' had been clearly rejected by Conservative leaders – but in its place agrarian 'demagogy' crept back in. The founding of the BdL provided the Conservatives with another challenge or opportunity. If in the end the power of governmental moderates was great and the trend towards populism was resisted, this was not without deep divisions that reveal the Conservative Party to have been more complex than the 'party of Junkers' left liberals and Social Democrats alleged it to be.

The Struggle to Accommodate Agrarian Populism

Stöcker's departure in 1896 from the Conservative Party ended any chance that anti-Semitism would reshape the party, and came as the electoral fortunes of independent anti-Semitism were waning. Even after 1896, anti-Semites were recognized as ideological relatives of the Conservatives and as acceptable members of local anti-socialist and nationalist coalitions, but their influence over party policy and candidate selection was extremely limited.[47] Instead, the numerically larger, more centralized, and economic-interest-oriented BdL loomed large in internal Conservative decisions. Populism's lasting impact on the party was by way of the agrarian organization. The overlap between the League and the party occurred mainly at the local level, for both had their core strength in the Protestant north and east. The interdependence of the two was reflected in the greater number of German Conservatives endorsed by the League than members of any other major party.[48]

The BdL provided the German Conservatives, organizationally the least developed of major Wilhelmine political parties, with an agitational instrument and a mass membership base. This helped the party to survive and hold its electoral position in mass politics without having to create a modernized, bureaucratic structure. Some even suggest that the BdL made possible 'the drive into new classes of the electorate, and at the same time the transformation into a party of the modern type with a broad base.'[49] This service to the Conservatives, however, is often seen as having created a dependence on the League; one historian claims 'it was impossible for a Conservative election committee to set itself against the only mass organization that supported it,'[50] and that in the end the interest group 'took over' the party.[51] In the last analysis, the BdL is often seen (much as contemporary left liberals saw it) as a manipulative device of the 'Junker' aristocracy of eastern Prussia, designed to secure leadership of smaller landowners and institutionalize the 'Junker' hold on rural society and on the Conservative Party. However, this view underestimates the seriousness of conflicts between governmental leaders and agrarians, between *Honoratiorenpolitik* and radical agitators within the party, conflicts which were spread across the German countryside in the campaigns of 1898–1903.[52]

The Agrarian League represented a substantial compromise with the new politics. While it did contain aristocrats, its significance was that it was the first agrarian interest group in whose founding 'a middle-class farm agent ... and a middle-class estate owner' played a leading role, a sign of 'the shift from landed aristocracy to a landowner class.'[53] It compromised with populism in adopting anti-Semitic ideas, in providing members with opportunities to participate (at least symbolically) in local meetings and as subscribers to newsletters, and in its election campaigns, which required candidates to bind themselves to a specific program in order to earn the League's endorsement. The implication of the BdL's agitation was that agrarians had to support agrarian candidates and candidates pledged to an agrarian program. This contradicted the traditional trust in community leaders that was the basis of *Honoratiorenpolitik* and of the traditional appeal of Conservative aristocrats to their electorate; and as such, it contradicted what governmentalists and government ministers wanted. It also had the effect of taking specific issues and policies out of the circles of parliaments and notables and placing them in the hands of agitators and voters. There was a participatory egalitarianism in all this that involved real elements of populism, not mere manipulation.[54] This is clearer when seen in a larger context, for the BdL was only one agrarian organization within a spectrum of populisms.

Populist strains of agrarianism flourished at the regional level in Wilhelmine Germany.[55] The Bavarian Peasants' League, for example, ran its own Reichstag candidates and tore peasant voters away from the Centre Party in Catholic Bavaria. The Peasants' League offered a combination of fierce anti-clericalism and what the *Kreuzzeitung* called 'particularism, anti-Prussianism, anti-militarism, and democracy.' This anti-authoritarian program had an ideological continuity with liberal-populist traditions – and, in fact, the Bavarian peasants considered political alliance with the left-liberal German People's Party against their Centre Party opponents.[56] The fierce campaigning of the Peasant League in undermobilized rural seats led to breakthroughs in the Reichstag elections of 1893–1903. A measure of the League's success is that it undid the positive statistical correlation between the rural population and Centre voting in Bavaria. Whereas rural voters could previously have been predicted to be Centre voters, in the years of the Peasants' League's success no such generalization could be made.[57]

The Bavarian Peasants' League's fiery 'democratic' slogan 'No more nobles, officials, or clericals!' alienated it from the Centre Party, governmental liberalism, and the BdL alike. The Peasants' League denounced the BdL as a 'conservative/anti-Semitic Junker association' – language that tried to associate the BdL with governmentalism, reaction, Protestantism, and northern Germany, in a way that would inspire Bavarian peasants to revulsion. One political poet expressed the Bavarian Peasants' League's appeal as follows (in colourful regional dialect) during the 1903 Reichstag campaign:

> Rise up peasants, stir yourselves
> There's no more use in chatter
> Now the paying [taxation] comes to a stop
> We won't put up with anything more.
>   'Courage, go to it!
>   Long live the Peasant League!'
> We're going to get the ministers
> All together they must flee
> Simple peasants must get in
> They must be the excellencies.

The peasants' movement stood for a kind of radical parochialism, mistrustful of all outsiders and emphasizing the self-mobilization of peasants in their own cause.[58] Peasants' leagues of the Bavarian model were not about to be manipulated by 'Junkers.' While the BdL increased its membership outside of eastern Prussia after 1896, including in Bavaria, it is not clear that this implies an extension of 'Junker' influence. Rather, it appears that, in Bavaria at least, the BdL succeeded in establishing itself only where it cooperated with pre-existing and independent agrarian movements, and never did manage to penetrate Catholic areas. Except for penetrations into Protestant Franconia, the BdL was squeezed out by the vigorous and dynamic politics of the numerous independent peasant movements.[59]

The 'democratic' tendencies of the peasant leagues were anathema to Conservatives, and even the BdL was suspect. Conservative dissenters from agrarianism argued for a renewal of close cooperation with the government, based on the anti-socialist cause and a prudent balancing of agrarian interests against broader governmental ones. In the period 1896–8, the Conservative Party press reveals a growing suspicion of the political style of the BdL and especially of its agitators.[60] In the 1898 campaign, the exact relationship of the interest group to the political party was still unclear, but by 1903 two events had served to distinguish acceptable from unacceptable agrarianism in the eyes of the party establishment. The first was the Mittelland Canal issue in the Prussian Landtag, beginning in 1899, which saw the emergence of open conflict between the kaiser and the BdL, with the threat of dismissal of Landräte who did not toe the anti-BdL line.[61] The fierce tariff debates of 1902 provided the second acid test of governmental loyalty. The lines were drawn between moderate agrarians satisfied with the 1902 tariff law and extremists (including BdL agitators) who demanded in addition their so-called 'great measures' (große Mitteln) to help agriculture, such as bimetallism and a state monopoly in grain trading. The quiet resistance displayed by the government to agrarian sectionalism in the 1898 Reichstag campaign became firmer, shutting out those agrarians who demanded still more concessions.

The ultimate test of conservatism, it was reiterated during the tariff controversy, was loyalty to the government. The Schlesische Zeitung noted that it was not the demands of the BdL that made it radical (that was merely interest politics), but the methods:

Radical on the other hand is the way that ... these demands are fought for in the press and in meetings, the way that people try to persuade the rural population that the government and the compromise parties lack good faith ... , the way that one by these means ... undermines trust and authority. The slogan 'All or nothing!' is radical, threats against allegedly 'soft' conservatives are radical.

'The radicalism we are fighting in the agrarian camp,' said the governmental paper, 'is flesh of the flesh of democracy, it is the fruit of ... democratic agitation methods and lies far away from conservatism, which always carries respect for legitimate authority on its banner.' The paper proclaimed, 'Away from Radicalism!' as a slogan for the right, and reiterated that 'a conservative party as a party of fundamental opposition with radical allure is an absurdity.'[62]

As the Conservative Party remained ambiguous about its exact position between governmentalism and agrarianism, both sides attempted to supply it with electoral help in a way that would further their own particular interests within the party. Government officials, as already noted, helped moderate Conservative candidates by arranging the support of other parties for them and by donating money, pamphlets, and press support to their campaigns. On the other side, the BdL frequently put its mass agitation behind Conservative candidates. This accentuated the divisions. For one thing, the BdL in its election propaganda stood for a vicious anti-liberalism, something that simply could not be accommodated in the framework of government-sponsored cooperation among the *Kartell* parties. One exemplary Agrarian League leaflet appealed to 'German Voters' in the 1898 main ballot, suggesting that such voters ask their candidates, 'How do you want to help us?' It continued:

There are many who will answer you, 'I want to extend the political rights of the people, want to assure and extend for you freedom of speech, freedom of the press, and freedom of assembly.' Then say to them:
    'We don't need you!'

According to the BdL, 'German Voters' already had all the rights '*which are honourable and compatible with religion and good morals.*' Promises of freedom of occupation, free trade, freedom of stock exchanges, and freedom of commerce (in short, liberal ideas) were allegedly the same for the farmer as '*freedom to hunger!*' and amounted to the '*tyranny of stock-exchange big capital ... [the] economic slavery of honourable labour ...*'[63] Such anti-capitalist, anti-liberal, anti-urban *Mittelstandspolitik* differed only marginally from the anti-Semitic appeal, and certainly was nothing the government could condone, considering electoral and parliamentary realities. The League's response to the charges of 'one-sided interest politics' was ingenuous: 'Who doesn't pursue interest politics today?'[64] The government (and governmentalist Conservatives) could not go along with this without breaking necessary anti-socialist coalitions with National Liberals and left liberals.[65]

The BdL, and particularly in its well-prepared campaigns of 1898 and 1903, drove a wedge between the governmentalism and the agrarianism of the German Conservative Party. Conservative candidates in rural areas were faced with having to pledge themselves to the League program, regardless of government priorities, and face the possible behind-the-scenes resistance of the government's officials if they joined the radical agrarian camp. In many constituencies, the tension was not unmanageable; in the large-landowning areas of the north and east, the Conservative Party and the BdL appeared to be a single unit. Agrarianism (like anti-Semitism before it) did not split from the Conservatives with significant opposition candidacies in these strongholds either in 1898 or in 1903.[66] But in other areas, the Conservatives needed to appeal for the support of liberal elements against the SPD, and here agrarian sectionalism was a disadvantage to the party. It was in such seats that Prussian officials resisted agrarian candidacies and struggled to find moderate governmental representatives; and it was in such seats that anti-Semites and the BdL most frequently broke away from the governmental camp and nominated their own candidates. In Protestant, 'German' rural seats not dominated by great holdings, the Conservatives lost ground and all the *Kartell* parties as well as the left liberals lost votes and seats, while the anti-Semites and the BdL, on the one hand, and the SPD, on the other, gained. The seven seats lost by the Conservative Party (DKP) were reflected in the seven gained by anti-Semitic and agrarian populists.[67] In majority-rural seats that also had a substantial urban population, the SPD was able to exploit the other parties' divisions and the agrarian issue to become by far the largest single party (38 per cent of the vote in 1903 compared to 29 per cent for all the *Kartell* parties together), entering the run-off in numerous cases and winning ten seats. The conservative parties lost ground here as well.[68] Agrarian sectionalism complicated the anti-socialist cause in just those seats where the latter needed to be most effective, namely mixed urban/rural seats where agrarian elements plus non-socialist elements in the towns together had a majority.

The divisions within conservatism were explicit by the time of the 1903 elections. In Prussia and Saxony, Conservative Party leaders tried to preserve the old *Kartell* strategy by reining in agrarians in National Liberal Hanover just as in Conservative eastern seats.[69] But the BdL simply repeated in 1903 that 'the present economic policy of Germany since the beginning of the nineties has benefited the development of industry in a completely one-sided way'; the 'peasantry' would have to continue the fight for greater protection, even though 'in this struggle we are left in the lurch by the government.' The extreme agrarians had been limited and contained, but they had not been assimilated.[70] Political observers wrote of the 'gulf' between the crown and the agrarians shortly after the Reichstag elections, and of the gloomy foreboding that next time real conservatives would 'go down before the renewed onslaught of the most extreme Agrarian Leaguers, of left liberalism and of Social Democracy, and monarchical sentiment would be destroyed.'[71] Seen in this electoral context, the kind of *Sammlungspolitik* articulated by Miquel and echoed by Conservatives in some regions, represented an attempt to reconcile the contradictory aspects of the anti-socialist and agrarian-protectionist causes. Miquel's claim that the two coincided was a hopeful attempt to synchronize them, not a statement of reality. Conservatives, in arguing that 'aid to hard-pressed sectors' was necessary for the stability of the state, were trying to legitimize agrarian sectionalism and make it a respect-able patriotic cause, and thereby to preserve both their party's patriotism and its agrarian, rural base. Their success in doing so was mixed: during 1898–1903 agrarianism strengthened the Conservative Party in its core areas, but weakened it in marginal seats. The result was a smaller, more compact, more contained, and more agrarian Conservative Party.

Conservatives and Voters, 1898–1903

In the midst of the controversy over agrarian demands, the Conservatives did not 'drive into new classes of the electorate' as advocates of a right-wing 'people's party' hoped, but were driven back into the regions and groups that had always provided the core of their support. They lost ground outside rural eastern Prussia, became less geographically and socially representative, and did not recover until the economic issues of 1898–1903 had been put behind them and they again had the chance (in 1907) to fight a 'national' campaign. Agrarian issues hampered the Con-servatives' regional and national campaigns; encouraged renegade candi-dates and populist competitors in marginal areas; gave rise to ambivalence on the part of the government; and provided the Social Democrats and left liberals with a potent and effective election issue.[72] It is not a coincidence that the height of the political agrarian movement during 1898–1903 saw the worst electoral performance of the Conserva-tive Party. On the other hand, agrarianism strengthened the Conservatives in the middle term as a sectional or regional-interest party. Agrarianism made the Conservatives, in electoral terms, into a more Prussian party. This occurred in stages. In 1890, as we have seen, 74 per cent of seats won by Conservatives were in Prussia (which had 60 per cent of Reichstag constituencies). In 1903, with an election focused on the tariff issue and agrarianism, the Conservative seat total hit its lowest level in two decades. As part of this loss, the SPD overwhelmed the Kingdom of Saxony (winning 22 of 23 seats, the Conservatives losing all 5 that they had held previously), and the Conservatives won only one seat in southern Germany. *Ninety* per cent of the party's seats were now in Prussia. Even the otherwise successful 'national' elections of 1907 failed to restore the party to the position it had enjoyed after the previous 'national' elections in 1893.[73] The Conservatives retreated from the cities, from the 'fragmented' battlegrounds of middle Germany, and from the south into the aristocratic strongholds of the north and east. Conservatism suffered a double blow, evident by 1903, to its governmentalist moderation and at the same time to its electoral breadth. But this was not entirely a weakness: if the Conservative grouping in the electorate was smaller and more regionalized, it was also firmer.

During 1893–8 the SPD had made some noteworthy penetrations into the large-landowning districts of northeastern Germany, where the party hoped to arouse agricultural labourers against big landlords. Some of the party's successes were startling and imply a certain potential for the party to win not just rural but actual agricultural voting support – and just at the time when this was a major doctrinal controversy between revisionists and orthodox Marxists in the party (see chapter 7).[74] But while the agrarian issue helped the SPD rally and solidify support in many areas of the Reich, in these northeastern, core Conservative regions the reverse was true. The SPD's penetration was slowed in 1903, and in the 'national' campaign of 1907 utterly crushed, so that the levels of SPD support in those seats won during 1898–1903 were not regained. In its core areas, German Conservatism became *stronger* as the agrarian movement was integrated into the party, restoring once again an almost homogeneous Conservative environment in these constituencies.

The success (and limitations) of Conservatism in retaining its electoral base during 1898–1903 is reflected in multiple regression analysis of the Conservative popular vote (table 6). The regression coefficients show a party with a clearly defined social-economic base. The negative correlation of Conservative support with Catholicism was highly significant. The German Conservatives were without question highly Protestant in their

TABLE 6
Multiple Regression for German Conservative Popular Vote, 1890–1912

	Var. type	1890	1893	1898	1903	1907	1912
% Catholic	C	**−0.273**	**−0.250**	**−0.215**	**−0.220**	**−0.220**	**−0.216**
		−7.68	−7.63	−7.08	−7.58	−7.50	−7.52
% Employed in	C	**0.249**	**0.264**	**0.236**	**0.154**	**0.255**	**0.235**
agriculture		4.20	4.65	4.45	3.05	5.27	5.27
Large land-	D	**11.6**	**13.9**	**10.7**	**15.8**	**20.3**	**13.0**
ownership		3.80	4.82	3.90	6.07	8.01	5.57
% Turnout	C	**−0.441**	*−0.212*	*−0.132*	**−0.314**	**−0.469**	*−0.135*
		−4.36	−1.80	−1.54	−3.09	−3.10	−0.881
Prov. of E.	D	**28.7**	**33.6**	**32.4**	**31.6**	**38.7**	**18.5**
Prussia		6.01	7.48	7.86	7.88	9.81	5.10
Brandenburg	D	**18.4**	**19.0**	**23.4**	**9.34**	**7.17**	*5.65*
		4.21	4.62	6.10	2.52	1.96	1.68
Pomerania	D	**20.7**	**13.0**	**22.5**	**19.3**	**20.7**	**22.0**
		3.65	2.54	4.75	4.22	4.58	5.32
Silesia	D	*4.62*	**10.8**	**14.8**	**14.2**	**12.7**	**10.2**
		1.40	3.47	5.11	5.07	4.57	4.00
Schleswig-	D	**−12.9**	**−13.5**	**−14.0**	**−16.0**	**−15.9**	**−8.86**
Holstein		−2.20	−2.46	−2.75	−3.22	−3.27	−1.97
Hanover	D	**−15.3**	**−13.3**	**−8.44**	*−6.31*	*−6.97*	*6.68*
		−3.43	−3.16	−2.16	−1.67	−1.87	−1.96
Kingdom of	D	**16.8**	**13.8**	**13.4**	*4.88*	*5.21*	*1.84*
Saxony		3.98	3.47	3.63	1.36	1.46	0.571
Adjusted R^2		.478	.485	.500	.501	.585	.488
$F(18/378\ DF)$		21.1	21.7	23.0	23.1	32.0	21.9

Source: Multiple regression based on the author's constituency-level Reichstag election data; see Appendix C. Independent variables which did not show significant t-ratios at the 5 per cent level in at least two elections are not shown.

Note: The dependent variable is the percentage of the vote for the German Conservative Party (DKP). In the body of the table, the regression coefficient is on the top, and the t-ratio beneath (378 DF); significant coefficients are shown in bold, and the insignificant ones in italics. (See Appendix D for explanations of terms and abbreviations.)

electoral base. However, this negative correlation was stronger during 1890-3 than it was thereafter.

The Conservative vote was positively correlated, on the other hand, with the percentage of the population employed in agriculture – the Conservatives were and remained a party associated with Protestant rural Germany. This correlation was weaker, though, in 1898 and especially 1903 than before or after. It is plausible that this apparent weakening of agricultural support in these particular elections was a result of breakaway Agrarian League and other agrarian candidacies. At the same time, in addition to higher support in agricultural areas overall, they were especially strongly represented in the areas of large landownership, and this association was strongest during 1903–7. In those same years, 1903–7, Conservative votes tended to come from less-mobilized seats that had lower voter participation. Both of these patterns suggest that in 1903 and the following election, the Conservatives effectively capitalized on their support in their core areas, the large-landholding areas of the north and east, where voters were less highly mobilized – and that, correspondingly, they did less well in other rural seats, including those where the population was strongly politicized. Despite the fluctuations during 1898–1903, the Conservative base in these kinds of environments was cracked only in 1912, when the *Kartell* broke down for good and National Liberals began widely contesting them.

Regional factors beyond those accounted for by the social and demographic statistics were also strong determinants of the Conservative vote. Conservative voting was even stronger in East Prussia, Brandenburg, Pomerania, Silesia, and (before 1903) Saxony than one would expect from the demographic characteristics of those regions. The strength of Conservative support in East Prussia and Pomerania remained rock-solid, as indicated by the coefficients, which is especially impressive given that these were *also* provinces dominated by large landholdings. In other words, the two variables were working together: the Conservatives did better, because of the landholding structure, than they did in other regions; and other regional factors not apparent in the social-economic statistics gave them an additional boost of 13 to 39 per cent of the vote in the seats in these regions. In Brandenburg, on the other hand, the Conservatives enjoyed a special regional dominance of similar magnitude but only until 1903, when their special advantage was sharply reduced. In this case, the main factor was probably the spread of Social Democratic voting outward from the cities into the surrounding towns and countryside; at the same time, the seats were becoming more urban. Also, some of the governmental candidacies in the province went over to the Imperial Party, whose performance in Brandenburg improved (see below).

The situation in the Kingdom of Saxony was even more dramatic. It had been a region of unusually strong Conservatism right up until 1903, when it was submerged in the Social Democratic tide of that year and in the massive protest, using the Reichstag suffrage, against the regressive changes in the state suffrage (see chapter 7). In Schleswig-Holstein and (until 1903) Hanover, voters 'should' (according to the social-economic and demographic predictions) have voted more frequently Conservative than they did – here the regional variables turn up strongly negative. These were largely rural, largely Protestant provinces, which is why the regression predicts that, but for specific regional factors, the Conservative share of the vote would have been higher. Instead, National Liberals, left liberals, and Social Democrats dominated the electorate in these provinces. Hanover was a particular National Liberal stronghold, until a falling-out with the Agrarian League in 1898 and 1903. Schleswig-Holstein had a distinctive pattern of oppositional, Social Democratic voting until the Weimar Republic.[75]

These trends show some particular fluctuations during 1898–1903 – the change to a stronger concentration in areas of large landownership and low turnout, the decline in Brandenburg, the collapse in Saxony, the improvement in Hanover – but overall the picture is one of stability until 1912. Despite the agrarian storms of the turn of the century, and the advance of Social Democracy, the Conservatives maintained their electoral identity in terms of confession, economic interests, and regions. They remained, in Stanley Suval's terminology, a coherent 'social grouping,' and, one might add, with somewhat greater emphasis than Suval did, a regional grouping as well.[76]

The problem for the Conservatives was that their consistent support came in a growing electorate increasingly dominated by the SPD. As the electorate grew and became more urban, the firm Conservative electoral strongholds were more and more a minority. This clearly affected the Conservative popular vote, which declined to just 11 per cent in 1898 and 10 per cent in 1903, the lowest totals since the party's reorganization in the mid-1870s. The lack of redistribution of constituencies protected Conservative rural seats to some degree even as the Conservatives' overall percentage of the vote fell; but lack of redistribution alone was not enough to protect all Conservative seats. As towns grew into cities, they changed formerly rural constituencies into more urban ones; and larger cities spilled out into the surrounding constituencies, as in Brandenburg and Saxony, colonizing the countryside. With the growth of cities came Social Democratic voters. The Conservatives retained or even strengthened their identity, while winning fewer votes and seats. In the 1898 elections, they won just 56 seats, compared with 73 in 1890 and 72 in 1893. The new, lower level of representation proved permanent. In 1903 the Conservatives fell further to 54 seats, and never regained the levels of the

TABLE 7

Multiple Regression for the Imperial Party Popular Vote, 1890–1912

	Var. type	1890	1893	1898	1903	1907	1912
% Catholic	C	−0.0900	−0.0981	−0.0579	−0.0445	−0.0465	−0.0422
		−3.39	−4.25	−2.71	−2.34	−2.09	−2.39
Prov. of W. Prussia	D	12.1	11.5	17.7	16.0	12.9	21.2
		2.75	3.01	5.00	5.09	3.50	7.29
Brandenburg	D	5.22	0.145	3.11	10.7	13.2	10.7
		1.43	0.0460	1.06	4.10	4.30	4.42
Posen	D	15.6	16.8	17.7	13.3	11.8	8.70
		3.72	4.62	5.27	4.44	3.38	3.14
Silesia	D	11.1	8.66	5.62	4.93	5.22	5.05
		3.93	3.53	2.48	2.43	2.21	2.70
Prov. of Saxony	D	5.96	17.0	15.2	9.51	4.32	4.11
		1.65	5.42	5.22	3.67	1.43	1.71
Schleswig-Holstein	D	1.82	3.60	10.9	11.8	4.49	1.12
		.362	0.827	2.72	3.27	1.07	0.337
Rhineland	D	5.73	6.47	7.69	3.75	1.79	1.44
		1.91	2.48	3.19	1.75	0.711	0.725
Adjusted R^2		.084	.146	.169	.167	.0966	.167
$F(13/383\ DF)$		3.80	6.21	7.18	7.12	4.26	7.10

Source: Multiple regression based on the author's constituency-level Reichstag election data; see Appendix C. Independent variables which did not show significant t-ratios at the 5 per cent level in at least two elections are not shown.

Note: The dependent variable is the percentage of the vote for the Imperial Party (RP). In the body of the table, the regression coefficient is on the top, and the t-ratio beneath (383 DF); significant coefficients are shown in bold, and the insignificant ones in italics. (See Appendix D for explanations of terms and abbreviations.)

early 1890s. Thus the Conservative adaptation to populism and mass politics can hardly be judged a complete success, either by the standard of popular support or by the standard of Reichstag representation.

Not surprisingly, a multiple regression on the Imperial Party's popular vote (table 7) shows much less coherence. The adjusted R^2 value of 0.169 or less signifies that all the predictors, demographic and social-economic indexes as well as regional dummy variables, 'explain' at most 16.9 per cent of the variation in the party's vote. There was a significant negative correlation of Imperial Party voting with Catholic population – it was a Protestant party – but this relationship was a great deal weaker than for the German Conservatives, and declined during 1898–1903. The weakness of the negative correlation with Catholicism probably has to do with the number of examples where governmental candidates chose to stand for the Imperial Party to unify the 'German' vote in areas of mixed confession or Polish, Alsatian, or Guelph minorities (minorities who were or included Catholics). In other words, while the Imperial Party was a Protestant party, there was a secondary tendency for its candidates to run where Catholics or Catholic ethnic minorities (also, of course, other 'enemies of the Reich') were a political factor.

In any case, social-economic factors like rural or urban population and agricultural or industrial employment define nothing at all about the Imperial Party base. It represented no social grouping definable by the available statistics. But regional patterns do show up: the party's support was higher in West Prussia, Posen, Silesia, and Schleswig-Holstein (all areas of battles between 'Germans' and particularists) and in certain periods in Brandenburg, the Prussian province of Saxony, and in the Rhineland. This regionalization, without a clear social-economic base, is characteristic of the old-fashioned parties. In terms of the available demographic, social-economic, and regional information, the Imperial Party failed to establish an institutionalized identity and did not adapt in an era of adaptation. Its popular vote dwindled from little to very little – less than 4 per cent in 1903. But the party consistently won twenty-odd seats in every Wilhelmine election save 1912. There is no contradiction in this: its candidacies were opportunistic, in the sense that candidates were put up only where prospects were good for rallying support from governmentalists. This dependence on external support also shows the Imperial Party's failure as a political party of the modern type.

In Wilhelmine Germany, and particularly during 1898–1903, conservatives lost any broad geographic or social-economic representative ambitions they may have had. The Imperial Party represented no definable interests and little in the way of policy. The German Conservatives declined to become a 'people's party,' to break out of the mould of *Honoratiorenpolitik* and of defensive electoral coalitions like the *Kartell*, but the party at least succeeded in stabilizing its core areas of electoral support. Anti-Semitic and agrarian surges indicated the potential for electoral dynamism on the right, but this potential was not wanted or not realized. Anti-Semites and radical agrarians broke away from the conservative camps in the 1890s and early 1900s, weakening the moderate and governmental cause. It is true that such breakaway populisms dealt no fatal blow to conservatism within the Wilhelmine period; but their existence, and the failure to integrate them, revealed the limitations of the established

German right wing in an era of emerging mass politics. The activists who sought a populist-nationalist conservatism had to seek alternatives and bide their time; many of them re-emerged in the Weimar Republic. Majoritarian conservatives, rejecting populism, were left with the handicap of an unresolved dualism between their governmentalist and agrarian tendencies: they suffered electorally from being associated with both the government and with agrarian-protectionist interests, without being able to exploit the electoral potential of radical nationalism or radical agrarianism. The result was a party whose numerical power and national representative claims had been significantly reduced.

One chief difference between the broad conservative and liberal groupings in Wilhelmine politics was that conflicts between 'notables' and 'populists' emerged *within* the conservative camp, and there were efforts to resolve the resulting conflict. Despite the turbulence and complexities of trying to find a workable electoral synthesis between agrarianism and governmentalism, the German Conservative Party did hold on to its core regions of strength. Whatever its losses in marginal areas, the German Conservative Party tightened its hold on agrarian seats in northeastern Germany by its alliance with agrarian interests. The electoral grouping redefined in this way had sufficient cohesion to help the party largely stabilize its representation in the Reichstag after the losses in 1898. Even in 1912, when the National Liberals finally broke governmental ranks and attacked the Conservatives in these core seats, the loss of votes and seats was not altogether ruinous for the Conservatives. In maintaining their core electoral strength and sustaining a link even with a geographically restricted social milieu, the German Conservatives did better than Germany's liberal parties. Liberals, by contrast, had few strongholds anywhere, found no coherent social-economic grouping, and failed to produce an electoral populism of their own.

5

The Low Ebb of Liberalism

The transformation of German politics that was in progress at the turn of the century was problematic for German liberals. Not only the development of more integrated, mass party structures, but also the increasing orientation of issues and parties along the lines of social-economic cleavages conflicted fundamentally with the liberal conception of politics and representation. Liberals had been the quintessential practitioners of the politics of notables in Germany. To the extent that they could not adapt fast enough to the new age, the crisis of *Honoratiorenpolitik* necessarily involved a crisis of liberalism. The electoral fortunes of Germany's liberal parties declined as mass electioneering developed; liberals did not put up as candidates populist 'men of the people,' and did not have mass party organizations or mass propaganda. Liberals continued, often, to try to fit their ideas into the old patterns of leadership: leaders as finders of compromises in the overall national interest, leaders as representatives of abstract and nationalistic causes. They excelled, typically, at exploiting the cleavages of the era of national unification – fighting against clericals and ethnic minorities – but failed to find a formula to turn the cleavages of industrialized society to their advantage. Most liberals rarely spoke the language of classes, interests, popular rights, and fairness of taxation burdens. There were exceptions, both regionally and among the different liberal parties. But, in general, liberals were vulnerable – and their opponents took delight in exposing them – to charges that they were a remote elite isolated from the simple *Volk* and from the lower classes. If Conservatives were caricatured by the image of Junkers, liberals were represented by their critics as men of privilege from the circles of the educated and business leaders, out of touch with the common people.[1] Such an image was hardly an asset in an era of mass politics, and it is no surprise that the years surrounding the turn of the century were years of liberal failure. Long and agonizing as this crisis may have been, liberalism reached its lowest electoral ebb during 1898–1903.[2]

This said, the weakness of liberalism should not be overemphasized. The electoral support of the liberal parties reached a trough during 1898–1903 but recovered somewhat before 1914. Even in that trough, liberals of many kinds together garnered almost a quarter of the votes, making them still one of the four strong groupings in Wilhelmine politics – stronger, together, than all the right-wing and conservative parties, about as strong as the Centre and particularists, not yet too far behind the SPD. And liberals remained influential in many spheres, particularly in civic governments.[3] The problem, in elections, was twofold. First, liberal votes were spread too thinly and divided among too many parties, many of which fought against each other. Liberal parties mostly lacked secure regional bases like the German Conservatives or the Centre – the National Liberals in places like Hesse were an exception – or secure social-economic environments like the SPD enjoyed in most of the large Protestant cities. Second, and perhaps more importantly in the long term, it was no longer clear what liberalism as an electoral program stood for; thus the twenty-odd per cent of voters casting liberal ballots did not necessarily share anything substantially in common.[4] Votes for National Liberals were indistinguishable in some areas from conservative governmental (sometimes even from conservative agrarian) votes, because of the party's tactical alliances. Left-liberal support in some cities overlapped with SPD support and appeared to shift back and forth. Refusing to orient themselves around social-economic cleavages within the Protestant, 'German' electorate, liberals lost coherence, even as they continued to advocate unity and the national good.

Liberal Decline

From winning 40 per cent of votes or more in the 1870s, and performances in the mid-30 per cent range up to 1890, the liberal parties fell sharply to 24 per cent in 1898 and 23 per cent in 1903. The number of Reichstag seats they won was also less than in the 1880s and earlier.[5] For liberals the elections of the 1890s verged on catastrophe. Their average level of support of 23 per cent was not only low; it also represented votes spread thinly among many seats, unlike other parties (especially the particularists and the Centre) whose votes were sufficiently concentrated to benefit from the winner-take-all electoral system. With 23 per cent, liberal candidates could win only in exceptional cases, where other parties were extremely divided and favourable coalitions were possible on the second ballot. The loss of a few per cent more across the electorate as a whole could mean that liberals would fail to hang on even to second place in many seats, and, by failing to make it to the second ballot, lose much of their remaining representation.[6] Poor performances in elections also created a kind of vicious circle, providing ammunition for opponents – the SPD press ridiculed liberals for being unable to survive on their own strength, that is, without second-ballot support from others – and thus undermining the credibility and appeal of the liberal parties.

This was an uncomfortable position for liberals, who had been the first political movement organized in Germany, and who had conceived of themselves originally as the representatives of the whole public. Prior to unification, liberals claimed the mantle of representing 'the people' – or the enlightened interests of the same – against the state, which was associated with privilege and absolutism. In this vague, dichotomous conception, the liberal party was defined neither by rules, structures, and formal policy, nor by competition within civil society against other parties. German liberals believed their doctrine to be the only legitimate political orientation, the only philosophy that represented the interests of the people against the authoritarian and bureaucratic principles of the state. Liberals believed they had a moral mission to provide political leadership, that they represented the best of the nation's talent, education, and achievement.[7] In short, they were trying to assert 'hegemony' in the emerging public sphere of politics and discussion: liberals would articulate what the interests of the people were. This concept of party persisted after unification, so that even at the turn of the century, liberal newspapers reported on the progress of 'the' liberal party, at a time when four separate organizations and many independent candidates existed. One might say that the individual liberal parties displayed a low degree of institutionalization – and in fact were reluctant to become more institutionalized. This reluctance represented a latent claim that their 'party' was more than a mere faction or organization, that it represented informed opinion and the enlightened interests of the nation, while more formalized and agitational parties were merely sectarian and divisive. Max Weber, a German nationalist, commented that the Centre and the SPD – Imperial Germany's largest and most mass-oriented parties – 'have, from their inceptions, been minority parties and have meant to be minority parties.'[8] In the liberal hegemonic conception, the fact that these parties consciously appealed to coherent interests – to social-economic cleavages – made them inherently illegitimate. While liberals clung to this view, however, they did not succeed in making others share it.

With the exception of the liberal victory of 1881, every Reichstag election since unification brought a lower combined share of the vote to the liberal parties. From the high of 47 per cent in 1871, liberals had been reduced by 1898–1903 to half that amount, and to less than half the number of seats.[9] There were both long- and short-term aspects to the liberal decline; liberals lost nearly as much popular support in the two elections of 1893 and 1898 (a total of 10 per cent) as they had lost in the previous two decades. The expansion and increased politicization of the electorate, the gradual fading of unification issues in favour of social-economic ones, the disunity of the 'middle classes' to whom liberalism looked for leadership and support: all these could be mentioned as factors in the long-term decline. Two factors in particular exacerbated liberalism's long-term problems in the 1890s: the agrarian movement and the SPD. To the extent that these new movements brought forward new issues, liberals were at a disadvantage.

The weakness of liberalism can also be viewed in part as the strength of its competitors, and especially their better adaptation to the circumstances of mass politics. Germany's other main political groupings found reliable means to hold or even extend their electoral support. The conservative parties, it is true, fell from levels of support as high as 27 per cent in 1878 to 19 per cent in 1898 and 16 per cent in 1903. But the conservative decline was not, like the liberal one, an across-the-board deterioration, but a process of concentration assisted by firmer ties with the agrarian, Protestant environment of the north and east of Germany.[10] This allowed them to maintain respectable seat totals and political influence even while their popular vote declined. Liberalism mostly did not have such stable core areas, nor a movement like agrarianism to revitalize its electoral campaigns, nor a social grouping defined by firm community ties to which it could appeal. The Centre (and the Poles) fared even better than the conservatives, mobilizing nearly enough new voters to keep their electoral support constant in spite of the growing electorate. So firm were the communities to which they appealed that only the SPD could break into them, and that only slowly. If the SPD rode the crest of a wave of electoral support in the 1890s, these other groupings, all except the liberals, at least managed to keep their heads above water.

The advance of the SPD neatly paralleled the liberal decline. From 1890 to 1903 the liberals and the SPD nearly reversed positions in the electorate, from 34 per cent and 20 per cent respectively in the last election overseen by Bismarck to 23 per cent and 32 per cent in the first election of the twentieth century. Protestant urban constituencies once typically won by liberals were now being taken by Social Democrats, pushing the liberals back to more rural bases of support at exactly the time agrarianism and anti-Semitism were causing problems for liberal candidates in rural areas. In Protestant cities (type 4 seats – see Appendix A), National Liberals and left liberals had fought 18 run-offs and won 17 seats (both ballots) in 1890; in 1903 they fought only 10 run-offs and won only 6 seats in total. The SPD had picked up the difference, increasing from 20 to 34. By 1903 the SPD's *average* level of support in Protestant cities was 57 per cent, allowing it to win many seats on the first ballot. Accordingly, the total number of second-ballot contests declined sharply in these seats, and the liberals did not even get the chance to organize second-ballot coalitions.[11] In seats that were not completely urban, but still contained a city, the SPD advance was slower, but the trend was the same. In 1890 the liberal parties still dominated, fighting 38 run-offs against the conservatives, the SPD, and each other, and splitting 45 per cent of the popular vote. The SPD in 1890 received only 17 per cent and won no seats. By 1903, as both urban settlements and SPD support spread into new constituencies, the liberals made it into the run-off in only 26 cases, compared to 37 run-offs and 12 seats for Social Democrats. Liberals now received only 27 per cent of the vote; the SPD 35 per cent.[12]

In the countryside, matters were only a little better for National Liberalism, and possibly worse for left liberalism. The large-landownership Protestant constituencies of the north and east were solidly in the grip of the Conservatives; rural Catholic constituencies were loyal to the Centre (or, in old Bavaria, went to the Peasants' League); and the remaining rural regions included many of the ones most affected by agrarian and anti-Semitic extremism.[13] In Protestant rural areas (type 2), liberals had managed 50 per cent of the vote and 16 seats in 1890 (by far the strongest party grouping), while by 1903 they were reduced to 26 per cent and 11 seats – fewer votes than the Social Democrats, barely more seats than the anti-Semites and radical agrarians. The biggest losers were the left liberals, who had been stronger than the National Liberals in such rural seats in 1890, both in votes and seats won, and were behind in both categories by 1903.[14] In the Social Democratic and agrarian waves of the 1890s, all liberals lost out in the cities, and all liberals, but especially left liberals, declined in the countryside. The new issues, interests and 'fairness' questions, were not well suited to liberal programs in either town or country. What they were left with was the middle ground – neither city nor country

FIGURE 9
National Liberal Popular Vote, by Constituency Type, 1890–1912

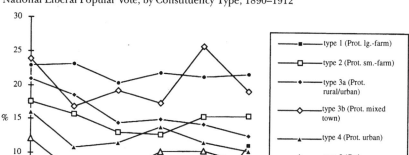

Comments: National Liberals did best on a Reich-wide basis in types 3a and 7b (mixed rural-urban and mixed-confession) seats, and worst in Catholic rural seats and, until 1912, in the type 1 rural seats that were dominated by the Conservatives.

Note: For clarity of presentation, type 6 and type 7a seats are not shown.

– and no clear issues. The similarities and differences in the electoral trends for the two varieties of liberalism are evident in figures 9 and 10. (The main liberal groupings are discussed in more depth below.)

The continued reliance of the National Liberals on confessional issues – a 'national' polarization exploiting the original cleavages surrounding unification – is evident in figure 9. Where neither confession had a commanding majority, the tension between Protestants and Catholics tended to remain the focus of electoral battles, perpetuating a style and content of politics that favoured National Liberalism. In four of the six general elections of the Wilhelmine period, the National Liberal popular vote was higher in constituencies of mixed confession (type 7b) than in any other category. In such seats the party won, on average, over 20 per cent of the vote from 1893 to 1912 – significantly above its Reich average of 13–15 per cent. During 1898–1903 such seats provided the party with one-quarter to one-third of its deputies (15 of 46 in 1898, 14 of 51 in 1903) and involved the party in twenty-odd run-offs in each case. In these seats, where an older pattern of 'national' politics persisted, and in these seats alone, popular support for the National Liberals remained roughly constant throughout the Wilhelmine period.

In other seats, National Liberalism suffered. Its other main strongholds were in Protestant seats that were neither wholly urban nor wholly rural (type 3), and in rural seats not dominated by large farms (type 2). This mixed, rural and small-town Protestant base, generally in 'middle Germany' away from the Catholic and particularist fringes of the empire, was not a coherent social grouping. The National Liberal base, statistically speaking, was somewhat in the backwaters of Germany. This reinforces the image of electorally successful National Liberals as notables from provincial towns and cities able to exert some influence on the immediately surrounding rural area, but who in more purely agrarian settings were vulnerable to the competition of the populist right, and in more purely urban ones to the competition of the SPD. In the Protestant urban seats (type 4) increasingly dominated by the socialist labour movement, the National Liberal vote dipped after 1890 and stayed low. In the Protestant rural seats dominated by large landholding (type 1), the National Liberals were not even in the contest. With the effective persistence of the *Kartell* electoral coalition until 1907, the National Liberals left these seats to the conservatives. Still, with the exception of the more urban Protestant seats, figure 9 shows the National Liberals not much worse off in 1912, after recoveries in certain areas, than they had been in 1890; and, of course, in the type 1 seats they did immensely better once they ceased cooperating with the conservatives in 1912.

On the basis of the electoral strengths indicated in figure 9, it is perhaps surprising that the National Liberals were perceived as a party of industrial interests, when their vote was strongest in towns and the countryside, and in confessionally based 'national' struggles. And one could ask a second, related question: why did the party not shape its support into a coherent social grouping, by indulging in a small-town populist movement of its own? After all, these were environments (type 2 rural seats and type 3 mixed rural-urban ones) where anti-Semites and radical agrarians had some success doing just that, a phenomenon that highlights the National Liberal failure. There are two answers to this question of why the National Liberals failed to develop a rural populism. The first is that a party and its electoral support are two different things – and particularly so with older-style parties in the era of modernization of politics. The National Liberal leadership included eminent industrialists and moderate governmentalists; many of its activists were dedicated (urban-intellectual) nationalists. As a party they were committed (as they stressed again and again in election programs) to putting the national interest ahead of all regional and sectoral interests, and therefore to reaching a

FIGURE 10
Left-Liberal (FVP, FVg, and DVP) Popular Vote, by Constituency Type, 1890–1912

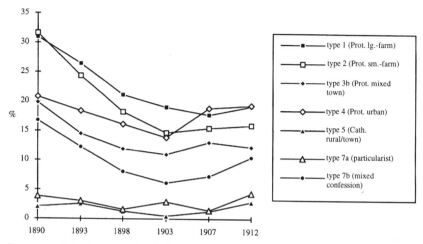

Comments: Left liberals did best in Protestant seats, and worst in Catholic and particularist seats. Their steepest proportional decline was in rural Protestant seats.

Note: For clarity of presentation, type 3a and type 6 seats are not shown. Type 3a ran close to 2 until 1903, then with 1 and 4 at the top; type 6 ran among the bottom three lines.

compromise between agriculture and industry. The National Liberal dilemma in the 1890s was precisely to try to remain a party of the national interest, in an age of sectoral and interest politics.[15] Given this outlook, National Liberal leaders did not want to redefine their party in terms of social-economic issues and groupings. But the second answer is that, in the regions where it was most successful, the National Liberal Party was, indeed, a rural and agrarian party, contrary to its national image: in the Grand Duchy of Hesse, in the Prussian province of Hanover, in rural Oldenburg, in Baden. Hesse is an interesting example. One of the long-time National Liberal deputies from Hesse was Wilhelm Haas, well known as a founder and leader of agricultural cooperatives, which were especially strong in the duchy from the 1880s on.[16] Thus, in areas where it was strong, the party *did* have a rural populism of a sort, or at least a capacity to adapt to the times and integrate its supporters through new kinds of organizations and movements. These regional pockets underpinned the party's electoral performance in Wilhelmine Germany; without them, the National Liberals would have been simply a party of broad but shallow support – campaigning in many seats, winning few on the first ballot – much as the left liberals were.

In contrast to the National Liberals, the situation faced by the various left-liberal parties was more grim. As indicated in figure 10, their support declined precipitously in virtually all kinds of constituencies up until 1907, and the recovery in 1907 and 1912 was more in the way of a levelling off than a dramatic upswing. The curious feature of figure 10 is that it shows left liberalism to have been strongest, in electoral terms, in Protestant rural areas, even though left liberals were even less seen as rural or agrarian than were National Liberals. Indeed, left liberals won many votes from rural seats as a whole; but they finished first in scant few of these. Particularly in the large-landholding areas (type 1), the left liberals were a perpetual opposition party, winning votes but no seats. Similarly, their third-strongest showing over the six Wilhelmine elections was in Protestant urban seats (type 4), which were more and more often being won by the SPD. In both rural and urban seats, then, the left liberals were confirmed as everyone's second choice. In an electoral system with run-off ballots, this meant they could still win seats – if other parties' supporters helped them. In a straight plurality system of election, the left liberals would have been completely wiped out in the 1890s. Some of this second-ballot support later became institutionalized as first-ballot support: witness the improvement of left-liberal support in Protestant cities in 1907 and 1912. By this point it was clear that only left liberals had any hope of success against the SPD in most cities, and their support increased as they garnered the anti-socialist vote.

Only shrewd alliances prevented the extinction of liberalism in many constituencies. More and more liberals were elected only in run-offs and only by the tactical voting of other parties on the second ballot. By the 1903 elections, 36 of left liberals' 36 seats and 46 of National Liberals' 51 were won in run-off battles.[17] Even successful liberal deputies in long-time liberal seats could garner only a minority of votes on the first ballot, a poor show of their ability to attract the primary allegiance of voters. Many of the liberal candidates who won seats did so with only 25–30 per cent of first-ballot votes, generally through anti-socialist second-ballot combinations.[18] Considerations of local tactics further exacerbated liberals' internal divisions, for they were under pressure to lean left in one area for support, right in another. Unable to decide on a consistent nationwide policy about whether working-class reform votes or patriotic German votes were more important, about whether 'Junkers' or 'subversives' were the enemy, one liberal party was set against another, one region against another. Decline reinforced disunity.

Unlike conservatives, Catholics, particularists, or socialists, liberals frequently opposed other liberals in election campaigns. Not only did National Liberals and left liberals often oppose one another, but even the small left-liberal parties managed to find constituencies where they could conflict.[19] This 'fragmentation' had two important effects. First, it damaged the effectiveness of the liberal campaign and discredited liberalism's claims to be a single coherent philosophy or party. And second, even where liberalism remained strong, multiple liberal candidacies in a single constituency split the liberal vote and gave other parties the opportunity to enter the run-offs. This was apparent in constituencies like Wiesbaden Land–Obertaunus, which the left liberals managed to win in 1890 and the National Liberals only narrowly lost in 1893, both times in run-offs against the SPD. After 1893 no liberal ever made it to the second ballot again, simply because the liberal vote was split. Instead, all the liberal parties watched from the sidelines as the better-organized Centre and SPD fought for the seat in every election from 1898 to 1912. In order to have a chance, liberals had at least to make it into second place, and without unity it was increasingly difficult to do so.

The Quest for Liberal Unity

Liberals' difficulties stemmed at least in part from the formative years of their political movement. The original, vague self-conceptions of liberalism as an enlightened movement of the people helped broaden and legitimize liberalism's claims in the mid-nineteenth century, but they hindered any pragmatic approach to the electoral problems of 1898–1903. The naïve claims of liberals to represent 'the people' were now being tested by new ideas about how to organize popular support.

By the 1890s liberals were aware of their difficulties. Their speeches and writings reveal gloom about the future of liberalism and, by association, of parliamentary politics and responsible government. The feeling of fatalism, particularly the feeling of inevitable SPD victory, pervaded the liberal campaigns, left and right, in 1898 and 1903. The impression given by National Liberal leader Ernst Bassermann in one of his campaign speeches is illuminating:

Social Democracy is assisted by an election slogan, popular and arousing; today we lack any such [slogan].

... in the face of this movement the middle class [*Bürgertum*] stands disunited and splintered; the struggle between *Mittelstand* and big capitalism has been kindled; the distress of agriculture is knocking at the door of the state; religious and racial divisions are making themselves felt ...

Liberals and the national interest they tried to represent were divided; their opponents were not.[20]

Liberals fought for a conception of public life which was refuted by the very existence of phenomena like Social Democracy and agrarianism. Liberals assumed that the *Bürger* to whom they appealed was a rational, independent individual concerned with the national interest; they could not easily bring themselves to use appeals based on divisive social-economic categories. They fought for the general interest embodied in the independent citizenry, against the 'particular' interests like Catholicism, working-class socialism, or agrarianism, so that the struggle for liberal unity in the 1890s tended to become the same as the struggle against interest politics. Left-liberal publicists attacked 'clericals, agrarians, and Social Democrats' as the 'three main interests' fragmenting the German nation. Such 'interests' were anathema for liberals because they did not reflect the liberal notion of a rational community of independent and detached citizens. 'One feature is common to all of our interest-parties,' said a leading left-liberal paper, 'namely that they are unable to recognize the concept of the political citizen. For them there are really only comrades of their own class [*Standesgenossen*], either religious-clerical or purely economic.'[21] The links forged by other parties with coherent social groupings, the key to those parties' electoral success, were seen by liberal commentators as the source of political chaos. In defining themselves as the party of the general good against the parties of the interests, liberals were framing their self-conception in anti-pluralist terms. All of their competitors (Catholics, socialists, conservatives) were lesser and fragmentary; only liberalism was above self-interest, bias, and ideology.

Many German liberals turned in the 1890s to proposals for regeneration and unity, and the 1898 and 1903 campaigns – perhaps because they were the worst ever for liberalism – illustrated these efforts. The process was set in motion in 1897 when the leader of the [South] German People's Party (Deutsche Volkspartei, or DVP) proposed a committee among the liberal parties that would negotiate an end to competing candidacies. Also in 1897, the small Left Liberal Union (Freisinnige Vereinigung, FVg) proposed to meet with the other main north German left-liberal party, the Left Liberal People's Party (Freisinnige Volkspartei, FVP) led by Eugen Richter, to reach an agreement based on the existing distribution of seats between them.[22] One newspaper called for a revitalized liberalism to be the 'rallying-point' (*Sammelpunkt*) of all the broad and intelligent classes that disagreed with 'conservative-agrarian-clerical politics.' Elsewhere liberals called for a 'liberal *Kartell*.' Like the proponents of *Sammlungspolitik*, liberals feared the fragmentation of the middle classes and strove for a coalition to reunite them; but theirs was to be a rallying to the old liberal banner of responsible citizenship, not an economic *Sammlung*.[23]

The tone of the appeals for liberal unity is illustrated by the left-liberal *Berliner Tageblatt*, which near the beginning of the 1898 campaign called for liberals to stand together in the 'struggle against reactionary appetites and agrarian Junker domination.' It greeted with enthusiasm the program of the FVg, a party that stood midway in style, structure, and content between the National Liberals and the rest of the left liberals. 'Every liberal-minded [*freigesinnte*] politician' could agree with the moderate FVg program, according to the left-liberal paper, whether such a politician belonged to the FVg itself, to Richter's FVP, to the south German DVP, 'or to the left wing of the National Liberals.' Not only was it possible for these groups to agree, it was essential: 'liberalism will stride united to the ballot box, or it will no longer exist at all.' The paper's proposal was to save liberalism by constructing an alliance of the Protestant centre directed principally against the Protestant agrarian right.[24] The same call was repeated, even more emphatically, in the 1903 Reichstag campaign, when the paper declared that the forces of reaction were the 'chief enemy of the *Bürgertum*' and went so far as to suggest it was the 'duty and responsibility of liberal voters' to support a socialist in the run-offs where this was necessary to defeat a 'reactionary.'[25] The call to support socialists over agrarians only underscored the differences among liberals, since many National Liberals still cooperated effectively with conservatives and even agrarians.

In constituencies across Germany, liberals negotiated to try to ensure that only one liberal candidate contested each seat. These scattered local initiatives, however, depended heavily on tactical situations, and faced the formidable disincentive to cooperation embodied in the two-ballot electoral system. If a liberal candidate refused to back down, he might make the run-off, and then other liberals would virtually be obliged to support him. The central link in any renewed liberal alliance would have to be between the FVP and the FVg, for these two parties were the mainstays of left liberalism, and their overlapping electoral bases inside Prussia provided much of the internecine conflict among left liberals. For ten years from 1884 to 1893, the two had been united, splitting apart exactly when Caprivi's 'New Course' and rising agrarian opposition to it were heating up party politics. The FVP had by far the greater organizational breadth and depth, but the smaller FVg was, in electoral terms, a crucial bridge to reaching National Liberal notables and voters. In also contained important personalities like Theodor Barth and, from 1903, Friedrich Naumann.[26] The essential minimal accord between the FVP and FVg was announced towards the end of May 1898, late in the campaign and long after the left-liberal press had begun its agitation. In essence, it was a left-liberal copy of the *Kartell*. The party leaderships recommended that wherever only one liberal had been nominated, no second candidate was to be nominated by the other party. Second, wherever both had candidates, and because of their division were likely both to be excluded from the run-offs, the candidate with less favourable prospects was to withdraw. Finally, where no candidates had yet been nominated, the two parties were to nominate one jointly. And where no unity could be achieved, liberals were still to refrain from 'embittered press polemics' against one another. If this agreement had been observed, a nucleus for a liberal coalition could have been created in 1898.[27]

The agreement, however, was not binding on local liberal associations. The *Frankfurter Zeitung* noted that conflicts among left liberals in the constituencies were continuing, despite the recommendations of their party leaders. The liberal parties were simply too weakly structured for decisions of the central leaders to be enforced in the localities. Liberal parties disputed whose candidate had priority by virtue of being nominated first, as in Königsberg, where the FVP refused to withdraw in favour of the FVg; or they disputed who had the best chance of winning, as in Schwarzburg-Sonderhausen, where the FVg, though smaller, insisted its candidate was more likely to win because the National Liberals were more likely to support him on an eventual second ballot.[28] Left liberals united best where their cause was hopeless, and continued to quarrel where their share of the vote was large enough for winning to be within sight. Not even a coalition between the two leading left-liberal groups, let alone one drawing in National Liberals, could be sustained.

Where left liberals hoped unity would come through repudiation of *Reaktion* and agrarianism (that is, through a left-liberal-style constitutional, anti-militarist, free-trade campaign as in the 1860s), within National Liberalism there was some recognition that a regeneration of liberalism would require a new set of issues, not just organizational reconciliation. The 'Young Liberals' attempted from 1898 onwards to propose a new liberal agenda, a sort of social liberalism that would provide new vigour and dynamism in the party. Originating in the Rhineland in the aftermath of the Prussian Landtag elections in the fall of 1898, the National Liberal youth movement spread rapidly, from the first club founded in Cologne in January 1899 to the formation of a Reich-wide federation in October 1900.[29] The growth of Social Democracy in 1898 and 1903 helped drive National Liberal reformers to the conclusion that a social-reform program was required to revitalize the party's support. They took the view that a new program must be substituted for the tired national and constitutional issues that had once sustained liberalism, but which were increasingly lost in the pluralistic interest politics of the Wilhelmine era. The new program had to include suffrage reform (perhaps even female suffrage), inheritance taxation, and the sinking of roots in the working classes. Such a program would mean abandoning *Sammlungspolitik* and governmentalism, and moving left to rejoin the rest of the liberal parties. 'Liberalism will be social,' claimed one writer in the traditional apocalyptic style used in turn-of-the-century politics, 'or it will not exist.'[30]

The idea of a social program for National Liberalism paralleled another current of thought, that of Naumann and his tiny National-Social movement, which was absorbed in 1903 into the Left Liberal Union (FVg). Naumann hoped to preserve the 'national' causes and principles of the middle parties and wed them to a social reform program. This would reinvigorate the fragmented middle classes, extend their social appeal to the working classes, and create a reformist block from the SPD to the National Liberals – 'from Bebel to Bassermann.' Like the Young Liberals, however, Naumann's tiny group failed to have any actual impact on the way in which the major parties selected their candidates and ran their campaigns in the constituencies. Even at the Reich level, right-wing National Liberals and the DVP dissociated themselves from the social-reform ideas of Young Liberalism and of the National-Socials, while Richter and his anti-militarist FVP remained abidingly suspicious of the emphasis on national power in Naumann's group, in the FVg, and in the National Liberals. Naumann's blend was no true synthesis of liberalism since one wing of liberals suspected the 'national' part, and the other, the 'social.'[31]

The basis of liberalism's sought-after unity, its broad and universalist traditions, served instead as a seedbed that nurtured competing strains of liberalism; it even provided nourishment for socialist and anti-Semitic weeds.[32] In the hothouse politics of the 1890s, the strains of liberalism evolved along diverging paths, making it even more difficult to find the one 'true' liberalism. Variations like 'social liberalism,' the National-Socials, or the 'liberal *Kartell*' did not take root. Ahead of all other factors, one single issue pulled liberals apart: the question of their relationship to the state. National Liberals were pulled to the right by their willingness to cooperate with the government and the conservative parties; left liberals were pulled to the left by their campaigns against 'Junkers' and 'reaction.'

Fragmentation: National Liberalism and the Right

The National Liberals had been formed out of the broader pre-1866 liberal movement as the liberal party most willing to accommodate itself to the new order created by Bismarck, accepting, as it were, the fulfilment of the nationalist demands of the liberal movement (and subsequently many of its legal and economic ones) as a satisfactory step towards the implementation of all liberal demands, including constitutional ones. National Liberalism was strongest outside of Prussia and in the territories annexed by Prussia in 1866. In these regions, national unification and cooperation with the new Reich government did, indeed, represent progress in the context of the older liberal fight against absolutist state governments.[33] Inside the older provinces of Prussia, more of the liberal movement remained committed to the old Progressive program, in the tradition of the constitutional conflict of the 1860s, and this corresponded to a sharper polarization in electoral politics between left liberals and conservatives. These differing regional experiences, related to liberals' willingness to cooperate with the Reich government, underlay lasting distinctions between the National Liberals and the rest of the liberal movement through to the turn of the century.

The National Liberals were also considerably more apt to be anti-clerical than were any other liberals and conservatives. The left-liberal FVP was on quite good terms with the Catholic Centre and concluded mutually advantageous electoral pacts (see chapter 6); this would have been out of the question for National Liberals in some regions, especially in the mixed-confession areas of the west and south. However, while the National Liberals won many votes as an anti-Catholic party in constituencies that were predominantly Catholic or of mixed confession (types 5, 6, and 7b – see Appendix A), it was not able to win many seats in, at least, the first two of these three types. Organizing small Protestant minorities against Catholic majorities, as in Catholic centres in the Rhineland, gave the party's anti-clerical activists perhaps a 'national' aura, but few seats. In 1898, with 95,000 votes in predominantly Catholic 'German' seats (type 5 and 6), the party elected only a single deputy. In the mixed-confession seats (type 7b), the party won 240,000 votes in 1898 and elected 12 deputies. But the rural Protestant vote (as in Hanover, Hesse, Oldenburg, and so on), and the help of right-wing parties in run-offs against the left, elected more National Liberals yet. Also in 1898, 120,000 votes in type 2 seats were enough to elect 15 deputies. The National Liberals received many votes as a competitor to the Catholic Centre; but won most of their seats as a rural, patriotic party in Protestant areas.

There were also differences in the National Liberal leadership compared with that of the other liberal parties. Both National Liberals and left-liberals had comparatively broad and urban leaderships, dominated by professionals, officials, businessmen, and some landowners. But left-liberal deputies were almost invariably urban, whereas National Liberal caucuses (like the National Liberal electorate) included more agrarians. National Liberal leaders tended to be of higher status – there were more senior officers and officials, more prestigious academics, and, to some extent, more powerful industrialists. Left liberalism was associated to a greater degree with humbler elements of the educated middle classes, especially teachers, lower officials, smaller businessmen, and artisans.[34] In regions where National and left liberals competed head-on, as in Oldenburg, the National Liberals tended to represent the bigger property owners, and showed less ability than the left liberals to depart from the structures of *Honoratiorenpolitik* to achieve a broader social and political integration.[35]

However, it was the status of the National Liberals as a governmental party that most clearly separated them from the other liberals, and this status proved repeatedly to be both the party's greatest strength as well as its greatest weakness in electoral politics. Bismarck's turn to the conservatives and to protectionism during 1878–79 had presented the National Liberals with a basic choice about whether once again to unite with the rest of the liberal movement to oppose the government. Instead they moved to the right with the Heidelberg Declaration of 1884, in which south German National Liberals showed their willingness to cooperate with the government on the basis of 'national' causes and anti-socialism, and to accept tariff protectionism (on which they could not themselves agree) as a 'closed' debate. Declaring the tariff debate closed, however, did not make it so; and the resurgence of the tariff issue in the 1890s added considerably to National Liberal discomfort. Unable to agree internally or with the government on economic policy, National Liberals chose to cement their governmental legitimacy and their unity with the 'national' glue of colonies, military issues, and anti-socialism. At the same time, such a program, in reverting to the 'ideal' issues typical of the unification era, foreswore any modernization or centralization of the party and its electoral appeal. It implicitly sanctioned continued dependence on regional *Honoratiorenpolitik* .[36]

The reward for this strategy came in 1887 when the National Liberals joined the conservatives in Bismarck's *Kartell*. The 'national' elections of that year were based on an issue favourable to the National Liberals, the renewal of the military budget and a war scare with France. In each constituency, the *Kartell* parties consolidated their first-ballot support behind the candidate with the greatest chance of winning.[37] As part of the *Kartell*, the National Liberals won more votes in 1887 than ever before or after, and more seats than any time after 1878. For twenty-five years the *Kartell* approach, and the desire to recreate the success of 1887, dominated the party's strategy. Practical benefits remained for the National Liberals even after the *Kartell* collapsed as an effective coalition within the Reichstag in 1890. By and large none of the *Kartell* parties made a systematic attempt to expand beyond its 1887 base, until 1912: the *Kartell* as an electoral coalition remained quietly in force. The *Kartell* parties also continued to receive behind-the-scenes assistance from Prussian political officials (as described in chapter 3), especially in persuading conservatives and agrarians to maintain *Kartell*-style coalitions and refrain from challenging National Liberal incumbents. This was undoubtedly a factor in enabling the party to retain some control of its rural strongholds, especially where it proved possible to control the Agrarian League. National Liberal credentials as supporters of the government and as nationalists at least limited the conflict with the Agrarian League, even though their inability to deal with the tariff question antagonized many agrarians. In remaining part of this coalition, however, the National Liberals were diminishing their role as an nationwide party independent of government, and continued to divide themselves from the rest of the liberal movement.

If the benefits of the *Kartell* were greatest in 1887, the cost of the pact with Bismarck was deferred. National Liberalism, propped up by the *Kartell* and by Prussian officials, did not much modernize its structure, did not expand into new regions or segments of the population, and was not well able to position itself as a champion of any kind of reform. As time wore on, the handicaps began to outweigh any benefit from the *Kartell*. As indicated above, the party was shut out of conservative-dominated rural seats in the large-landholding area, was increasingly shut out of the cities by the SPD (the agitational social-reform party *par excellence*), and retained a base only in a nondescript assortment of non-urban, generally

TABLE 8
Multiple Regression for the National Liberal Popular Vote, 1890–1912

	Var. type	1890	1893	1898	1903	1907	1912
% Catholic	C	**−0.149**	**−0.146**	**−0.109**	**−0.107**	**−0.130**	**−0.111**
		−4.71	−4.96	−3.99	−4.17	−4.04	−3.76
Large	D	**−6.76**	**−6.65**	**−6.80**	**−6.33**	**−6.51**	*0.113*
landownership		−2.34	−2.40	−2.63	−2.59	−2.16	0.0433
% Turnout	C	**0.257**	**0.235**	**0.252**	**0.290**	*0.211*	**0.411**
		2.84	2.25	3.25	3.29	1.24	2.61
Brandenburg	D	**−15.8**	**−10.6**	**−9.78**	*−4.65*	*−4.69*	*−3.82*
		−4.18	−2.91	−2.94	−1.46	−1.18	−1.12
Hanover	D	**20.3**	**21.6**	**19.2**	**20.2**	**20.1**	**14.3**
		5.22	5.78	5.59	6.14	4.93	4.08
Rhineland	D	**8.73**	**8.02**	**6.39**	**10.3**	**8.00**	**8.01**
		2.68	2.55	2.21	3.75	2.33	2.71
Catholic Bavaria	D	**19.0**	**11.9**	*4.78*	**11.1**	**10.4**	*5.79*
		5.17	3.32	1.49	3.63	2.59	1.77
Mixed-Confession	D	**23.6**	**23.3**	**17.9**	**13.1**	**9.07**	*4.85*
Bavaria		5.86	5.99	5.01	3.86	2.15	1.34
Württemberg	D	**12.2**	**11.2**	*6.59*	*6.43*	*1.98*	*0.0798*
		3.03	2.88	1.85	1.90	0.460	0.219
Baden	D	**21.2**	**25.9**	**27.9**	**25.7**	**21.9**	**17.8**
		4.66	5.97	7.00	6.74	4.61	4.32
Hesse	D	**24.1**	**26.2**	**19.6**	**28.1**	**17.4**	**14.6**
		4.50	5.00	4.11	6.22	3.10	3.02
Adjusted R^2		**.338**	**.316**	**.311**	**.314**	**.196**	**.163**
$F(17/379\ DF)$		12.9	11.8	11.5	11.7	6.67	5.54

Source: Multiple regression based on the author's constituency-level Reichstag election data; see Appendix C. Independent variables which did not show significant t-ratios at the 5 per cent level in at least two elections are not shown.

Note: The dependent variable is the percentage of the vote for the National Liberal Party. In the body of the table, the regression coefficient is on the top, and the t-ratio beneath (379 DF); significant coefficients are shown in bold, and the insignificant ones in italics. (See Appendix D for explanations of terms and abbreviations.)

not entirely rural areas (fig. 9, above). Any effort to change the party's electoral orientation – a 'social liberal' program, alliance to the left with the left liberals, geographic expansion to contest more conservative seats, a more agitational style and party organization – would conflict fundamentally with the party's governmentalism, and hence with the course followed since the Heidelberg Declaration and the *Kartell* elections of 1887. Not until the 1912 elections did the National Liberals shake off the shackles of the *Kartell*. In 1898 and 1903 they were still paying the price for not doing so sooner.

The multiple-regression data in table 8 provide statistical support for the picture of the National Liberals as a party with a poorly defined electoral base and no corresponding social grouping. The adjusted R^2 of only slightly over 0.3 (even lower for 1907 and 1912) indicates that all of the predictor variables together explain barely more than 30 per cent of the variation in National Liberal voting strength from constituency to constituency. The majority of the variation was a result of other, perhaps purely local, factors for which one presumably cannot account. Social and economic statistics are of very little help in explaining National Liberal support; regional ones are somewhat better, but the adjusted R^2 is still low. The weak relationship is a statistical expression of the 'splintering' of the party among regions and interests in the 1890s and 1900s. Or perhaps one should allow the National Liberals to put a brave face on it: they succeeded in their ideal of not representing particular interests in an age of interest politics.

There was a definite negative correlation of National Liberal voting with Catholicism; this is to be expected for an almost purely Protestant and in part anti-clerical party. But the National Liberals, the party of the *Kulturkampf* and the party that, in regions like the Rhineland, attracted most of Germany's anti-Catholic activists, showed a weaker negative correlation with Catholicism than did the German Conservatives, who were more friendly to Catholics. This relatively weak negative correlation must reflect the tendency of National Liberals to represent the Protestant-governmental cause in predominantly Catholic and mixed-confession constituencies. This conclusion is supported by Appendix A, which shows high National Liberal voting strength relative to other Protestant parties in type 5, 7, and, especially, 7b seats. The National Liberals were a Protestant party that tended, in certain regions, to run against Catholics. The significant positive correlation of National Liberal voting with high turnout might reflect the same phenomenon: turnout was higher in mixed-confession seats where confessional battles regularly occurred, and this might be what is reflected in the table.

The lack of any correlation with either rural or urban environments reflects the fact that the party had some urban strongholds, some rural ones, plus a certain tendency to do well in seats that were divided. The party was originally strong in some cities, but decreasingly so by the 1890s as these were being conquered by Social Democracy. It was not strong in most rural areas, either – except for special pockets like Hanover, Hesse, and Baden (see below). It was and remained disproportionately strong in seats of mixed rural-urban structure (type 3a; see Appendix A) and in seats of 'national' polarization (types 7a and 7b). In other words, the party tended to contest constituencies that were fragmented in social-economic or cultural terms, those not integrated into strong social groupings or dominated by a single environment. This, alongside the remaining rural strongholds and urban votes, may explain the lack of any urban or rural leaning to the party's overall support. The only other definable social-economic characteristic of the National Liberal electoral base is that it generally did not include the large-landholding areas of the north and east. The negative correlation with large landownership reflects the fact that National Liberals, as part of the *Kartell*, generally did not contest the conservative-dominated rural seats before 1912.

The most interesting feature of table 8 is what it says about the regional nature of the party's support. While the National Liberals remained a large national party in the sense of receiving some support in many constituencies, their support was strongly influenced by regional factors, following the pattern in this respect that was typical of the older parties. In 1898 and 1903, National Liberal support within Prussia came from a handful of regions, most notably the provinces of Saxony, Hanover, Schleswig-Holstein, and Hesse-Nassau.[38] In the multiple regression shown in table 8, only Hanover and secondarily the Rhineland show regional support greater than the socio-economic factors by themselves would predict. In the case of Hanover, the regional factor was large: it was as if National Liberals received a 20 per cent bonus in Hanoverian seats, compared to seats of similar social-economic construction elsewhere. This fits the pattern already noted, that National Liberal electoral strength was concentrated outside Prussia and in areas like Hanover that were only recently integrated into Prussia. Among the non-Prussian states, Hesse and Baden provided special regional bastions comparable to Hanover. Until 1912 the National Liberals were also disproportionately strong in Bavaria, especially the mixed-confession areas of the kingdom. The party's strength in the Rhineland and in Bavaria had to do in part with its anti-clerical, anti-Catholic appeal.[39] In many ways, the National Liberals remained the party of national unification three decades after national unification was accomplished, the party of the *Kulturkampf* two decades after the *Kulturkampf* had ceased. Thus the party of national unity thrived only in isolated pockets. While other parties organized the classes and the masses, the National Liberals were left (in electoral support as in philosophy) as the compromise party of what remained, the Protestant 'German' middle, for whom nationalism and not any one interest was the unifying cement.

The National Liberals' role as a party of nationalism may not have won them a distinct social-economic niche, or increased voter support during 1898–1903, but they did maintain close connections with the activist cadres of Germany's nationalist pressure groups, and received some indirect organizational benefit. These 'parallel action groups,' as they have been called by Anthony O'Donnell, may have helped the party's *Honoratioren* make up for the deficiencies of their own mass organization. Such groups rarely took an autonomous role in election campaigns in 1898 or 1903, but they provided a circle of contacts for National Liberal candidates and a reservoir of personnel and ideas, plus a certain small but loyal 'national' audience among the public. They were not as large, as mass-oriented, or as effective in the electorate as the BdL, but they did provide an underpinning for the party's structure and philosophy. Given the lack of unity among National Liberals on social and economic issues, it could only help that the pressure groups accentuated the 'national' in public debate and in formulation of public opinion. This was another advantage of the party's nationalist and governmental commitment, but to judge by the party's inability to put forward national issues when it wanted to, as in 1898, it was not always a large advantage.[40] The national issues on which the National Liberals relied did not dominate politics at the turn of the century.

Instead of national issues, the political agenda in the late 1890s and early 1900s was dominated by the tariff question. Just as during 1878–84, the tariff issue divided the National Liberals both among themselves and from the more clearly united, free-trading left liberals. In 1894 the party tried to define its basic program in a resolution at the Frankfurt party congress, and tried to do so by de-emphasizing the tariff issue to make it just one of a numberof national policies within the framework of measures to support and strengthen the empire. The Frankfurt statement emphasized the fight against Social Democracy and against ethnic minorities, structural support for peasants and artisans, and nationalist colonial causes. Such a program clearly provided for cooperation with the right and for nationalist agitation. In 1898 the National Liberals tried to stick to this program, campaigning on their record as a governmental party (boasting of positive accomplishments in naval legislation and *Mittelstands-*

politik) and on their opposition to the 'danger threatened by Social Democracy,' 'Ultramontanism,' and the 'national Polish' movement. Again in 1903, the party campaigned on the government's record, including the tariff, army, and navy laws of the preceding session, and simultaneously emphasized the fight against enemies including the SPD, Ultramontanism, and, now, economic interests.[41]

The addition in 1903 of economic interests to the list of National Liberal enemies reflects the disastrously undermining effect that the agitation of the BdL had on the party's attempts to stick to this program. While the election declarations tried to emphasize favourable issues, National Liberals were forced again and again to talk about tariffs and protection for agriculture, issues that had divided them for decades. While providing some help for agriculture or artisans was hardly against the party's principles, the polarized debate tended to force the party to choose either free trade or protectionism, and this the National Liberals had never been able to do. The more agriculture demanded protection, the more industrial and commercial interests advocated the need for trade treaties to ensure access to world markets; and both sides demanded clear commitments. The best the National Liberal Party could do in 1898 was to produce a hasty and cumbersome compromise wording, inserted in the program and reproduced word for word in National Liberal leaflets and pamphlets across Germany: the party acknowledged 'that in the conclusion of future trade treaties the interests of agriculture must be better protected than previously,' but that, on the other hand, 'account must be taken ... of the requirements of industry and trade' for concluding treaties of long duration that facilitated export. The party neither explicitly accepted nor rejected *Sammlungspolitik*, but instead stated that protectionism was acceptable 'only on this basis' of combining greater agricultural protection with continued access to foreign markets.[42] This awkward and possibly contradictory formula was out of step with interest groups, newspapers, and public opinion that tended to be clearly for or clearly against the agrarians; and out of step with the other parties, whose campaigns all took clear positions either for or against higher tariffs. Matters became only slightly easier in 1903 following the passage of the tariff law, as the National Liberals could now once more assert that the tariff was a closed question, even if agrarians, among others, did not agree with them on this point.[43]

The governmentalism of the National Liberals, and their compromise position on the tariff question, contributed to a perception that National Liberal leaders dallied with 'reactionaries' and 'Junkers,' an impression that further divided the party from the reformist and oppositional left, and deepened liberal divisions. In Fürth-Erlangen (Franconia) in 1903, the unification of the liberals foundered on this subject after they had agreed in principle on a common candidacy. The *Frankfurter Zeitung* charged that the National Liberals backed out of the arrangement only in order to cater to agrarian opinion that found the left-liberal nominee too 'radical.' A separate BdL candidacy was threatened unless a right-wing liberal contested the seat.[44] In Weilburg in Hesse-Nassau, the FVP rejected a National Liberal nominee because 'no satisfactory binding statement' could be obtained from him 'regarding his position on trade treaties.' The common ground the liberals possessed in emphasizing the importance of trade treaties for business was of no practical importance when governmental principles and electoral base required National Liberals to compromise with protection.[45]

In spite of the importance of the National Liberals' claim to be a governmental party, and the behind-the-scenes benefits it brought them, it was of no assistance when it came to formulating a unified campaign or an effective electoral program. National Liberals described hopefully how the opposition had had 'the wind taken out of its sails' by the 'new men' in the Reich leadership and the great events of 1898: the occupation of Kiaochow, *Weltpolitik*, the fleet, events they believed had aroused the masses. But the government did nothing to accentuate such issues in either campaign, and both the abstention of most other parties from nationalist appeals and the failure of the National Liberals to increase their support imply that the masses were *not* aroused. In public campaigning, governmentalism was a handicap during 1898–1903, and extreme nationalism had a limited appeal beyond the already-converted National Liberal electorate.[46]

In 1898 and 1903 the National Liberals paid the price for their governmentalist commitment – partly in votes (in 1898 they lost half a percentage point and seven seats), partly in lost opportunities (they remained at a long-term low in support), mostly in internal unity.[47] The behind-the-scenes aid that was provided by officials and pressure groups only helped counterbalance the deep damage done to the party's popular appeal by its association with controversial policies, its unmodernized structure, its lack of a social-economic program in a social-economic age, and its self-limiting electoral *Kartell* with the conservatives. In 1898 and 1903 the party had all the disadvantages of being a governmental party, scorned by the SPD, Centre, left liberals, and particularists for its complicity in taxes, tariffs, armament spending, resistance to suffrage reform, and so on, while receiving few of the advantages, given the government's own silence and lack of an election program. The best that could be said is that, at the cost of disunity and the forgoing of broader representative ambitions, the National Liberals were able to slow their decline and, from 1903, stabilize their support, retaining an importance in the government's calculations. Stability, even at low levels, is more than can be claimed for the left liberals.

Fragmentation: Left Liberalism and the SPD

Just as National Liberals were discredited with their potential liberal allies during 1898–1903 because of their cooperation with 'reactionaries,' left liberals were criticized by the governmental parties for their connections with the *opponents* of the state, a group which included (according to some) the Catholic Centre, and certainly the Poles and the SPD. This was partly an allegation that they received electoral support from such parties (which, in the run-offs, was frequently true), and partly an observation about the 'democratic' family resemblance between left liberalism and Social Democracy. As with the relationship between the BdL and the National Liberals, the SPD and the left liberals overlapped intimately in many constituencies in a way that made them both allies and enemies in different places, depending on the local tactical circumstances. Also, the left liberals, like the National Liberals, had to bend towards an extreme of which many liberals disapproved (in this case, agitational policies and style) in order to hold their support.

The left liberals were organized into three main groupings – the Left Liberal People's Party (FVP), the Left Liberal Union (FVg), and the [South] German People's Party (DVP) – which differed both in policy and in political technique. The FVg was, in personnel and philosophy, the descendant of the National Liberal 'Sezession' of 1880–1, the left wing that had split away when the main party moved right. Although it had been united with Richter's FVP from 1884 to 1893, it still possessed certain features similar to National Liberalism: an emphasis on national power, a commitment to a highly regionalized *Honoratiorenpolitik*, and a possibility of cooperating with the government. Richter, on the other hand, until his death in 1906, kept his group firmly committed to an emphasis on an institutionalized, agitational party employing the propaganda and techniques of mass politics – all wedded to consistent opposition to the government. The difference between the two was evident, for example, in the 1903 Reichstag elections in the province of Brandenburg. Richter's FVP set up eleven candidates in the twenty seats even though it had not a single incumbent, while the FVg ran only two candidates to defend its two seats. The former tried to mobilize the greatest possible mass support independent of the other parties, while the FVg banked on opportunistic calculation, aiming to attract National Liberal support and forswearing any claim to be a mass representational party. The DVP was different again, south German rather than Prussian in its support, clearly distinct in its lower-middle-class democratic, particularist, and anti-clerical blend as well as its predominantly rural base.[48]

Of these groupings, Richter's FVP has the most interesting electoral and party history, both because it was the largest left-liberal party and because it was the only liberal party with ambitions to develop a modern, mass-membership, agitational base. The FVP had a well-articulated policy and structure of local associations and national congresses. It engaged in mass campaigning, using left-liberal-affiliated peasant leagues where it could in the countryside and workers' organizations in the cities. And, like the SPD and the Centre, it tried to spread its campaign into as many constituencies as possible, putting up *Zählkandidaturen* (multiple candidacies – one person contesting many seats at the same time) where necessary to extend its influence over the electorate and in the calculations of the other parties, rather than necessarily to win. Richter's personal contribution to the liberal movement was an emphasis on centralization and bureaucratic structures that was distasteful to many other liberals, perhaps because it bore too obvious a resemblance to the SPD's own techniques. In the catch-phrases of the time, Richter was known for his 'radicalism' or 'democratic' tendencies, or (to sympathizers) his 'resolute liberalism,' in contrast to the 'moderate liberalism' of the FVg and the National Liberals.[49]

Richter's FVP also adopted some of the characteristic issues of a mass party, emphasizing several points common to SPD and Centre electoral programs. Successful campaigns like those of 1881 and 1890 had seen left liberals heap scathing criticism on government taxes, tariffs, wasteful military spending, and denial of popular rights.[50] During 1898–1903 the FVP opposed *Sammlungspolitik* in exactly the same terms as did the SPD, as 'exploitation of the masses' through regressive taxation (tariffs), and similarly opposed military and naval spending.[51] But by 1898–1903 the socialists pressed the same themes more widely and more vehemently. Left liberals qualified their social reform demands with statements of opposition to 'state socialism,' attempted to show that they were in their own way loyal to kaiser and Reich, and tried to cater to anti-socialist opinion by asserting their moderate option was the best way to fight socialism. The SPD had clearer and firmer stands on every important left-liberal cause; its propaganda was more distinctive as well as more strident, and received a reverse kind of legitimacy from the way the governmental parties singled out the SPD for abuse. Demoralized liberals were left to lament that the SPD popular rights and taxation platform was 'not Social Democratic, but liberal.'[52]

While the FVP had a fairly firm party structure and a commitment to an agitational style, it lacked the array of extra-parliamentary auxiliaries that made the SPD and the Centre so formidable. It also did not have the help of officials, important interest groups, or 'parallel action groups' such as those of the other middle-class parties to reinforce its message. However, the party did have some connections with social and economic groups. Left-liberal peasant leagues like the Bauernverein Nord-Ost (North-East Peasant Association) helped in the fight against conservatism, but were only a drop in the agrarian ocean of the 1890s. The left-liberal Hirsch-Duncker Trade Unions contributed to left liberalism's credibility in the cities, but by the middle of the 1890s were far outstripped by the SPD Free Trade Unions in membership and influence. The attempt to form a free-trade interest group in 1900 to balance the tariff lobbying of the BdL resulted only in the HVV (Trade Treaty Association), an elite lobby group with no mass membership and no mass- agitation function other than the sponsoring of a few pamphlets in 1903. While the left liberals adapted, then, to the age of socio-economic programs by working with class and interest groups, the measure of their adaptation was unequal to the challenge.

Tables 9 and 10 indicate what multiple regression can show about the electoral bases of the two north German left-liberal parties. The FVg (table 9) showed the negative correlation with Catholicism that was typical of all the parties except the Centre and the particularists, although the magnitude of this negative correlation was even less than for the National Liberals. It is interesting that the FVg, which originated as a National Liberal splinter and remained more 'national' than the other left-liberal groups, continued to exhibit a profile resembling the National Liberal one: a Protestant party, but only weakly negatively correlated with Catholicism (indicating that its candidates reasonably frequently ran where Catholics were present), with support strongly determined by regional considerations, and with no coherent social grouping. In the FVg's case, the variation in the party's support was almost exclusively

TABLE 9
Multiple Regression for the Popular Vote for the Left Liberal Union
(FVg), 1890–1912

	Var. type	1893	1898	1903	1907
% Catholic	C	**−0.0604**	**−0.0421**	**−0.0361**	**−0.0361**
		−4.26	−3.58	−2.76	−2.63
Pomerania	D	**18.2**	**21.1**	**18.2**	**13.1**
		6.91	9.63	7.51	5.15
Schleswig-	D	**17.6**	*3.29*	*4.39*	**13.2**
Holstein		6.24	1.41	1.69	4.83
Kingdom of	D	**−4.66**	**−3.40**	*−2.76*	*−2.94*
Saxony		−2.35	−2.07	−1.52	−1.54
Western Small	D	**7.72**	**3.97**	**7.88**	**11.0**
States		3.55	2.20	3.93	5.23
Hansa	D	**16.9**	**9.73**	*6.78*	**18.6**
		4.27	2.98	1.88	4.90
Adjusted R^2		.312	.298	.214	.258
$F(14/382\ DF)$		13.8	13.0	8.69	10.8

Source: Multiple regression based on the author's constituency-level
Reichstag election data; see Appendix C. Independent variables which
did not show significant t-ratios at the 5 per cent level in at least two
elections are not shown.

Note: The dependent variable is the percentage of the vote for the Left
Liberal Union (Freisinnige Vereinigung, FVg). In the body of the table,
the regression coefficient is on the top, and the t-ratio beneath (382
DF); significant coefficients are shown in bold, and the insignificant
ones in italics. (See Appendix D for explanations of terms and abbreviations.)

determined by regional factors. It was disproportionately strong in Pomerania, the small states of western Germany (Brunswick, Lippe, and so
forth), and in the Hansa cities.

The FVP (table 10) showed less of the National Liberal/FVg pattern
(i.e., weak non-Catholicism, regional factors, no other significant statistical correlations) and some faint hint of a definable base for the party's
vote. There was a strongly significant negative correlation of FVP votes
with the percentage of Catholics in the population. This is interesting
because there was a pact between the FVP and the Centre Party regarding
certain regions (see below) – some of the avoidance of campaigning in

TABLE 10
Multiple Regression for the Popular Vote for the Left Liberal People's Party (FVP),
1890–1912

	Var. type	1890	1893	1898	1903	1907	1912
% Catholic	C	**−0.343**	**−0.190**	**−0.152**	**−0.131**	**−0.133**	**−0.165**
		−18.0	−11.8	−10.6	−10.1	−7.92	−8.55
% Employed in agriculture	C	**−0.268**	_−0.0304_	**−0.135**	**−0.185**	**−0.279**	_−0.145_
		−3.23	−0.442	−2.19	−3.35	−3.90	−1.77
% Rural	C	**0.167**	_0.0835_	_0.0965_	**0.126**	**0.189**	**0.169**
		1.99	1.17	1.51	2.18	2.53	1.97
Constituency size	C	**−5.92**	_−0.744_	_−1.90_	**−2.27**	_−1.16_	**−1.98**
		−2.05	−0.362	−1.31	−2.23	−1.11	−2.12
Berlin	D	**18.4**	**13.6**	**15.7**	**11.4**	**17.1**	_0.198_
		3.18	2.83	3.71	3.01	3.51	0.0354
Pomerania	D	_−6.66_	**−9.77**	**−9.25**	**−7.33**	_−4.75_	_0.812_
		−1.88	−3.24	−3.44	−3.03	−1.52	0.226
Silesia	D	**9.73**	**9.68**	**9.02**	**9.09**	**5.79**	_1.95_
		4.33	5.09	5.31	5.94	2.93	0.856
Hanover	D	**−16.4**	**−10.0**	**−8.27**	**−7.43**	**−9.16**	**−10.3**
		−5.42	−3.91	−3.61	−3.60	−3.45	−3.36
Kingdom of Saxony	D	**−18.4**	**−7.85**	**−9.73**	**−6.48**	**−7.55**	**−8.95**
		−6.18	−3.11	−4.32	−3.19	−2.88	−2.96
Württemberg	D	**−18.9**	**−10.1**	**−7.73**	**−6.02**	**−5.89**	**6.95**
		−6.04	−3.80	−3.27	−2.82	−2.15	2.20
Adjusted R^2		**.511**	**.312**	**.326**	**.323**	**.251**	**.233**
$F(12/384\ DF)$		35.5	16.0	17.0	16.7	12.0	11.0

Source: Multiple regression based on the author's constituency-level Reichstag election
data; see Appendix C. Independent variables which did not show significant t-ratios at the
5 per cent level in at least two elections are not shown.
Notes: (1) The dependent variable is the percentage of the vote for the Left Liberal People's
Party (Freisinnige Volkspartei, FVP). The name is that current during 1898–1903; the same
liberals were part of the 1884–93 Deutsch-Freisinnige Partei (German Left Liberal Party)
and, after 1910, Fortschrittliche Volkspartei (Progressive People's Party). (2) In the body of
the table, the regression coefficient is on the top, and the t-ratio beneath (384 DF); significant coefficients are shown in bold, and the insignificant ones in italics. (See Appendix D
for explanations of terms and abbreviations.)

Catholic areas was tactical. Among the liberal and conservative parties, then, it may be that a strong negative correlation with Catholicism marks the parties that got along best with political Catholicism, like the FVP and in some regions and elections the German Conservatives; the weakest negative correlations were the Protestant parties that most often fought Catholics, like the National Liberals. If this is so, then the weakest negative correlations with Catholicism indicate the most aggressively Protestant parties: a finding that might greatly complicate sociological-functionalist interpretations of regression results!

The FVP vote tended to be lower the greater the proportion of the population employed in agriculture; and higher, the greater the proportion of rural residents. These contradictory results are of borderline statistical significance. They may indicate that the party tended to have support where rural areas contained other activities alongside farming – small rural cities and towns, perhaps, little affected by urbanization and heavy industry, with many tradespeople and shopkeepers. The negative correlation in three elections with the population of the constituency may be a related matter: the FVP won a higher proportion of the votes in small constituencies, which were, mainly, quiet rural and small-town seats that experienced little industrialization. These results are of too little significance to draw a firm conclusion. It is also possible that the party simply had no coherent base definable by these variables. The FVP was stronger than average in Berlin and Silesia, weaker than would otherwise be predicted in Pomerania, Hanover, the Kingdom of Saxony, and Württemberg (where the People's Party represented the left-liberal cause). The adjusted R^2, indicating how much of the variation in the FVP share of the vote is actually explained by all these factors, is only a little greater than for the other liberal parties.

Left-liberal support during 1898–1903 was even more scattered and shallow than that of the National Liberals. If there was any significant regional concentration, it was as the alternative, opposition party to the conservatives in eastern Prussia; in a more 'democratic' form in the DVP's strongholds in rural southern Germany; and in the scattered 'small states' of Thuringia, the Hansa cities, and the north.[53] Left liberalism's highest and most stable popular vote in any general category of constituencies during the period 1890–1903 was won in the overwhelmingly Conservative and agricultural constituencies of northern and eastern Prussia, where large landed estates dominated a Protestant countryside (type 1 seats; see Appendix A). Here (and during 1898–1903 *only* here, of the categories of analysis used in this study) left liberals averaged over 20 per cent of the popular vote – yet won only four seats in 1898, and in 1903 only two. In the latter year, the SPD surpassed the combined liberals in popular vote in these seats. In other Protestant 'German' rural seats where large estates did not dominate (type 2), left-liberalism had exceeded 30 per cent of the vote in 1890, but as anti-Semitism and agrarianism gathered momentum this plummeted in the 1890s and bottomed out at barely over 15 per cent of the vote in 1903. Left liberalism was strongest in rural areas, but this was exactly where it was hardest hit. The left-liberal rural vote collapsed in the 1890s, somewhat less so in the large-landownership areas – but those were the hardest to win.[54] In the same way that National Liberalism was pushed out of the cities and acquired a proportionately more rural electorate just when agrarianism was growing in strength, left liberalism collapsed in the face of agrarianism and retreated into the cities just when socialism was making breakthroughs there.

By contrast to the countryside, left-liberal support in Protestant cities (type 4) declined a great deal less, and after 1903 recovered to its 1890 average of over 20 per cent – and considering the massive urbanization of the era this represented not so much a stability of support as an ability to keep attracting *new* voters, and many working-class ones at that.[55] In type 3a seats (which also contained cities), the left liberals increasingly faced Social Democrats in the run-offs. Although they did not capture a large share of the votes in these seats, the fact they could make it into the run-off, then win as an anti-socialist second choice, gave them numerous mandates. This tended to open a growing gap between how the left liberals won their *votes* and where they could win their *seats*. In type 1 seats, as just mentioned, left liberals won only 4 seats with 21.1 per cent of the vote in 1898, because of the heavy Conservative domination of these areas. In type 3a seats the same year, left liberals won (on average) 17.1 per cent of the vote, but won 11 seats. Thus while left liberals still won many votes as an anti-conservative, opposition party, they increasingly won their seats as an anti-socialist party and with the help of non-socialist supporters from other parties.

Electoral evolution brought left liberalism face to face with urban socialism, and what seats left liberals (particularly the FVP) won after 1890 were won increasingly from the SPD and much less frequently from National Liberals or conservatives. In this process, the left liberals were robbed of their most effective mass appeal, their appeal as a party of opposition, of defence of popular rights, of resistance to taxation, and of social reform. With the SPD taking the left liberals' former role as the party of popular-democratic urban opposition to the government, there was little populist ground left for progressive liberalism. What there was room for, however, was anti-socialism.

Left Liberalism and Anti-Socialist Calculation

On the national level, left liberals led a marginal existence by 1898–1903, surviving as a result of advantageous local configurations of parties and run-off alliances. Increasingly, tactical considerations deprived left liberals of any real strategic options or clear programmatic directions – instead of trying to persuade the voters of left liberalism's merits, they had to worry about positioning themselves to be acceptable to other parties' voters in the run-offs. Of necessity, left-liberal strategy varied with the circumstances, but given the constellation of Wilhelmine politics, certain overall patterns emerged. Successful left-liberal candidates were those who slipped through in a three-way battle within a constituency (or a more complex one still, but these were rare) and made it into the run-off, where they could count on the support of the third-place party (or parties) to elect their deputy on the second ballot. By 1903 not a single left-liberal managed to be elected anywhere in Germany by any procedure other than a second-ballot compromise.

Even in their strongest and most consistent seats, left-liberal support was gradually overshadowed by the rise of the SPD, and they were forced to depend on run-off votes from the right. In seats like Liegnitz-Goldberg-Hainau, the left liberals had defeated the conservatives in 1890 on the main ballot and in 1893 in the run-off, gaining the votes of the then third-place SPD to do so.[56] As SPD strength grew, however, the Social Democrats pushed the conservatives out of the run-off in 1898, and from this time onward the FVP needed the support of the right against the challenge from the left.[57] In 1903 the SPD surpassed the liberals to become the largest single party on the first ballot. In seats of a more urban composition, the transformation was more dramatic, and such seats included many of the most important left-liberal constituencies. In Berlin-Centre, the left liberals were still able to win a narrow majority in 1890, 53 per cent on the first ballot, but had declined by 1903 to 33 per cent as the SPD gained. The latter was in the run-offs against the liberals every year from 1893 on, its first-ballot vote increasing steadily, 26 per cent in 1890, 27 in 1893, 29 in 1898, then 41 per cent in the 1903 breakthrough, when the party came within four hundred votes of the FVP in the second ballot.[58] In Richter's seat of Hagen in Westphalia, the SPD again advanced to become the largest single party in 1903 (38 per cent of the vote to Richter's 29 per cent) and was defeated in the run-off only with the help of National Liberal and Centre votes.[59] These were, it is to be recalled, among the strongest left-liberal seats in all of Germany, yet even here the SPD broke through during 1898–1903.

Liberalism's greatest staying power against the SPD was where it could sink roots in a stable rural and agricultural electorate, as both left liberals and National Liberalism did in the two Protestant constituencies of the Grand Duchy of Oldenburg. Yet only special circumstances enabled the enduring liberal victories in Oldenburg – above all, the fact that left liberals and National Liberals here achieved strict second-ballot unity against the SPD. The regional strength of liberalism in Oldenburg was the result of unusually effective liberal cooperation, of a dominant and stable rural society that slowed the intrusion of Social Democracy, and of the traditional roots of liberalism in clearly defined rural interests. The overall pattern, however, was only different in degree and timing from the Reichwide one.[60]

Across Germany, left liberals found themselves increasingly dependent by 1898 on seats where steady Social Democratic advance was transforming the balance among the parties. There was an intimate interrelationship between the left-liberal and Social Democratic urban electorates, manifested in comparatively easy shifting of votes in either direction, and especially in run-off support of one party for the other. The examples of SPD run-off support going to left liberals when the latter were fighting a party of the right are so numerous and so clear-cut as hardly to need elaboration; the throwing of SPD support to the left liberals was public and explicit. Much more interesting are the examples of left-liberal first-ballot votes going to the SPD on the second ballot, for officially this was discouraged by the party leadership in most areas. In 1898 there were eight examples in which the SPD gained 15 percent or more in the second ballot as compared with the first. In seven of the cases, they fought a right-wing opponent; in seven of the cases, left liberals were at least one party holding the 'balance of power'; and in four of the eight, left liberals had 20–30 per cent of the vote and were the *only* other significant force from which extra SPD support could have been drawn.[61] The SPD's penetration of left-liberal electoral environments thus created a certain symbiosis between the parties, with each having at least a good chance of some run-off support from the other if it was needed against the right.

This also meant, conversely, that the left liberals (the FVP, in particular) were the party best able to *compete* with the SPD for votes. On the

main ballot or in the run-off, a left liberal gave voters a moderate oppositional, reformist option, a second way of protesting against tariffs and
Reaktion. In addition, the left liberal could, if necessary, gather right-wing
anti-socialist votes. Statistically speaking, left liberals were Wilhelmine
Germany's most effective anti-socialist candidates. Of 98 run-offs in which
the SPD participated in 1898, 30 were against conservatives, 33 against
National Liberals, 20 left and independent liberals, 7 Centre, 6 agrarians
and anti-Semites, and 2 particularists. The *Kartell* parties managed only a
65 per cent rate of run-off victories, presumably a result, in part of the liberal and particularist support or benevolent neutrality which the SPD
might gain when running against *Reaktion*. The left liberals, however, had
an 88 percent success rate, indicating that they of all the conservative and
liberal parties could best fight the SPD head-on. This opened the possibility of a new role for the FVP, as an anti-socialist rather than an anti-*Kartell*
party. Increasingly Richter, particularly, engaged in a propaganda war
with the SPD. His *Gegen die Sozialdemokratie* (Against Social Democracy) of
1896 was an important step in his development as an anti-socialist propa-
gandist, but was exceeded in biting sarcasm by his 1903 *Sozialistenspiegel*, a
vicious 'A-B-C' of socialist errors that ran from 'Agitation Style'— 'excitement of class hatred ... envy, jealousy, and ill-will ...' – through 'Expropri-
ation (see "Peasant")' to 'Private Property (abolition of same).' To judge
by the anger of the SPD press response, these caricatures hit a sore spot.[62]
    In the context of the growing SPD threat and the opportunity provided
by the efforts of the government to organize anti-socialist coalitions, the
FVP came to accept what was called its 'honourable mission' to do battle
with socialism on behalf of the united *Bürgertum*. For their part, the government and the governmental parties were driven at the turn of the century to concede that, as one left-liberal paper put it, 'the middle-class
opposition is in truth state-supporting.' Although liberals were still bitterly divided, the way was prepared for the left liberals' acceptance as governmental allies in 1907, with scores of run-off battles in 1898 and 1903
having demonstrated their effectiveness in defeating socialism. Yet
another barrier to any deeper unification of left liberals or of the overall left was thereby created, for Richter's FVP, with probably the most
left-wing program of any northern liberal party (judging by its anti-
militarism) and with a certain agitational and mass-orientated style,
became more and more committed to fighting the SPD openly, just when
the FVg, the National-Socials, and left-wing National Liberals were hoping for a more conciliatory approach to the socialist working classes.[63]
    Left liberalism's electoral predicament also led to other, at first glance

strange, bedfellows. One of the firmest of all explicit alliances among parties in the 1898 and 1903 campaigns was that between the FVP and the Catholic Centre Party. Karl Bachem of the Centre corresponded with Richter and exerted his influence within his own party to bring about first-ballot alliances in many parts of Prussia. Such alliances were not easy to organize, for party supporters in each constituency liked to have a separate candidate on the first ballot to show their strength and fly the party flag. Nevertheless, both parties considered such an alliance essential. It was especially important to the left liberals considering their weak support and the necessity that they make it into the run-offs. For the Centre, the important consideration was the FVP's stand on constitutional issues; the party could be relied upon to oppose 'exception laws' and suffrage revisions. The net result was that the liberal free-traders and the clerical protectionists cooperated – an important qualification to the oft-quoted argument that 'rigid' Wilhelmine parties never compromised with each other.[64] Two of the parties most unlikely to agree on ideology nevertheless agreed on pragmatic electoral interests, driven, above all, by the shared interest in ensuring a Reichstag majority that would defend democratic rights.

But this, too, strained liberal unity. The liberal parties could not bring themselves in 1898 to forgive each other's electoral alliances. In 1897 the National Liberals charged 'democracy' with responsibility for cooperating with and increasing the strength of the Reich's enemies; here the enemy referred to was the Catholic Centre Party. A left-liberal paper issued the slogan 'National Liberalism is the enemy,' echoing denunciations at the time of the *Kartell* that 'the National Liberals have betrayed the liberal cause,' were 'allies of Junkers,' and that the FVP was 'the only liberal party.' Only in 1903, with the tariff law passed, the BdL exorcized from governmental ranks, and the anti-socialist cause finally a paramount consideration, is there any clear indication of reduced hostility, a precursor of the cooperation that was to prove possible and so very effective in 1907.[65]

Superficial liberal unity would only maximize the possibilities inherent in a declining electorate. Unity might lead to more effective propaganda, more votes in some places, and many more seats, but could not necessarily address the reasons for the long-term decline in the *total* share of the popular vote won by all the liberal parties put together. It is an indication of liberals' true position that the solutions their parties attempted were, in essence, merely more efficient techniques of electoral cooperation. No liberal party attempted (or probably could have agreed upon) a fundamental revision of program, an aggressive party-building drive in the localities, an aggressive geographic or social extension of campaigns, or a basic alteration of political style. The terms in which electoral politics were viewed were defensive ones, a matter of making do and preserving incumbents through one more election. Most of all, liberals had little effect on the main issues around which the campaigns revolved. Tariffs, tax levels, economic interests, popular rights, and the defence of the Reichstag suffrage were the order of the day, issues that revolved around the status polarizations of industrial society – not liberals' cherished nationalism, or traditional appeals to thoughtful voters to trust wise men to make choices on the people's behalf. Where liberalism succeeded, it was frequently by adapting in only the most minor ways the old style and content of politics: as in its stable rural bastions, or its fights against clericals, socialists, and other 'enemies of the Reich.' This limited the liberal parties more and more to a minority of constituencies where favourable conditions lingered. Other parties, however, did adapt sufficiently, finding new structures, policies, and electoral appeals. Among the nonsocialist parties, the most successful at the turn of the century was the Catholic Centre.

6

Fortress Mentalities: The Catholic Centre and Particularists

The Centre Party and other particularist parties in Germany had their origin, as described in chapter 1, in the resistance of minorities, the periphery, and the Catholic Church to the 'national revolution' of the 1860s and 1870s. They were formed, that is to say, along the lines of cleavages created by the process of state modernization. Yet their electoral support remained remarkably stable beyond the turn of the century, even as social-economic cleavages resulting from industrialization became more and more the axes around which electoral politics revolved. This is testimony to the enduring significance of region, ethnicity, and confession in shaping electoral behaviour, even in an industrial age. The small particularist parties, especially, enjoyed tightly knit communities of support that seemed able to ride out the differentiating and destabilizing effects of industrialization among their electorates. But the Catholic Centre was a large party – over the course of the empire, it was *always* one of the top two parties in its share of the votes – and it could not so easily escape the disintegrating impact of social-economic cleavages. The explanation of the Centre Party's electoral stability is not its lack of change, but its following its own unique path to party modernization and interest mobilization. From its parliamentary nucleus in the 1860s and 1870s, by the turn of the century the Centre had spread out to develop a dense network of contacts with extra-parliamentary affiliates throughout the country, its own mass-political auxiliaries, and a new leadership group or 'dominant coalition' ambitiously focused on the power-political realities of the day. It was these changes that led contemporaries to characterize the Centre alongside the SPD as one of the 'parties that ruled the masses,' a party incorporating the populist dynamics of a new age.

Particularist parties generally argued for minority rights, opposed Prussian or German nationalistic centralism, and were based around the geographic fringes of the empire. In the eastern provinces there were the Poles (and tiny splinter groups like the Masurians, who ran their own candidates in a few constituencies). In the south and west was the bulk of the Catholic population, not to mention independent-minded Bavarian parties. Near the French border there was a separate Alsatian party. In the north were the Danes. In recently annexed territories of Prussia, there were those who still protested the demise of state independence: the strongest being the Guelph dynastic loyalists in Hanover, but there was also the Hessian Rights Party in the portion of Hesse that Prussia had taken. All of these groups had their own parties and candidates in Reichstag elections, and, together, the deputies they elected made up a substantial portion of every Reichstag. The term 'separatism' does not describe what they wanted; and while all dissented in some respect from the imperial political culture, some did so on the basis of religion, others on that of nationality, others according to dynastic factors, and some on the basis of regional rights. The term 'particularism' captures something of what they had in common: asserting the rights of a minority that was somehow left out of the Prussian-German status quo, cultivating a distinct regional base, representing a particular population of people with one of their own kind as a representative to Berlin. While many of these parties were small, it is worth remembering that their particularism as a whole was a significant phenomenon in Germany, and they were not to be written off as 'comical remnants' as some of them have been dismissed.[1] Within their seats and their communities, they were important forces, and together they represented a cleavage between the centre and the localities in German politics.

The clearest cleavage in German politics – certainly the one most easily measured by statistical means – was that between the Protestant majority and the Catholic minority, the latter represented more or less monolithically by the Centre Party. The Centre Party was for all the history of the empire the largest or second-largest party in popular support, and after 1881 usually the largest in Reichstag representation. The stability of its support made it virtually unassailable and gave it, as the governmental parties declined, a 'key position' in the composition of Reichstag voting blocs. Unlike all the other particularists, the Centre's strength and size eventually won it respect as a 'German' party, considered by many conservatives and some liberals to be an ally in building and defending the empire against its enemies. It was the only party to move from opposition into a more governmentalist role during the twenty years from 1887 to

1907; and the key years in this transition were 1898–1903. The Centre makes a fascinating study by virtue of its unique social-cultural roots, popular institutions, and, not least, its success in adapting to mass politics at the turn of the century, effecting at least a partial transition from a particularist party to a modern Catholic social-populist party. There is no parallel to the Centre Party in the political cultures of Anglo-Saxon and most European countries, and perhaps this is what makes the Centre so difficult to categorize.

The Centre fits only with difficulty into left-right, class-based schemata, but historians generally fit the Centre into the right wing of German politics. According to a classic history of political parties, the 'spiritual foundation of Catholicism is the strongest traditionalism; from that ensues a conservative character.'[2] The party's conservatism gradually became apparent from the 1890s onward as it cooperated more with the government and sought increased recognition as a governmental ally. The period 1894–1906, when the Centre dominated the Reichstag and moved from opposition to legislative cooperation with the government, is seen as a step towards the 'Blue-Black Coalition' with the conservatives in 1912. This coalition summed up a natural alliance, in the same way as the parallel leftist bloc 'from Bebel to Bassermann.' Recent historians have presented similar views, arguing that the party's increasing conservatism represented the sociological character of its electoral base, notably among peasants, shopkeepers, and artisans. It evolved in the 1890s and early 1900s into 'a moderate conservative social party on a Catholic foundation.'[3] Another historian groups the Centre with the 'parties of the "corporatist/pre-industrial" ... social strata' and concludes that, therefore, 'pre-industrial' parties held sway in Germany, outnumbering the progressive 'parties of the industrial revolution.'[4]

The question of the Centre's right-wing nature comes into better focus if one defines the issues according to which left and right are judged. The Centre did favour tariff protection for agriculture and advocated *Mittelstandspolitik*; it supported state intervention to help the 'ailing sectors' of society. In the debates over the *lex Heinze* in the 1890s, the party showed support for state intervention in cultural matters to preserve public morality. On economic and cultural questions, it appeared to be conservative. But one should beware of teleology, reading the 'Blue-Black Coalition' of 1912 (or the right-wing machinations of certain Centre party leaders near the end of the Weimar Republic) backwards in time to redefine this conservatism as an innate or predetermined tendency of the party's development. At the turn of the century, the Centre was also an agitational mass party that consistently defended and advocated the constitutional rights and suffrage of the Reichstag, and that generally refused to be drawn into right-wing electoral alliances. A better formulation would be that the Centre was right-wing on most economic questions, but rather more left-wing on constitutional ones – which had a decisive impact on the empire's evolution, insofar as the Centre helped forestall reaction and repression.

The line of argument that presents the Centre Party as a pre-industrial conservative party is not particularly helpful in interpreting the 1898 and 1903 elections, perhaps because this was a period of flux when the party's identity was being redefined, and certainly because the issues in the elections were not only the ones upon which historians have concentrated. During 1898–1903 an electoral alliance between Catholics and conservatives was favoured only by small groups within those parties, and discussed only within very restricted regions of the Reich. Conservatives were committed, with the prodding of Prussian officials, to an alliance with the frequently anti-clerical National Liberals. The Centre Party was committed, despite compromises it struck in the Reichstag, to protecting popular democratic rights, preserving the freedoms guaranteed by the constitution, and mobilizing the anti-centralist feelings of its Catholic constituents. It campaigned in these elections in defence of the Reichstag suffrage, denouncing conservatives as reactionaries and National Liberals as *Kulturkämpfer*. And these issues – the threat of reaction, the defence of the suffrage – were important popular causes at the turn of the century. As part of a deliberate strategy, the Centre formed its tightest electoral alliances with the left-liberal FVP and with regional particularist parties; and it devoted more energy to discussing cooperation with the SPD than with the conservatives. And out in the countryside, in election campaigns, it was no defender of the government. In these respects, it was unlike the conservative parties of the same period.

Contemporaries viewed the Catholic Centre Party as a mass party, like the SPD, with a modern (to liberals and conservatives, distasteful) style of agitational popular politics. Within the Reichstag, it was a party with which governments could bargain; outside, in the constituencies, it was seen as one of the rabble-rousing, 'demagogic' parties, alien in substance and style. It certainly received little governmental assistance, and some thought it should still be considered an 'enemy of the Reich.' Here, out in the constituencies, the Centres most resembled Germany's assortment of other particularist parties. Like other particularist parties, the Centre had a concentrated and rigidly defined electorate and stood as a defender of federalism and of popular rights against Prussian centralism and against threats of political repression. Like them, it was considered an enemy by 'national' activists and ideologues, and by liberals whose chief concerns were national, centralist, or cultural rather than constitutional. Most particularists were based like the Centre in economically 'backward' areas and favoured protectionist economic policies. These similarities led to regular cooperation between the Centre, on the one hand, and Guelphs and Poles, on the other, both in the Reichstag and in the constituencies. The Centre's most important difference from these other parties was, however, that the minority it represented constituted fully a third of Germany and spread over many regions. Political Catholicism therefore had a strength, a security, and an opportunity for exercise of influence not shared by the small particularist parties.

The Centre Party and Catholic Solidarity

The Centre Party's peculiar mystique was that of minority Catholic solidarity and strength, symbolized in two propaganda phrases repeated endlessly during 1898–1903: 'the Centre tower' (*Zentrumsturm*) and 'the Centre Party's decisive position' (*ausschlaggebende Stellung*). The imagery bound up in these phrases was a potent electoral tool in 1898 and 1903 for a party that rarely campaigned on individual issues and was confined to a tightly knit and already well mobilized social grouping. In a few words, such slogans told German Catholics that they were strong, united, and important. Even more significant, by using such slogans the Centre's leadership was able to legitimize a new course for the party in the 1890s without altering its rhetoric or its electoral image. The *Turm* into which Catholics retreated in the *Kulturkampf* became a social platform for achieving 'parity' with Germany's Protestant elites, a parity realized symbolically in the Centre's own increasing acceptance by the government.[5]

   'Stronger after every shower / standeth our Centre tower,' proclaimed election propaganda in banal verse.[6] The roots of the Centre Party lay in the coming together of a powerful and revitalized Catholic social grouping in the 1860s and 1870s. The particularism of that era, the sectional defence of the local community against outside attack, remained institutionalized in the party and in its electoral appeal.[7] The real or assumed threat of renewed repression, and the continued need to work at undoing restrictions and civil-rights disabilities left over from the 1870s, kept the *Kulturkampf* alive in election platforms for a generation after it ended. Among the specific grievances that still remained in the 1890s was the

Jesuit law of 1872, which suppressed the order and banned its members from Germany. In addition, many of the small and middle states of north Germany retained discriminatory legislation, and questions like taxes for confessional schools provided lasting aggravation to Catholics. Finally, there was discrimination against Catholics in the civil service, professions, and universities.[8] In retrospect this may not seem like an especially oner-ous sort of discrimination, given the harsher treatment of Jews, Poles, and Social Democrats. Yet the Centre's more extreme propagandists con-stantly repeated that a 'silent *Kulturkampf* was in progress and spoke of 'forceful Protestantization' of parts of Germany. Statistics were collected to show that government subsidies and appointments disproportionately favoured Protestants.[9]

The *Kulturkampf* was also kept alive by anti-clericals, especially those associated with National Liberal circles. The more successful the Centre was in exerting political influence, the more strident this minority became – providing the Centre with further ammunition for its election campaigns. Thus in 1903 an 'electoral union for fighting Ultramontan-ism' issued an election declaration on 1 April complaining that 'Centre is trump! The progress of Ultramontanism cannot be denied.'[10] The anti-clericals were concerned that 'the Centre exercises ever-greater influence on law-making and administration,' the effect of which was to undermine national consciousness and intellectual freedom (classic liberal con-cerns). 'The energies of our people are made serviceable to an interna-tional and anti-national system of rule' – the Catholic Church. This sort of thing had sounded plausible, perhaps, in 1874; but in 1903 it was an anachronism. Ironically, it was an anachronism that helped the party it attacked by keeping alive the unity of Catholics.

Characteristically, the Centre Party's regional election declarations were wordy and vague, replete with old-fashioned and high-sounding phrases that implicitly or explicitly recalled the *Kulturkampf*.[11] According to the Westphalian Centre's proclamation in 1898, Catholics should sup-port the party because of the 'holy cause which called the Centre into being, the glorious history which it can ... look back upon, the esteemed, often decisive position that it assumes in parliament ...' The regional party could dismiss in a single sentence the arguments about interest pol-itics, agrarianism, tariffs, and so on, which had become an obsession of the Protestant liberals and conservatives: the Westphalians merely stated that the Centre had set itself the goal 'to serve the whole German people, to further the just compromise of all interests.' This resembled the claim put forward by the National Liberals, but the Centre's claim to be a party of all strata and interests was solidified by its emotive appeals to Catholic loyalty and traditional community solidarity.[12]

The need for the unity and strength of the Centre electorate was highlighted by dwelling on the number and ferocity of the party's foes, by stressing its isolation. Many parties used the language of 'battle' to describe Wilhelmine elections, but the Centre more than any represented elections as battles between separate communities, battles in which Catholics always closed ranks. 'Let us therefore exert these energies to the utmost,' urged the 1903 Westphalian election platform, 'let us go to the last man to the ballot boxes and let us give our votes unanimously to the candidate recommended unanimously or at least with a great majority by our authorized and [duly] convened constituency committee.' The emphasis on 'unanimity' went beyond that of some other parties in at least one significant respect. The Centre really was not just concerned with winning; it advocated loyalty to Catholic candidates even where these stood no hope of victory, and regularly put up *Zählkandidaturen* so that local Catholic voters would have a Centre man to vote for. This was a tactic pursued in the main only by the mass-orientated parties, which did not count it as a wasted effort to spread the party's agitation and to encourage identification with the party by sympathizers everywhere. This had tactical uses, explained a Westphalian paper affiliated with political Catholicism, 'for, first, with the great fragmentation of the other parties our candidate might be brought into the run-off even where Centre members find themselves in a minority and then, in the end, win after all, especially in constituencies where we would only have to fight Social Democracy; and second, it is also of great importance and lasting effectiveness that the total strength of our party come completely to the light of day.' All Catholics were urged to turn out and vote for the Centre no matter what the local tactical situation, in order to show 'that the Centre voters in fact form the strongest political party in the whole German Reich.'[13]

Apart from local penetrations by other parties in particular regions and types of constituency, the Centre was Catholic Germany's *only* political party.[14] The electoral discipline of Catholics in Imperial Germany was legendary. It was reported in 1903 that of the 175 eligible voters in the upper Bavarian village of Hollenbach, 174 had turned out at the polls, and 172 of these voted for the Centre. Two voted for the Peasants' League, and the one who did not vote was ill and confined to bed. In Ingolstadt a man of more than one hundred years of age was led carefully to the poll by his relatives to vote. These, it should be noted, are cases where a Centre victory was absolutely assured; these people were voting on principle, not because the campaign was close.[15] Across the Reich as a whole, it has been estimated that more than 80 per cent of Catholic voters voted for the Centre during the *Kulturkampf*; this declined during 1884–90 to around 70 per cent and remained stable at that level through to 1903.[16] Indeed, the party rarely received any but Catholic votes. No other social or economic correlate 'explains' Centre voting as well as does confessional composition of the population, and in certain regions the correlation increased in the 1890s to achieve 'an astonishingly high degree' of mobilization of Catholic voters.[17]

The degree of Catholic solidarity is reflected in table 11, which shows a multiple regression concerning the party's popular vote. The correlation of the party's popular vote with the percentage of Catholics in the population is remarkable. It suggests that for every 10 per cent more Catholics in one constituency as compared to another (with all other variables held constant), the party could expect 8 or 9 per cent more support – about as close to a one-to-one correlation as one would expect to find in this kind of data.[18] The table also shows that the party did better in smaller constituencies and slightly better in rural areas – the 'backwaters' of Germany in an economic and demographic sense. This likely reflects the fact that there was some success by the Social Democrats in recruiting Catholic voters in large cities, while more purely rural environments remained secure. The negative correlation with the large-landownership districts apparently reflects another such minor penetration of the Catholic electorate by a different party. Most of the territories in the east where large landholdings were common, and that were Catholic, were in the Polish provinces. The voters here generally, in most of the regions, saw themselves as Poles first and Catholics second, and supported a Polish particularist rather than a Catholic one. The relationships with the Social Democrats and the Poles is dealt with at greater length later in this chapter.

Regional factors of various kinds were significant in causing variations in the Centre Party's vote. Although the party won Catholic votes in high proportions, it did so less effectively in certain regions. In table 11, only two coefficients are positive: those related to the percentage of Catholics in the population, and the percentage of rural residents. Thus the 'baseline' prediction of the computer model is that Centre votes were a function of the Catholic and especially rural Catholic population. The table then shows nine regions with negative coefficients – regions where the party's actual performance deviated downward from the otherwise pre-

TABLE 11
Multiple Regression for the Centre Party Popular Vote, 1890–1912

	Var. type	1890	1893	1898	1903	1907	1912
% Catholic	C	**0.859**	**0.906**	**0.876**	**0.850**	**0.807**	**0.800**
		38.1	39.5	40.5	43.2	37.7	34.2
Large landownership	C	**−5.36**	**−4.84**	**−5.73**	**−5.77**	**−5.26**	**−4.94**
		−2.55	−2.20	−2.87	−3.09	−2.55	−2.36
% Rural	C	**0.100**	**0.110**	**0.0861**	**0.119**	**0.130**	**0.118**
		3.16	3.17	2.69	4.02	4.12	3.75
Constituency size	C	*−2.89*	*−3.59*	*−3.16*	**−2.75**	**−2.46**	**−1.73**
		−1.07	−1.49	−1.83	−2.20	−2.23	−2.00
Prov of W. Prussia	D	**−29.5**	**−33.1**	**−28.4**	**−29.3**	**−29.1**	**−27.7**
		−7.61	−8.31	−7.74	−8.62	−7.78	−7.30
Posen	D	**−51.8**	**−55.8**	**−47.9**	**−49.6**	**−50.2**	**−49.0**
		−13.9	−14.7	−13.7	−15.1	−14.1	−13.6
Silesia	D	**−7.66**	**−10.2**	**−7.35**	**−11.5**	**−15.4**	**−17.6**
		−3.45	−4.36	−3.45	−5.79	−6.88	−7.83
Hanover	D	*−5.09*	**−6.64**	**−6.58**	**−5.28**	*−5.22*	*−4.25*
		−1.79	−2.21	−2.41	−2.07	−1.86	−1.48
Catholic Bavaria	D	**−10.0**	**−22.8**	**−29.6**	**−20.7**	**−9.53**	**−15.4**
		−3.66	−7.88	−11.5	−8.54	−3.40	−5.69
Mixed Bavaria	D	**−7.67**	**−10.0**	**−10.3**	*−4.94*	*−4.74*	**−13.3**
		−2.60	−3.20	−3.63	−1.86	−1.62	−4.50
Baden	D	**−21.1**	**−23.0**	**−14.6**	**−10.4**	**−13.6**	**−14.7**
		−6.32	−6.54	−4.58	−3.49	−4.15	−4.38
Hesse	D	**−12.4**	**−17.3**	**−15.3**	**−7.49**	**−10.4**	**−12.9**
		−3.17	−4.11	−4.03	−2.12	−2.69	−3.27
Alsace-Lorraine	D	**−67.6**	**−68.5**	**−66.4**	**−59.9**	**33.0**	**−57.3**
		−20.3	−19.4	−20.9	−20.1	−10.1	−17.2
Adjusted R^2		.880	.861	.879	.887	.857	.851
$F(19/377\ DF)$		153	130	152	164	126	119.6

Source: Multiple regression based on the author's constituency-level Reichstag election data; see Appendix C. Independent variables which did not show significant t-ratios at the 5 per cent level in at least three elections are not shown.

Note: The dependent variable is the percentage of the vote for the Centre Party. In the body of the table, the regression coefficient is on the top, and the t-ratio beneath (377 DF); significant coefficients are shown in bold, and the insignificant ones in italics. (See Appendix D for explanations of terms and abbreviations.)

dicted performance, regions where the party did not live up to its potential to mobilize Catholics. Most of these regions were contested by other particularist parties: West Prussia, Posen, and Silesia were Polish; Hanover was contested by Guelphs; and Alsace-Lorraine was home to its own Alsatian particularist party. In Posen and Alsace-Lorraine, it was as if the Centre Party collapsed completely, and the Catholic population supported the alternatives almost completely. In the other particularist regions, the coefficients are smaller in magnitude, reflecting the fact that the situation in these provinces was more complicated. We know from other evidence that the Centre Party sometimes cooperated with the Guelphs or Poles in these areas, sometimes opposed them; was sometimes successful with its own candidates, and sometimes not. The other regional variations from the trend have different origins. In Bavaria, the Centre was the 'established' party, seen as tied to the elites, to state government, and to the church; so that instead of championing a minority against the centre, it was itself vulnerable to attack by the populist Bavarian Peasants' League and by liberals. In Baden, the Centre Party was, historically, not well organized, and that state remained a relative weak point even after 1898. There are, then, particular factors that led the party to be less successful in mobilizing Catholics in the cities and in certain regions; but, overall, the remarkable feature is the degree of Catholic support.

In mobilizing Catholic voters, the Centre could rely on established leadership and social institutions of Catholic communities. The clergy were indispensable allies. Priests sat on local Centre committees, legitimated the party, and helped its leaders reconcile conflicting interests within it. Their confidence and support was an essential factor in the stability of the party's electoral base. In certain cases, the clergy were the decisive agents of party discipline. One historian has interpreted the loyalty of the Rhenish clergy to the Centre Party as the decisive factor in the defeat of rebel Catholic agrarians in the 1898 and 1903 elections.[19]

The liberal anti-clerical press was highly suspicious of the electoral agitation of the Catholic clergy. It was rarely shown that anything the clergy did was illegitimate, but it was often partisan, and the liberals were often the victims. In 1903 a National Liberal paper reported that the Centre election committee in Konstanz had sent a circular around the local clergy which argued that 'the already-ignited struggle against our holy church' would, 'after a defeat of the Centre, develop with a ruthlessness never seen before' into an all-out confessional war. The clergy ought therefore to help the party by identifying 'self-sacrificing men' to serve as *Vertrauensmänner*, and to fill out a questionnaire about the state of the election campaign in their communities. The liberal paper claimed that such instructions made the clergy into 'subordinate servants of the Centre leadership.' The same source quoted numerous examples of priests delivering political speeches in support of the Centre and charged that they were misusing their pulpits and their sermons to do so. Where such a practice was likely to be challenged, the priest simply arranged for election meetings to be held on Sundays, which emphasized his religious authority without requiring him to speak from the pulpit during a service. Even government officials complained of such 'election influence' by the Catholic clergy 'against the National Liberals.'[20]

The content of the clergy's speeches can perhaps be judged from the example of 'Herr Stadtpfarrer Schließl,' who addressed a Centre meeting in Munich in May 1903. Schließl asked the audience, 'Why should we vote? For whom should we vote?' and proceeded to answer his own question:

In the thirty years since the beginning of the Reichstag, many laws have been made which have harmed our holy religion and which the church still feels heavily today. Even if in the coming Reichstag no religious questions should come up, nevertheless there are many questions to be dealt with which have a profound effect on the life of our people and which for the good of the people must be solved on a religious foundation.

'Only the Centre has the right to call itself a true people's party,' argued the priest, in contrast to the liberals, who were self-interested outsiders, 'the party of big capitalism.'[21] In presenting itself as the party of the people, instead of the party of big capitalism or of the state, the Centre was assuming the so-called 'democratic' or 'demagogic' mantle.

But while the clergy were essential to the party, in agitation and in legitimation, this is not the same as saying (as the liberals did) that the Centre was 'a clerical party.' The Centre had clearly demonstrated its independence of the church in tactical matters, particularly in its opposition to Bismarck's military bills.[22] Even in its period of active legislative cooperation with the Reich government, it remained a 'people's party' aiming to represent the interests of the Catholic community in Germany – political, social, and economic, not just religious. While confession legitimized the party and helped cement its electoral base, and while the clergy played an important role in the party's structure and campaigns, the growth of mass politics and of new issues in the 1890s also challenged the party to justify itself to its voters in new ways. The old 'national' and confessional issues did not retain their sole dominance within the party, and this relates to the Centre's success in an era of change. With the decline of national issues and the rise of interests and fairness issues, the liberals foundered; but not (during 1898–1903) the Centre. Like the other established parties, and better than most of them, the Centre adapted to the new conditions of electoral politics.

The Centre Party and the Aspirations of the Masses

The counterpart to the mystique of Catholic security embodied in the 'tower' symbolism was the language of responsibility, influence, and importance contained in the boasts about the Centre's 'decisive position' in German politics. Considering itself limited to the minority Catholic population, the Centre could nevertheless hope for an important political role. 'The Centre can clearly never win an absolute majority,' reasoned one Centre newspaper, 'since Catholics are in a minority in the German Reich. But it can remain the decisive party, and the efforts of its leaders are primarily directed to preserving this position ...'[23] Correspondingly, the notion of the Centre's role in defending against a *Kulturkampf* gave way before the idea that the Centre's job was to win 'parity' for Catholics, integration on equal terms with Protestants in business, professions, and public life. The 'key position' of the party and its 'double majority' possibilities were to be used to achieve greater equality for Catholics. The Centre allied to the left to defend popular rights, and to the right to participate in the government's social, economic, and fleet legislation. The central element in the Centre's success was the way in which its leaders created an effective populist style and image, while preserving the freedom to manoeuvre in committing their party to legislative projects.[24]

By the end of the 1890s, a new leadership of younger men, mostly middle-class urban professionals, controlled the party. They were led by Ernst Lieber until his death in 1902, and by men like Peter Spahn, Karl Trimborn, Adolf Gröber, Georg Baron von Hertling, and Aloys Fritzen. The gradual victory of this new leadership over the aristocratic wing, which was deeply entrenched in provinces like Silesia, came about in two main stages in the 1893 Reichstag elections and in the run-up to the 1898 campaign. In 1893 numerous Catholic aristocrats broke with the party leadership and campaigned (in accordance with Rome's wishes) in support of the military bill over which the Reichstag had been dissolved – hoping to accommodate the German state and so reduce tensions. The aristocratic

rebels were soundly defeated, a key step in the establishment of the
party's discipline and independence. The second milestone came in
1898, when Lieber's success in carrying the bulk of his Reichstag caucus
with him in support of the naval law, against strong resistance and the
defection of Bavarian deputies, confirmed his effective leadership of the
party. As Matthias Erzberger commented, it was 'wholly clear that the ...
transition from the more oppositional activity to a more positive one
[did] not come off without internal disturbances in the party' – yet,
under Lieber's guidance, it did come off.[25] In terms of Panebianco's
analysis of political parties, this represented a reshaping of the 'dominant
coalition' within the party – and with the reshaping came not only a new
group of leaders but also new issues and a new style of politics.[26]

Lieber and his colleagues did not abandon the Centre's confessional
appeal. The 1898 and 1903 election platforms continued to emphasize
the historic associations of the party. Neither did they de-clericalize the
party at the level of local committees and campaigns. They continued to
regard their electorate as defined and limited by the Catholic population
of Germany. All of these 'particularist' features were maintained, but the
party's size and 'key position' presented unique opportunities for legislative participation. Lieber and his colleagues were determined to realize
those opportunities, but doing so required changing or supplementing
the idea that the party was a Catholic 'tower.' The broadening of Catholic political goals and consciousness was later summed up in Karl
Bachem's 1906 appeal, *Wir müssen aus dem Turm heraus!* (We must leave
the tower!).

The idea of achieving 'parity' for Catholics provided the intellectual
link between the social-reform appeal of the party at the grass roots and
the aspirations of its Reichstag leaders to participate in exercising power.
First raised as a major issue at the 1891 national assembly of Catholics in
Mainz, parity became the subject of a concerted campaign during 1897–9,
the crucial years when Lieber was charting the party's new parliamentary
course.[27] Parity was expressed in confessional terms as removal of the
remaining disabilities suffered by Catholics, while in social terms it reaf-
firmed the broadening of the party's program from narrow clerical pre-
occupations to expressed concern for the welfare of all Catholics in all
economic sectors and all roles; and, in political terms it expressed and
was symbolized by the influence wielded by the Reichstag caucus in its
partnership with the government.[28]

The transition during the 1890s in the party's leadership, legislative
strategy, propaganda, and public image was paralleled by an evolution in

its organizational basis, an evolution that served the party well in the battles of 1898 and 1903. The Catholic solidarity shaped by the *Kulturkampf*
and represented politically by the Centre was based on separate Catholic
occupational, professional, and social associations throughout Catholic
Germany. These organizations linked the Centre, which possessed no
regular structure of committees, delegates, and conferences, tightly into
all aspects of life in Catholic communities. Thus one of the most rudimentary or informal of party organizations in Germany was based on one
of the most highly articulated foundations of social, economic, and community institutions.

Catholic peasants' associations had spread widely in the 1880s, providing a powerful rural base for political Catholicism and one which helped
to contain Catholic agrarianism within the party. Where such peasant
leagues were strong and well organized, as in the Rhineland and Westphalia, breakaway agrarian groups found little electoral support. In the
heartland of Catholic Bavaria, where the party and its rural affiliates were
less developed, the Peasants' League became, instead, the chief benefi-
ciary of agrarian populism. In most regions, Catholic agrarians sought
response to their grievances within political Catholicism rather than outside it and were satisfied with their party's acceptance of protectionist tariffs. One reason for the Centre's relative success in placating agrarians,
except the Bavarian peasants, may have been the party's organizational
base in the countryside.[29]

The second problem for the Centre in electoral politics in the 1890s
was the urban working class. The Centre's response to the spread of
Social Democracy was more effective than that of any other party, assisted
to be sure by the cultural barriers involved in the solidarity of the Catholic community. The founding of the People's Association for Catholic
Germany (Volksverein für das katholische Deutschland, or VkD) followed the call for a new social policy by Catholic bishops in 1890 (legitimized the following year by Leo XIII's *Rerum novarum*). Between 1891
and 1903, the VkD grew from 109,000 to 322,000 members and adopted
an important role as one of the Centre Party's chief agencies for mass
election agitation. In the mid-1890s, its membership was heavily concentrated in the urban areas of the Rhineland and Westphalia, where it organized the working classes in ways older Catholic organizations could not.
Its growth was associated with the rapid development from the 1890s
onward of Catholic workers' organizations, including regional federations founded in Munich in 1891, Berlin in 1897, and Mönchen-Gladbach
in 1904.[30] The VkD provides a clear example of political Catholicism's

adaptation to the new social, populist, and 'fairness' issues exploited with such success by anti-Semitism and by Social Democracy. Up to 1898 the VkD distributed some 23,629,000 pieces of printed material, including 4,929,000 'social-political leaflets' in 1898 alone. Also by 1898 the VkD maintained twenty-eight bureaux throughout Germany. All of this was essential in mass-political and particularly in electoral terms, and had a distinctive anti-socialist coloration. A Centre Party handbook explained the usefulness of mass meetings in inoculating workers against Social Democracy:

In *popular meetings* to which everyone has free entry, the worker, who during the week is at work and often assailed by enemies, sees hundreds or even thousands of Christian comrades around himself. From capable and distinguished men he hears refuted and exposed the errors and impossible aims of Social Democracy ...

It was characteristic of the Centre's new orientation that, as 'parity' and social policy waxed and as the battle-imagery of the *Kulturkampf* waned in importance, so too the SPD replaced the National Liberals as the chief enemy and competitor.[31]

VkD pamphlets were explicit presentations for 'the peasant, artisan, or worker' to hear 'what all has occurred, especially through the Centre, for correcting his economic distress' – explanations, that is, of what made the Centre a socially responsive *Volkspartei* and an effective parliamentary force. In urban Catholic constituencies, where Centre and SPD voting proportions had moved in almost exactly inverse fashion (Centre tending downward and SPD upward), the period from 1890 to 1893 saw a stabilization of Centre support. This corresponds to the initial impact of Catholic social activism and of the VkD's agitation.[32] This initial success among the working class in the early 1890s, however, was difficult to sustain in the long term given the party's simultaneous commitments to other interests.

The Centre Party had Catholic peasant leagues and tariff policy to offer to agrarians, workers' associations and social reform to the urban population, and the VkD together with an extensive network of Catholic newspapers for mass propaganda. Not to be outdone in any aspect of social policy, it also adopted *Mittelstandspolitik* to protect artisans. The Centre played an important role in the legislation of the 1890s against unfair competition, regulating stock markets, monopolies, cartels, and consumer cooperatives; in the stengthening of guild structures; and in other projects favoured by the government and intended to aid the embattled traditional lower middle classes.

The Centre's claim to be a social-reforming 'people's party' was based on providing something for everyone, including both an organizational means for integrating each major group and interest, and policy concessions in the party program. This inclusion of all classes was something the Protestant liberal parties, especially the National Liberals, would have liked to accomplish, but could not. They lacked the strong basis in social-economic organizations and in communities, they lacked the willingness to follow the path of social-reformist policies and populist organization, and they lacked the appeal to Catholic solidarity that still worked so well for the Centre. The old confessional appeal, revamped with social and power-political overtones as 'parity,' helped tie the divergent policies together. No other German party was quite so balanced as the Centre, in these years, in having both well-developed agrarian and working-class organizations and policies. Other parties had to ride just one horse at a time; the Centre straddled the two most spirited social movements of the day. Still, in an age of bitterly conflicting economic interests there was a complex acrobatic act to be performed within the party. Organized workers in the Catholic political movement, in particular, argued that the Centre's middle-class leaders did not do enough for them; but the workers were opposed by the party's aristocratic and clerical traditionalists. There was, in the long term, a basic difficulty in the party's attempts to satisfy so many divergent interests. This is what made it useful for the party to campaign on an issue like parity, which could, potentially, subsume the social-economic aspirations of all Catholics.[33]

The Centre was not altogether immune to the 'fragmentation' experienced by other non-socialist parties in the 1890s and early 1900s. As memories of the *Kulturkampf* waned there was the threat of decreasing loyalty among the Catholic population, and, as already mentioned, there were indications of a downward trend in the proportion of voting Catholics who voted for the Centre Party. This trend stabilized in the 1890s after the founding of the VkD and the party's new reformist emphasis, but worsened again after 1903. By 1912 one estimate suggests that nearly half of Catholic voters voted for parties other than the Centre.[34] One aspect of the party's problem was the SPD's ability to win the allegiance of the Catholic working population in the cities, for though SPD penetration was slower than in Protestant cities it was nevertheless steady. This was the greatest single threat to the Centre's electoral base and to its claim to be a *Volkspartei* representing all classes. The SPD's huge victory in 1903 had to be a worry for Centre leaders. But, second, the Centre had to deal during 1893–1903 with rebel agrarians in its ranks and with the external challenge of the Bavarian Peasants' League, who also represented a kind of radicalism that complicated the internal bargaining among interests in the party and especially its appeal to the working classes. And finally, the resurgence of Polish nationalism challenged from a different perspective the Centre's claim that Catholics had more in common than dividing them. New breakaway Polish candidacies hurt the Centre significantly in 1903 and thereafter both in eastern Prussia and in the Ruhr. While these challenges were neither crippling nor national in scope, and still left the party with many safe seats (unlike the liberals), they do reveal that even the Centre's adaptation to mass organization, mass appeal, and sectional interests was stormy and incomplete.

Balancing Diverging Interests, 1898–1903

'The Centre as a true people's party embraces all circles and all classes of the people,' proclaimed the Hessian party for the 1903 elections. 'In the Centre are united agrarians and businessmen, industrialists and trades-men, workers and great landowners, producers and consumers from north and south.' Like the liberals, the Centre party attempted to stand 'above the interests.' Accordingly, the party accepted the protectionist demands of agriculture for aid in its plight, but tried to balance this by offering complementary measures to help other sectors. The enemy in this endeavour, as for the National Liberals, as for the government, was extremism: 'extreme agrarians and Social Democrats work hand in hand to make trade treaties impossible,' observed the Hessian Centrists. And, also like the National Liberals, the Centre preferred to minimize eco-nomic issues by saying as little as necessary about them. The 1903 national Centre Party platform, for example, listed the issues as (in order) defence of the federal constitutional order, defence of the Reichstag suffrage, criminal law reform including abolition of duelling, frugality in govern-ment expenditures, lightening of military burdens, and peaceful coexist-ence of confessions with greater equality for Catholics. Only after these first six points, popular and non-sectional (and touching on popular-rights 'fairness' issues), did the party present its grab-bag of economic policies to help all interests.[35]

By the time of the tariff-oriented campaigns of 1898–1903, it had become essential to the party's internal unity to accommodate as well as contain protectionist demands. The issue of 'agricultural distress' forced the Centre to be solicitous towards Catholic peasants and aristocrats, responding both with propaganda and with advocacy of protective tariffs

to their sometimes noisy demands. Praise, at least, was cheap and relatively easily incorporated into the image of a broad social-reform party:

The peasant class is counted with justice as one of the main supports for throne
and altar ... Nothing so heavily endangers the whole state existence as [does] a
deep disturbance of the most conservative element of the state, the peasant class
... From this it is self-evident that the preservation of healthy, energetic peasantry
belongs to the most important tasks of state authority.

The party further conceded that 'this class finds itself today in hard-
pressed circumstances, in a true state of distress,' and advocated higher
tariffs, reform of inheritance law, insurance against natural disasters, and
a central European customs union as appropriate answers. In short, the
Centre exploited the language and social analysis of *Mittelstandspolitik*
(the idea that lesser property owners were 'state-supporting') and associated itself with the demands of agrarianism. It dissociated itself, however,
from the BdL's program and from the BdL-sponsored Kanitz proposal
for a state grain monopoly. It would commit to specific and limited policies to help agriculture; but it would not become an agrarian party or
endorse 'boundless' agrarian demands, as critics called them. In this way,
the party attempted, like the Protestant conservative moderates, to preserve its latitude to cooperate with the government.[36]

Lieber and other leaders of the party were attacked by Centre agrarians, to the extent that Lieber complained of a 'war of extermination'
against him by the party's agrarian press. Catholic peasant leagues and
prominent agrarian aristocrats were willing to adopt populist political tactics in order to further their own and agriculture's claims. Felix Baron
von Loë-Terporten of the Rhenish Peasants' Association proposed in
1898 that a 'direct representative of the class interests [*Standesinteressen*]
of Rhenish agriculture' be nominated as a Reichstag candidate, and suggested his right-hand man, Franz Schreiner, editor of the *Rheinische
Volksstimme*. In May 1898 at a meeting of local farmers, it was decided that
'[agrarian] comrades [*Standesgenossen*] should give their votes within
their political parties only to such candidates as recognize the specially
formulated demands of Rhenish agrarians.' The party proper resisted
this direct interest-representation as antithetical to its own ideas of leadership. 'Lively disagreements' at party meetings resulted in the overruling
of Loë and his peasant movement by the majority.[37]

Later in the campaign, agrarians attempted to explain that they were
not rebelling against the Centre as the political representative of all

Catholics, and yet insisted that they distrusted its leaders and wanted more agrarian spokesmen in the party. 'We are not working against but for the Centre,' assured the agrarians. 'But what we desire and demand is that sufficient men enter the Centre who are not only friends of, but also experts [*Kenner*] in agriculture ... And with that belongs having felt on one's own foot where the shoe rubs. Above all it must be experts in agriculture who make their influence felt in the leading bodies.' This claim for direct agrarian representation within the party paralleled the claims of the BdL and the anti-Semites for direct agrarian representation within the Reichstag and the state – you can't represent farmers unless you've walked in their shoes. The populist thrust became apparent at a meeting of agrarians in Cologne at which both Loë and Wilhelm Count von und zu Hoensbroech refused to stand as candidates in the elections, insisting instead on the less exalted Schreiner. The National Liberal interpretation of Schreiner was that he offered 'a certain popularity [*Volkstümlichkeit*]' by virtue of his willingness to cater to 'the most impossible hopes and untenable plans' in a way that 'out-trumped the tone of the Agrarian League.' He was, in other words, one of the rabble-rousers and demagogues. Clearly the aristocrats felt it was more important for a man of the people and an effective agitator to take the field in the Reichstag campaign.[38]

In 1903 the line became more sharply drawn between Catholic moderates and Catholic agrarians, just as it did the same year between Protestant governmentalists and the BdL. In that year 250 Rhineland agrarians 'of the Schreiner tendency' (as the press called them) were reported to have decided on a separate slate of candidates and a separate election machine by April. Their policy was still to approach the local Centre association and first give it the opportunity to adopt agrarian demands, but explicit provision was made for separate agrarian candidacies. This more radical approach led to a split within the peasant league, to the resignation of its chairman, and ultimately to the isolation of the extremists. *Germania* estimated that Schreiner captured 13 executive members, 141 committee members, and 3,037 other members, but his opponent, the ex-chairman Count Spee, counted 66 executive members, 794 committee members, and 20,264 others. The split illustrates both that the Centre Party was vulnerable to the same kind of sectional agrarian pressures as other parties, but also that it could accommodate and contain them.[39] The party made programmatic concessions to the 'distress of agriculture,' but in the selection of candidates it preserved the independence of its leadership from particular interests and with that it maintained its claim to be a 'people's party.' The rebel Rhenish farmers' candidates were unsuccessful, proving that without the legitimacy and the organization of the official party machine and the patronage of the Catholic establishment, candidates could not get very far in Centre constituencies. When in 1903 the strength of the Bavarian Peasants' League began to fail as well, it became apparent that the Centre tower had weathered another storm.[40]

The Centre was simultaneously pulled in a different direction to satisfy the demands of Catholic workers' organizations. But because of its predominantly rural base, the party was less vulnerable to working-class radicalism than to agrarian extremism. Only a small proportion of 'German' (i.e., non-Polish, non-Alsatian) Catholic seats were highly urbanized (even though these seats had a lot of voters), whereas many Catholic seats were rural. Accordingly the party would not bend quite as far to satisfy the particular demands of workers as it bent to placate the agrarians. In fact, the extent to which the Centre had to cater to Catholic agrarians complicated its fight with the SPD for the allegiance of urban workers.

The Centre did have a legitimate, organized working-class constituency, more so than any other party besides the SPD. The Christian Trade Unions had corporate privileges within the party and were consulted about the social reform sections of the party program. The question of their cooperation with non-Catholic trade unions, however, stretched the party's commitment to workers to its limits. The conflict became acute after the turn of the century when growth and formalization of structure and policy created increasing pressure to come to an explicit decision. The party's orthodox hierarchy, its Berlin leadership, and its aristocratic elements and corporatists could agree to 'a workers' movement on Catholic principles,' and that social reform to address 'the modern workers' question' was a priority 'of morals and religion.' Such things could be incorporated into political speeches and election platforms. But they disagreed with the proposition that Catholic trade unions should be organized according to the same rationale as socialist ones and participate in parallel with the latter in collective bargaining. The Christian trade union movement continued nonetheless to grow in size and organization. In 1902 a general secretariat was established, and in 1903 a non-socialist 'German Worker's Congress' was held in Frankfurt, which added its voice to the call for legal trade union rights. The union movement and its demands helped convince the Centre to negotiate with the government and participate in some modest reform measures. This was not enough, however, to prevent a steady and somewhat worrisome leakage of Centre party support in urban seats to the SPD.[41]

The unity of the Centre's electoral grouping was also complicated by the heating-up of the ethnic conflict between Germans and Poles at the turn of the century, which divided Catholics in eastern Prussia and in the Ruhr and led to electoral difficulties more serious than those caused by the Rhenish agrarians and more immediate than the trickling away of support to the SPD. The Polish electoral appeal was straightforward: 'We are Poles! These words encompass our entire political program,' declared the Polish electoral association for Upper Silesia in 1903. 'The community of blood and faith, the equality of the beloved Polish mother language, the equal customs and practices of all Poles from Putzig to Myslowitz make up the bond that unites all Poles into an indivisible whole.'[42] In response to the growing German-Polish polarization, loyal Centrists stressed the primacy of confessional over national affiliation and were supported in this by the clergy. Provost Gajowiecki of Kolmar told a meeting of German Catholics in Wirsitz-Schubin (District of Bromberg, Province of Posen) in 1903 that the seat was contested by 'a Catholic, a non-Catholic, a Pole, and finally a socialist.' 'You are certainly not allowed to vote for a socialist ,' Gajowiecki told his listeners, 'because socialists have no religion ... You must, therefore, declare for a Catholic or a non-Catholic, for a Pole or a German. I ask you: what is more important in human existence, religion or nationality? Is it not religion? ... From that follows that we Catholics must stick together, are not allowed to betray our religion, and are obliged to vote for a Catholic.' Similarly in Czarnikau-Filehne voters were told that 'in Reichstag elections nationality ceases; we have the duty to vote Catholic,' and that anyone who did not do so was 'no Catholic' at all.[43]

At the same time, Poles had begun organizing in the Ruhr, where inmigration of workers from the east was creating a sizeable Polish minority. In the spring of 1898 there were numerous meetings to discuss the Reichstag elections, and the Polish-language press worked to arouse national consciousness. Propagandists argued that 'the war of the Germans against the Slavs has lasted without cessation into our times,' and that the Poles were sorely beleaguered. Good-natured, fewer, poorer, less educated, 'everything is against them, only God and God's justice is with them.' The Polish press insisted that because of this Poles must organize themselves separately, that they must stay away from election meetings organized by the German parties. In 1898, however, this injunction applied particularly to 'all varieties of *Hakatisten*' – the National Liberals and the conservatives. Two days before the voting, the Polish press declared that the Centre had issued 'the required declaration' in favour of Polish demands and that therefore all barriers to voting for the Centre had been removed. For that year, in the Ruhr region, where the Polish organizations were new and small, the rift was healed.[44]

The growing radicalism of the Polish national movement diverged from the Centre's growing governmentalism, and the divisions were deeper in 1903. Poles began to oppose Centre candidates in the formerly solid Centre district of Oppeln, Province of Silesia, in 1903, taking 18 per cent of the district vote and one seat; in 1907 they took four more seats. The Polish electoral association for Silesia declared that 'it is finally time' for Poles to take the future into their own hands and 'not let themselves be led' by political Catholicism. The slogan 'away from the Centre!' drew crowds to public meetings. In the Ruhr, meanwhile, relations also had worsened. Instead of merely holding aloof until the last minute, as in 1898, the Polish political movement was determined to field separate candidates if the Centre did not accept all the Poles' demands. This 'new Polish course' worried the Centre press, which noted that in the Ruhr, whose confessional structure was mixed, the loss of a few per cent to the Poles could lose several key marginal seats for the Centre. This was all the more ominous as the Poles demands were 'self-evidently ... unacceptable.' First, the Centre was to give up all its candidacies in the Polish areas of East and West Prussia, eastern Pomerania, Posen, and Upper Silesia, and was to instruct all German Catholics there to vote for Polish candidates. Second, the church was to provide services in Polish, and third, refrain from German-language church meetings and newsletters that were believed to contribute to the 'Germanization' of Poles. Finally, the Centre was to obtain the removal of all official restrictions on the Polish language, especially in the mines of the Ruhr and Silesia. Needless to say, given the anti-Polish thrust of Reich and Prussian policies, the Centre could never pursue such priorities without compromising its ability to be an ally of the government.[45]

Traditions of Catholic unity were not sufficient to keep Bavarian peasants, Rhenish agrarians, working-class trade unionists, and Poles from rebelling to various degrees against the Centre's political hegemony in Catholic Germany. Instead, the party needed a tariff program, a social-reform program, organized peasant and working-class interest groups, and the mass agitation of the VkD to retain its mass electoral base and its image as a *Volkspartei*. There were some cracks in the edifice of political Catholicism at the turn of the century, but fortunately for the Centre Party's dominant coalition, the divisions in each region were different.

Internal rebellions or intrusions by other parties remained localized; the party's popular vote held nearly stable through 1903 and, indeed, 1907 as well; and, in any case, the Centre maintained its level of representation in the Reichstag. The Centre had adapted successfully for its time to the challenges of mass organization, of working-class reformism, and of agrarian sectionalism. What divisions remained could be plastered over with the rhetoric of the *Kulturkampf* or, increasingly, of *Mittelstandspolitik* and anti-socialism. This left the party's leaders with a freedom to manoeuvre that was unique among the parties during 1898–1903, a freedom to tack alternately on the winds of popular rights or of agrarian protection, to ally left or right, with the opposition or the government, according to the dictates of strategy. They elaborated this into a coherent electoral and parliamentary policy.

Election Strategy: The 'Double Majority,' 1898–1903

In its policy and in its electoral appeal, the Centre relied in part on the traditional, defensive, particularist concerns of German Catholics, and in part on the newer style of a social-reforming *Volkspartei*. Its national leaders, however, also embodied a growing desire to be accepted and integrated in the life of the state, a desire they legitimated by talking of the Centre's 'decisive position' and the possibility of achieving 'parity' for Catholics. These two considerations, the need for popularity and electoral appeal, on the one hand, and for recognition by the state, on the other, could only be reconciled by a particular electoral and parliamentary strategy, the strategy of the double majority. To the left (roughly), the Centre could band together with Social Democrats, with Richter's FVP, and with the Poles and other particularists – in short, with all the other parties that styled themselves as *Volksparteien* and courted mass popularity – to defeat 'exception laws' and prevent limitation of popular rights. To the right, the Centre could participate with the governmental parties in what its propagandists called 'positive' legislation and provide the government with the majorities it needed for its important measures. This strategy required, however, that the Centre balance between government and opposition and ensure that neither got a majority in its own right. It had necessarily to oppose *Sammlungspolitik* because of the threat that it would produce a majority for the *Kartell* parties, and so in 1898 and 1903 it sought to prop up the moderate left by supporting the left liberals. As the threat from the SPD grew, moreover, the Centre had to pay increasing attention to preventing a simple polarization between socialism and conservatism. This was another reason to help out the liberals, and also to resist Social Democracy.

By the turn of the century, the Centre came to play a role in the party system in many respects equivalent to that of the National Liberal Party, exploiting the central position and attempting to use moderate governmentalism to gain influence over and recognition from the state. It also resembled National Liberalism in having (by the end of the 1890s) a largely urban, educated, professional elite leading a substantially rural party and trying to act as mediators among competing social-economic interests in the name of a superior loyalty. It is not surprising that the two were referred to as Wilhelmine Germany's two centre parties, one Protestant and one Catholic. But there were two important differences between them: sectional divisions within the Centre Party were successfully contained, diverted, or diffused during the period in question – the Centre party *was* a 'people's party' by the standards of the time; and the Centre did actually *act* as a centre party, balancing left and right, exploiting its middle position, influencing decisively the parliamentary balance and the course of law-making with a minority of seats. The National Liberals, on the contrary, were unable to break themselves out of the *Kartell* with the right and became increasingly dependent, at least up to 1903, on right-wing support. It was in no small measure the haggling of the Centre with the government that gradually raised the importance and influence of the Reichstag and took Wilhelmine Germany part way down the road to parliamentary government. Ironically, it was the detested clerical party that succeeded at liberalism's own game.

The considerations of this 'game' guided the Centre's electoral strategy during 1898–1903 in a consistent and rational way. The Centre, which rejected Miquel's *Sammlungspolitik*, had more in common with Miquel in crucial economic policies than did the National Liberals, many of whom accepted it. The Centre favoured tariff protection; it adopted *Mittelstandspolitik* in all its respects; and it desired both to cooperate with the government and to fight Social Democracy, though not by an 'exception law' or other political coercion. Nevertheless, *Sammlungspolitik* was treated by the party and its press with deep suspicion. 'Ostensibly this "call to *Sammlung*" was directed against Social Democracy,' said a party policy book. 'But in fact this *Sammlungspolitik* had in mind the restoration of the one-time *Kartell* parties ... A majority in the Reichstag without the Centre was to be brought about, the Centre driven from its decisive position.'[46] This was merely Bismarck's old policy warmed up and served again, a declaration of war on German Catholics. The Centre press emphasized (again the apocalyptic rhetoric of the age) that the coming elections would be 'of ... decisive importance for the course of our internal politics' because of the threat that an 'absolutist-reactionary era' might ensue. The appropriate response to this threat was to preserve 'the possibility of a double-majority combination.'[47] And indeed, if an 'absolutist-reactionary era' could be prevented by popular mobilizing, then this is what was accomplished by the Centre Party along with the SPD and the left liberals at the turn of the century.

The national Centre Party did this by making the 'defence of the Reichstag suffrage' a cornerstone of both its 1898 and 1903 campaigns. In each case, this policy was the basis for a strong popular-rights appeal to the electorate, for emphasizing the Centre's position of strength *vis à vis* the government, and for keeping open the leftward option of the double-majority strategy. In 1898, the Centre deputy Müller-Fulda created a minor sensation in the press by announcing that a draft proposal for changing the suffrage had already been written and was in the hands of a government official. Whether Müller's information was meaningful or not, the publicity campaign he created served to legitimate both him and his party as defenders of popular rights. Lieber endorsed Müller's campaign and noted that the party that lives by parliamentary technique must defend the means of its influence: 'it is only the general, equal, direct suffrage that has made possible for the Centre this position in parliamentary life.' Throughout May and June 1898, the Centre press ran lead articles about 'the endangered Reichstag suffrage,' and the party placed the issue prominently (alongside the defence of the constitution itself) at the head of its national program. When the Reich government issued a denial, the party press kept the issue alive by asking, What about the Prussian government? Did officials there have plans for a *coup d'état* in their desk drawers? In 1903 the Centre again made an ostentatious defence of the suffrage, referring to the party's record on the subject in the first lines of the preamble to its election platform, and emphasizing this 'most important right of the German people' as the first point in the body of the program.[48] This time there were no rumours of plans to revise the suffrage, but the issue was kept alive by controversies over state suffrage reform, and perhaps by the 'parties of the masses' themselves, since it was so helpful to them.[49]

The emphasis on fighting *Reaktion* and defending popular rights hindered any cooperation of the Centre with the conservatives, and especially with agrarian conservatives. This was all the more weighty a factor given the Centre's problems with its own agrarians and the corresponding need to draw a clear line between acceptable demands and unacceptable extremism. Bachem wrote to Felix Porsch in May 1898 concerning the party's relations with the conservatives and with the left liberals in Silesia, and argued that a first-ballot alliance with the BdL would be 'fatal' and 'would compromise our entire position in relation to the Agrarian League.' He asked his colleague 'urgently' to 'do what you can so that this does not happen!' 'We have in m[y] o[pinion] every interest in preventing a shift in the overall orientation of the Reichstag towards the right,' he argued in a subsequent letter, 'for then we could easily be driven out of our decisive position. We must therefore support left liberalism where[ever] we can.' The considerations of 'double-majority' thus exerted pressure on the party to refrain from electoral cooperation with conservatives even in regions like Silesia where some local basis existed for it.[50]

The Centre maintained its traditional alliance with the FVP in 1898 and in 1903. In late May and early June 1898, Bachem discussed twenty-three first-ballot deals between the two parties – deals in which one party would forgo a candidate in order to help the other party to win the seat or at least reach a second ballot. These included constituencies in the Ruhr area, in Hesse-Nassau, in Silesia, in Baden, and in scattered areas across the Reich. In some the two parties stated clearly that what they intended to create was 'a resolute front against the policy of *Sammlung.*' This union persisted precisely because it was convenient: unlike the more old-fashioned parties, both the FVP and the Centre had a policy of contesting seats where they could not win majorities, making alliances necessary; and both habitually jockeyed for position with other minority parties with an eye to winning in run-offs what they could never win alone. In all likelihood, the FVP gained more seats from the alliance, but given the considerations of the 'double-majority' this did not necessarily matter to the Centre. However useful the arrangement, it was still difficult for Bachem, Müller, Richter, and others who negotiated such alliances to make their local committees follow them faithfully: the sacrifice of a first-ballot candidacy was tantamount to sacrificing a sense of identity.[51]

The Centre's alliance with the moderate left complemented its other systematic alliances, notably with regional particularist parties. These, too, could be relied upon in a double-majority calculation to oppose 'exception laws,' centralism, or political repression, and were in their particularism not unlike the Centre itself. In the case of Hanover and Brunswick there was in fact a substantial Catholic population, but given the strength of the Guelph dynastic particularists separate Centre candidates would have split the anti-*Kartell* vote seriously. Accordingly, the Centre maintained first-ballot support for Guelph candidates. The relationship became strained in 1903 when the BdL appealed to Catholics to join it instead of the Guelphs, but the national and Rhenish party press strongly defended the traditional Centre-Guelph alliance and the ostracism of the BdL.[52]

The alliance with the Guelphs (and, where possible, with the Poles) was a stable element in Centre strategy, and the alliance with left liberals was not only stable but grew somewhat more urgent as the left liberals declined in strength. Müller for one argued for an alliance with the SPD · as well, and on the same basis – that it would uphold the Reichstag suffrage and vote against repressive legislation. He proposed a general public statement applying to Hesse, Hesse-Nassau, and Thuringia, at least, to support the SPD in the run-offs where it opposed the *Kartell* parties. This would have been a logical extension of the 'double-majority' concern, but it also conflicted with the Centre's growing anti-socialist rigour. Bachem objected that being instructed to vote for a Social Democrat, even in a run-off, would 'demoralize' the Catholic workers' movement – implying that anti-socialism was a chief element of the party's hold on its working-class supporters – and that it must be a fixed principle of the party never to encourage votes for the SPD. Müller proferred other options, such as 'indirect' help for SPD candidates. In the language of the day, this meant encouraging voters 'under no circumstances' to vote for a *Kartell* candidate, but then remaining silent about whom else they could support or whether it was permissible to abstain. Bachem replied just as firmly that this was out of the question. The Centre was strictly neutral between the SPD and '*Kartell* people.'[53]

Some regional leaders in the party were less easily kept in line than was Müller. In Baden, Theodor Wacker entered into an alliance with the SPD, and in several constituencies neutrality or pro-*Kartell* agreements were undermined by a perceptible drift of votes to the SPD. In Bavaria, the Centre and the SPD concluded a highly successful electoral compact in the state elections of 1899, providing the prototype of a common assault based on the suffrage issue against the liberal parties, who were clinging to power by means of unreformed voting rules. In general, southern Germany offered much more fertile ground for cooperation in both state politics and Reichstag elections, partly because of the lesser degree of polarization, partly because of the shared interest in suffrage reform and overturning of liberal dominance.[54] There was a regional basis, then, for national cooperation, and the 'double-majority' analysis suggested it was an appropriate moment for such. After the 1898 elections, the Centre deputy Reinhard Schmidt pointed out that the balance in the Reichstag had swung to the left, and that therefore the Centre should institutionalize its cooperation with the left by arranging for a deputy from that side of the chamber to be chosen as vice-president of the Reichstag.[55]

The swing to the left remarked upon by Schmidt, represented, potentially, a bigger threat than a *Kartell* victory. The increasing strength of the SPD, at the expense of the other Protestant parties, threatened at least to polarize Reichstag politics in a way that would impede the Centre's freedom to manoeuvre. Possibly, if it continued long enough, it could eventually destroy the possibility of a 'double-majority' situation by making the left disproportionately strong. The SPD, if it continued its huge victories along the lines of 1898 and 1903, was the greatest long-term threat to the Centre's 'decisive position.' The Centre's electoral interest was essentially in preserving the status quo, for it already enjoyed the maximum representation and the maximum influence it could realistically expect to attain. This was an additional reason, therefore, to prop up the left liberals: they constituted not only a counterweight to the *Kartell*, but a barrier on the left between the Centre and the SPD. Or as Bachem told Müller, 'it would be highly uncomfortable for us if left liberalism disappeared altogether and we came to sit so closely beside the soci[alist]s, without a buffer between us, and therefore I, too, will do what I can to preserve as many left liberals as possible.' He repeated the same argument with only a little less frankness in trying to persuade a Centre constituency leader that it was essential to conclude a first-ballot alliance with the FVP: 'it is thoroughly advisable for us to support the left liberals again this time according to [our] ability, first because of the struggle against the Social Democrats, in which they do us the most valuable service, then also in order to preserve our own decisive position in the Reichstag.'[56] Desiring maximum influence on and participation in government, Centre leaders were committed to limiting both extreme left and right in order to preserve the tactical position of the Centre.

The Centre and the SPD had much in common, at least in the eyes of contemporaries, and, indeed, perhaps the problem was that they had too much in common to cooperate with one another. Both were considered the 'parties that ruled the masses,' with powerful party or affiliated institutions that permitted large-scale agitation not only at election time but between campaigns as well. Both cultivated a more intense sort of identification or membership among their supporters than other parties could

achieve among theirs. Both promoted 'fairness'-orientated popular platforms in election campaigns, concentrating on defence of the suffrage,
on fairer taxation, and on different versions of social reforms. In 1898
and 1903, they had similar interests in opposing *Sammlungspolitik* and
Reaktion. Their potential electorates also overlapped in the cases of Catholic workers and Catholic cities. But in spite of and because of these similarities, the two parties became increasingly bitter enemies during the
1898 and 1903 campaigns and during the naval and tariff debates that
preceded them.

Lieber's policy of cooperation with the government from a position of
independence conflicted irreconcilably with the SPD's '*Obstruktion*' in the
Reichstag. The 'pure opposition' of Social Democratic deputies repelled
many of the Centre's pragmatic, middle-class leaders nearly as much as it
did those in the liberal caucuses. The differences between the two
approaches bring to mind Max Weber's contemporary essay on the difference between the politics of absolute ends and the politics of pragmatic
results.[57] Also, in electoral politics, the tariff, *Mittelstandspolitik,* and other
socio-economic issues of the 1890s drove a deep wedge between the two,
for the Centre's base in less-urbanized and less-industrialized regions
(plus its commitment to being a *Volkspartei* of all classes) committed it to
compromises with protectionism that could never be acceptable to the
SPD and its more urban, wage-earning, consumption-oriented electors.
The SPD was also the only major party in Germany that could make persistent inroads into Catholic regions, even if these were largely confined
to a number of major Catholic cities. While the number of *seats* involved
was perhaps not large for the moment, the potential number of *votes* the
Centre might lose among the working classes would damage its claims to
representativeness and social neutrality. In line with these conflicts over
style, policy, and voters, a new kind of Centre rhetoric ('demagogy,' as
one historian calls it) was clearly emerging at the turn of the century, in
which the SPD and class conflict gradually supplanted the old enemies of
liberalism and confessional prejudice.[58]

Radical Centre propagandists accused the SPD of opposing all practical
measures, of misusing workers' funds, and of inciting industrial disturbances, which led to job losses:

... we have seen how Social Democracy uses the workers' moneys entrusted to it;
how it was and is ready to prevent any improvement of the position of the working
class ... how it is its most ardent desire to see the peasant class destroyed; how it
strives equally for the destruction of the artisanal class; ... how ... claiming to have

sworn opposition to capital, [it] still supports big capital against the *Mittelstand*; ...
how it is without religion and hostile to religion ... that it wants to overturn family
life ... that it is guided by Jews ... led by rich capitalists; ... that it wants to achieve its
final goals by bloody, revolutionary means ...[59]

New leaders like Matthias Erzberger in Württemberg (elected as the
Reichstag's youngest deputy in 1903) resorted to 'frightening the pious
peasant voters with the red bogy,' as it has been characterized.[60] The
aggressiveness of the propaganda attacking Social Democrats as manipulative 'outsiders' was now a part of the Centre's own populist appeal.

The net result of this growing competition and bitterness between Germany's largest Protestant and largest Catholic parties is difficult to judge.
On the one hand, contemporary observers estimated that only some 11
per cent of SPD votes came from Catholics, and that the 'resistance of
German Catholicism ... against the Social Democratic movement is stronger than the resistance of economic and social backwardness' against its
advances – meaning that it was not just small-town Catholic Germany, but
Catholic urban workers as well, who resisted Social Democracy. Many historians agree that the confessional divide remained the sharpest social,
economic, or cultural divide in German politics; one judges that 'a real
breakthrough into the region of domination of the Centre did not succeed.'[61] Yet confession alone was serving the Centre less and less well as
an integrating force, and only the SPD consistently gained against it in
head-on competition. Social Democratic growth was slower in Catholic
cities, but growth it was. To contemporaries during 1898–1903 the picture
was one of unrelenting Social Democratic advance, in spite of application, in turn, of force, reason, and patriotic appeals. This symbolized a
new pattern of cleavage, a new style and content of politics, a new popular-democratic opposition, which compelled resistance or imitation from
all the other parties.

7

The Rise of Social Democracy

It was not only Robert Michels, Moisei Ostrogorski, and Max Weber – along with political scientists decades later – who saw the Social Democratic Party of Germany as the characteristic mass party of the new century.[1] This was also how most contemporaries saw it, and for non-socialists and anti-socialists the prospect was disturbing. The SPD incorporated all the features of the new politics: the mass-membership, bureaucratic organization; the use of popular-democratic language to attack elites and the state; and the conscious articulation of social-economic cleavages to mobilize a mass electorate. The party had shaped these tools since its origin in the 1870s and seen them hardened in the fire of repression in the 1880s, but it was in the 1890s that the mass electoral breakthroughs came. The capstone to this series of election triumphs was the 'three-million victory' of 1903, when the SPD captured more than a quarter of the voters, 50 per cent more than the Centre and well over double the total of any other Protestant party. But while studies of the party have focused on its organization, other factors such as electoral strategy and tactics, issues, and patterns of alliances are important in explaining its success.

An overview of the SPD's voting trends (fig. 11) shows a picture of almost uniform advance, except for 1907, in all types of constituency. The SPD did best in Protestant urban seats, worst in Catholic rural ones. It did poorly as well in seats where particularist parties were strong: first, because it was difficult to introduce its class-based mobilization where older patterns of 'national' polarization persisted; and second, because these seats tended to be 'backward' in relation to the trends of industrialization and urbanization. There are only two notable discrepancies in figure 11, both of which relate intimately to what was happening in the 1898 and 1903 elections. First, until 1898 the growth curve of Social Dem-

FIGURE 11
SPD Popular Vote, by Constituency Type, 1890–1912

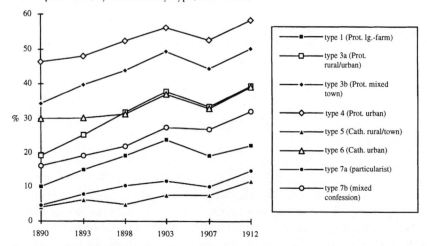

Comments: The SPD did consistently best in highly urbanized and Protestant seats, worst in rural Catholic and particularist seats.

Note: For clarity of presentation, type 2 seats are not shown.

ocratic votes was flat in Catholic cities (type 5 seats – on the constituency typology, see Appendix A). This was the period in which the VkD became active and undertook mass propaganda, and in which the Catholic workers' movement began to develop. But beginning in 1898, the SPD's growth curve in Catholic cities paralleled its upward trend in Protestant cities. From 1898, the SPD was able to recruit a growing share of Catholic urban votes. Second, the party's performance in rural seats dominated by large landholdings – where many agricultural labourers were located – dropped off after 1903. To summarize these two changes in the otherwise consistent trends, 1898–1903 was a period when the SPD became more of an urban workers' party, including, increasingly, Catholic workers; and when it lost any real potential it may have had to be a rural party. Both developments were related to the campaign issues and the SPD's own strategic choices, about which more is said in this chapter.

The SPD's general approach to election campaigning was utterly unlike the approaches of the other parties. Elections were part of the task of building a workers' movement and demonstrating its strength, and the party did not particularly intend to use the deputies it elected or the number of seats it won to bargain with the government, as the Catholic Centre did. This stance of opposition to the regime certainly appears not to have hurt the Social Democrats' election performance. Indeed, a basically negative policy seems to have struck a responsive chord.

'Negative Integration' and Electoral Politics

The sense of separateness embodied by the SPD was, like the strong sense of Catholic particularism, the product of conflict and past repression. Even after the anti-socialist law was permitted to lapse in 1890, the SPD's sense of isolation and its radicalism were continually reinforced by harassment at the hands of employers and officials. Laws regarding *lèse-majesté* were used to prosecute Social Democratic publicists and leafleteers. A social bias was apparent in court proceedings, in which witnesses could be discredited by their appearance or their Social Democratic connections; and perjury charges could be laid against witnesses who contradicted testimony given by police. After a brief lull during 1897–8, such partiality became more evident as Social Democracy advanced in strength and confidence.[2] This persistent 'class justice' led party propagandists to conclude: 'it is as if two different nations lived in the midst of [the same] people, who hardly understood each other any more.'[3]

Verbal aggressiveness by the party provided a chief outlet for the resentment and frustration experienced by politicized workers, by trade union organizers, and by SPD officials and writers. It also appealed to the broader frustrations of workers stuck in the 'ghetto' of low social mobility and a rigidly segmented society.[4] Propaganda substituted for class war, with unrelenting and bitter opposition to every aspect of the status quo serving to sum up the frustrations of the party's sympathizers and mobilize them for political action. The SPD press thrived on scandals that seemed to illuminate the decadence of established society and hinted at its decline. Prominent scandals included embezzlement by the conservative deputy Wilhelm Baron von Hammerstein, editor of the *Kreuzzeitung*, during 1895–6; the 'Twelve Thousand Marks Affair' of 1900, in which the CDI donated funds to the Ministry of the Interior for propaganda about a bill on 'industrial working conditions'; and a long series of attacks on the powerful Krupp family culminating in the 1902 exposure of Fritz Krupp's homosexuality. Polemics on these and more general subjects were psychologically satisfying to workers who otherwise felt powerless.[5]

The second aspect of the feeling of being 'two nations' was an internally directed impetus towards more and more intensive organization. The simple framework adopted by the party in Halle in 1890 evolved by the end of the decade into a more complex hierarchy. New regional structures developed, including special agitation districts for Reichstag campaigns that permitted regional planning and funding.[6] With the removal of the *Verbindungsverbot*, a certain centralization was possible, which was furthered by the organizational statutes adopted in Mainz in 1900 and Jena in 1905.[7] This increasing hierarchical or vertical differentiation was complemented by the horizontal differentiation of Social Democratic organizations for nearly every aspect of working, recreational, and cultural life. The 1890s saw the founding of Social Democratic choral groups, cycling clubs, gymnastic associations, hiking groups, libraries, and drama companies.[8] The purpose of these organizations, however, was not the propagation of any distinctively revolutionary or even working-class culture; one contemporary critic commented that 'the overwhelming majority of the songs customarily performed has little or nothing to do with the states of mind associated with the struggling proletariat.' What was proletarian about these organizations was not the content of their meetings, but the simple fact of their membership: they provided the working classes with substitutes for opportunities denied to them within the larger framework of society. As one historian has put it, they were 'conceived more as a counterweight to ... civic disabilities than as a crystallization of ... anti-capitalist sentiment.'[9]

The explosion in the party's size and structures in the 1890s made it the archetypal mass party of the new age. Observing this process, Robert Michels concluded that 'from a means, organization becomes an end,' so that the party proceeded endlessly with self-perpetuating activity. 'We now have a finely conservative party which ... continues to employ revolutionary terminology, but which in actual practice fulfils no other function than that of a constitutional opposition.'[10] Whatever else this did for the party, it helped create an integrated electoral grouping comparable or superior in its emerging unity to the Catholic grouping represented by the Centre Party.

The SPD's growth required its leaders to reconcile its role as a representative and inclusive social institution with its originally professed role as an agent of revolution. It did this during the 1890s through what Karl Kautsky explained as the concept of a 'revolutionary but not a revolution-making party.' According to 'Kautskyianism,' the SPD's role was to organize the working classes while waiting for an eventual revolution that would occur as a result of the internal development of capitalism. The party's policy amounted to 'revolutionary *attentisme.*' The idea that one day the revolution would come on its own served to reconcile the 'verbal radicalism' of the party with its simple 'organizational patriotism.'[11] The party preserved a radical allure, while being excused from actually organizing any revolutions: it was free to concentrate on simply building big-ger and bigger working-class organizations, mobilizing more and more voters. This synthesis, however contrived it may appear, was essential to the unity and growth of Social Democracy. There were revolutionary ele-ments on the left wing of the party that did not accept the compromise, notably Rosa Luxemburg and others who later broke away to form the German Communist Party; and there were those on the right wing whose concerns were purely pragmatic, and had not even any rhetorical use for Marxist theory. Kautskyianism, however, was the ideology of the domi-nant coalition, a partnership of intellectuals like Kautsky, trade union officials, and venerable and popular politicians like party leader August Bebel. Bebel himself summed up his whole party: politically a realist, ded-icated to his working-class constituency, not strong on Marxist theory. Max Weber paid Bebel a tribute, perhaps not condescendingly, as a genu-ine leader 'through temperament and purity of character, however mod-est his intellect. The fact that he was a martyr, that he never betrayed confidence in the eyes of the masses, resulted in his having the masses absolutely behind him.'[12]

Some historians have seen signs in the SPD's response to exclusion, in its dedication to organization, of a 'negative integration' of the working classes into German society. Excluded from influence in normal social relations – therefore not positively integrated – the working classes were instead organized, bureaucratized, compensated, and satisfied (the argument runs) by the Social Democratic 'subculture.' The subculture therefore blunted their frustrations and revolutionary potential and 'inte-grated' them indirectly. They were given a stake in society through their socialization and welfare funds; their desire for recognition was partially satisfied and therefore their radicalism was weakened; they were taught to be disciplined and wary of authority; and their material needs were allevi-ated. All of this helps explain why, when the opportunity came in 1918, Social Democrats displayed so little revolutionary zeal.[13] But is this the right question to ask about the pre-1914 party? Is 'integration' of any kind the best way to characterize its relationship to the dominant social sys-tem? The sociological functionalism of the 'negative integration' inter-pretation has been under attack for some time now.[14] If society is seen, as functionalism postulates, as a steady-state, machine-like system, then by definition almost any major institution will turn out not to threaten 'the' system. Surely the desire to undertake armed revolution is not the only kind of non-integration that matters. What is missing, from the histo-rian's point of view, is an appreciation for process, contingency, and the perceptions of the people involved in history. In elections, Social Democrats were not 'negatively integrated,' but were (even without revolution) challenging the government, the regime, and its allied parties for legitimacy and for hegemony in civil society.[15]

German politics was reshaped by perceptions of Social Democracy. Both the government and other parties were troubled by the success of the Social Democratic movement at mobilizing mass support behind ideas and approaches that delegitimized the state and the established parties. The extent to which politics came to be structured around status cleavages reflects at least partial success by Social Democracy in its challenge to the regime. The government did not want politics to articulate these particular cleavages; yet increasingly, all the non-socialist parties were compelled to respond to the SPD. The growing strength of Social Democracy forced conservatives out of cities, provided (alongside agrarianism) a serious electoral blow to German liberalism, undermined the Centre's claims to represent working-class Catholics, and made a mockery of the government's attempts at harassment and containment. This was a basic electoral, social, and ideological challenge, and, while it was not insurrectionary, that is not to say it was a stabilizing influence. The story in 1898 and 1903 was one of intense social and political change, and the rise of the SPD was the sharp edge of the changes that were overtaking German society.

Contemporaries, unlike present-day historians, had no idea where this would all end. The perception of a boundlessly growing and unstoppable socialist movement was fundamental to the attitudes of anti-socialists and deeply conditioned their gloom about democratic suffrages, parliamentarism, and the future. Others, of course, saw in it hope for change in German society. Nor was the Social Democratic movement quite as tightly knit as a historical analysis might suggest: even in 1914, the movement did not yet have the rigidity for which it became known in the Weimar years. During 1898–1903 the affiliates of the party – the choirs and bicycling clubs and all the rest – were small and dispersed, uneven in size and distribution, with large regional variations in intensity. Microcosmic studies, especially those of the Ruhr, emphasize fragmentation and division, between Catholic and Protestant, Polish and German, natives and in-migrants, village and city. No monolithic 'working class' existed at the turn of the century; rather, the SPD and its social, economic, and cultural 'parallel action groups' were in the process of *creating*, and not least by election agitation, a new and cohesive social grouping. While conditioned by socio-economic circumstances, this grouping became real and effective only to the extent that it was mobilized by specific mechanisms in specific circumstances into a cultural and political unit. It is appropriate that one recent work self-consciously abandons the terminology of 'subculture' in favour of the broader and less connotative 'social-cultural milieu.'[16]

The 1898 and 1903 elections helped develop mechanisms that defined and integrated the Social Democratic grouping. Since the elections of 1893, the party had officially repudiated the policy of appealing to the peasantry with a special agricultural program, which Georg von Vollmar and other southern German leaders advocated. With agrarianism and tariffs as major campaign issues, the party basically chose to exploit the polarization between rural producers and urban consumers by concentrating on the latter. If the penalty paid was the loss of the party's slight inroads into the peasant electorate, the bonus was two massive breakthroughs in urban and working-class environments. Unifying the SPD's anti-agrarian, anti-tariff stance was a wider emphasis on defence of popular rights and of popular incomes. Contrary to assumptions, the SPD appealed to voters (by whose numbers its strength was customarily measured) not solely on the basis of the 'verbal radicalism' of the preamble to the Erfurt program, but perhaps even more with a basic, limited, election platform whose main emphases were civil liberties and fair taxation. It is in this respect that Michels's comment on the SPD's character as a 'constitutional opposition' is relevant: the electoral appeal of Social Democracy was based concretely on advocacy of popular democratic rights, opposition to indirect taxes, opposition to military expenditures, and practice of populist mass politics.

Making a Social Grouping

Contemporaries, as well as some who have written about the history of the party, have characterized the SPD's electorate as proletarian – a term that connotes low-skilled male factory workers in heavy-industrial cities. This follows the party's practice of taking the SPD popular vote as a proxy for the 'true strength' of the socialist, industrial, urban working classes. How 'proletarian' was the SPD's support at the constituency level? Perhaps surprisingly, it is hard to tell. Identifying the 'working class' in any specific way raises a host of technical and definitional problems.[17] The most reliable social-economic index to be derived is the proportion of individuals in each constituency engaged in agriculture.[18] As will be shown, it is safe to say the SPD had little agricultural support, but the working non-agricultural population from which it did draw its support is difficult to characterize in general terms.

There are numerous indications that the SPD did not represent a homogeneous class of proletarians, but instead a diverse group of localized and sectionalized supporters. Skilled crafts, trades, and possibly salaried employees were prominent among the party leadership, membership, and electorate.[19] There is a legitimate point to a contemporary analyst's comment that 'a *socially unified* party of this strength is *probably impossible* under current conditions.' He asserted that 'workers in small-scale industry' provided 'the strongest group, perhaps the majority of the Social Democratic party; the big-industry workers are numerically hardly stronger in German Social Democracy than the middle-class elements.'[20] Much of German industry consisted of small workshops in small towns, while many of Germany's biggest enterprises were in the Polish and Catholic provinces of Silesia, the Rhineland, and Westphalia, where Social Democratic support was weak. Recent research tends to emphasize the extent to which the 'working class' was fractured along lines of region, confession, and – not least – gender. Accounting for such factors, according to one historian, 'reveals the necessity of disengaging the history of the working class from the language of class and the teleology of class consciousness.' The moments 'when the social identity of class overcame gender and regional or religious divisions' should be weighed against those when it did not.[21] In terms of the present study, perhaps we should not assume that Social Democratic success *represented* the unified strength of a social grouping. Perhaps there was no such underlying unity; perhaps the success of the party was that it effectively (if temporarily, superficially, and only on particular issues) bridged the basic divisions in the working classes. Perhaps class consciousness, to the extent it existed, was a product of organization, institutions, mechanisms – and Reichstag campaigns. Cleavages in society may be made by industrialization, but the corresponding cleavages in politics are made by politicians. Seen in this light, the making of the German working class was well advanced by 1898–1903.

Reichstag elections were the chief focal points of Social Democratic mass campaigning, and the party's preparations were exhaustive. Issues and strategy were debated by the national party congress in the year before elections were due. Thus the congress in Hamburg in October 1897 set the policy for the elections that came the following June. In his introductory speech, party leader Bebel emphasized the basic strategy of building the movement by maximizing votes: 'Reichstag elections have always been the most important event for us as a party of struggle, because they give us the opportunity to champion our ideas and demands with all energy, [and] because we can establish from the election result how the development of our party has [progressed] in the period that has passed; they have been and are for us the indicator of how far the party has pushed ahead on its march to victory.' Votes, not deputies, offices, or members, were the party's chief objective. But not every election was of equal importance, nor was organization the only ingredient for success. Issues and strategy mattered, as Bebel made clear. 'The next elections will be of ... decisive importance,' he also told the 1897 congress, because 'not just one single question calls the German people to the ballot box, but rather a whole series of questions of deeply serious and highly political nature. The next election campaign will be more intensive than any before.' Bebel outlined the importance of two major issues: the new trade treaties, whose form would be decided by the next Reichstag, and the threat to the Reichstag suffrage. He proposed a three-point checklist for giving support to non-SPD candidates in run-offs: first, they must support the Reichstag suffrage; second, they must oppose 'exception laws'; and third, they must oppose any new indirect taxes or tariffs. Bebel's strategy illustrates how the party's view of election issues and strategy depended on short-term issues and led to flexible electoral alliances for the run-offs. The party did not, in fact, base its election campaigns on the Marxist theory of the Erfurt program's preamble, nor exactly on the long-term policy of that programme's second part, but on the current issues facing the German nation, although it understood these current issues to be of far-reaching importance.[22]

The significance of elections for the party was made even clearer at the 1898 congress in Stuttgart, where the Reichstag campaign earlier in the year was reviewed. The report of the party leadership emphasized three related points. The first was that new state, provincial, and regional organizations had emerged to conduct the agitation and had been very successful. These operated on a wider scope than just a single constituency, coordinating propaganda and leafleting campaigns across a coherent area.[23] A second feature of the successful campaign had been the policy of standing candidates everywhere possible, regardless of the chances of winning, in order to give local party adherents the opportunity to cast their votes for the SPD. The report emphasized that victory was not to be measured in seats won, but in popular vote. Finally, a 'substantial portion' of the party's increased support was judged to have come 'from the circles of rural small-ownership and proletariat [agricultural wage labourers].' To the extent the party had received support from peasants, this was attributed to the party's opposition to militarism and taxes. The organizational extension and show of political strength achieved in 1898 had taken place alongside an election program that emphasized 'liberties.' Unfair taxes and wasteful military and naval policies were (the leadership stated) merely part of the general constitutional issue that the party had placed at the centre of its strategy. This was what had permitted it to broaden its support.[24]

For the 1903 elections, the conditions were similar, although this time the party decided (at its Munich conference in September 1902) to give greater relative weight to its anti-tariff and anti-agrarian policies, in a conscious effort to focus on the working classes and win them away from the other parties. The Centre was now considered the chief target. The review the next year in Dresden reported that this strategy had been successful: a 'powerful protest movement went through the Reich' objecting to the tariff law passed by the Reichstag majority and swelling the ranks of SPD voters. At the same time, the party's technical performance had been improved. The form of electoral organization remained the same as in 1893 and 1898, but the central office had succeeded in producing and distributing 632,800 copies of the national party's election declaration, as well as sending out some 6,000 sample pamphlets to local party organizations for reprinting and some 4,500 copies of the party policy handbook. Clearly this was a great organizational success, but equally clearly, in the minds of the party leaders, the correct choice of strategy and issues had been of fundamental importance.[25]

All of this was completely unlike the election campaigns of any other party. None of the others chose their issues and strategy so far ahead, planned so carefully, created such elaborate special-purpose organizations to conduct the campaigning, or distributed so much literature. For other parties, a short statement a few paragraphs in length, a few weeks before the elections, made up the platform; and backroom deals, a few handshakes and letters, made up the tactics. For the SPD, the platform was the subject of intense national-level debate as much as a year in advance. Both the party's long-term program and, above all, short-term issues and alliances were taken into consideration. Central policies for campaign tactics were established – whom to support and under what circumstances. Regional campaign organizations were created that could distribute tens of thousands of pamphlets in a day. At the turn of the century, the SPD was the epitome of 'agitation.'

Handbooks and pamphlets distributed to local propagandists concen-

trated on current issues and the business before the Reichstag.[26] More
theoretical approaches or those emphasizing revolutionary rhetoric were
few. These theoretical treatises included a brochure developing the
party's policy from, as it were, Marxist first principles, beginning with definitions of property and of the factors of production and proceeding to
surplus value, exploitation, and the increasing misery of the working
class. It then dealt with particular issues and the party program, and
appended the full text of the Erfurt program. In 1902 Kautsky and Bruno
Schoenlank published a new edition of the Erfurt program with commentary. This contained no major policy statements on tariffs or navalism,
thereby ignoring two of the biggest issues of the time in public opinion
and in the SPD's own electoral platform.[27] Theory was plainly an object of
reverence and an arcane field for the party's intellectuals, not the focal
point of its mass propaganda. A typical election platform started with just
a whiff of Marxism – a short reference to the bourgeois parties or propertied classes – then dealt with concrete issues. The party's practical,
popular-democratic emphasis is not surprising when one considers
contemporary estimates that only 10 per cent of the party members —
members, not voters – understood Marxist theory.[28]

The SPD press, like the party's election brochures, was theoretical in
inverse proportion to its circulation. The organs with larger audiences,
notably *Vorwärts*, were distinctly agitational. In 1898 the paper focused on
the Reichstag elections for months on end. It published the election declaration of the Reichstag caucus on the occasion of the fixing of the election date (27 April); tactical instructions to party organizers, who were
told on 19 April to keep the campaign peaceful by staying away from
opponents' meetings; lead articles on key issues throughout May ('Bread
Prices and Agrarians,' 'The Endangering of the Reichstag Suffrage');
and election news from individual constituencies. By early June, this
expanded to some three pages per issue concerning the elections – in
stark contrast to more staid governmental papers which relegated election news to the back pages.[29]

Even the party press, however, was primarily an organ for the SPD's
convinced supporters. Whereas the party press might reach a few hundred people in a community, and mass meetings would draw in a few
hundred up to a few thousand, intensive leafleting could reach many
more with the party's message – especially as leaflets had to be distributed
to homes and were often discussed there with the voters. In May 1898,
50,000 leaflets were distributed in Magdeburg, 100,000 in Breslau, and
181,000 in Hesse, as reported by *Vorwärts*. A police report in 1903 noted

that 40,000 leaflets were distributed in Elberfeld on a single day, and a newspaper reported 60,000 handed out in Düsseldorf one Sunday.[30] These mass-distribution leaflets were invariably short, usually a single side of a single sheet, and generally fell into one of three categories, all of which were heavily concerned with immediate issues and those contingent on what other parties did. First, there were leaflets attacking other parties; second, those refuting other parties' attacks; and third, those presenting the main issues as seen by the SPD, which reflected the decisions of the party congress.

Leafleting penetrated workers' lives with a coherent view of politics and issues that they might otherwise never have encountered. Consider the story told by Nikolaus Osterroth, a clay miner, who was eating lunch one April day in 1898 when an SPD election leaflet was passed through his window. Until that election, Osterroth had been a loyal Catholic and a Centre Party supporter. 'I began to read,' he later recalled. 'Sentence by sentence there was an indictment against the government and the bourgeois parties, against armament expenditures that had been driven to unbearable heights, against the insanely increasing debt burden of the empire, against the excess of the new naval appropriations that oppressed the people, and against the plundering of the masses by tariffs and indirect taxes.' The populist critique of the nation's elites gripped Osterroth's attention and aroused his fury at the inequitable economic treatment of people like himself. 'Suddenly I saw the world from the other side, from a side that up to now had been dark for me. I was especially aroused by the criticism of the tariff system and the indirect taxes. I'd never heard a word about them before! In all the Centre Party speeches they kept completely quiet about them. And why? Wasn't their silence an admission ..., a clear sign of a guilty conscience?'[31] Osterroth's recollection of that April day illustrates the way the SPD wove election issues together into a coherent package of 'popular rights' questions and questions of social-economic fairness, articulating the status cleavages in German society in a way that made instant sense to ordinary working people like Osterroth.

Also, as the above example illustrates, in these two elections it was particularly the Centre that drew the ire of SPD propagandists. This was in line with the growing competition between the two parties, the Centre's increasing accommodation with the government, and the strategy decided at the SPD's 1902 congress to draw Catholic workers away from the Centre by using the tariff issue. Leaflet after leaflet launched scathing attacks on the Centre for its governmentalism and contrasted its policies for workers unfavourably with those of the SPD. 'The Centre has *betrayed* the interests of the people,' declared one Social Democratic pamphlet in an effort to prove the SPD's superior populist credentials; 'once an opposition party, it has ... earned the name of a *government party*.' Another leaflet asked whom the German people should blame that the nation 'steered towards an adventure-policy' in world affairs, requiring 'huge amounts' of money; who was responsible for the erosion of the rights of the people; who could be thanked for the fact that 'sooner or later the tax screw will again be set in motion.' The Centre Party was blamed for all of this. Where it campaigned against the Centre, the SPD was determined to exploit the full advantage to be derived from the Centre's willingness to be associated, to a degree, with unpopular policies.[32]

The other parties, of course, were equally lively in their attacks on Social Democracy and compelled SPD propagandists to spend a certain portion of their energy in warding off damaging allegations and returning the discussion to, as they saw it, the proper issues. One systematic 1898 attack, *Was wollen die Sozialdemokraten?* (What do the Social Democrats want?), required a point-by-point response from the SPD printing presses. The attack had catalogued a whole series of the most common anti-socialist arguments: Social Democrats wanted to abolish private property, Social Democrats were atheists, Social Democrats were unpatriotic, Social Democrats undermined marriage and the family. To this extent, the party's Marxist rhetoric constituted an electoral disadvantage. The SPD's response was to deflect or deny these criticisms by saying abolition of property, atheism, and so on did not represent its formal policy, and to return to the issues it *was* campaigning about.[33]

Probably the single most damaging charge, to judge by the quantity of critical propaganda and the intensity of the SPD's response, was the allegation that the SPD was 'in league' with capitalists in welcoming the destruction of the peasantry and of the artisanal classes, that it was unresponsive to the concerns and demands of agriculture and trades.[34] The truth in this was that the agricultural question constituted a particular policy problem for the party. In the 1890s, official policy offered peasants 'cooperative organization of agricultural labour' and 'socialization of land,' which excited little support even among small peasant landowners and did not address their perception of their own needs and future. In line with party policy, SPD writers sometimes presented an unflattering picture of the peasantry as a declining and degraded class, and problems were only made worse when the tariff controversy led the party to promote cheap grain for consumers.[35] SPD mass propaganda for rural audiences, therefore, was especially careful and defensive. Its main concern was to refute the charges that the party was atheistic (sometimes trying to base socialism in biblical charity) and to emphasize the two program points held in common with peasant populists: anti-militarism and opposition to indirect taxes.[36]

Much SPD propaganda engaged in particular arguments with opposing parties, representing them as elitist protectors of wealth and privilege, and dismissing their claims about the philosophy and 'ultimate goals' of Social Democracy. The two related points hammered again and again by SPD propaganda were, first, defence of popular rights, and, second, fairness of the tax burden. 'What burdens does the Reich lay on the working people?' asked an 1898 pamphlet. 'Every year the tax collector comes into your house,' the leaflet told voters, but he skipped the homes of the rich. 'If you are an *enemy of the suffrage* and a *friend of new warships, new taxes,* and further *bread price increases,*' concluded the leaflet, 'then vote for the National Liberal, conservative, Centre man or anti-Semite.' In 1903 the tax-fairness aspect was even more prominent in much SPD propaganda. The government and its allies were blamed not only for the tariff, but for desiring to increase consumption taxes on beer and tobacco and to impose an army tax on those who were not serving in the armed forces. Militarism and navalism were criticized by drawing attention to their great cost, and then noting that 'for *Reich expenditures* the *lowest worker contributes as much as the millionaire.*' It was still claimed in 1903 that 'the Reichstag suffrage is heavily threatened.' In its main emphases, then, the SPD mass electoral propaganda of 1898 and 1903 showed a clear and consistent emphasis on the civic rights of the masses and the fairness of taxation policy.[37]

In election campaigns, the SPD willingly entered into direct engagement with the other parties over specific current issues and tried to represent a distinctive position. It chose, more often, more consistently, and more extremely than other parties, to present a forceful image of being a *Volkspartei* and of opposing the government. With the Centre's accommodation over key pieces of legislation, and left-liberal reluctance to engage in *Obstruktion* in the Reichstag, the SPD was better able to do this than any other party. But its rhetoric was no more extreme, no more apocalyptic, no more aggressive than that of other parties. Anti-Semitic diatribes; the calls to arms of Catholics against *Kulturkämpfer,* of Poles against Germans, of National Liberals and conservatives against 'enemies of the Reich'; the rousing calls for anti-socialist unity; the strident attacks by left liberals on the Agrarian League – all of these appeals used the language of battle and glory, of historic destiny and the need to strike down foes. This was a general aspect of the political culture, a widely adopted means of arousing more intense loyalty among partisan constituencies, an adaptation to urgent electoral needs. It was not a qualitatively different aspect of the image of the SPD. Social Democrats approached the electorate during 1898–1903 not as violent revolutionaries, but as populists advocating social justice. This left open the *possibility* for voters of any class or background to vote for the SPD on the basis of its advocacy of popular rights and fair taxation, limited only by the comparative effectiveness of other parties in mobilizing those other constituencies. The reality remained that the grouping most responsive to the SPD's appeal lay within the emerging social-cultural environment of the urban working classes, and this provided the basis for two electoral successes of proportions that had to seem alarming to other parties.

The Popular Response to Social Democracy

Neither the Social Democrats nor their opponents were in any doubt that the SPD was the chief winner in the general elections of both 1898 and 1903, and that this represented a triumph of mass election organization. The large and steady increase in the SPD vote, which occurred virtually across the board, in regions and constituencies of every type (apart from a few the party had not yet penetrated and those already mobilized to the maximum extent), was the most dramatic feature of these elections both to contemporaries and in retrospect. These victories were striking precisely because they were the culmination of a long series of electoral gains and because they occurred in spite of the growing anti-socialist stridency of the government and most of the other parties. As *Vorwärts* commented in 1898,

In no country in the world is socialism shown such malice ... In no other country is the socialist movement persecuted so uninterruptedly, so systematically, surely also so indiscriminately, as in Germany – and in no country has Social Democracy advanced so uninterruptedly and so systematically and has it taken on such a powerful growth.[38]

The spread of SPD electoral support was achieved by the party's policy of putting up as many candidates as possible, even hopeless candidates and candidates standing in multiple constituencies. The SPD did this more than any other party and took it as an expression of the party's organizational breadth. In June 1903 the party press boasted that the SPD with 395 candidacies in Germany's 397 seats easily led all other parties in this regard: the Centre (in second place) had 218, the National Liberals 187, the left liberals 119, the conservatives and anti-Semites 112 and 107 respectively. Seventy-three of the SPD candidacies were multiple candidacies, also more than any other party, and, indeed, among the other parties *only* the Centre (57), the anti-Semites (57), and the Poles (22) made significant use of the device of *Zählkandidaturen*.[39]

The use of multiple candidacies was one of a number of 'populist' features of the SPD's campaigns. As discussed in chapter 2, the use of multiple candidacies was a key feature of the new, mass style of campaigning. Candidates were put up even where they had no chance of success, because the votes they won would inflate the party's national totals and increase its claim to be a party of the people. It was clearly implied or stated in campaign literature that only a workers' party could represent workers – another populist idea, unlike the old premise of *Honoratiorenpolitik* that a wise community leader could represent all people in the community. And the issues upon which the SPD focused, issues of defending popular rights and opposing unpopular taxes, tariffs, and military expenditures, were populist issues oriented towards the rights, feelings, and pocketbook of the common man. While quite different in many respects from right-wing populism, this, too, was the cultivation of the image of a 'people's party.'

By following a populist electoral program and strategy, the SPD extended its geographic bases of strength, establishing nuclei of agitation and voting support that grew steadily during the 1890s. By the turn of the century, the SPD was Germany's only truly nationwide party, contesting nearly all constituencies, mounting campaigns in all regions, even breaching the confessional barrier to a perceptible extent.[40] It was also the only party to exhibit so large and so steady an electoral advance: from 19.7 per cent of the popular vote in 1890, when the anti-socialist law lapsed, to 23.3 per cent in 1893, to 27.2 per cent in 1898. The 1898 figure represented a breakthrough in a number of ways. First, the SPD now received not only more votes than any other single party, but nearly as many as any other major party *grouping*: even all the *Kartell* parties together polled only 28.0 per cent. Secondly, the SPD had broadened its support significantly into some new seats, spreading outward from regional urban strongholds into surrounding towns and villages. And thirdly, the SPD had attained levels of support that put it in second place in more constituencies than ever before, edging out (most commonly) liberals to enter the run-offs.[41]

Yet if 1898 was a minor breakthrough, 1903 was a major one. The 'three-million victory' of 16 June 1903 dismayed the government's allies and left Social Democrats elated. They identified three jewels in their crown of victory: Berlin, because a particularly strong joint effort by the non-socialist parties of the capital, led by the FVP, had been defeated ('revenge for the treacheries of Eugen Richter'); Essen, where the kaiser's friend, Krupp, had beaten the workers' party in the previous two elections, but which was now an SPD seat; and Saxony, where twenty-two of twenty-three seats went to the SPD ('Saxony red! ... The *Kartell* of "order" smashed to pieces ...').[42] The 1903 victory vindicated the party's strategic choices, including its concentration on separate organization and candidacies in all constituencies. By not becoming dependent on allies, even by alienating potential allies and losing run-offs, the SPD had built up its popular strength to the point where it could now frequently win by its own unaided effort on the first ballot, or perhaps on the second by an intensive feat of voter mobilization to draw out a few more SPD voters. This process was exemplified in the national capital, where in Berlin II, Berlin III, and Berlin V the SPD won with 55–60 per cent of the first-ballot vote, whereas in 1898 it had had to fight run-offs and, indeed, had won only one of these three seats.[43] Other aspects of the victory are equally illuminating, particularly the breakthrough in Saxony.

The Saxon victory of 1903 was exceptional. The SPD had never won so great a proportion of the votes in the state or so many seats before, and never did so again, even though across the rest of the Reich its performance generally improved after 1903.[44] While the SPD campaign against the tariff and in defence of the suffrage had been successful among the politicized workers of Saxony, political commentators were agreed that the difference there was provided by the state politics of the preceding years. The governmental parties paid the price at the polls in the Reichstag election of 1903 for a number of state scandals, including particularly the regressive Saxon suffrage revision of 1896. Since Saxon elections involved polling a third of the seats every two years, in 1898 little of the state had any experience of the new Prussian-style three-class suffrage.[45] By 1901 the entire state had, and by 1903 the SPD campaign against it was in high gear. The Reichstag elections provided an effective means to express protest using an equal suffrage; and the SPD, with its record of vigorous rhetorical defence of the democratic suffrage, was the main recipient of the state's popular protest vote.[46] Bülow commented that it was 'highly regrettable' that Saxon voters had shown their 'bad temper' by voting for the SPD, and that the answer lay in subordinating criticism of the government and confessional strife to the fight against Social Democracy.[47]

The SPD successes of 1898 and 1903 showed that the Protestant urban working classes, above all, had been solidly won by the party. This is not quite the same as saying the SPD was strong only in Germany's big cities; by 1903, substantial Social Democratic support could be found in essentially all but purely rural areas. Support for Social Democracy was highest by far in large Protestant cities (type 4 constituencies – see Appendix A concerning the constituency typology, and figure 11, p. 210). In such constituencies, the party climbed from 47 per cent of the popular vote in 1890 to 57 per cent in 1903. With 34 deputies elected from such large cities, the party received about 40 per cent of its parliamentary representation.[48] This was followed by Protestant mixed urban-rural environments (3a and 3b), where SPD support was lower but increasing on a similar curve to that in the large cities, and slightly closing the gap. The party did penetrate, that is to say, environments where one small city was a centre for a predominantly rural seat, and where towns predominated over both city and country (type 3b, a pattern typical of portions of Saxony, where the SPD was particularly strong). The spread of the SPD into these less-urban seats also reflects the progress of urbanization: the constituencies themselves were changing and becoming more urban. Altogether these three environments (4, 3a, 3b) containing substantial Protestant urban populations accounted for 77 per cent of the seats won by the SPD in 1898 and 74 per cent of those won in 1903. In large Catholic cities (type 6), the SPD advanced much slower, though it still advanced. While the confessional barrier, on the one hand, and the strength of the Centre and the VkD, on the other, clearly hindered the party, the SPD did gain importantly on the Centre in Catholic cities by 1912, steadily winning more and more Catholic city voters to its cause.[49] It also did better in Catholic cities than it did in rural environments of any type, Protestant or Catholic.

The question of whether confessional or social-economic factors had a stronger effect on the party's vote is extremely difficult to answer, because these variables are interrelated. The Catholic areas of the German Empire were also, overall, much more rural, much less industrialized, than the Protestant ones; the confessional and social-economic factors worked together in hindering the SPD vote in these regions. Given that the SPD did badly in Catholic rural areas, how much of this was on account of Catholic culture, and how much was a result of the ruralness of the seats? The best way to answer such a question is to put all the variables together into a multiple regression; the coefficients and signifi-cance of the variables can then be compared to see which had a greater effect on the outcome, that outcome being the percentage support for the SPD.

These different factors affecting support for the SPD – working-class population, urban demographic structure, confession – are compared with each other and with regional and other variables in the multiple regression presented in table 12. The most highly significant predictor of SPD support was the confessional factor – the greater the percentage of Catholics, the lower the percentage of SPD support – and this increased in magnitude and significance during 1898–1903. Looking back on figure 11 (p. 210), we can see that this was likely the result of the dropping off and stagnation of support in Catholic rural seats (type 5), which were by far the majority of Catholic seats. In these elections, when the SPD solidi-fied its urban support and made some inroads into the Catholic working class, it lost any chance of further penetrating more rural Catholic envi-ronments; also, the increasingly anti-socialist counter-propaganda of the Centre, the church, and other Catholic organizations was most effective in the rural areas. Also very significant – and of greater magnitude (i.e., larger coefficients) – were the interrelated variables concerning percent-age of rural population, size of constituency, and percentage employed in agriculture. Across different constituencies, the SPD did better as the pro-portion of rural residents was lower, as the total population of the constit-uencies was larger (as it was in the great cities), and as fewer people were employed in agriculture. The coefficients for these variables are larger than those for the Catholic variable; in other words, the variation of SPD support from one seat to another was more greatly affected by differences in demographic and economic structure than by differences in confes-sional structure. Agricultural communities, rural communities, and small constituencies posed a greater barrier than the confessional factor by itself. The coefficient for size of constituency declined steadily over time, implying that the party's support was steadily spreading outside the larg-est centres.

Table 12 also indicates a number of regional deviations from the pre-dicted Social Democratic share of the vote. The regional variables show that SPD support was also conditioned by regional political cultures, and was not a simple function of the statistical make-up of the population. In six regions, the party's vote was noticeably less than would be predicted based on the confessional and social-economic considerations alone; and in three regions, it was stronger. Distinct factors of regional politics and

TABLE 12
Multiple Regression for the Social Democratic Popular Vote, 1890–1912

	Var. type	1890	1893	1898	1903	1907	1912
% Catholic	C	**−0.0786**	**−0.0957**	**−0.150**	**−0.187**	**−0.154**	**−0.174**
		−4.39	−5.90	−9.09	−12.0	−10.6	−10.7
% Employed in agriculture	C	**−0.202**	**−0.207**	**−0.203**	**−0.246**	**−0.227**	**−0.310**
		−3.01	−3.34	−3.25	−4.02	−4.13	−5.29
% Rural	C	**−0.241**	**−0.233**	**−0.248**	**−0.219**	**−0.227**	**−0.200**
		−5.03	−5.20	−5.43	−4.93	−5.72	−4.73
Constituency size	C	**8.84**	**7.58**	**5.34**	**4.48**	**3.42**	**2.37**
		4.25	4.60	3.98	4.39	4.63	3.89
Prov of E. Prussia	D	**−5.51**	**−6.56**	*−2.04*	*−3.96*	**−8.81**	**−13.0**
		−2.24	−2.86	−0.886	−1.76	−4.35	−6.02
Prov. of W. Prussia	D	*−5.32*	**−6.73**	**−10.4**	**−9.68**	**−10.5**	**−11.8**
		−1.90	−2.63	−3.91	−3.82	−4.58	−4.86
Pomerania	D	**−7.80**	**−5.25**	**−10.5**	**−11.5**	**−10.4**	**−12.77**
		−2.82	−2.10	−4.15	−4.68	−4.66	−5.40
Posen	D	**−6.07**	**−7.71**	**−10.1**	**−11.2**	**−11.7**	**−13.7**
		−2.23	−3.11	−3.96	−4.54	−5.30	−5.89
Westphalia	D	**−8.98**	**−10.8**	**−12.3**	**−10.2**	**−9.63**	**−10.8**
		−3.67	−4.74	−5.31	−4.51	−4.73	−4.95
Rhineland	D	**−6.31**	**−10.0**	**−10.1**	**−8.95**	**−10.1**	**−11.2**
		−3.37	−5.69	−5.72	−5.19	−6.37	−6.75
Kingdom of Saxony	D	**9.76**	**9.62**	**7.63**	**11.9**	**4.39**	**4.01**
		4.27	4.52	3.56	5.65	2.31	1.99
Thuringia	D	**7.64**	**13.6**	**12.8**	**9.69**	**6.71**	**9.65**
		2.70	5.16	4.82	3.72	2.85	3.86
Alsace-Lorraine	D	*−2.01*	*4.66*	**5.71**	**4.85**	**4.85**	**8.14**
		−0.768	1.89	2.33	2.02	2.21	3.52
Adjusted R^2		.712	.754	.782	.812	.815	.818
$F(19/377\ DF)$		52.5	64.9	75.7	91.2	92.6	94.9

Source: Multiple regression based on the author's constituency-level Reichstag election data; see Appendix C. Independent variables which did not show significant t-ratios at the 5 per cent level in at least three elections are not shown.

Note: The dependent variable is the percentage of the vote for the Social Democratic Party. In the body of the table, the regression coefficient is on the top, and the t-ratio beneath (377 DF); significant coefficients are shown in bold, and the insignificant ones in italics. (See Appendix D for explanations of terms and abbreviations.)

culture lie behind these deviations. East Prussia and Pomerania, two of the areas of weakness for Social Democracy, were regional strongholds of the German Conservatives. In these places, the opposition party was historically the left liberals. The SPD appeared to have difficulty breaking into this regional political culture. The other regions where Social Democracy was relatively weak all involved regions of either 'national' or confessional polarization of politics. West Prussia and Posen were Polish provinces where the 'national' polarization of politics remained dominant, and such Polish regions were among the worst for the SPD anywhere in Germany. The SPD's appeals to the Polish working classes have been judged as 'completely hopeless.'[50] And it is interesting that the Rhineland and Westphalia appear in the table as weak points for Social Democracy. This finding confirms other studies that indicate SPD support in this part of Germany lagged behind what was achieved in places of comparable confessional and social-economic structure elsewhere. One of the problems for the SPD in the Rhineland and Westphalia may have been the *mixture* of confessions, which contributed to a longer persistence of confessionally based politics than in seats that were predominantly of a single confession. There is evidence from regional studies of the Ruhr, for example, that confessional divisiveness augmented the anti-clerical appeal of National Liberals to Protestant workers, thus entrenching a Centre–National Liberal polarization that made it difficult for a party not greatly concerned with confessional issues to establish itself.[51] Politics based on sectional ethnic conflict created a political culture in which the SPD found little support.

As for regions of unexpected Social Democratic strength – not explainable, that is to say, merely on the basis of the urban or economic structure – table 12 reveals the strength of the SPD in the geographic middle of the German Empire, namely in Thuringia and in the nearby Kingdom of Saxony, areas generally noted for widespread artisanal production in towns rather than for heavy industry. The Saxon protest vote of 1903 shows up in the table as an especially large coefficient for that year. Alsace-Lorraine, on the other hand, became a relative Social Democratic stronghold only in 1898, as the party made breakthroughs into a pattern of politics previously dominated by liberals and particularists. Since Alsace-Lorraine was largely Catholic, the positive coefficient here likely indicates that the SPD did a better job attracting Catholics in Alsace-Lorraine than would otherwise be predicted by the Reich-wide regression equation.

Although the SPD did less well in rural areas, this does not mean it attracted no rural support. By 1898 the SPD was a large party and represented many diverse elements. A substantial number of votes were cast for the party in local environments that were not exceptionally urban nor industrial, by people who, though possibly working-class, were unlikely to have been industrial proletarians.[52] In 1898 more than a quarter of SPD votes were cast in communities of fewer than two thousand people, and nearly half came from communities of fewer than ten thousand. Small towns in agricultural regions provided some 14 per cent of the votes received by Social Democracy. In Mecklenburg and in northeastern Prussia, as well as in peasant areas of Hesse, central Württemberg, and the northern Palatinate, the SPD made important breakthroughs in 1898, in some cases doubling or more than doubling its share of the vote and entering run-offs where it never had before. Apart from Mecklenburg and some of the eastern Prussian constituencies, this increased support came from regions surrounding SPD urban strongholds: the highest small-town votes for the SPD were found in the vicinity of Hamburg, Hanover, Berlin, Magdeburg, Halle, Leipzig, Chemnitz, Dresden, Breslau, Danzig, Königsberg, Munich, Stuttgart, Nuremberg, and Frankfurt am Main. Overall, the failure to break through into deep agricultural areas, especially in Bavaria, was a disappointment to SPD leaders in 1898 and helped convince them to give up on any ambitious agrarian program.[53] The attempt to cultivate some agrarian populism for the SPD, epitomized by Georg von Vollmar, was effectively abandoned. This was made clear when party ideologue Karl Kautsky issued *The Agrarian Question* in 1899, which returned to the Marxist orthodoxy that peasants were economically inefficient and would be eliminated, and that the SPD had no interest in promoting or protecting the interests of agriculture.[54] Parallel to this conclusion, the SPD chose during 1902–3 to emphasize its opposition to agricultural tariffs in order to win the votes of urban consumers. As the party turned from an agrarian program and fought bitterly against the 1902 tariff law, any advance in agricultural constituencies was checked.

The SPD's footholds in agrarian Germany stagnated in 1903, and a large number were almost eliminated in 1907. In table 12, the negative coefficient for the percentage of the population employed in agriculture becomes greater in magnitude and more significant in 1903, and remains that way until 1912. The SPD's 'three-million victory' of 1903 confirmed and strengthened its non-agricultural base of support. At the same time, the internal unity of other parties in rural Germany was greater in 1903 than in 1898 because of the completion of the tariff debates, the isolation of agrarian extremists, and the continued weakening of independent anti-Semitic and agrarian campaigns, not to mention anti-socialist propaganda. This unity was greater still in 1907, when a 'national' campaign greatly hurt the SPD outside its core areas and helped its opponents. This was most dramatic in the large-landownership rural areas of the Baltic region, where the fall of the SPD vote in 1907 was not subsequently made up. In constituencies like Rastenburg-Gerdauen-Friedland and Ragnit-Pillkallen (both in East Prussia), the SPD had broken through during 1898–1903 with 19–24 per cent of the vote, compared to 4 per cent or less previously, only to see this collapse in 1907 to 12–13 per cent and not recover before the war. The German Conservative hold on these constituencies increased.

Given the setbacks in some rural areas, it might have been that the SPD's rapid growth was nearing a limit; but the graph in figure 11 (p. 210) shows a party still improving in 1912 in every category of seat. The regression in table 12 (p. 228) shows a party that was concentrated in urban areas, but evidence shows it was not shut completely out of rural ones. And there were particular regions like the Rhineland and Westphalia, the Polish territories, and the east in general where the party was disproportionately weak and could grow in the longer term, if the existing regional political culture were to be undermined. Only a simplistic, functionalist view – asserting that the SPD mobilized only Protestant 'proletarians' and that all such had been mobilized by 1912 (both questionable assertions) – would hold that the Social Democratic movement was hitting some kind of ceiling in Wilhelmine Germany. The political situation seemed rather to bear out Friedrich Engels's remark in 1895 that 'German workers ... showed the comrades in all countries how to make use of universal suffrage.' At that time, Engels had predicted that if the progress continued, 'by the end of the century we shall ... grow into the decisive power in the land, before which all other power will have to bow, whether they like it or not.'[55] The 1898 and 1903 elections had come close to bearing out Engels's vision. If the other parties did not want to work with Social Democracy, then fighting it was going to have to become their chief preoccupation.

Reactions to Success

The SPD press summed up the 1903 triumph in language that mocked opponents' attacks on the party and its policy:

Republicans now represent almost all [princely] seats of the most monarch-rich country in the world; only Potsdam and Schwerin are still barely preserved from humiliation ... We barbarians hold the red flag above the most meaningful centres of science and art: Berlin, Leipzig, Munich, Halle, Königsberg, etc. We deadly enemies of militarism rule amidst the swarming barracks of the cannon-state. We opponents of the adventurist world policy enjoy the trust of the Hansa cities. We destroyers of religion penetrate even into the vestments of clericalism ... In short, all the cultural centres of Germany and all the cultural elements are ours.[56]

If Social Democracy consisted of 'barbarians,' *Vorwärts* was saying, then Germany itself consisted of barbarians.

Maximilian Harden, the essayist, made a similar point. He reflected on the public attention given to the kaiser, his court, his monuments and ceremonies; and contrasted this to the very different Germany revealed by the election results. Events were staged where workers professed their loyalty to the kaiser, and the kaiser thundered (as he did in December 1902) against the Social Democrats: 'you, as honourable men, should and must have nothing more to do with such people, not let yourselves be led around by them anymore!' Yet six months later, the cities where he made such speeches voted overwhelmingly for the SPD. Concluded Harden: 'The masses [take] pleasure in the kaiser spectacle. But, when things get serious, they vote Social Democrat!'[57] The reality was summed up for Harden in Hamburg in 1903 when a crowd of Social Democrats celebrated the election results across from the huge new memorial to Wilhelm I. The crowd mocked the fine society due to assemble for the North German Derby the next day: '*Heil Dir im Siegerkranz*,' they sang, 'who in our old homeland is sending all these Reds to the Reichstag?'[58]

The scale of the SPD victory badly undermined the old argument that Social Democracy was a movement of a tiny minority of 'agitators' who whipped up voters with demagoguery. Much criticism of the universal suffrage hinged on the way a well-organized 'minority' like Social Democrats was thought to 'tyrannize' the 'majority.' According to this view, Social Democrats won victories only because their fanatical minority turned out in greater proportion than the majority of voters. Germany's non-socialist notable-politicians looked to an elusive silent majority to crush the Social Democrats, if only they, too, could be mobilized to vote. Past successes in 'national' elections, notably 1887, when increased turnouts corresponded to increased governmental support, seemed to bear out such an interpretation. But in 1903, the huge SPD success had been achieved with an increase in voter turnout, which now stood at 76 per cent, nearly as high as it had ever been in the history of the Reich. The party press remarked, '... our glorious victory is not to be traced somehow back to the indifference of middle-class "non-voters."'[59]

The non-socialist press therefore groped for explanations and reassurance. The nationalist *Rheinisch-westfälische Zeitung* noted the day after the main ballot that 'the growth in Social Democratic votes is nothing short of colossal' and joined many other papers and politicians in blaming this on the government's slackness and lack of positive direction.[60] A few days later, however, the paper had recovered its composure and published a denial that any 'swing to the left' had occurred at all. On closer analysis, the 'pale pink colour of the left liberals of all three species' had simply faded away into 'the crass red of the Internationals.' It was, therefore, no crisis at all, except for left liberalism. The paper then went on to emphasize that the gains made by the Poles necessitated a further sharpening of the anti-Polish campaign.[61] The *Kreuzzeitung* also tried to downplay the SPD gains. In 1898 it had commented 'that Social Democracy did indeed achieve successes' but comforted itself with the claim that these were 'not of the scope hoped for' by the party. In 1903 it, too, argued that the real losers were the left liberals and noted the 'complete dissolution' of the agrarians and anti-Semites and the victories of the Centre. Buried deep in the article was the fourth observation, that 'without any doubt Social Democracy achieved the most powerful successes.'[62]

Predictably, the SPD's success increased right-of-centre doubts about the Reichstag suffrage. The *Kölnische Zeitung* observed in 1898 that Social Democratic victories damaged the reputation and respectability of the Reichstag and of politics in general. As the paper phrased it sarcastically, 'in the big cities the conviction is gaining ground that any old cigar-worker can necessarily, through the consecration of election, achieve the ability to understand and represent the interests of a prosperous community life.' The middle classes had, the paper argued, to reassert their leadership for the good of society and could no longer 'wait for a remedy from the government.' The SPD was getting weaker (the paper gave no evidence of this); the *bürgerliche Parteien* could defeat it. Other papers agreed: the suffrage was the problem, and the non-socialist parties were too scared of the masses to do anything about it.[63] However, in spite of the bourgeois grumbling, the day had, indeed, arrived when 'any old cigar-worker' could make a mark on German politics. At root, what the conservative and right-wing liberal press objected to was a fundamental change in German politics and society, and one that was irrevocable.

The disillusionment and yearning for action on the right was matched by even greater aimlessness in the middle and left-liberal press. Here columnists observed simply that the 1903 result 'definitely disappoints but does not surprise.' As to the causes, the *Berliner Tageblatt* stated rather fatalistically that 'with the workers' battalions ... grow today, almost parallel, the battalions of Social Democracy.' The left-liberal press, however, like the rest of the non-socialist press, refused to believe that the SPD vote totals actually represented adherents of the party's doctrines. The 'veering to the left' represented by nearly a third of the Reich being threatened by the SPD in the 1903 run-offs would be of 'fateful importance for the continuance of our state order,' *except* that 'one knows perfectly well that among the Social Democratic–voting masses of the electorate all those countless generally dissatisfied are to be found' who only wanted to express 'the sharpest protest' against government policies. The results were explained as the consequence of 'imponderables' in the public mood. In their horror at the extremism and barbarism they thought Social Democracy represented, they perhaps overlooked the fact that much of the SPD's agitation was perfectly gauged for the role of a legitimate populist and social-protest party – a role no liberal party understood adequately.[64]

The deficiency of non-socialist analysis of Social Democracy reflected fundamental assumptions, prejudices, and mental blockages. In 1903 arch-conservative Paul Mehnert of Saxony rushed to write a letter to the chancellor the day after his home state voted overwhelmingly for the SPD. For once the SPD's victory could *not* be blamed on the 'fragmentation' of the other parties, for 'the unification of the anti-socialist parties' had been realized almost everywhere. But Mehnert had no better explanation and wrote vaguely of 'a never-before-experienced shortage of candidates'– respectable figures were too disillusioned to run for office – and about bitter divisions engendered by the tariff debates, Protestant hostility aroused by concessions to the Centre, and insufficient press censorship that had permitted scandals to be sensationalized and monarchical loyalty to be undermined. Bülow's reply was vaguer still, attributing the results to the 'ill humour' of the voters, the fickleness of the masses, and the adverse effects of constant niggling criticism of the government by all the parties. The Württemberg envoy got the same impression of the chancellor's beliefs: the election results included 'a plentiful dross of general dissatisfaction.'[65] Statements by Bülow and other leaders indicate that they did not perceive the social and political changes that lay behind the SPD's success, above all the rise of mass politics and the effectiveness of the party's populist appeal.

In Essen, the Krupp firm conducted a special inquiry into the loyalty of its employees in order to determine whether they were responsible for the SPD victory there in 1903. Using poll-level voting results, a company brochure argued that areas where Krupp workers lived had swung less towards the SPD than other areas; the firm was exonerated, its workers (relatively) loyal. The blame was laid 'at least in large part' on 'circles of the population ... which have nothing to do with the work force' of the Krupp plants, but came instead from new arrivals in the constituency, masses of shiftless, dissatisfied, rootless labourers. The company argued that such elements had migrated to Essen in the prosperous years of the 1890s expecting good wages, and then, disillusioned in the slump of 1901, had turned to Social Democracy. The theory, however comforting for the firm, had one large drawback: even the twenty-one polling areas unusually thickly settled with Krupp *Kolonien*, in which eleven thousand enfranchised Krupp workers lived, voted in equal parts for the Centre, the 'national parties,' and the SPD.[66] Even Krupp's employees were one-third Social Democrats.

In the last analysis, the government and its supporters had no clear idea of who voted for Social Democrats, or why, and could merely observe (as Bülow did in his memoirs for 1898) that elections 'brought fresh progress to the Social Democrats.' There was little more to be said. But the chancellor reflected another current of opinion when he wrote that the 1903 results stirred him to action:

To me it was less the Socialist gains which seemed significant, than the belief, now gaining ground all over Germany ... that the Socialist movement could never be brought to a standstill, but must roll ahead like some elemental force – like the sea or an avalanche. I therefore sought an opportunity for a reckoning with the socialists.

In other words, whether or not they understood the SPD, leaders like Bülow were increasingly convinced that something had to be done about it. His action, in the first place, was an aggressive series of speeches against Social Democracy in the Reichstag in December 1903, designed to give leadership and 'enthusiasm' to the anti-socialist cause. The speeches were published by the well-connected nationalist firm of Mittler and Son. Bülow's new approach reflected a belief that the SPD could be resisted neither by repression (as in the 1880s) nor by passivity, by leaving the fight to the established party organizations (as in the 1890s), but that a new offensive was necessary to engage the SPD with 'intellectual weapons.'[67] Elsewhere Bülow commented that the SPD could not be defeated, and that instead the purpose of anti-socialist efforts was to neutralize it by separating intellectuals and liberals from it, and by limiting its parliamentary strength.[68]

Anti-socialist propaganda had frequently exhibited a rather crude form of condescension, corresponding self-evidently to the assumption that, since only manipulation could lead people to Social Democracy, only a manipulative appeal to loyalty was required to win them back. One pamphlet from the early 1890s illustrates this perfectly. The reader, addressed intimately as *Du*, is asked whether he really believes 'property is theft.' 'Is that the talk of a sensible person, and does your heart agree? Now listen, you must do your best for your homeland that has been dear to you from your ancestors onward ...' If you believe in 'joy in the things with which you work' and 'joy in saving for you and your own,' then 'you are no Social Democrat.' Such soft and clumsy approaches remained standard ones for anti-socialist publishers; in 1898 one finds a nationalist publisher distributing 'In the Pub at Peterwitz, or, What Mayor Großmann Thinks of Social Democrats' ('certainly the most *popularly* written brochure in the fight against Social Democracy,' emphasized the publisher). In the pamphlet's storybook format, a local boy goes off to the big city and comes back a Social Democrat, claiming that 'the city people have made me smart.' The village authority figure, Großmann, sternly reminds him that the SPD opposes religion, inheritance, and families, and wants to turn everything into cities and factories. The chastised local son repents, and the fatherly mayor tells him, 'You are a child of Peterwitz; I didn't think it was in your blood to be a Social Democrat.'[69]

Another effort in 1898 and 1903 was 'The Worth of Social Democracy for the Workers: Experiences of a Comrade Who Was Active in the Party.' While this assumed the form of a popular confession, it was perhaps a little more sophisticated than most predecessors. Again a story format was adopted, telling how the author became a Social Democrat and once again stressing the malign and alien influence of the city. Young and alone in Berlin, the first-person narrator was drawn in by a socialist circle and indoctrinated ceaselessly with slogans, political discussions, and criticism of the state, until his faith in God was undermined and his respect for humanity turned into grumbling. 'Out of the pious, happy upper Franconian a dissatisfied person was made' – probably a realistic representation of how non-socialists understood the process. This state of dissatisfaction was then used by unscrupulous, self-interested SPD agitators to manipulate him, to get him to give them money, to get him into trouble with the police. In the end, they abandoned him. The moral of the tale was that the party spread only hate, undermined everything happy or honourable, and lined its pockets with the money of workers. The publishers commented that this leaflet was well suited to mass door-to-door distribution 'to fight [the SPD's] methodical arousal of hatred among the voting masses with the same means.' It drew favourable reviews from the right-wing press.[70]

Publications such as these were numerous in the 1890s and early 1900s. Considering the reference to 'voting masses' as well as the timing of their publication, they were clearly intended to influence material for election campaigns. Assuming that common folk were humble, such publications treated them with condescension. But many publications abandoned the storybook formats, the dramatic dialogues or exhortations to readers to be loyal, and took on a serious and methodical polemical style. Not all of these were for mass distribution, but they reflect increasingly the desire to *argue* against Social Democracy, to *prove* it wrong, to employ the sort of 'intellectual weapons' to which the chancellor referred, to *persuade* workers and others to be loyal. In this they implicitly accepted the awareness of the working-class audience and the fact that it would make its own judgments about its self-interest. The trend of getting 'real' workers to denounce the SPD, instead of using fictional dialogues and authority figures, continued during 1897–8 when Theodor Lorentzen ('a worker in the imperial dockyard at Kiel') published no fewer than four books as part of his effort to explain to his 'fellow workers' the true nature of SPD agitation and the emptiness of the promise of a *Zukunftsstaat* (state of the future). Lorentzen, whose circular suggested employers distribute his books to their workers, reiterated the standard argument that 'nowhere is such a terrorism exercised as that [coming] from Social Democratic comrades [themselves].' The real SPD was 'a great number of agitators ... who were never workers' and only wanted to stir up trouble.[71]

There were, increasingly, more factual and 'scientific' attempts to refute Social Democratic ideas. In 1893 Henry Axel Bueck of the CDI wrote to the government about SPD speeches in the Reichstag concerning their 'dreamed-of *Zukunftsstaat*' and said the CDI had decided 'to initiate mass distribution of those debates' as a way to bring down to earth the unreal promises of Social Democracy. This was followed during 1894–5 by leaflets like 'The Heaven of Social Democracy in Dream and Reality' and 'What Our Workers Can Expect from the Social Democratic *Zukunftsstaat*,' which (according to the publishers) showed 'in figures, in the most visual form and *in* the *language* of the *simple man*,' the 'emptiness' of Social Democracy's 'many slogans.' Another work of the same period also tried the resort to cold, hard facts, asking 'Are the Many Incorrect Statistical Assertions in Bebel's Chief Work Lies or Blunders?'[72]

For the 1903 elections, Admiral Tirpitz endorsed H.F. Bürger's *Social*

Facts and Social Democratic Teachings, which sought to use economic statistics to disprove predictions of Marxist theory, such as the decline of small business. Tirpitz asked if it appeared advisable 'to interest independent circles in securing wider distribution of this work in strata of the population that are infected by Social Democracy.' By 'independent circles,' he evidently had in mind something like the CDI campaign of 1894. Another enthusiast of the same work wrote to the minister of the interior suggesting indelicately that a circular signed by 'a few district administrators, *Landräte*, and mayors' could be sent around Prussian local officialdom to enable the latter privately to arrange orders for their jurisdictions. In fact, though the Prussian bureaucracy helped order approved election leaflets for the governmental parties in election campaigns, this kind of general political endorsement, in writing, of a general work was not done.[73]

Pamphlets alone did not constitute the kind of systematic mass agitation which nationalists advocated. No anti-socialist materials could be effective without the organization, funds, and volunteers to distribute them effectively, which is precisely what the governmental parties lacked in comparison with the SPD. The *Rheinisch-westfälische Zeitung* stressed this in 1903, stating the SPD was *the* issue in the Reichstag campaign and that members of the non-socialist parties must recognize 'the holy duty of all German citizens' to fight Social Democracy. Unfortunately, 'Social Democratic agitation rests on reckless incitement and on annihilation of every sense of authority, as well as unscrupulous servility and flattery,' and the national parties were unable to compete in such respects. The answer, nevertheless, had to be 'consequential mass work' to win back the voters. Government officials were also turning to the conclusion that no amount of repressing it, no amount of ignoring it, no amount of talking about it would make the SPD go away, but that instead 'a successful struggle against the Social Democratic movement will only be made possible by the route of an enthusiastic and indefatigable associational life.' In 1898 Posadowsky had tried to rally the governmental parties to do this themselves; veterans' associations had been deployed for a patriotic campaign. Yet the governmental parties had not risen to the challenge.[74]

The SPD success in 1903 finally discredited the governmental parties in the eyes of nationalists and officials as the possible agents of such a renewed 'enthusiasm' in 'associational life.' In a talk during the 1903 campaign, when the SPD's victory was already foreseeable, Posadowsky blamed it on the 'indifference' of 'our bourgeois society,' which had to learn to fight socialism without crying out for government aid. The 'state-supporting' parties 'would likely get their accounting for such dereliction of duty in the coming elections, in the growth of the radical parties.'[75] After four straight major defeats, it was clear that a different kind of anti-socialist organization was called for. This sentiment led directly to the founding shortly after the 1903 elections of the Reichsverband gegen die Sozialdemokratie (Imperial League against Social Democracy, RgS), a new nationalist pressure group which was to organize the sort of united, agitational mass movement which the parties had proven was beyond their competence. The perceived need for the League and the idea of its role both sprang directly out of the unsuccessful efforts to organize anti-socialist coalitions and propaganda in the Reichstag elections of 1890–1903.

At an organizational meeting in Halle on 30 September 1903, representatives of the three *Kartell* parties laid the basis for the Imperial League. Its purposes were to organize anti-socialists from all political parties, to collect money for agitation, to send out newsletters and speakers, and in all respects to offer organizational assistance to the 'national' parties in their anti-socialist campaigns. A special 'election fund' was to be collected to make sure that, next time, the fight was more favourable for the government. The new 'parallel action group' was a kind of holding company for agitators, propaganda, and funds designed to prop up the soft mass bases of the governmental parties. It replaced, supplemented, or coordinated what the CDI, the nationalist publishing firms, the individual propagandists, and government officials had learned to do in the preceding years and provided an agency for the kind of national leadership in the anti-socialist cause that the government had shown itself incapable (for reasons of image, prestige, and constitutionality) of providing.[76]

The RgS represented a developing partnership among nationalist agitators, interest groups, officials, and the non-socialist parties, a partnership formed out of bitter experience with the inadequacy of existing avenues of political action. It represented, implicitly, both an adaptation to the requirements of mass politics – the need to fight the SPD with its own weapons – and also an unfavourable judgment about the success of the liberal and conservative parties in adapting by themselves to those requirements. The Imperial League reflected a more urgent and acute consciousness of the need to deal with mass politics in new terms; but this was not underpinned by any deep understanding of the roots and nature of SPD successes. What the League tried to copy was the technique of the SPD, ignoring the populist platform, the social-reform image, the policies and language that underlay the party's agitation and that struck responsive chords in its communities of supporters. As nationalists saw it, the

SPD was spreading Marxism by organization and agitation, and patrio-tism merely needed the same tools at its disposal. Mass politics, the sway-ing of voters, was just a matter of pitting one side's 'terrorism' against the others. Events proved them wrong in this judgment. The one defeat inflicted on the SPD in Wilhelmine Germany, that of 1907, was accom-plished by a 'national' campaign allegedly directed against the Centre, which whipped up electoral enthusiasm using colonial and anti-clerical, and not just anti-socialist, slogans, and whose success was mainly the result of the decision to bring the left liberals into the governmental coa-lition. The Bülow Bloc's electoral success was rooted in the experiences of 1898–1903 and earlier, which demonstrated large advantages to includ-ing the left liberals in second-ballot anti-socialist coalitions. It was old-fashioned top-level coalitions and 'national' issues, not a grass-roots, mass-membership anti-socialist crusade, that made the difference in 1907. When these factors were gone in 1912, the SPD resumed its former growth curve.

The Social Democratic victories of 1898 and 1903 helped reveal the powerlessness and 'fragmentation' of the Protestant governmental par-ties, in the sense that these were unable to regain their lost ground or compete equally with the SPD's popular appeal and mass campaigning. The victories, and the refusal of governmentalists to accept those victo-ries, also helped to polarize politics even more in a socialist/anti-socialist sense, embodied finally in the Imperial League against Social Democracy. Against the general and increasingly solid opposition of virtually all other parties and of the government itself, the SPD demonstrated at the turn of the century that its particular combination of style and program, of mass agitation and choice of election issues, could score dramatic and impres-sive successes against the efforts of almost any other party. The impact of this fact on the 'national' parties was depressing and demoralizing. When Bülow wrote of the growing sense of inevitability of Social Democratic growth, about its advance like a 'tide' or an 'avalanche,' he caught the mood of many. By 1903 the comparative poverty of other political group-ings in mass appeal, save the Centre and regional parties, was exposed clearly for all to see. The day had arrived when 'any old cigar-worker' might indeed have a place in German political culture.

8

Conclusion

On 16 June 1898, 7.8 million ballots were cast; five years later it was 9.5 million. These millions of individual choices, made within particular historical and political contexts, revealed a cross-section of the German political nation on the cusp between centuries. The numbers and percentages did not reflect only sociological and social-economic groupings in the population. They also reflected the contextual factors of issues, images, strategies, and tactical voting; and they were conditioned by the particular institutions of mobilization and representation.

Far from being atypical, many of the trends in Wilhelmine Germany were similar to trends observed in other countries, and compatible with a development towards democracy – while not foreordaining such a development, as hindsight starkly shows. Richard Rose suggested a number of years ago that 'where strong linkages exist between national parties, or blocs of parties, and demographic groups, voting participation should be encouraged.'[1] This was the case for the party system in turn-of-the-century Germany. The class and cultural linkages of Social Democracy and of the Catholic Centre Party, especially, helped drive the strikingly high participation rates evident from 1903 onward. And (said Rose) where national parties correspond to different, meaningful cleavage groups, 'election outcomes take on an easily identifiable significance.' This also was true of Wilhelmine Germany: it was clear to voters who won and what they represented. High participation, coherent social groupings, and 'affirming' patterns of voting participation were taken by Suval to show that mass politics in Imperial Germany was modern.[2]

Change and Populism

Contrary to generalizations that have sometimes been made about the excessive rigidity or stagnation of German party politics, the party system was undergoing fundamental change at the turn of the century. Measured statistically, the 'volatility' of voting in Imperial Germany – the changes between parties in percentage vote – was second only to France and the Netherlands among ten European countries surveyed by Bartolini and Mair.[3] There was plenty of change in German mass politics, including the expansion of Social Democracy, the rise and fall of right-wing agrarian and anti-Semitic populism, and the changing fortunes of the liberal and conservative parties. The unchangingness of Imperial German parties is a myth. It is true, of course, that the trends did not usually change abruptly from election to election, and that the ideological characterizations and relationships of the parties remained similar; these characteristics are precisely what Suval used to demonstrate the development of modern, 'affirming' patterns of voting. Meanwhile, apart from the vote totals and basic ideologies, changes were occurring within the parties as well.

It was apparent at the turn of the century that the balance was shifting from *Honoratiorenpolitik* – the politics of notables – towards a new style of mass politics (chapter 2). The old style involved weakly institutionalized parties with no solid membership base and little permanent structure between elections; it involved appeals to voters based on deference rather than issues; and it offered voters only weak forms of symbolic participation. In the new politics – which was clearly perceived to be gaining ground – mass leafleting, meetings, and propaganda were carried out by agitational parties. Their organizations were more extensive, more permanent, more bureaucratic, with a new level of centralization or systematization among constituencies and among regions. Candidates and parties that followed the newer style of politics strove for a more intense identification between supporters and parties, integrating those supporters through mass membership, through parallel organizations like trade unions, interest groups, or cultural organizations, and by means of symbolic forms of identification between followers and candidates. In the process, they elevated the idea of the 'common man' to a new level. It became fashionable and popular for candidates to campaign as 'men of the people' and to style their parties as 'people's parties,' in opposition to the self-conscious elitism of the politics of notables.

Some of the same parties that exhibited populist style and form were also strongly influenced by class, culture, and region. Populism complemented and reinforced the roots of certain parties in particular social structures and groupings. It did not substitute for social affiliations, but rather strengthened them. The Social Democratic Party identified itself and was identified by others with the working class; the Centre Party with Catholics; the German Conservatives with agriculture, the aristocracy, and the Prussian northeast; regional and ethnic parties with their localities and minorities. Each of these groupings employed populism, at least sometimes, to mobilize its own audiences and to help weave them together into coherent social-political groupings. There is an occasional sense in the late twentieth century that 'populism' must denote the opposite of cohesion or structure, but this is not true of the kinds of populism illustrated at the turn of the century.

There were also new issues. The old 'national' polarizations between Protestant and Catholic, between 'Germans' and ethnic or dynastic particularists, and between regional parties and the centre lived on in certain corners of the Reich, and where they did, the older liberal and conservative parties continued to do comparatively well. But elsewhere during 1898–1903, the election issues were popular rights and the defence of the suffrage, fair tariffs, resistance to *Reaktion*, equity in taxation burdens – popular-rights and social-economic issues. These were 'fairness' issues concerning distribution of rights and power among social-economic interests and groups.

It was the Social Democratic Party more than any other that made such issues its own, especially challenging the denial of wealth and power to the working class. The SPD's success can be understood as one expression of the 'populist' drift of the times. Social Democrats stood for election in 'multiple candidacies' and campaigned even where they had no chance of success, because the votes they won would inflate the party's national totals and increase its claim to be a party of the people. The SPD embodied a claim that only a workers' party could represent workers – another populist idea, unlike the old premise of *Honoratiorenpolitik* that a wise notable would represent all classes. And the issues upon which the SPD focused, in Reichstag elections, were populist issues oriented towards the rights, feelings, and pocketbook of the common man: defence of the 'universal, equal, secret, and direct' Reichstag suffrage in contrast to restricted state suffrages; fighting agrarian tariff demands that (the SPD argued) would tax consumers; and opposing military expenditures that were financed through 'unfair' indirect taxes. While quite different in many respects from right-wing populism, this, too, was the cultivation of the image of a 'people's party.'

But the Social Democratic movement was not the only 'agitational' advocate of social-economic and popular-rights causes. Turn-of-the-century political language was laced with value-laden terms like *Demokratie* and *Demagogie, Volkspartei* and *Volkstümlichkeit* ('popularity'), *Radikalismus* and *Agitation,* which might pertain not only to the SPD but to tendencies within all of the other camps. The Catholic Centre Party (recognized by Chancellor Hohenlohe as the second of the 'parties that rule the masses') had long defended minority Catholics, especially their religion and schools – a cleavage issue of modernization. During 1898–1903, this appeal was given an enlarged character, as advocacy of the 'parity' of Catholics in access to wealth and power – a social-economic fairness issue, buttressed by the party's sectional promises to Catholic workers, Catholic farmers, and other economic and status groups. The party also campaigned during 1898–1903 in defence of the Reichstag suffrage. The Centre, when it needed to, conducted mass propaganda with the party press and with the People's Association for Catholic Germany (VkD). The dominant coalition in the party preserved its image as a people's party despite their political manoeuvring in the Reichstag, and the Centre remained the only substantial party to maintain its share of the vote in these elections in face of the SPD advance. The liberal parties evinced much less of the new populism, though the agitation of Richter's left-liberal FVP echoed in some respects that of the Social Democrats. Even among the Poles there was a 'People's Party' that challenged an older 'Court Party.' And on the right, populism blossomed. Anti-Semites tried to wed nationalism to the cause of 'reform' that would help the common people and were advocates of the democratic suffrage. Agrarians challenged agriculture's loss of wealth and power, demanding that their rural constituents receive more consideration. It was the agrarian movement, alongside the rise of Social Democracy, that most strongly affected the Protestant non-socialist parties in the elections of 1898 and 1903.

Agrarianism and Rural Populism

After Social Democracy, the agrarian movement was Germany's second important mass-political movement at the turn of the century. The axis around which the national agrarian movement turned was the issue of tariff protection for agriculture, which symbolized the feeling that agriculture and rural Germany were losing out in industrialization, and that state policy should redress the balance. Together with this went the classic populist idea that farmers had to organize, because their interests could be represented only by farmers themselves. The largest agrarian organization, and the most troublesome for the governmental parties, was the Agrarian League (chapter 4). The Agrarian League had been organized in 1893 and in 1898 fought its first well-organized election campaign – acting as an interest group, a sponsor of political candidates of other parties, and, in some places, as a political party in its own right. This, coupled with the continuation of the rural anti-Semitic surge that began in 1893, threw the rural-based Protestant parties into disarray. Both the League and the anti-Semites employed systematic techniques of agitation similar to those pioneered by the SPD, which proved both a challenge to more staid and old-fashioned governmental candidates and also an opportunity, if these groups could be engaged as allies. The bitter tariff debates of the 1898–1903 Reichstag, culminating in a new tariff law passed only half a year before the 1903 elections, set the stage for an even more polarized confrontation between agrarians and their opponents in 1903. The German Conservatives and the National Liberals, in particular, had to deal with acute pressures among their constituents. For the German Conservatives, this meant a kind of alliance, or in places almost a merger, with the League; for the National Liberals it meant alliances in some regions and competition in others. At the national level, this translated into painful internal divisions among National Liberals. A party which had not only rural but also industrial roots, commercial trade interests, and a nationalist philosophy struggled to accommodate sectional demands from agrarian and regional interests.

The tariff issue was brought to a boiling point by the campaigns of the Agrarian League and the heated debates over the tariff law of December 1902 (chapter 2). It was a dominant issue in both elections and incited not only breakaway agrarian candidates but also friction within and between the governmental parties. Ultimately the tariff issue hampered all efforts to create a united governmental coalition. The economic *Sammlungspolitik* of 1897–8 appears in context as a largely unsuccessful attempt both to placate and to contain radical agrarianism.

It is worth remembering, however, that the tariff was not the only agrarian issue, and the Agrarian League was not the only rural organization. Peasant leagues like the Bavarian Peasants' League, anti-Semitic agrarian candidates, and the agrarian wing within the Centre Party all have to be seen as part of a broader movement that goes beyond a single organization. Indeed, agrarian populists were the only significant challenge to the Centre Party's normal impregnability in its rural seats in these years, particularly in those regions of Bavaria where the Bavarian Peasants' League mobilized the peasantry. 'Simple peasants must get in / They must be the excellencies': the Peasants' League slogan summed up a populism more potent than any established party could accommodate. Farmers should be represented only by farmers; the 'people' (variously defined) should have a voice in making policy, and not only entrust this to dignified representatives; the political culture of the nation can be affected by mass organizing – key beliefs of the new populism, expressed within the agrarian context.

Officials and governmentalist politicians blamed 'agitators' and 'demagogues' for the emergence of the new politics in Germany. Perhaps they were right: the activists and campaigners, the mass organizations, and the new styles of speech and thought were creating a new structure of politics. But these 'agitators' and their parties were given much to work with by the cleavages in German society, both those dating from unification and state modernization in the 1860s and 1870s, as well as those heightened by rapid industrialization. Behind the various mass-political and populist phenomena of 1898–1903 lie, indisputably, social and economic issues, interests, and cleavages. Workers or farmers, *Mittelstand* or peasant, this was the age of interest politics. The Reichstag elections of 1898–1903 centred on questions of tariffs and taxes, Reichstag suffrage and popular rights, questions in which the social balance of wealth and power was at stake. It was the organization of social and economic interests that was driving the reorganization of politics and the change in political styles. The 'masses and the classes' had arrived on the political stage, with a vengeance.

The Mass Appeal of Social Imperialism?

In all of this, some issues were conspicuous by their absence from electoral politics. The 1898 elections seemed ideal for social imperialism: colonial ventures like the occupation of Kiaochow were in the news, the first Navy Law had just been passed, *Weltpolitik* and the fleet were favourite topics in some arms of the press, and nationalist pressure groups were active. Surely the time was ripe for the government and the right-wing parties to divert the attention of the electorate to foreign-policy issues, and away from the defence of the suffrage, the fairness of taxation, and programs of reform. Those who hoped to do so were sorely disappointed.

The National Liberal Party, almost alone, championed the fleet as an election issue. (It was joined, less stridently, by the marginal and fragmentary Imperial Party.) The government's campaign did nothing to accentuate the fleet. Other parties campaigned against the fleet (SPD, FVP) or

campaigned proudly on their record of having cut its cost (Centre) or
played it down as just another military issue in the traditional vein (German Conservatives, many of whom were not excited by the fleet). Nationalist pressure groups were strangely silent, leaving the field entirely to the
parties. Even though its explosive growth occurred just when the 1898
Reichstag campaign was under way, the Navy League was not a visible factor in the press or the party programs. The curious invisibility of even the
Navy League in mass electoral politics reinforces the conclusion that
nationalist activists belonged to a separate culture of their own making,
and their taste for party and electoral politics was slight. Meanwhile, the
abstention of most parties from nationalist appeals, together with the
unflattering election performance of the National Liberals – the worst
election result in their history – suggest that the masses were *not* aroused.
In public campaigning, governmentalism was a handicap during 1898–
1903, and extreme nationalism had a limited appeal beyond the already-
converted National Liberal electorate. Social imperialism did not happen
on a mass scale in the elections; and how effective can social imperialism
have been if it did not much affect elections?

The Passivity of the State

The government itself, by misunderstanding mass politics, by showing
reluctance to accept results of elections, and by its misguided attempts to
influence elections and promote unity among its preferred parties also
made things worse and provided grist for the populist mill. The Reich
government was caught more or less helplessly in the constellation of
issues, interests, and parties, and could hardly act without negative side-
effects (chapter 3). Fundamentally the problem was that large portions of
the politically organized electorate were critical or suspicious of basic governmental policies, such as its attitude towards democracy and its treatment of tariffs and taxation. Meanwhile the parties friendly to the
government were divided by the issues of the day. Behind the scenes the
government, through the Prussian state administration, continued its
clandestine aid to the governmental parties – the German Conservatives,
Imperial Party, and National Liberals, Bismarck's old *Kartell* of 1887. But
publicly the government was handcuffed by the divisions among its allies,
the ineffectiveness of all of them together against the SPD and against
agrarian populists and other rebels, and not least of all by its own inability
to understand the new politics and the new parties.

Sammlungspolitik, the 'politics of rallying together,' was a catch phrase invented as an election slogan to unify the governmental forces in the 1898 Reichstag campaign. The pro-agrarian, pro-tariff *Sammlung* conceived by Prussian finance minister Miquel turned out to be an albatross for the government, at a time when encouraging the agrarians and splitting the *Kartell* – for these were the effects of campaigning on the tariff issue – were the furthest things from the government's plans. The 1898 and 1903 elections, in fact, saw some of the worst examples of disunity among the governmental forces. Instead of finding unity on protectionist issues (the Miquelian *Sammlung*), a weak second-ballot strategy of anti-socialist cooperation was pursued – the Posadowskian version. This cooperation extended even to free-trading left liberals, and in this way the anti-socialist cooperation of 1898 and especially 1903 became a precursor for the Bülow Bloc of 1907.

The government was hardly neutral. It did everything it could to hinder its enemies, above all the Social Democrats and the Polish particularists. This included setting the timing of the elections, arranging statements about issues and government positions, encouraging the unity of the other parties, and working through its officials to do everything from distributing pamphlets to raising campaign funds. This manoeuvring makes a mockery of the government's claims that it acted 'above the parties' – it was hopelessly enmeshed in their affairs. In the last analysis, however, the remarkable thing is the degree to which the state felt constrained by the rule of law, backed as it was by the Reichstag majority. Despite its open partisanship, the state reined in its officials, kept to a narrow path of legality, and foreswore sensational and confrontational measures. The problem, as Germany's leaders saw it, was the heating up of mass politics. It was water, not gasoline, that they wished to throw on the flames. The best they could do was a quiet policy of official non-intervention in the campaigns, which at least had the virtue of minimizing the embarrassment to the government when the results came in. The governmental parties, on the other hand, felt that they had been abandoned.

Stress and Adaptation of the Parties

For the parties of the right – German Conservatives and the Imperial Party – the main problems were posed by agrarianism and anti-Semitism (chapter 4). After flirting with the latter, the German Conservatives discarded it; and during 1898–1903 the independent anti-Semitic parties declined in effectiveness and influence. Anti-Semitism was too 'agitational' for the establishment conservatives, requiring as it did that conservatism wed itself to populism and 'reform' if it were to be popular. Agrarianism was less socially threatening to the conservative elite, and certainly more unavoidable given the conservatives' rural base. Nevertheless, conservatives struggled to accommodate agrarian demands while freezing out agrarian extremists, and in doing so, they both gained and lost.

The German Conservatives solidified their hold on their core electoral base in northern and eastern Prussia, surviving the agrarian storm and even strengthening their base in electoral environments characterized by Protestant population, large landholdings, agricultural economy, and low voter turnout. This was an accomplishment, one that no other mainstream Protestant party could match at the turn of the century. The connection between the Conservatives and a particular, definable agrarian social-economic grouping was strengthened, which was one form of adaptation to the new politics. However, this social grouping was a factor in only a small minority of Reichstag seats. In confirming their northeastern, agrarian base, the German Conservatives actually lost ground in other areas and became more and more a Prussian and a regional party – with disproportionate influence in government, to be sure, but with no possible pretension to be a true nationwide party in Reichstag elections.

In no other election between 1874 and 1912 did the Conservative seat total decline as dramatically as in 1898, and 1903 brought no recovery. The Conservative vote declined across the Reich as a whole and collapsed, particularly, in the Kingdom of Saxony in the face of the SPD breakthrough there in 1903. Agrarianism, which helped the party in its core seats, hurt it in the peripheral ones; relatively poor campaign organization and lack of a genuine populist synthesis also contributed to the decline. The Imperial Party, meanwhile, hung on only as a flag of convenience for local governmental candidates who wished to rally the patriotic forces. It was hardly a party at all in the modern sense, outside the legislature, and had no really definable social-economic base.

Liberalism, by contrast with the German Conservatives, maintained its pretensions to be a national movement, but failed to win and hold any strong geographic core or social-economic grouping (chapter 5). These two elections were the worst in the history of the empire for the combined liberal forces. Tariffs, tax levels, economic interests, popular rights, and the defence of the Reichstag suffrage were the order of the day – not liberals' cherished appeals to nationalism. Liberals swam against the tide of interest politics and 'fairness' issues, instead holding out to try to represent the national interest against all lesser interests. They resisted the new politics (with the partial exception of Richter's Left Liberal People's Party, FVP). All varieties of liberalism noticeably failed to identify themselves with any coherent social grouping. Their electoral bases were scattered and shallow; their electorates not clearly definable in terms of social-economic or demographic characteristics; and regional strongholds were few and scattered. Perhaps most damaging of all, they could not achieve effective unity among themselves and continued to fight one another for the allegiance of a declining share of the electorate.

National Liberals were pulled to the right by their *de facto* involvement in the *Kartell.* In these elections, that connection was undoubtedly a disadvantage. While they had the help of governmental officials and the advantage of not facing many conservative challengers in their seats, the disadvantages were to be associated with governmental policy, to be unable to challenge the conservatives in their seats, to be retarded from developing a modern, agitational party organization, and to be compromised on the all-important tariff issue. The National Liberals, a party dedicated to trade agreements and to the reconciliation of economic interests, a party whose support was neither clearly agrarian nor clearly industrial, were trapped by a governmental policy that was seen to favour the protection of a single interest. While the National Liberals could cooperate with the Agrarian League in some regions, in others the agrarians broke from the governmental camp in order to fight the National Liberals. Liberal leaders were left to lament the supremacy of economic interests over their traditional issues of 'national' integration.

Left liberals did even more poorly in these elections. Under intense electoral pressure, they lost ground in rural areas as the agrarian movement ran its course, and in the cities to the SPD. Assailed by both of the major social movements of the turn of the century, left liberals had no equivalent populist appeal of their own. They campaigned vigorously against *Reaktion* and taxation, a formula that had won them victories earlier in the empire's history; but during 1898–1903 that platform had been taken by the Social Democrats. More and more, left liberals had to win run-off campaigns against the Social Democrats in order to win what seats they could. By the turn of the century, left liberals could gain election only with the compromise support of other parties' voters. Under these electoral pressures, Richter's FVP, in particular, became increasingly anti-socialist, paving the way for cooperation with the government in the 1907 elections.

The Centre Party, on the other hand, was one of the success stories in turn-of-the-century German politics (chapter 6). It succeeded in the act of internally balancing different interests – agriculture and industry, workers and aristocrats – to a degree the Protestant liberal parties could not manage. In this it was assisted by the powerful institutional base of political Catholicism in Catholic communities, through the clergy and through occupational and other organizations. The Centre Party could rely on the solidarity of Catholics even a generation after the *Kulturkampf*. The loyalty of Catholics to the Centre was legendary, and the percentage of Catholics in the population largely defined the party's electoral base and its limits. In maintaining unity among different Catholic intersts, it helped that the Catholic areas of Germany were less industrialized and less urbanized than the rest, which minimized the need for political Catholicism to deal with big-city mass politics. But another part of the Centre's success is that it succeeded in making specific changes and adaptations to the new mass politics. The People's Association for Catholic Germany (VkD) was the most important of these. Nevertheless, it was difficult even for the Centre to ride two horses at one time, and particularly to placate both agrarians and urban workers. The SPD was making inroads in the large Catholic cities. The Centre had made a viable adaptation to the mass politics of the turn of the century, for it represented and held together a coherent social grouping; but a constant effort was required to integrate divergent interests.

During 1898–1903 the Centre campaigned for 'parity' for German Catholics, a cause that symbolized the desire to remove civil disabilities and participate fully in German society. The campaign for parity reflected the slogan *Heraus aus dem Turm!* (Come out of the fortress!), which called Catholics to take their places in a new Germany where they were not disadvantaged. This appeal reflected the ambitions of a new group of middle-class party leaders, who sought not only to defend the Catholic interest as in the past, but to be accepted and win influence. Parallel to this the party argued that its 'key position' in the Reichstag must be maintained. By holding the balance of power, the party could exert influence on government and also block unfavourable measures. Centre strategy was dictated by the need to preserve this 'double-majority' capability, to block any repressive government measures by allying to the left, and to participate in positive legislative accomplishment by allying to the right. In the 1898–1903 elections, this meant that the Centre bitterly fought the *Kartell* and *Sammlungspolitik*, because these groupings opened the possibility of a right-wing majority without the Centre; and it agreed to an electoral pact to try to prop up the left-liberal FVP. There was some discussion of electoral cooperation with the SPD, but (except in southern

Germany) this did not occur. It was already apparent to some Centre leaders, like the young Erzberger, that the Social Democrats were the Centre Party's biggest competitors in the long term.

For the Social Democrats, these were the key elections in their march to popular legitimacy and numerical pre-eminence (chapter 7). The 1898 elections legitimated the SPD as the strongest of all parties or regular party combinations. The 'three-million victory' of 1903 made an even greater impression on contemporaries, coming as it did at the end of a long string of Social Democratic successes. The 1903 elections established the party as by far the largest single party in popular vote with nearly one-third of all votes cast, gaining it one-fifth of the Reichstag seats and clear status as the second-largest parliamentary delegation. With 81 seats in the 397–seat Reichstag, it was within striking distance of the Centre Party's 100 – the largest delegation in the chamber.

These victories were no accidents. The SPD had the most modern of party organizations: it chose its issues and planned its strategy almost a year ahead of the elections, and conducted its campaigning with a degree of central coordination and local agitation unmatched by any opponent. The issues, moreover, clearly caught the mood of the times: defence of the Reichstag suffrage, opposition to tariffs and consumption taxes, opposition to military and naval expenditures. The party's filibuster on the tariff law in 1902 gave it notoriety as the most determined opponent of the legislation. Its emphasis on the Reichstag suffrage issue in both elections was rewarded, particularly in Saxony, where the regressive new state suffrage of 1896 gave rise to a protest movement that could find effective expression only through the Reichstag suffrage. All of these factors – structure, agitation, and issues – combined to build and develop the party's base in an increasingly strong social grouping. Up until 1903 the negative correlations between SPD support and Catholicism were increasing, as were the negative correlations with employment in agriculture, the large-landownership area, and rural population (chapter 7). The Social Democratic advances of 1890–1903, then, including the two-million-vote victory of 1898 and the three-million-vote one of 1903, were associated with the SPD's deepening of roots in its strongest environments, which were Protestant cities and towns.

The Social Democrats succeeded in winning the solid support of the Protestant working classes and of other voters in urban Protestant Germany. In the process, they did lose some of the inroads they had made in rural and agricultural areas, but in electoral terms the close tie to a well-organized social grouping was important. This was the key to success in the politics of the day. Nevertheless, the Social Democrats also had the support of many small-town and rural voters. There were regions where Social Democracy had not spread to its potential breadth or depth because of the persistence of earlier patterns of confessional and 'national' politics. For these reasons, it was by no means clear that Social Democracy had reached any predetermined limit – quite the reverse. To contemporaries the Social Democratic advance seemed as relentless, and as opaque, as an avalanche or some other natural disaster.

One of the important outcomes of these campaigns was the coalescence of anti-socialist opinion, which contributed to the formation of the Imperial League against Social Democracy. While nationalists and those on the right did not understand the reasons for the success of Social Democracy, they were determined to fight it by borrowing its techniques. Since the government seemed unable to act and since the governmental parties were clearly ineffective at mass-political organizing, the Imperial League was founded to prop up the anti-socialist cause and make up for the organizational and agitational deficiencies of the governmental parties. The formation of the League, and the many other anti-socialist initiatives of the time, were a clear sign of impatience with the slowness of the older parties to react. It was, in its extreme, an expression of impatience with democratic party politics and with the continued 'fragmentation' of the non-socialist parties.

A 'Fragmented' Party System?

The stress caused to the party system by rising socialist vote totals, by the divisive effect of agrarian radicalism, by the continuation of old confessional and particularist divisions, and by new breakaway populisms was reflected in the perception of the 'fragmentation' of parties. Political life seemed to be disintegrating into competing interests. But how real, how serious, was the 'fragmentation'? Did it reflect a fragmentation of German political culture as a whole, a fragmentation at the base or at the top?

What seemed to fracture Germany's established Protestant parties during 1898–1903 was a concatenation of four problems: two that were immediate and identifiable, one structural and fundamental, and one that was too new for contemporaries to grasp in its entirety. The first problem was Social Democracy, easily named and identified, which by articulating class and status cleavages appeared to be splitting what liberals and conservatives had perceived as a unified electorate. The second specific and immediate problem was radical agrarianism, a disruptive force which, like Social Democracy, forced politics increasingly into channels related to abstract social-economic interests. To the extent that the older parties accommodated agrarianism, this played into the SPD's hands for its campaigns against privilege, tariffs, and regressive taxes. The third, underlying structural problem was the persistence of the conflicts of the old empire alongside the new: the confessional divisions, the particularist polarizations around the fringes of the Reich, the relations of liberals and conservatives, and the instability of the politics of notables. This list of unresolved business from the era of unification hampered the liberal and conservative parties in their majoritarian or hegemonic aspirations. The final problem was the emergence of the populist style of participatory mass politics. The established Protestant parties showed little sign of being able to adapt quickly to or understand the populist trend, and were slow to integrate the aspirations of the masses, either symbolically or substantively. There was a deficit in German politics, or a lag in adaptation of liberal and conservative party structures. This contributed to their relative lack of success compared with the SPD, the Centre, agrarians, and anti-Semites. For 'relative lack of success of the established Protestant parties,' one can read 'fragmentation.' The endless complaints about fragmentation really meant, primarily, that Wilhelmine Germany did not have the kind of electorate or party system that liberals and conservatives desired.

So how fragmented was the party system really, and in what ways? Looking first at the constituency level, table 13 quantifies the fragmentation of German parties, using the same index of concentration that was used in chapter 3 to analyse unity among the right-wing parties. The figures in table 13 show that after 1890 the indexes were lower, supporting the idea that voter support was more divided. More parties were contesting more constituencies and were more equal; one can see the same trend reflected in the growing number of run-off ballots needed to reach a decision. But it is not true that the party system in local constituencies was badly fragmented. The level of concentration of votes was about 0.44 at the turn of the century (a little greater in 1898, a little less in 1903). This is an average among constituencies. In a hypothetical 'average' constituency, this suggests that no party got much more than 60 per cent of the first-ballot votes, but also that the first-place party got at least 40 per cent.[4] A pure two-party system in which the parties got 40 to 60 per cent of the vote would produce an index in the range from 0.42 to 0.50, while a system of three competitive parties would tend to produce values around 0.30 to 0.35. Constituencies, then, had – on average – less than three-way

TABLE 13
Local Two- and Three-Party Systems (Herfindahl's Index Calculated Separately by Constituency and Averaged)

	Germany	Prussia	Bavaria	Saxony	Württemberg	Baden	Hesse
1890	.490	.489	.535	.454	.473	.435	.369
1893	.428	.438	.425	.405	.424	.367	.366
1898	.445	.469	.423	.425	.401	.406	.340
1903	.436	.451	.436	.463	.382	.388	.358
1907	.445	.455	.468	.439	.453	.406	.321
1912	.421	.428	.439	.419	.424	.403	.340

Note: Herfindahl's index (H), also known as the Herfindahl-Hirschman concentration index, was created as a measure of industrial concentration. Here it is used to measure the degree of concentration of votes among all parties. H is the sum of the squares of the individual parties' shares of the total vote, each party's share being a ratio from 0 to 1. The value of the index thus ranges from $1/n$, where n is the number of parties, up to 1. A single party with 100 per cent of the vote would produce an H of 1.00; two equal parties would produce an H of 0.50; and three equal parties an H of 0.333. Rein Taagepera and Matthew Shugart use this index (*Seats and Votes*, p. 79), while Jan-Erik Lane and Svante O. Ersson (*Politics and Society in Western Europe*, p. 177) refer to it as the Laakso and Taagepera index. Note that the values in the table are averages among constituencies in each region.

races in Wilhelmine elections. Choices for voters were clear and simple. One must be careful in that these figures pertain to averages among widely varying constituencies, and one would want to test the variation in these indexes – for example, the extent to which some seats in which one party received over 90 per cent of the votes (producing an index close to one) balanced off other seats in which five- and six-party races produced very low numbers. In general, however, these statistics support the observations from a number of regional case studies that point towards relatively stable regional systems of no more than three parties.

Table 13 hints at an important feature of turn-of-the-century German politics: fragmentation was not *within* constituencies, but *between* them. It was the Reichstag that was fragmented, not the local electorates and local party systems. Bearing in mind that some of these parties had family similarities and second-ballot electoral agreements with each other, can we say more about what *patterns* there may have been among these sets of choices – what similarities in the groupings of parties, even if the parties were not identical from one constituency to the next? In this book, the parties have been analysed according to four groupings: conservative, liberal, particularists (including especially the Centre), and Social Democrats. Even these four groupings were rarely present all at the same time. As a thought experiment, in order to visualize what these groupings mean, let us test a broad three-party model of Imperial German electoral politics and consider the proportion of the votes for which it accounts. Take only the largest liberal *or* conservative party in each seat (not both) the SPD and the largest among the Centre and particularist parties; add up their votes. What proportion of the total votes in the constituency do these three take? Simplistic as it is, the generalized three-party-group model nevertheless accounts for 73 per cent of all the votes cast in Germany in 1898 (78 per cent in 1903). In more than two-thirds of the constituencies (68 per cent and 75 per cent), the model accounts for more than two-thirds of the votes cast. One can, of course, group the parties various ways, and one could count more than three. But still, many constituencies are largely described by the formula: one liberal or conservative party, one particularist party, and the SPD. The real cause of the 'fragmentation' observed by contemporaries, then, was that between one region and another, between one constituency and another, it was not the *same* liberal or conservative party, not the same particularist party, that filled a spot in the spectrum of electoral choices. Presumably, without the two-ballot system, the fragmentation at the base would have been still less.

The fragmentation between localities and regions (not within them) did produce a Reich-wide party system that was fairly fragmented by today's standards. Table 14 shows the values of the index H calculated for the popular votes of all the parties. Interestingly, however, while H was quite low, it was in fact generally increasing through to 1912. In other words, measured by the objective, numerical standards of political science, the 'fragmentation' of the German party system was decreasing, not increasing. Once again, this should give pause for thought as to whether what liberals, conservatives, and government leaders meant by 'fragmentation' was the same as what they said. A number of relationships lie behind the changes in this statistic. First of all, the growth of the SPD meant, numerically speaking, less fragmentation, because more of the voters were united in a single party. Similarly the unification of the left-liberal parties and their improved performance in 1912 contributed to the increase in the index of concentration for that year. On the other hand, the 'national' campaigns of 1893 and 1907 provided the only declines in the concentration index. When the government campaigned against what it saw as political fragmentation, by fighting the mass-based Centre or SPD and helping its splintered liberal and conservative allies, it made statistical fragmentation worse.

TABLE 14
The Reich-Wide Multi-Party System, 1890–1912

	1890	1893	1898	1903	1907	1912
Index of concentration (H)	0.148	0.141	0.151	0.177	0.163	0.194
'Effective number of parties' $(1/H)$	6.78	7.07	6.64	5.65	6.13	5.16

Note: Concerning H, see note to table 13. H was calculated using the party shares of popular vote as recorded in G.A. Ritter and M. Niehuss, *Wahlgeschichtliches Arbeitsbuch*, pp. 40–2.

The second row of statistics in table 14 shows what is known as the 'effective number of parties,' a measure based on H that provides an abstraction of how many significant parties there were in the system.[5] One could say, then, that Wilhelmine Germany as a whole was consolidating from roughly a seven-effective-party system during 1890–8 down to what by 1912 was pretty much a five-party system; this, of course, ignores any family groupings or alliances among any of these parties. This may seem high to readers familiar with two-party systems, but the 1912 number is not so far off the average of 4.0 found by Lane and Ersson for sixteen western European democracies over the period 1945 to 1989. In fact, the Federal Republic of Germany during 1945–9 had an effective number of parties of 4.9, little lower than Imperial Germany in 1912. Modern Western European democracies with an effective number of parties of 6.0 or more have included France in the late 1950s, the Netherlands in the 1960s and 1970s, Switzerland generally since 1970, and Belgium in the 1980s, which at one time reached 8.9.[6] Perhaps Imperial Germany was an undemocratic place with little potential for responsible government; but it was not the multi-party nature or 'fragmentation' of its party system that held it back. Perhaps 'fragmentation' proved, indeed, that the representative system of the Reichstag suffrage was working, since the society being represented was diverse.

Though German parties were diverse, lively, and dynamic, could they really have supported a democratic government? In assessing the democratic potential in Imperial Germany, a central question has been whether the polarized, ideologically charged political parties were really competent to govern even if the constitutional system had offered them opportunities to do so. Sometimes, in the way this question is posed, there is still an assumption that multi-party systems must be unstable – reflecting essentially an Anglo-American viewpoint. It bears repeating that two-party systems are somewhat rare, and even where they are held to exist they 'are more of an abstraction than reality: even Great Britain,

Canada and New Zealand have only been two-party systems in some phases of their history because they were clinging to the idea of alternating governments to avoid coalitions.'[7] There is no point, then, in suggesting that Imperial Germany was deviant or unstable because its democratic procedures produced a multi-party system. One can more productively ask, what *kind* of multi-party system was it? Multi-party systems have been variously categorized according to whether they embody 'moderate' or 'extreme' pluralism, 'centripetal' or 'centrifugal' tendencies, less or more polarization. The key distinction in the literature is whether in a polarized pluralism the centre parties are still capable of governing – whether they are sufficiently large and unified, relative to extreme anti-system parties on the left and right. The classic example of polarized pluralism where no centre could govern is Weimar Germany.[8]

One intriguing result of recent research is that it suggests, depending on the behaviour of elites, that the kind of multiple, interest- and ideology-based parties exhibited by Imperial Germany can indeed sustain stable coalition governments. This is based on the observation that coalitions are most stable when the coalition partners are not direct competitors with each other, least stable when one of them sees others as threats to its existence. Following from this, it is found to be precisely 'in "segmented" societies in which the parties have non-overlapping electoral followings' that multi-party systems can give rise to stable governing coalitions.[9] In other words, one can argue that precisely because several parties in Wilhelmine Germany mobilized coherent groupings of 'affirming' voters, groupings that were in general mutually exclusive and ideologically rather closed, the system may have had the potential to support a stable 'consociative' multi-party democracy. Comparative electoral theory suggests that neither the multi-party system, nor the interest- and ideology-based affirming voting, nor the apparent 'fragmentation' of the electorate need in itself have been a barrier to democratic development. Indeed, the very same populist, cleavage-oriented, interest-mobilizing behaviour that repelled contemporary nationalists like Max Weber may have represented the best democratic potential in the party system.

The difference between a 'consociative' multi-party system and a centrifugal one is the attitude of elites: whether they are inclined to moderation and working towards shared interests, or whether they set one part against another until the whole system is ready to fly apart. There were approaches and alliances between parties in Imperial Germany; some, like the union of the SPD, the Centre, and the left liberals behind the peace resolution of 1917, and later behind the formation of the Weimar Republic, were clearly constructive and cooperative. In general, however, one has to have doubts whether the elites in German society had the will to make a consociative democracy work. The problem, according to this analysis, was not the frag-mentation of the electorate, the parties, the ideologies, or the social groups. The problem was the ineffectiveness or unwillingness of specific elites to pursue the accommodations necessary for democracy. The flaw in German society lay less at the bottom than at the top.

It may be, as is sometimes asserted, that the seeds of later 'centrifugal' party fragmentation in the Weimar era were sown in Imperial Germany. In the sense that a tradition of multiple parties was established, with no clear nationwide majorities or alternation of parties on the British or American model, this could be so. Ironically, the imperial electoral sys-tem may have buffered the adverse effects of fragmentation through its institutions of first-past-the-post election, run-off–ballot coalitions, and unchanging constituency boundaries – precisely the features of the impe-rial electoral law that are now widely regarded as undemocratic.[10] When proportional representation was introduced in the constitution of the Weimar Republic, this may have allowed existing divisions and tendencies in the electorate to be mirrored more directly in the parliament, allowing a latent polarized pluralism to come to full expression.

It seems too easy to assert, however, that the exclusiveness and ideolog-ical aggressiveness of turn-of-the-century parties somehow determined the catastrophic fragmentation of the 1920s. For one thing, the most ideological and rigidly organized of Wilhelmine parties – the SPD – was the most stable party in German politics (despite the split with the Com-munists), maintaining its identity and a large electoral following down to the present day. Supporters of democracy should only have wished for a similar degree of stability elsewhere on the political spectrum! The turbu-lence and chaos of Weimar politics was to come mainly in the middle and on the right, where liberals and conservatives had always struggled to maintain broad and flexible groupings, and to avoid social-economic and sectional commitments. Conservatives, agrarians, and Catholics managed to maintain firm, non-overlapping, clearly distinct electoral identities until the early twentieth century, but after that had no more success than liberals. Was the problem in German party politics really that there was too much appeal to material, ideological, and sectional interests – which is, to be sure, how German liberals would have seen it? Or was the prob-lem that the parties of the liberal centre generally failed, and those of the right enjoyed success only to 1914, in welding together coherent group-ings through populist and social-economic appeals? Perhaps it was the

lack or loss of social-ideological cohesion, not its excess, that left a problematic legacy for Weimar.

An Anti-democratic Culture?

The concept of political culture, introduced in chapter 1, was developed
as an analytical tool to investigate how societies in developing countries
create and sustain values and patterns of behaviour supportive of democracy. The general finding appears to be that, within a couple of decades
of introduction of mass suffrage, the population can have developed
knowledge about elections, judge the performance of parties, and have
developed belief in democratic institutions – depending on the role
played by elites in preparing the society for democratic and participatory
values. In other cases, it has been shown that populations could retain a
long-term faith in democracy even under unstable or undemocratic
regimes, depending on how political experience and political culture
have been shaped.[11]

In the context of these kinds of considerations, Imperial Germany presents a mixed bag, but with many more positive attributes than it has customarily been granted. Within a few decades of unification and mass
suffrage, there was a well-developed party system in relation to which voters demonstrated committed, participatory, 'believing,' and affirming
behaviour, and this was particularly true with respect to some of the larger
and more socially and economically coherent parties, as theory would suggest it should be. The elections of 1898 and 1903 do not seem to show an
authoritarian culture among voters. The victory of Social Democracy itself
in these elections, campaigning mainly on issues like popular rights and
equitability of taxation, is one indication that there were checks and limits
among the German people to the anti-democratic inclinations of some of
their leaders. The Centre Party's strength, too, also based in these years on
a commitment to democracy as well as to responsible conduct in parliament, would have to be taken as another supportive contribution to political culture. Even the lesser agitations and populisms show a dynamism
beyond the control of the state and challenging its authoritarian aspects:
from Eugen Richter's attacks on Junkers and militarism across to anti-
Semitic attacks on, in fact, much the same foes. Unhealthy as anti-Semites
and some agrarians may have been, they were not an authoritarian plot.
There was a volatility and dynamism among the electorate to which party
and government elites were compelled to respond.

Clearly a number of elites were indeed promoting values supportive of at least some aspects of democracy; but, on the other hand, the sense of tolerant pluralism, of accepting on some level the legitimacy of other parties and the interests they represent, was weak in some cases. Nevertheless, between the turn of the century and the First World War, electoral or parliamentary alliances, explicit or tacit, were concluded between liberals and conservatives (1903 *Kartell* parties, 1907 Bülow Bloc), among liberals (1912), between liberals and the Centre (1903, left liberal – Centre on first ballot in certain regions, and National Liberal – Centre in run-offs against the SPD), between the Centre and conservatives (Blue-Black Bloc, 1912), between the Centre and other particularist parties (standing cooperative arrangements with Guelphs, and where possible with Poles), between left liberals and the SPD (in isolated cases), and between the Centre and the SPD (in southern German states, for suffrage reform). For the fragmented and rigid splinter groups that Wilhelmine parties are supposed to have been, they did rather well at compromise. There was a great deal here upon which future German democracy could have built; but, on balance, there was one gulf that appeared to be not only deep but getting deeper, and that was the gulf between the SPD and its committed anti-socialist foes. The fact is significant that the state in its own mind did not accept the validity of the election results. There is nothing in mass political behaviour to suggest that German society as a whole was particularly authoritarian. Authoritarian, on the other hand, was the refusal of the state to accept the results.

State officials in Imperial Germany, especially its leading state, Prussia, distrusted democracy, resisted parliamentarism, and tended to question the legitimacy of a system that led to growing numbers of Social Democratic votes. Increasingly, after the turn of the century, radicalized anti-socialism was encouraged by the state and gained stronger footholds not only in the conservative but in the liberal and Centre camps. Excluding and attacking the largest party produced by free elections suggests lack of acceptance of democracy itself. The role of government and allied party elites in promoting anti-socialism was hardly unique to Germany, but perhaps the extent of anti-socialist mobilization, and the extent to which it was accepted by most of the non-socialist party elites, amounts to one clear way in which the kind of culture needed to support democracy was not developing – in which trends were, if anything, in the reverse direction. One could perhaps blame the Social Democrats for provoking this with their revolutionary language, or blame Bismarck for provoking them with his repression of their revolutionary rhetoric, but for present purposes that would be irrelevant. In many respects there were healthy signs

in turn-of-the-century Germany for a political culture that could potentially be supportive of democracy; but increasingly virulent anti-socialism
was a counter-indication.

At its root, the anti-socialist impulse was hopeless, because what the
anti-socialists objected to were not just features of Social Democracy, but
also fundamental social and political changes that were part of a wider
democratization of German society. The middle-class parties did not
accept that 'any old cigar-worker' could have opinions about politics and
get elected to represent them. Yet this was also what agrarianism was
about, and anti-Semitism, and other volatile movements of the day – the
idea that ordinary people should have opinions and should elect others
like themselves. These varieties of populism had that much in common.
Because of it, while one might inflict a defeat on the Social Democrats (as
was to follow in 1907), one could not turn the clock back. Moreover, in
enforcing the *Kartell* until 1903, then the Bülow Bloc in 1907, in promoting anti-socialist deals, in discouraging 'radicals,' in offering the assistance of government officials acting 'above the parties' – in all of these
respects, the state was discouraging the conservatives and National Liberals from developing autonomous, centralized, agitational, modern party
structures as fast as they might have done. In part because the governmental parties were too slow to modernize or were held back by the state,
the government turned to an increasing emphasis on anti-socialist strategies, of which the formation of the Imperial League against Social
Democracy following the 1903 elections was one expression.

Turn-of-the-century Germany had a flourishing mass-political culture.
It was responding to stress with adaptation, and was effectively creating
and representing interests and social groupings in the electorate. There
was dynamism, innovation, and conflict. Populists challenged authority
and old-fashioned assumptions, and the Social Democrats challenged all
others. Old groupings and allegiances did not persist out of any immov-
able rigidity but lasted only where they were renewed by new activity,
structures, and issues. While some parties were adapting more swiftly
than others – depending largely on whether they were held back by the
yoke of governmentalism, and whether they were enthusiastic to cultivate
the masses and the interests – all were changing. The diversity and energy
of German politics appeared to liberals as fragmentation, and to undemocratic officials as subversion. An increasingly uncontrollable realm of
electoral politics was disdained, but could not be dismantled, by right-
wing parties and officials who did not accept the premises of Germany's
new, mass electoral culture.

Constituency Typology

Typology of Electoral Environments, 1890–1912

The statistical analysis in this study relies for rigour on multiple regression analysis (see Appendices C and D). While this technique is excellent for isolating statistically significant relationships, tables of regression coefficients are not always the best way to communicate relationships to the reader. Accordingly this study uses a second, parallel methodology, grouping seats into categories based on definable social-economic and political characteristics. These groupings have proved to be statistically valid, many of them capturing geographic and cultural entities; and they are an intuitive way to grasp the different electoral contexts in different constituencies in Wilhelmine Germany. To a large degree, they incorporate social-economic with regional ways of looking at election results. In short, they provide a means to visualize and analyse discrete electoral environments, to go below the nationwide level of analysis without losing track of inter-regional comparisons.

On this basis, the Reichstag's 397 constituencies were grouped for this study into nine mutually exclusive categories or types, each of which aggregates constituencies of similar social-economic character and political culture.[1]

Summary of Constituency Types

1 *Large-Landownership Area.* Agricultural constituencies that were Protestant by a two-thirds majority, dominated by large landholdings, and where regional or ethnic particularists (see type 7a) were not strong ($N = 34$). Type 1 seats stretched in a belt roughly along the Baltic coast

from near Königsberg through Pomerania and the Mecklenburg duch-
ies to Schleswig-Holstein, plus a few pockets in east-central Prussia.
2 *Protestant Rural Seats.* Other Protestant non-particularist seats with more
than one-half of the population living in rural areas, no substantial portion living in cities, and not dominated by large holdings ($N = 63$).
3 *Protestant Mixed Rural/Urban Seats.* Protestant non-particularist constituencies of mixed rural-urban structure, including:
a) otherwise rural seats, with a rural majority, but containing one or
more cities ($N = 40$; typically a rural seat containing a district administrative and commercial centre);
b) seats where neither cities nor rural communities are a majority; i.e.,
a large population is in medium-sized towns ($N = 26$; type 3b constituencies were largely concentrated in the Kingdom of Saxony and in
nearby areas of Prussia and Thuringia).
4 *Protestant Urban Seats.* Protestant non-particularist constituencies dominated by one or more large cities ($N = 45$).[2]
5 *Catholic Rural / Small-Town Seats.* Constituencies that were Catholic by a
two-thirds majority, not particularist in their politics, and not dominated by one or more large cities ($N = 73$). Type 5 seats had both a cultural and a geographic unity, and were concentrated in a belt around
the southern, western, and eastern fringes of the Reich.[3]
6 *Catholic Urban Seats.* Catholic non-particularist constituencies dominated by one or more large cities ($N = 10$). These were located within
the same geographic areas as type 5 seats.
7 *Seats of 'National' Conflict.* Constituencies where electoral conflicts were
shaped by confessional, ethnic, or particularist struggles, including:
a) those where particularists were able to win at least one-third of the
vote in any Wilhelmine election ($N = 54$);[4]
b) those where neither confession had a majority of two-thirds or more
($N = 52$).[5]
These seats were spread mostly around the fringes of the Reich, away
from Protestant 'middle Germany,' in similar fashion and usually
adjacent to the Catholic type 5 areas.

These mutually exclusive categories count each Reichstag seat into
exactly one category. The categories can then be examined as electoral
environments and the differing performances of parties in them analysed.
    One immediate question must be the validity of such a categorization
by types. It may be, of course, that these categories are abstractions with

little power to explain the election results. Electoral performance of various parties varied greatly from one type to another, which is one sign that the categorization is a useful one. A somewhat more rigorous way to examine the validity of the types is to do multiple regressions using the statistics on which the types are based and, separately, dummy variables representing the different types. One can then examine the R^2 resulting from the regressions to see how much explanatory power was lost in going from one way of analysing the statistics to the other – the higher the R^2, the better the regression.[6] The results indicate that this typology is a reasonable way to understand the elections, especially for certain parties.

We read in table A.1 that different types of regressions produce better fits for different parties, but that using the constituency types is not far off the other techniques and is occasionally better. The German Conservative (DKP) and National Liberal (NL) popular votes are best predicted by regional variables; that of the Social Democratic Party (SPD) by social-economic statistics; and the Catholic Centre Party's vote (C) is slightly better predicted by the constituency typology. In any case, it is easier to work with the seven types of constituencies than with the twenty-odd regions represented in the bottom row of table A.1.

Survey of Constituency Types

The large-farm rural seats (type 1) made up a region heavily dominated by the German Conservative Party (DKP); of 204 deputies elected in these 34 seats in the six general elections from 1890 to 1912, no fewer than 146 were German Conservatives. This is reflected in the analysis of the popular vote in these seats (fig. A.1), which shows that the Conservatives had more than 40 per cent of the vote in these seats in every election considered here. Second place went to the left liberals – the small, loosely organized Left Liberal Union (FVg) did quite well in these seats in comparison with the larger Left Liberal People's Party (FVP) – until 1903, when the Social Democrats became the largest opposition party in these constituencies. These seats were the *only* electoral environment within which the German Conservatives' vote held up well from 1890 to 1912. Every other type of environment was weaker for the Conservatives, and in most other types they declined. In 1890 the DKP won 25 of its 73 Reichstag mandates (34.2 per cent) in type 1 seats; by 1912 it won 19 of its 43 mandates here (44.2 per cent). In effect, this meant that the Conservatives were increasingly retreating into a socially, economically, and

TABLE A.1
Multiple Regressions Using Constituency Types vs. Other Indicators (1898 and 1903)

	DKP 1898	DKP 1903	NL 1898	NL 1903	FVP 1898	FVP 1903	C 1898	C 1903	SPD 1898	SPD 1903	Partic. 1898	Partic. 1903
R^2 using social-economic statistics	.2794	.3164	.0821	.0653	.1540	.1734	.6624	.7458	.6991	.7379	.1457	.1783
R^2 using constituency types (dummy variables)	.2855	.3066	.0703	.0614	.1636	.1519	.7351	.7892	.5951	.6065	.6799	.7239
R^2 using geographic regions (dummy variables)	.3894	.3744	.2605	.2712	.2169	.2119	.4952	.5126	.4142	.4594	.6792	.6602

Note: The dependent variable is the percentage of the vote for the party indicated. All values of R^2 are significant at the 2.5 per cent level.

FIGURE A.1

Protestant Large-Farm Constituencies (Type 1), 1890–1912 (N = 34)

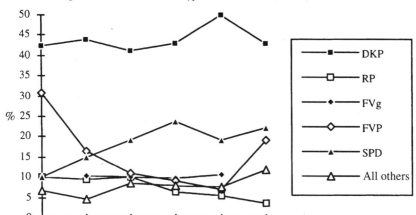

geographically restricted electoral environment. This is borne out by multiple regression analysis, which shows an increasing R^2 for the combined effect of confessional and agrarian structure in explaining the German Conservative share of the vote (chapter 4). The dummy variable representing 'large landownership' became more important as well as more significant during 1903–12 in explaining the electoral strength of the Conservatives.

The 'fragmentation' of the Protestant 'middle parties' was evident in Protestant rural seats. Type 2 constituencies had strong conservative, liberal, and SPD support, complicated further by a disproportionately large and effective right-wing populist vote – these seats were by far the strongest ones for Germany's anti-Semitic and agrarian parties (fig. A.2). The German Conservative vote did not hold up as well in these constituencies as it did in type 1 large-landownership areas, and the liberal parties' shares of the vote also declined until about 1903, followed by a noticeable resurgence in the 'national' campaign of 1907. The Social Democrats advanced in these constituencies to become, by 1903, the largest single party in popular vote with 27.6 per cent, surpassing the Conservatives' 18.1 per cent. The SPD appears to have done best in rural seats that were close to its urban strongholds. It is nevertheless important that, with its large victory of 1903, the Social Democratic Party was spilling over even into Germany's Protestant rural constituencies.

FIGURE A.2

Protestant Small-Farm Constituencies (Type 2), 1890–1912 (*N* = 63)

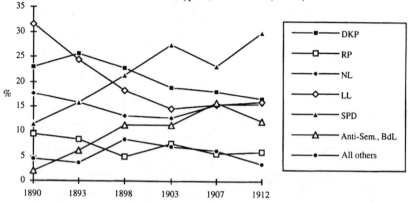

TABLE A.2

Mandates Won in Protestant Rural Seats (Type 2), 1890–1912 (*N* = 63)

	1890	1893	1898	1903	1907	1912
DKP	22	21	16	15	14	12
RP	5	7	4	5	6	5
NL	9	14	15	11	13	8
FVg	–	6	4	4	6	–
FVP	21	3	9	8	6	15
SPD	0	0	2	7	0	11
DVP	2	3	3	1	1	–
Anti-Sem.	3	8	8	7	11	8
BdL/WVg	–	–	0	3	4	2
Other	1	1	2	2	2	2

The net effect of these trends, in terms of seats won and lost, was instability among the parties, conservative losses in 1898 that were not later made good, and liberal losses (table A.2). The relative strength of anti-Semitic parties in these seats is noteworthy: in each and every election, the mandates won by the anti-Semites in type 2 seats constitute half or more of all the mandates they won.

Type 3a seats (Protestant mixed rural-urban – rural majority but containing a city) also provided fairly evenly divided opportunities for conservatives, liberals, and the SPD, and somewhat less foothold for agrarians and anti-Semites than did the type 2 seats (fig. A.3). Here the trend was away from the left liberals, in particular, and towards the SPD, which in the 1898 and 1903 elections clearly outdistanced all the other parties in

FIGURE A.3
Protestant Mixed Rural/Urban Constituencies (Type 3a), 1890–1912 (N = 40)

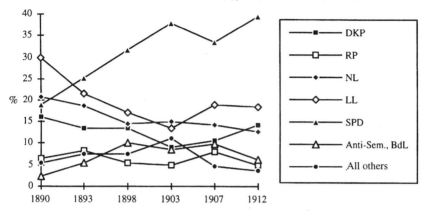

TABLE A.3
Run-offs and Liberal and Socialist Parties in Type 3a Seats, 1890–1912 (N = 40)

	1890	1893	1898	1903	1907	1912
Total run-offs	23	29	33	33	24	35
NL: seats won (both ballots)	10	9	8	11	10	8
Run-offs fought	15	15	10	11	7	11
LL: seats won (both ballots)	17	12	11	6	8	7
Run-offs fought	16	13	12	7	6	8
SPD: seats won (both ballots)	0	2	6	10	0	16
Run-offs fought	8	13	20	29	15	30

popular vote. The growth in the Social Democratic share of the vote in these seats lagged behind the growth in fully urban (type 4) seats but nevertheless exceeded 35 per cent in 1903 and 1912. The urban element in these seats went together with lesser support for the conservative parties than in type 1 and type 2 constituencies, and relatively greater support for the left liberals and National Liberals, who were second and third in popular vote in these seats during 1890–1907. Many of the constituencies came down to liberal-socialist battles in the run-offs – and run-offs were frequent. Fully 177 of the 240 contests in these seats from 1890 to 1912 had to go to a second ballot to be decided (table A.3). First-ballot fragmentation of party support was greatest in 1898 and 1903, when 33 of the 40 contests went to run-offs, and in 1912, when there were run-off elections in 35 of the type 3a seats. The pattern in these seats was increasingly

FIGURE A.4
Protestant Mixed Town Constituencies (Type 3b), 1890–1912 (N = 26)

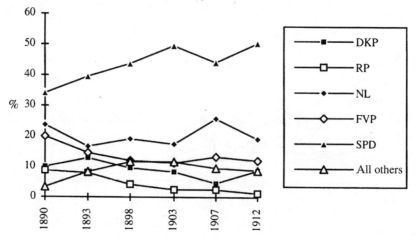

one of liberal-socialist confrontations and fierce two-ballot contests. The liberal parties clearly benefited from the high proportion of contests against Social Democrats – constituency-level results suggest that liberals garnered support from the right-wing parties to win their seats.

Type 3b constituencies – those which had neither a rural nor an urban predominance, but which were evenly balanced or dominated by mid-sized towns – illustrate a pattern similar to that in the type 3a seats, except that the Social Democrats did better, sooner, in these seats and reached a plateau of some 50 per cent of the vote by 1903 (fig. A.4). With this commanding share of the vote, the SPD won 11 of these 26 seats in 1898 and 15 in 1903. By 1912 they won 21 of 26 type 3b seats. Most of these seats were in Saxony and nearby parts of Prussia and Thuringia, where the Social Democrats' opponents were often National Liberals.

Protestant urban (type 4) constituencies were far and away the strongest for the Social Democrats. Already in 1890 they approached winning half the popular vote (46.4 per cent) in Germany's Protestant city constituencies, and this continued to increase to 58.5 per cent in 1912 (fig. A.5). The other parties essentially declined, except for a minor anti-Semitic surge during 1893–8 – they won 6.4 per cent of the votes in these constituencies in both of those elections – and a left-liberal recovery in 1907 and 1912. Most of these seats were growing rapidly; total votes cast in the 45 type 4 constituencies increased from 1.35 million in 1890 to 2.73 million in 1912, with relatively high turnout levels in all elections. To judge by the

FIGURE A.5
Protestant Urban Constituencies (Type 4), 1890–1912 (N = 45)

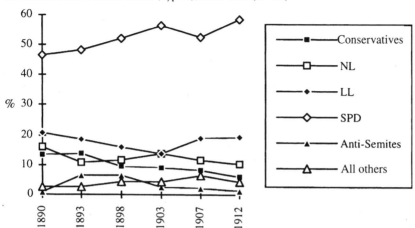

increasing Social Democratic share of the vote even as the total vote was increasing, Social Democrats must have been relatively better at mobilizing the growing electorate than was any other party. Only the left liberals after 1903 really kept pace.

Some key changes occurred in these seats in the 1898 and 1903 elections. While in other sorts of Protestant constituencies the non-socialist parties still had some hope of combining to defeat SPD candidates, in Protestant urban seats the SPD achieved levels of support that began giving it the lion's share of the seats. The 50 per cent level was of course critical, since 50 per cent plus one vote in a given constituency gave a party an immediate victory on the first ballot and gave opponents no hope of combining against it. When the average SPD vote in type 4 constituencies moved significantly beyond the 50 per cent level, it began to win the bulk of these seats. Thus in 1898 the SPD surpassed the 50 per cent level for the first time (52.3 per cent, up from 48.1 per cent in 1893), and the number of SPD candidates elected jumped to 28 from 23 in 1893. In 1903 the SPD vote advanced to 56.3 per cent, and the party won 35 of the 45 Protestant urban seats. The 'fairness' campaigns of 1898–1903, in the midst of the agrarian and tariff issues, were the campaigns that delivered the Protestant cities to the Social Democrats. That the SPD's position was not absolutely unassailable was shown in 1907, when it won only 52.7 per cent and 21 seats, but this recovered to 58.5 per cent and 40 of 45 seats in 1912.

Even more so than the Protestant cities, the Catholic rural / small-town

FIGURE A.6
Catholic Rural/Small-Town Constituencies (Type 5), 1890–1912 (N = 73)

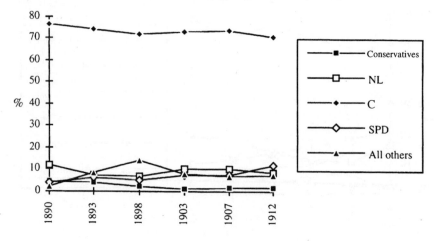

(type 5) constituencies were the preserve of a single party: in them the Catholic Centre won more than 70 per cent of the vote and at least 68 of 73 mandates in every election from 1890 to 1912, with no real sign of weakening over the time period (fig. A.6). The only other party to win more than one of these seats in a single election was the Bavarian Peasants' League, which scored some breakthroughs, most notably in 1898.

The type 5 seats were the worst electoral environment for the SPD, combining as they did Catholicism with a rural, agricultural population – three elements which correlated negatively with SPD support (chapter 7). In fact, a multiple regression using dummy variables to represent constituency types indicates that *only* type 5 correlated negatively with SPD support.[7] This large category of seats, then, the stable core for what was from 1890 to 1911 the largest delegation in the Reichstag, was alone of all types of constituency immune to significant Social Democratic penetration during the life of the Kaiserreich. The sorts of breakthroughs scored by the SPD in 1898 and 1903 did not extend to these seats.

Germany's Catholic cities (type 6 seats) did not make up a large group of constituencies, but are of significant interest. These seats showed a markedly different pattern from the rural type 5 seats. Here, the Social Democrats were consistently strong, with around 30 per cent of the vote during 1890–8, breaking through in 1903 to challenge the Centre Party and finally in 1912 slightly to surpass it, with 39.3 per cent of the vote to the Centre Party's 39.1 per cent (fig. A.7). The seats were split in 1912

FIGURE A.7
Catholic Urban Constituencies (Type 6), 1890–1912 ($N = 10$)

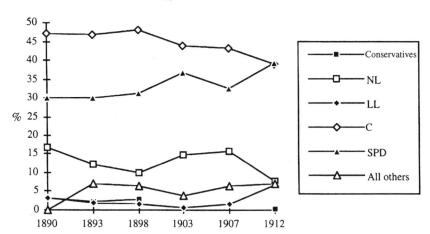

such that the Centre won five to the SPD's four; the National Liberals also won one.

To judge by the declining Catholic share of the vote and the increasing Social Democratic share, in urban areas the confessional factor was less and less important after 1898. Overall the SPD was a strongly Protestant party that rarely breached the confessional divide; but the variables related to employment in agriculture and rural population produced the coefficients of greatest magnitude, suggesting that these factors explain more of the Social Democratic performance than does the confessional structure of the seats (chapter 7). That the SPD did well in Catholic cities is therefore not too surprising: ruralness was a bigger barrier to the party than was Catholicism by itself.

Type 7a seats were dominated by national conflict, reflected in the proportion of the popular vote won by particularist parties, meaning parties representing ethnic or regional minorities: Poles, Alsace-Lorrainers, Guelphs in Hanover, etc. (fig. A.8). These seats were defined as those in which a particularist candidate attained one-third of the popular vote in *any* general election during 1890–1912. The fact that the *average* particularist vote in these constituencies exceeded 40 per cent for *all* elections is a general indication of how greatly concentrated and consistent the particularist votes were. This in turn enabled them to win 194 of the 324 contests in these seats over the six elections.

Two points are worthy of note with respect to the type 7a seats. First, in

FIGURE A.8
Particularist Constituencies (Type 7a), 1890–1912 ($N = 54$)

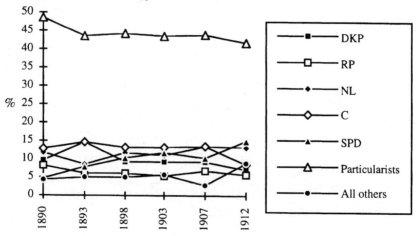

these seats *every* election tended to be a 'national' election, regardless of the issues at the Reich level. While conflicts between liberals and conservatives or between socialists and the old parties did enter into the picture, the main dynamic was a competition between the local particularist party and (perhaps on the second ballot) the strongest local representative of the so-called 'German' parties. Just about any liberal, conservative, or Centre party candidate counted as 'German.' In figure A.8, then, the commanding lead shown for the particularists is misleading insofar as the different particularist parties are here aggregated while the 'German' parties are not. In any given constituency, the race was likely to be much closer between the local particularist candidate and the local 'German' candidate. Second, however, what the performance of the individual German parties shows is that, at least until 1907, the older liberal, conservative, and Centre parties did not decline (as they did in the Reich overall) but maintained their vote with some consistency. In other words, in the presence of constant 'national' mobilization and the absence of polarization on the basis of 'fairness' questions, the old parties maintained their strength and the SPD advanced far slower than in other constituencies. The fact that many type 7a seats were more often Catholic and agricultural than the Reich average undoubtedly also hindered SPD penetration of these areas.

Similarly in regions of mixed confession (type 7b, many of which were in the Rhineland, Baden, Württemberg, and western or northern

FIGURE A.9
Mixed-Confession Constituencies (Type 7b), 1890–1912 (N = 52)

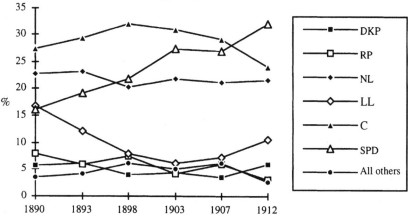

Bavaria), the 'fragmentation' was a bit less than in most of the Protestant seats, perhaps because the dynamic of confessional conflict helped reinforce the old party lines. The overall pattern pitted the Centre against liberal or, secondarily, conservative opponents (the dominant opposition being Centre–National Liberal) with the SPD overtaking the other Protestant parties (fig. A.9). The same relationships are reflected in the seat totals. Over the six elections, the most mandates (89 of a possible 312) were won by the Centre Party, which had the advantage that, though Catholics had no secure majority in these seats, at least there was only a single party normally wooing their votes. The Protestant parties were more divided, but the National Liberals won the most mandates (89 over the period 1890–1912), followed by the SPD (56). Interestingly, the Imperial Party won a substantial number of mandates (27) to come fourth, ahead of the German Conservatives and the left liberals, who, on the national scale, were much more substantial parties. This may reflect the tendency of 'national' election committees in some areas to select an Imperial Party candidate to attempt to serve as a non-agrarian, non-liberal, straightforward patriotic candidate rallying the whole non-socialist and non-Catholic field. The Imperial Party was similarly stronger than the norm in the type 7a seats, though not to as great a degree as in type 7b, and anecdotal evidence supports the notion that the Imperial Party sometimes served as a compromise patriotic party.[8]

In summary, the usefulness of these categories of analysis is partly contained in the fact that several of them were dominated overwhelmingly by a single political party or grouping, revealing a degree of homogeneity in political culture and behaviour. The Protestant large-farm areas of the northeast (type 1) were a firmly German Conservative environment. Protestant cities (type 4) were solidly SPD by this period, as increasingly were the Saxon-style mixed non-urban and non-rural seats (type 3b). Catholic rural and small-town environments were overwhelmingly committed to the Centre Party (type 5). In addition, the seats of particularist conflict were dominated, as a whole, by the various particularist parties. These four types of environments – Protestant large-holding rural areas, Catholic small towns, Protestant cities, and particularist communities – represent the stable pivots of Wilhelmine electoral politics, where party and social grouping were so intertwined as to be nearly unshakeable, although some changes began to become evident in 1912. These environments were the core areas for the most consistently strong parties.

By contrast, the other types defined here – the more middling or peasant-based Protestant rural areas and mixed rural-urban seats (types 2 and 3a) – were jumbled in amongst each other in 'middle Germany,' the broad (and jurisdictionally jumbled) area from Hessen to Thuringia. Middle Germany was surrounded by the mixed Protestant-Catholic seats (type 7b) and by the Conservative, Centre, and particularist strongholds on the peripheries, and dotted with cities that were centres of SPD strength. There were regional clumps within this area that were dominated more by one party than another – it appears that National Liberal concentrations, in particular, were quite localized – but these clumps rarely comprised more than a handful of constituencies. Considered as a whole, these categories appear as the environment in which the 'fragmentation' of the Protestant 'middle parties' was most evident. The small-scale, widely varying, 'fragmented' middle German environments (types 2 and 3a) were the ones where liberals eked out their existence, when other parties had built solid supra-regional blocs of support covering large parts of Germany.

Constituency Concordance

Constituency Number	Region	Number within Constituency Name		Type (see App. A)
Kingdom of Prussia				
Prov. of East Prussia				
1	Königsberg	I	Memel-Heydekrug	3a
2		II	Labiau-Wehlau	1
3		III	Stadt Königsberg	4
4		IV	Königsberg Land-Fischhausen	1
5		V	Heiligenbeil-Preußische Eylau	2
6		VI	Braunsberg-Heilsberg	5
7		VII	Preußisch Holland-Mohrungen	2
8		VIII	Osterode-Neidenburg	2
9		IX	Allenstein-Rössel	7a
10		X	Rastenburg-Gerdauen-Friedland	1
11	Gumbinnen	I	Tilsit-Niederung	3a
12		II	Ragnit-Pillkallen	2
13		III	Gumbinnen-Insterburg	1
14		IV	Stallupönnen-Goldap-Darkehmen	2
15		V	Angerburg-Lötzen	1
16		VI	Olctzko-Lyck-Johannisburg	2
17		VII	Sensburg-Ortelsburg	7a
Prov. of West Prussia				
18	Danzig	I	Marienburg-Elbing	1

19		II	Danziger Niederung-	
			Danziger Höhe	7b
20		III	Danzig City	4
21		IV	Neustadt-Karthaus-Putzig	7a
22		V	Berent-Stargard-Dirschau	7a
23	Marienwerder	I	Stuhm-Marienwerder	7a
24		II	Rosenberg-Löbau	7a
25		III	Graudenz-Strasburg	7a
26		IV	Thorn-Kulm	7a
27		V	Schwetz	7a
28		VI	Konitz-Tuchel	7a
29		VII	Schlochau-Flatow	7a
30		VIII	Deutsch-Krone	7b

Berlin

31	Berlin	I	Berlin-Centre	4
32		II	Outer City, South and Southwest	4
33		III	Inner City, South	4
34		IV	Outer City, East	4
35		V	Inner City, North	4
36		VI	Outer City, North and Northwest	4

Prov. of Brandenburg

37	Potsdam	I	Westprignitz	3a
38		II	Ostprignitz	2
39		III	Ruppin-Templin	1
40		IV	Prenzlau-Angermünde	1
41		V	Oberbarnim	3b
42		VI	Niederbarnim	4
43		VII	Potsdam-Osthavelland	4
44		VIII	Westhavelland-Brandenburg	4
45		IX	Zauch-Belzig-Jüterbog-	
			Luckenwalde	2
46		X	Teltow-Beeskow-Storkow-	
			Charlottenburg	4
47	Frankfurt a.O.	I	Arnswalde-Friedeberg	2
48		II	Landsberg-Soldin	3a
49		III	Königsberg	2
50		IV	Frankfurt-Lebus	4
51		V	Ost- und Weststernberg	2

52		VI	Züllichau-Krossen	2
53		VII	Guben-Lübben	3a
54		VIII	Sorau	3a
55		IX	Kottbus-Spremberg	3a
56		X	Kalau-Luckau	2

Prov. of Pomerania

57	Stettin	I	Demmin-Anklam	1
58		II	Ueckermünde-Usedom-Wollin	2
59		III	Randow-Greifenhagen	1
60		IV	Stettin City	4
61		V	Pyritz-Saatzig	1
62		VI	Naugard-Regenwalde	1
63		VII	Greifenberg-Kammin	1
64	Köslin	I	Stolp-Lauenburg	1
65		II	Bütow-Rummelsburg-Schlawe	1
66		III	Köslin-Kolberg-Körlin-Bublitz	1
67		IV	Belgard-Schivelbein-Dramburg	1
68		V	Neustettin	1
69	Stralsund	I	Rügen-Franzburg-Stralsund	1
70		II	Grimmen-Greifswald	1

Prov. of Posen

71	Posen	I	Posen	7a
72		II	Samter-Birnbaum-Obornik	7a
73		III	Meseritz-Bomst	7a
74		IV	Buk-Kosten	7a
75		V	Kroeben [Gostyn-Rawitsch]	7a
76		VI	Fraustadt	7a
77		VII	Schrimm-Schroda	7a
78		VIII	Wreschen-Pleschen	7a
79		IX	Krotoschin	7a
80		X	Adelnau-Schildberg	7a
81	Bromberg	I	Czarnikau-Kolmar	7b
82		II	Wirsitz-Schubin	7a
83		III	Bromberg	7b
84		IV	Inowrazlaw-Mogilno-Strelno	7a
85		V	Gnesen-Wongrowitz	7a

Prov. of Silesia

86	Breslau	I	Guhrau-Steinau-Wohlau	1
87		II	Militsch-Trebnitz	1
88		III	Groß Wartenberg-Oels	1
89		IV	Namslau-Brieg	1
90		V	Ohlau-Nimptsch-Strehlen	1
91		VI	Breslau City East	7b
92		VII	Breslau City West	7b
93		VIII	Breslau Land-Neumarkt	7b
94		IX	Striegau-Schweidnitz	7b
95		X	Waldenburg	3b
96		XI	Reichenbach-Neurode	7b
97		XII	Glatz-Habelschwerdt	5
98		XIII	Frankenstein-Münsterberg	5
99	Oppeln	I	Kreuzburg-Rosenberg	7a
100		II	Oppeln	7a
101		III	Groß Strehlitz-Kosel	7a
102		IV	Lublinitz-Tost-Gleiwitz	7a
103		V	Beuthen-Tarnowitz	7a
104		VI	Kattowitz-Zabrze	7a
105		VII	Pleß-Rybnik	7a
106		VIII	Ratibor	5
107		IX	Leobschütz	5
108		X	Neustadt	5
109		XI	Falkenberg-Grottkau	5
110		XII	Neiße	5
111	Liegnitz	I	Grünberg-Freistadt	3a
112		II	Sagan-Sprottau	2
113		III	Glogau	2
114		IV	Lüben-Bunzlau	3a
115		V	Löwenberg	2
116		VI	Liegnitz-Goldberg-Hainau	2
117		VII	Landeshut-Jauer-Bolkenhain	7b
118		VIII	Schönau-Hirschberg	2
119		IX	Görlitz-Lauban	4
120		X	Rothenburg-Hoyerswerda	2

Prov. of Saxony

| 121 | Magdeburg | I | Salzwedel-Gardelegen | 2 |
| 122 | | II | Osterburg-Stendal | 3a |

123		III	Jerichow I and II	2
124		IV	Magdeburg City	4
125		V	Wolmirstedt-Neuhaldensleben	2
126		VI	Wanzleben	3b
127		VII	Aschersleben-Kalbe	4
128		VIII	Oschersleben-Halberstadt-Wernigerode	3b
129	Merseburg	I	Liebenwerda-Torgau	2
130		II	Schweinitz-Wittenberg	2
131		III	Bitterfeld-Delitzsch	3a
132		IV	Saalkreis-Halle City	4
133		V	Mansfelder See- und Gebirgskreis	2
134		VI	Sangerhausen-Eckartsberga	1
135		VII	Querfurt-Merseburg	1
136		VIII	Naumburg-Weißenfels-Zeitz	3a
137	Erfurt	I	Nordhausen	3b
138		II	Heiligenstadt-Worbis	5
139		III	Mühlhausen-Langensalza-Weißensee	3a
140		IV	Erfurt-Schleusingen-Ziegenrück	4

Prov. of Schleswig-Holstein

141	I	Hadersleben-Sonderburg	7a
142	II	Apenrade-Flensburg	3a
143	III	Schleswig-Eckernförde	1
144	IV	Tondern-Husum-Eiderstedt	2
145	V	Dithmarschen-Steinburg	2
146	VI	Pinneberg-Segeberg	3b
147	VII	Kiel	4
148	VIII	Altona-Stormarn	4
149	IX	Oldenburg-Plön	1
150	X	Herzogtum Lauenburg	2

Prov. of Hanover

151	I	Emden-Norden	3a
152	II	Aurich-Wittmund	2
153	III	Meppen-Bentheim-Lingen	5
154	IV	Osnabrück	7a
155	V	Melle-Diepholz	7a

156		VI	Syke-Hoya	7a
157		VII	Neustadt-Nienburg	7a
158		VIII	Hanover-Linden City	4
159		IX	Hameln-Linden	2
160		X	Hildesheim	3a
161		XI	Einbeck-Northeim	7a
162		XII	Göttingen-Münden	7a
163		XIII	Goslar-Zellerfeld	3b
164		XIV	Gifhorn-Peine	7a
165		XV	Uelzen-Lüchow	7a
166		XVI	Lüneburg-Winsen	7a
167		XVII	Harburg-Rotenburg-Zeven	3a
168		XVIII	Stade-Blumenthal	2
169		XIX	Kehdingen-Neuhaus an der Oste	3a

Prov. of Westphalia

170	Münster	I	Tecklenburg-Steinfurt-Ahaus	5
171		II	Münster-Koesfeld	5
172		III	Borcken-Recklinghausen	5
173		IV	Lüdinghausen-Beckum-Warendorf	5
174	Minden	I	Minden-Lübbecke	2
175		II	Herford-Halle	2
176		III	Bielefeld-Wiedenbrück	3b
177		IV	Paderborn-Büren	5
178		V	Warburg-Höxter	5
179	Arnsberg	I	Wittgenstein-Siegen	2
180		II	Olpe-Meschede-Arnsberg	5
181		III	Altena-Iserlohn	3b
182		IV	Hagen	4
183		V	Bochum-Gelsenkirchen-Hattingen	7b
184		VI	Dortmund	7b
185		VII	Hamm-Soest	7b
186		VIII	Lippstadt-Brilon	5

Prov. of Hesse-Nassau

187	Wiesbaden	I	Landkreis Wiesbaden-Obertaunus	7b
188		II	Wiesbaden City	7b

189		III	Unterwesterwald-Rheingau	7b
190		IV	Ober- und Unterlahnkreis	7b
191		V	Dillkreis-Oberwesterwald	2
192		VI	Frankfurt a.M. City	4
193	Cassel	I	Rinteln-Hofgeismar	2
194		II	Cassel-Melsungen	4
195		III	Fritzlar-Homberg-Ziegenhain	2
196		IV	Eschwege-Schmalkalden	2
197		V	Marburg-Frankenberg	3a
198		VI	Hersfeld-Rotenburg	2
199		VII	Fulda-Schlüchtern	7b
200		VIII	Hanau	3b

Prov. of the Rhineland

201	Cologne	I	Cologne City	6
202		II	Cologne Land	6
203		III	Bergheim-Euskirchen	5
204		IV	Rheinbach-Bonn	5
205		V	Siegkreis-Waldbröl	5
206		VI	Mühlheima.Rh.-Wipperfürth-Gummersbach	5
207	Düsseldorf	I	Lennep-Mettmann	3b
208		II	Elberfeld-Barmen	4
209		III	Solingen	7b
210		IV	Düsseldorf	6
211		V	Essen	7b
212		VI	Mühlheim-Duisburg City	7b
213		VII	Mörs-Rees	7b
214		VIII	Kleve-Geldern	5
215		IX	Kempen	5
216		X	Gladbach	6
217		XI	Krefeld	6
218		XII	Neuß-Grevenbroich	5
219	Koblenz	I	Wetzlar-Altenkirchen	2
220		II	Neuwied	7b
221		III	Koblenz-St. Goar	5
222		IV	Kreuznach-Simmern	7b
223		V	Mayen-Ahrweiler	5
224		VI	Adenau-Kochem-Zell	5
225	Trier	I	Daun-Prüm-Bitburg	5

226		II	Wittlich-Bernkastel	5
227		III	Trier	5
228		IV	Saarburg-Merzig-Saarlouis	5
229		V	Saarbrücken	7b
230		VI	Ottweiler-St. Wendel	7b
231	Aachen	I	Schleiden-Malmedy-Montjoie	5
232		II	Eupen-Aachen Land-Burtscheid	5
233		III	Aachen City	6
234		IV	Düren-Jülich	5
235		V	Geilenkirchen-Heinsberg-Erkelenz	5
236	Hohenzollern-Sigmaringen	I	Sigmaringen	5

Kingdom of Bavaria

237	Upper Bavaria	I	Munich I	6
238		II	Munich II	6
239		III	Aichach	5
240		IV	Ingolstadt	5
241		V	Wasserburg	5
242		VI	Weilheim	5
243		VII	Rosenheim	5
244		VIII	Traunstein	5
245	Lower Bavaria	I	Landshut	5
246		II	Straubing	5
247		III	Passau	5
248		IV	Pfarrkirchen	5
249		V	Deggendorf	5
250		VI	Kelheim	5
251	Palatinate	I	Speyer	7b
252		II	Landau	7b
253		III	Germersheim	7b
254		IV	Zweibrücken	7b
255		V	Homburg	2
256		VI	Kaiserslautern	3a
257	Upper Palatinate	I	Regensburg	5
258		II	Amberg	5
259		III	Neumarkt	5

260		IV	Neunburg v.W.	5
261		V	Neustadt a.W.N.	5
262	Upper Franconia	I	Hof	3a
263		II	Bayreuth	3a
264		III	Forchheim	7b
265		IV	Kronach	7b
266		V	Bamberg	5
267	Middle Franconia	I	Nuremberg	4
268		II	Erlangen-Fürth	4
269		III	Ansbach-Schwabach	3a
270		IV	Eichstädt	7b
271		V	Dinkelsbühl	2
272		VI	Rothenburg a.d.T.	2
273	Lower Franconia	I	Aschaffenburg	5
274		II	Kitzingen	7b
275		III	Lohr	5
276		IV	Neustadt a.d.S.	5
277		V	Schweinfurt	5
278		VI	Würzburg	6
279	Swabia	I	Augsburg	6
280		II	Donauwörth	5
281		III	Dillingen	5
282		IV	Illertissen	5
283		V	Kaufbeuren	5
284		VI	Immenstadt	5

Kingdom of Saxony

285	I	Zittau	3b
286	II	Löbau	3b
287	III	Bautzen-Kamenz	3a
288	IV	Dresden r.d. Elbe	4
289	V	Dresden l.d. Elbe	4
290	VI	Dresden Altstadt-Dippoldiswalde	3b
291	VII	Meißen-Großenhain	3a
292	VIII	Pirna	2
293	IX	Freiberg	3b

294	X	Döbeln	2
295	XI	Oschatz-Grimma	3a
296	XII	Leipzig City	4
297	XIII	Amtshauptmannschaft Leipzig	4
298	XIV	Borna	2
299	XV	Mittweida-Burgstädt [Rochlitz-Flöha]	3b
300	XVI	Chemnitz	4
301	XVII	Meerane-Glauchau	3b
302	XVIII	Zwickau	4
303	XIX	Stollberg-Lößnitz-Schneeberg-Hartenstein	3b
304	XX	Sayda-Marienberg	2
305	XXI	Annaberg-Schwarzenberg	3b
306	XXII	Kirchberg-Auerbach	3b
307	XXIII	Plauen	3b

Kingdom of Württemberg

308	I	Stuttgart	4
309	II	Cannstatt-Ludwigsburg	3b
310	III	Brackenheim-Heilbronn	3a
311	IV	Böblingen-Leonberg	2
312	V	Eßlingen-Kirchheim	3a
313	VI	Reutlingen-Tübingen	3a
314	VII	Nagold-Neuenbürg	2
315	VIII	Freudenstadt-Oberndorf	7b
316	IX	Balingen-Rottweil	7b
317	X	Gmünd-Göppingen	3a
318	XI	Hall-Oehringen	2
319	XII	Gerabronn-Künzelsau	2
320	XIII	Aalen-Ellwangen	7b
321	XIV	Ulm	3b
322	XV	Ehingen-Laupheim	7b
323	XVI	Biberach-Waldsee	5
324	XVII	Ravensburg-Saulgau	5

Grand Duchy of Baden

325	I	Konstanz-Überlingen	5
326	II	Donaueschingen-Villingen	5

327	III	Schopfheim-Waldshut	5
328	IV	Lörrach-Müllheim	7b
329	V	Freiburg	7b
330	VI	Lahr-Wolfach	5
331	VII	Kehl-Offenburg	5
332	VIII	Bühl-Rastatt	5
333	IX	Pforzheim	7b
334	X	Karlsruhe	7b
335	XI	Mannheim	7b
336	XII	Heidelberg	7b
337	XIII	Bretten-Sinsheim	7b
338	XIV	Adelsheim-Buchen-Tauberbischofsheim	5

Grand Duchy of Hesse

339	I	Gießen	3a
340	II	Friedberg-Büdingen	2
341	III	Lauterbach-Alsfeld	2
342	IV	Darmstadt-Groß-Gerau	4
343	V	Offenbach-Dieburg	7b
344	VI	Erbach-Bensheim	2
345	VII	Worms	7b
346	VIII	Bingen-Alzey	7b
347	IX	Mainz	7b

Grand Duchy of Mecklenburg-Schwerin

348	I	Hagenow-Grevesmühlen	1
349	II	Schwerin-Wismar	4
350	III	Parchim-Ludwigslust	1
351	IV	Malchin-Warin	1
352	V	Rostock-Doberan	4
353	VI	Güstrow-Ribnitz	1

Grand Duchy of Saxe-Weimar

354	I	Weimar	3a
355	II	Eisenach-Dermbach	3a
356	III	Neustadt a.d. Orla	2

Grand Duchy of Mecklenburg-Strelitz

357			1

Grand Duchy of Oldenburg

358	I	Oldenburg-Lübeck-Birkenfeld	3a
359	II	Jever-Westerstede	2
360	III	Vechta-Kloppenburg	7b

Duchy of Brunswick

361	I	Brunswick-Blankenburg	4
362	II	Helmstedt-Wolfenbüttel	3a
363	III	Holzminden-Gandersheim	2

Duchy of Saxe-Meiningen

364	I	Meiningen-Hildburghausen	2
365	II	Sonneberg-Saalfeld	3a

Duchy of Saxe-Altenburg

366			3a

Duchy of Saxe-Coburg-Gotha

367	I	Coburg	3a
368	II	Gotha	3a

Duchy of Anhalt

369	I	Dessau-Zerbst	4
370	II	Bernburg-Ballenstedt	3b

Principality of Schwarzburg-Sondershausen

371			3a

Principality of Schwarzburg-Rudolstadt

| 372 | | | 2 |

Principality of Waldeck

| 373 | | | 2 |

Principality of Reuß Elder Line

| 374 | | | 3b |

Principality of Reuß Younger Line

| 375 | | | 3b |

Principality of Schaumburg-Lippe

| 376 | | | 2 |

Principality of Lippe

| 377 | | | 2 |

Free Hansa City of Lübeck

| 378 | | | 4 |

Free Hansa City of Bremen

| 379 | | | 4 |

Free Hansa City of Hamburg

380	I	Hamburg East	4
381	II	Hamburg West	4
382	III	Geest- und Marschlande	4

Reichsland Alsace-Lorraine

383	I	Altkirch-Thann	7a
384	II	Mühlhausen i.E.	7a
385	III	Colmar	7a
386	IV	Gebweiler	7a
387	V	Rappoltsweiler	7a
388	VI	Schlettstadt	7a
389	VII	Molsheim-Erstein	7a
390	VIII	Straßburg i.E.	7b
391	IX	Straßburg Land	7a
392	X	Hagenau-Weißenburg	7a
393	XI	Zabern	7b
394	XII	Saargemünd-Forbach	7a
395	XIII	Bolchen-Diedenhofen	7a
396	XIV	Metz	7a
397	XV	Saarburg-Salzburg	7a

Data Base and Methodology

Numbers are notoriously less precise and certain than they appear to be. While Imperial German statisticians were meticulous, there is nevertheless more than one way to count even the basic raw numbers they compiled, including election returns.

For this study, constituency-level electoral statistics for the Reichstag general elections of 1890–1912 (six elections in all) were taken from the governmental publications noted in the Bibliography (mostly the *Statistik des Deutschen Reichs*, where these were available to the author; and the *Anlagebände* to the *Stenographische Berichte über die Verhandlungen des Deutschen Reichstages*, where not). Reichstag reports of by-election results between general elections were also collected, but were mostly not used in this study. For provincial- and national-level election results, particularly for results before 1890, Ritter and Niehuss's excellent *Wahlgeschichtliches Arbeitsbuch* was used.

The raw constituency-level election data are affected by judgments of contemporary statisticians. No candidate receiving fewer than twenty-five votes was listed separately (the votes were put under 'other'), so that the 'other' category contains scattered votes for all parties. These votes were not, of course, reflected in the parties' nationwide vote totals. Also, this was an era of less formality in party identification than is today the case; and this was particularly true where *Honoratiorenpolitik* still held sway. Officials used their discretion and local knowledge in assigning party allegiances like 'liberal,' 'democrat,' and 'moderate liberal' to various candidates. Where calculations for 'left-liberal' totals are made in this study, they normally include the first two of these three designations.

In collecting the data, several conventions were followed which affect the statistics somewhat and could cause discrepancies when compared with other published sources. First, the statistics used were those for the *final* elections in each seat, the ones that resulted in a deputy taking up a mandate in the Reichstag. Sometimes the initial election proved invalid, either because a candidate was elected in more than one seat at a time, or because the results were declared invalid by the Reichstag election verification commission as a result of some abuse, or because the deputy died or resigned for personal reasons shortly after the election. In all of these cases, by-elections followed closely after the general election. This raises an issue for statisticians: if one counts only the ballots that were cast on general-election day, then the seat totals will not match the actual results, and some of the votes counted will be votes cast under proven situations of manipulation, coercion, and deception, later washed out by the verification committee's rulings. For this study, the election results tabulated were those that took effect, even if they were weeks or months after general-election day, possibly under political circumstances different from those in which the other constituencies had voted. There is no good answer to this dilemma, and it underlines the fact that, at root, voting should not be taken to be a sociological function, but a constructed process dependent on time, place, and institutions. Any procedure for assessing the results of voting has to contain some arbitrary elements.

Also, anti-Semites, agrarians, particularists of certain kinds, and various shades of liberals have been combined in many calculations. In most places in the text, it has been made explicit when this was done. There are also questions at the level of the basic data. One could, for example, maintain regional distinctions in the data among different kinds of anti-Semitic candidates (including German-Social and German-Social Reform candidates); but this was not done (only the Christian-Socials were separated from the others). An important part of the body of this study lies in finding various ways to combine similar kinds of party votes in order to arrive at meaningful generalizations across regions.

The social-economic and other statistics used in defining constituency types and as predictors in multilinear regressions were collected from a variety of sources. Voter turnout and constituency population were taken from the election results; the constituency size variable was normalized by putting the constituencies on a scale from one to one hundred, instead of from 11,000 to 340,000 as it would be using the raw data. Information on the confessional and urban/rural make-up of constituencies was also available in the *Statistik des Deutschen Reichs* election results after the turn of the century. The percentage of Catholics was the only confessional variable used, since Catholics and Protestants together accounted for 99 per cent of the population in almost every constituency. The rural/urban information indicated how many people lived in communities of 10,000 or more people ('cities,' as I have called them in the text), 2,000–9,999 ('towns'), or centres of 1,999 and fewer ('villages' or 'rural'). These numbers are likely highly accurate, but they do not necessarily reflect the culture of the community. Some 'towns' of 9,000 are factory suburbs dominated by heavy-industrial workers; and there is a great difference beween a 'city' of 11,000 and a city of 300,000. Perhaps for this reason, the rural and urban variables are not generally strongly significant in the regressions, although seen in combination with constituency size and percentage of agrarians (related statistics), they are still instructive.

The occupational statistics are the ones in which one has to have least confidence. The categories of percentage of the workforce employed in 'industry,' 'commerce,' and 'agriculture' do not seem, intuitively, to reflect meaningful social categories, except perhaps for the broad and at the time politicized distinction between agriculture and other sectors. This study uses only the 'agriculture' variable, whichs seems the most reliable of the three.

Other variables were dummy variables, meaning those that were given a value of zero in most constituencies, but a value of one in certain 'tagged' constituencies. For political regions like provinces, this is unambiguous – it is clear which constituencies are to be 'tagged' – but the variable for 'large landownership' needs explanation. Extensive information on landholding structures is available (see Hesselbarth in the Bibliography), but the author did not find any effective means to break these statistics down by Reichstag constituency. The region of large estates stretched across many provincial and state boundaries. The large-landownership variable was therefore defined by an extremely crude method: visual comparison was done between maps from Hesselbarth showing regions where large landholdings (those over one hundred hectares) made up more than half of all landholdings, and maps of Reichstag constituencies. The variable was assigned a value of one where the constituency appeared to lie mainly within the defined area. Naturally this method leaves room for judgment and error all around the boundaries of the large-landownership region: inclusion of the wrong seats or, more likely, exclusion of some that should have been included. However, to judge by the strong significance of the variable in several of the regressions, it is accurate enough to capture a genuinely meaningful social-economic structure. However, a good research project for someone would be to find a proper way to relate statistics on agricultural structure to voting results.

Another defect in the social-economic data is that they tend not to capture changes over time. For this study, the statistics used centred on 1898. Thus, the occupational census of 1895 was used for employment statistics, and the urban, rural, and confessional statistics relate to 1898–1900. These are probably fairly accurate for the two elections that are the focus of this study; but for the regressions on earlier and later elections, they will overestimate or underestimate the degree of urbanization and industrialization in some constituencies where changes were rapid. It is possible, then, that changes in regression coefficients for these earlier and later elections will reflect the imperfections of the data – for example, that the correlation of a party's vote with percentage of urban residents may appear stronger, when it was not stronger at all; it was the actual proportion of urban residents in each case that was higher than the statistic used.

The raw constituency-level results obtained within these various conventions and limitations were typed into a computer, where they were manipulated with special software to do the calculations used in this work. The data were screened automatically for obvious errors on input such as impossible values (e.g., percentages over 100) or sums that would not check, but also for improbable values, like 30 per cent turnout rates or 99 per cent run-off victories – both of which, incidentally, actually occurred in a few cases. This data-screening turned up a very small number of arithmetical or typographical errors in the official statistics, about which nothing could be done. Other errors in the data set, despite the author's best intentions, could possibly remain, but given the screening such errors should not be of large magnitude.

The software and hardware used for analysing the statistics went through several technological revolutions. The author began by using his own programs written in compiler BASIC and in assembly language on a machine with 64K of memory, 128K diskettes, and a CP/M operating system. From these stone knives and bearskins, the data ended up on an Apple PowerBook Duo 230 with 8 MB of memory, 80 MB of hard-drive storage, and all of the convenient graphical, statistical, and multi-tasking features for which Apple systems have been noted. (It is odd to watch a manuscript grow, slowly, as the computer shrinks around it down to something no bigger than a book itself, weighing three pounds.) The underlying analysis and sorting out of constituency types was done with the BASIC programs, but all the real statistical work was done later using SHAZAM (available from the University of British Columbia) for the multiple regressions and the basic statistics, and Microsoft Excel for the tables and charts. The author would be happy to share the data in electronic form with serious researchers, if this can be done efficiently and conveniently.

Understanding Multiple Regression

Those familiar with multiple regression techniques can certainly skip the first of the following sections but may want to consult the second portion of this appendix. As this work is intended for all those interested in the history of Wilhelmine Germany, the author does not presume a prior knowledge of statistical techniques.

A Layperson's Guide to Multiple Regression

Multiple regression is a powerful technique for identifying significant relationships in complex sets of statistics. The idea of a regression is to take a set of data and find a mathematical equation that 'predicts' another set of numbers. If the prediction works (in other words, if the equation comes close to giving the real answer in a lot of cases), then this indicates that, in reality, there is some important connection between the two data sets.

The simplest case to visualize is one in which there is one dependent variable (for example, the vote for party Y) which is to be examined in light of one independent or predictor variable (let us say X, the percentage of people of a certain demographic category within each voting district, like the percentage employed in agriculture). If we can find an equation that closely predicts Y when X is given, then we can take it that the vote for the party is a function of X – in short, that party Y's vote is affected by the number of people of type X who are present in each constituency.

There is a way to visualize what is going on in a regression: linear equations describe straight lines on a graph. In the example just given, one could measure the variable X on the horizontal axis of a graph, Y on the vertical axis, and plot the resulting points – the values of Y (party vote) associated with each level of X. If there is a good linear mathematical relationship between the two, then the points that are plotted will tend to fall near a single straight line. How close the points are to the best-fitted line (the best line minimizes the sum of squared errors) is an indication of how closely the variables are correlated. The computer (few people would attempt to do this by hand) draws the best possible straight line through a scattering of points that relate the two variables to one another. If the line closely matches the points of the actual data, we conclude that the underlying equation expresses a relationship between the variables. If the points are scattered randomly (i.e., the line does not closely match the points), we conclude that no statistically significant relationship exists between the variables.

In a linear equation, the dependent variable Y is modelled as a function of a predictor variable X multiplied by some coefficient (usually represented by the letter β or beta), plus a constant and an error term. The coefficient beta is the number that appears in the regression tables; it is the key to the regression and the way that the relationship between the variables is analysed. The higher the beta, the bigger the change in the dependent variable for a unit change in the predictor variable. A beta of zero means no relationship between the variables. Betas can be positive or negative, indicating positive or negative effects of the presence of X on the value of Y.

So far so good – but of course life rarely comes down to just two variables. This means that instead of plotting a line on a two-dimensional graph, the computer is plotting a line on an n-dimensional graph, where n is the total number of variables involved. In this study, some 30–40 predictor variables were used. (This is another good reason to let computers do the work.) Adding multiple variables into a regression is what turns simple regression into multiple regression, and it makes it a vastly more powerful technique. Essentially, the more variables are added in, the more information the computer has; and in trying to create the best fit to the actual data, it will discover which variables are meaningful and which are not. This permits the researcher to judge the significance and magnitude of one predictor variable compared with another, to discard what is not significant, and thus to determine which factors are really important (in the present case, important to determining how people voted). The researcher can determine not only that there is a correlation, but (with enough data) which correlations are more meaningful than others. For example, chapter 7 in this book contains a discussion of whether confessional allegiance or social-economic categories better explain Social Democratic voting support. Without multiple regression, such a discussion is virtually impossible because the variables (confession and social-economic structure) are interrelated.

The complicated part of multiple regression is judging whether results are statistically significant. A regression equation is a model that best fits a given set of observations. But those observations are only a subset of a real-life population that (especially in history) can never be known in its entirety. How do we know that the correlation we observe is not just an aberration present only in the observed values, and which does not exist in the 'real' population? These sorts of problems are addressed through analysis of error, the most complicated part of regression.

Briefly, what is done is to test the hypothesis, for each predictor variable, *that there is no real relationship between the predictor variable and the dependent variable* and estimate the probability that such a hypothesis can be rejected. 'No relationship' is equivalent to 'a coefficient or beta (for the predictor variable) equal to zero,' so that what is done is to assume for the sake of the test that the 'real' coefficient in the population at large is zero, and that the coefficient estimated by the regression is only a random error that deviates from this true value. Error (based on many assumptions) is held to follow a 'normal distribution' around a mean. The normal distribution is an abstraction and depends on some important assumptions, but it is based on long experience with social statistics. In essence, it says that errors fall symmetrically around the mean, more of them close to the mean than further away, producing a humped curve clustered around the mean value, with two long 'tails' that stretch out to each side. If the estimated coefficient falls under the 'hump,' where a large number of random errors could fall if the coefficient really were zero, then there is a good chance that random error alone could produce the estimated coefficient. In that case, the result (the estimated coefficient for that predictor variable in that regression) is said not to be statistically significant. But if the estimated value falls far out on one of the 'tails' of the normal distribution, then there is only a small chance that it could have been generated by error alone, without a real correlation existing. And one can say just what that chance is, based on the areas under the curve of the normal distribution. If the estimated value falls in an area on the tail of the curve where only 2.5 per cent of errors would normally lie, then this means there is only a 2.5 per cent chance that the result is due to error. One then says that the estimated coefficient is 'statistically significant at the 2.5 per cent level.'

In this study, the analysis of significance is done using t-ratios generated by the regression (these are based on the sum of squared errors, and they are shown in the tables of regression results in this book) and comparing these to 't-tables' that show the distribution for such t's. The significance tests used in this study are all 'two-tailed tests,' which means that the value from the t-table is doubled to allow for the error to be either positive or negative. Any t-ratio that exceeds the number from the table (doubled) is then statistically significant at the level indicated. (Higher absolute value is more significant.) The numbers from the t-tables also depend on the 'degrees of freedom' in the regression, which is related to the number of variables involved. In this study, the numbers of variables are quite large. The degrees of freedom (DF) can be found in the notes to each table.

No regression ever proves a causal connection. Any result could be the result of random error, or (more importantly) of problems in the data, such as failure to allow for important variables. The data set used for this study is large – 397 constituencies, 10 or so dependent variables tested individually against 20 or 30 predictor variables for each of 6 elections – which ought to reduce the probability of *random* factors producing illusory correlations. A random error might produce a coefficient that appears significant, but it would be remarkable for it to do so in six elections in a row, all of similar magnitude and sign.

In fact, the regressions presented in this study may tend to be on the cautious side, for an obscure reason. In Imperial German elections, there were few parties that contested all or even a large proportion of the Reichstag's 397 seats. This means that the vote for most parties is zero in most cases. Thinking of the analogy of drawing a line on a graph, imagine drawing a line through a set of points, most of which are at zero. Even if all of the non-zero cases fell onto a perfectly straight line – even if a party's vote, where it campaigned, was *perfectly* a function of the predictor variables – the relationship would be estimated as a weak one, because all the zeroes would not be explained. The line would tend to go through the middle of the graph, between the zeroes and the other results. Of course, one should also want to find social-structural explanations of why parties did not campaign in certain places and received no votes there; but to the extent that arbitrary personal and institutional factors influenced the choices of where certain parties campaigned, these arbitrary factors obscure what might be real social-structural explanations of why people did vote for the party when they were given a chance to do so.

Another problem is imperfect predictor variables. Every effort was made for this study to include every possible predictor variable; then those that were not useful in the regressions were eliminated, and the tables of coefficients as used in this book were composed. But if the real determinants of parties' performances were variables not used in this study, this could affect the results. And, indeed, the predictor variables are quite imperfect. This is, above all, true of the occupational statistics. Imperial statisticians recorded in their occupational censuses mainly whether people were employed in 'industry,' 'commerce,' or 'agriculture,' and most respondents were forced into these categories. For the modern researcher (interested, for example, in the effects of class or stratification on voting behaviour), these categories are woefully inadequate. In the present study, *only* the category 'employed in agriculture' was used as a predictor variable, the others being judged too unreliable. Even the agriculture statistics, of course, combine impoverished, migratory, landless labourers with prosperous peasant farmers and even Junker aristocrats. Given imperfections like these, one feels it is remarkable if any statistically significant correlation appears at all. There is also the possibility that where a statistically significant correlation appears, it is a result, not of the particular predictor variable under examination, but of some third variable that is accidentally or causally correlated with it. This is always a danger.

The other point to be mentioned about the variables used in this study is the inclusion of dummy variables for regions. These are variables that are either 'present' or 'absent' – 0 or 1. They are set to zero for all constituencies not located within the particular region. The regions used were Prussian and Bavarian provinces, the middle states, and groupings of the small states (Thuringia, Western German small states, Hansa cities). Introducing these variables into the regressions gives the computer an opportunity to allow for purely regional factors that are not explainable in terms of the other predictor variables. In effect, this allows the computer to consider regional culture as a predictor alongside more conventional social-economic statistics; and, of course, to compare the impact of region and social-economic factors against each other. Such variables were found to be significant in many cases, but see below for special considerations in interpreting their coefficients. The use of these dummy variables can be viewed as a crude but effective way of including regional factors not measured by any other means in the equation.

Reading the Regression Tables in This Book

When reading regression tables (tables of estimated coefficients) in this book, the reader should bear in mind the following:

1 The note to each table indicates what the *dependent* variable is – in other words, the variable that is to be 'predicted' by the variables listed in the left column of the table.[1]

2 The predictor variables listed in the left-hand column of each table are those that produced statistically significant coefficients.[2]

3 The second column generally indicates what kind of variable each predictor variable is. Variables are denoted as 'C' (continuous) or 'D' (dummy). The continuous variables run from 1 to 100 and can assume any value in between; the dummy variables can be only 0 or 1, and usually denote a region. Note that a continuous variable with a coefficient of 0.2, which seems small, might affect a party's vote as much as a dummy variable with a coefficient of 20, which seems large. This is because the continuous variable might vary from 0 in one constituency to 100 in another, causing a 0.2 × 100 = a 20 per cent difference in the dependent variable between the two constituencies. The dummy variable can never be greater than one, so that the greatest impact it could have in this case would be 20 × 1 = 20 per cent.

4 The remaining columns are usually one for each election (six elections, 1890–1912). A separate regression was run for each individual election, and the differences between one election and another can be analysed by comparison between columns.[3]

5 On the row beside each predictor variable are the 'estimated coefficients' for that variable in each election. The size of the coefficient shows how big an impact the predictor variable had on the dependent variable (which is usually the percentage vote for some party). A coefficient of 1 indicates a one-percentage-point increase in the party's performance for every 1-unit increase in the predictor variable; a –2 indicates a two-percentage-point decrease in performance for every 1-unit increase in the predictor variable. These coefficients can assume any value. Where the *t*-ratios indicate the coefficient is significant at at least the 5 per cent level (see below) it is in **bold**; where not, it is in *italics*.

6 Below each coefficient and in smaller type, the tables show the corresponding '*t*-ratio.' The magnitude of the *t*-ratio is an indication of how unlikely it was that random error alone produced the estimated coeffi-

cient.[4] A large positive or negative t-ratio suggests that the coefficient is statistically significant, and that the predictor variable has a real impact on the dependent variable. In general, the absolute value of the t-ratio should be above two for a relationship to be significant. Because the degrees of freedom are similarly high in all the regressions shown, the relevant t-ratio is the same for all tables: results are significant at the 5 per cent level when the absolute magnitude of the t-ratio is 1.96 or more; at the 2.5 per cent level when the absolute magnitude of the t-ratio is 2.58 or more (2-tailed test).

7 In the bottom row of each table is shown the adjusted R^2 (R-squared) for each regression.[5] The closer the R^2 approaches 1, the more completely the dependent variable (the vote for the party in question) has been explained by the variables used. An R^2 of .75 could be interpreted as showing that 75 per cent of the variation in votes for the party concerned has been explained by the predictor variables, and that 25 per cent is a result of other factors not accounted for by the variables examined.

8 Below the R^2 is an F. This number is compared to a t-table to test the hypothesis that all the betas (except the constant) are really zero. The higher the F, the less the chance the betas were produced by the effects of error alone.[6]

An important point to bear in mind is that these are *multiple* regressions: all of the predictor variables were tested at the same time in a combined regression equation. Thus the coefficients in the table are produced by all the variables working together, not by each of them in isolation from the others. This is a powerful technique because it eliminates spurious results that can appear when variables are tested one at a time – it tends to sort out overlapping variables and determine which ones are really meaningful. But it can also lead to subtleties of interpretation. When a table shows one variable as acting in a strongly negative way, for example, this means that it causes a negative deviation *from the value that would have been predicted by the other variables alone.*

Readers particularly have to observe the special character of the regional dummy variables that appear in the regressions ('Berlin,' 'Brandenburg,' and the like). These do not indicate the regions where the party in question was strongest (or weakest). They indicate where the party's *share of the vote* was *higher or lower than was to be expected* given the other variables in the regression. Thus, if a party is strongly supported by the farm population and its support is found to be high in an agricultural region, this is only to be expected. The dummy variable for that region may not be found to contribute much to explaining the variation in the party's vote, even though it is strong there. But if the level of support is greatly different in a region for no reason that is apparent from the other statistics used in the regression, then it will appear as a significant predictor variable with a bearing on the party's performance. If the estimated coefficient for the regional variable is found to be, for example, 10, this is like saying the party in question got a 10 per cent bonus in the seats in that region compared to what would be estimated on the basis of the other predictor variables. It could be, however, that a party's strongest or weakest region would not appear in the table as either positive or negative – if that strength or weakness was explainable by the other predictor variables. If farmers supported the party in question everywhere but in one region, this might appear as a general positive correlation of the party's support with farming, but a specific negative coefficient for its support in that region. And the level of support in that region, despite the negative coefficient, could still be higher than it was in a third region that does not show up in the table at all. The regions only show up where they are *different* from the trend produced by the other variables.

It is also worth remembering that the regressions in this study are based on the *share* of the vote won on the *first* ballot. Since constituencies varied greatly in size, it is possible that parties could win a majority of their votes where their share was low; the regression would nevertheless show them as being weak in those kinds of seats. And where they *won* their seats is another question entirely. Anything could happen in a run-off ballot, with victory not necessarily depending on the share of votes won on the first ballot.

Guide to Abbreviations

Abbreviations Used in Main Text

BdI	Bund der Industriellen (League of Industrialists)
BdL	Bund der Landwirte (Agrarian League)
CDI	Centralverband Deutscher Industrieller (Central Association of German Industrialists)
DVP	Deutsche Volkspartei ([South] German People's Party)
FVg	Freisinnige Vereinigung (Left Liberal Union)
FVP	Freisinnige Volkspartei (Left Liberal People's Party)
HVV	Handelsvertragsverein (Trade Treaty Association)
RgS	Reichsverband gegen die Sozialdemokratie (Imperial League against Social Democracy)
SPD	Sozialdemokratische Partei Deutschlands (Social Democratic Party of Germany)
VkD	Volksverein für das katholische Deutschland (People's Association for Catholic Germany)

Abbreviations Used in Appendices, Notes, and Bibliography (in Addition to Above)

State Agencies

LA	Landratsamt [Landrat District]
LR	Landrat
MdA	Ministry of Foreign Affairs
MdI	[Prussian] Ministry of the Interior
Min. State	[Prussian] Ministry of State
OB	Oberbürgermeister

OP   Oberpräsident [provincial governor]
RdI   Reich Ministry of the Interior
RP   Regierungspräsident [district governor]
RT   Reichstag[1]

Political Parties and Organizations
C   Centre Party
DKP   German Conservative Party
LL   left liberal(s)
NL   National Liberal(s)
RP   Imperial Party
WVg   Wirtschaftliche Vereinigung (Economic Union)

Archives (See Bibliography)
BAK   Bundesarchiv Koblenz (ZSg: Zeitgeschichtliche
            Sammlung)
BAP   Bundesarchiv, Abteilung Potsdam (RLB PA: Reichs-
            landbund Pressearchiv)
BHSA
  Munich   Bayerisches Hauptstaatsarchiv München (Abteilung II,
            Geheimes Staatsarchiv, unless otherwise noted)
GStAPK   Geheimes Staatsarchiv Preußischer Kulturbesitz, Berlin-
            Dahlem[2]
HASK   Hauptarchiv der Stadt Köln
Hess. SA
  Marburg   Hessisches Staatsarchiv Marburg
HSA   Hauptstaatsarchiv (Düss.: Düsseldorf; Hann.: Hanover;
            Stutt.: Stuttgart)
LASH   Landesarchiv Schleswig-Holstein
RWSA
  Münster   Rheinisch-Westfälisches Staatsarchiv Münster
SA Bremen   Staatsarchiv der Freien Hansestadt Bremen
SA Münster Nordrhein-Westfälisches Staatsarchiv Münster

General Abbreviations Referring to Archive Collections
Best.   Bestand
CB   Centralbüro
HB   Hauptbüro
no.   *document* number (Blatt)
Nr.   *file* number

Präs.	Präsidialbüro
Reg.	Regierung
Rep.	Reperatorium
Verz.	Verzeichnis

Newspapers

BT	*Berliner Tageblatt*
Corr. d. BdL	*Correspondenz des Bundes des Landwirte*
DTZ	*Deutsche Tageszeitung*
FZ	*Frankfurter Zeitung*
Germ.	*Germania*
KöVZ	*Kölnische Volkszeitung*
KöZ	*Kölnische Zeitung*
KZ	*Kreuzzeitung (Neue Preußische Zeitung)*
NAZ	*Norddeutsche Allgemeine Zeitung*
NZ	*Nationalzeitung*
RWZ	*Rheinisch-westfälische Zeitung*
VW	*Vorwärts* (Berlin edition)

Note: Dates are given in the form day/month/year. The *edition* is specified immediately after the date, as follows:

1BB	Erster Beiblatt (First Supplement), etc.
ev	evening
m	morning (m1: first morning edition; m2: second; etc.)
n	noon/afternoon
S	Sunday

Academic Journals

CEH	*Central European History*
CJH	*Canadian Journal of History*
EHQ	*European History Quarterly*
ESR	*European Studies Review*
HJ	*The Historical Journal*
HZ	*Historische Zeitschrift*
JEEH	*Journal of European Economic History*
JMH	*Journal of Modern History*
MM	*Militärgeschichtliche Mitteilungen*
PP	*Past and Present*
SH	*Social History*

Notes

Chapter 1: Democratic Participation in an Undemocratic State

1 Germany had a democratic suffrage for men before any of the other fifteen Western European countries examined by Lane and Ersson in 1991, with the exception of the French and Swiss suffrages of 1848 (Jan-Erik Lane and Svante O. Ersson, *Politics and Society in Western Europe*, p. 300).

2 It approached 'universal,' of course, only among men twenty-five years of age and older, a suffrage which earned the term 'universal' a century ago given the highly restricted gender assumptions of the time. The founding constitution and basic laws of the 1871 German Empire carried over a number of institutions, including the suffrage, from the 1867 constitution of the North German Confederation.

3 For example, Hans-Ulrich Wehler, *Das Deutsche Kaiserreich 1871–1918*; Ralf Dahrendorf, *Society and Democracy in Germany*. More examples could be cited, but these two synthesize many of the others.

4 Joseph Schumpeter, *Capitalism, Socialism, and Democracy*, esp. pp. 269ff. On 'the modern "economic" theory of democracy' or rational-choice model of voting, see Angelo Panebianco, *Political Parties: Organization and Power*, pp. 40ff; and Martin Harrop and William Miller, *Elections and Voters: A Comparative Introduction*, pp. 145ff.

5 Note that by some definitions, Imperial German parties – though they served as models in the development of party theory – were not really 'political parties' at all! Joseph LaPalombara and Myron Weiner, for example, include in their definition of a party a 'self-conscious determination of leaders ... to capture and to hold decision-making power alone or in coalition with others, not simply to influence the exercise of power' ('The Origin and Development of Political Parties,' in Joseph LaPalombara and Myron Weiner, eds., *Political*

Parties and Political Development). For a much more nuanced appreciation of the ambiguity of party, see Kenneth Janda, 'Comparative Political Parties,' in Ada W. Finifter, ed., *Political Science: The State of the Discipline II*, pp. 165–6.

6   For example, Seymour Martin Lipset, *Political Man: The Social Bases of Politics*, pp. 75–8.

7   Alan Ware, *Citizens, Parties and the State: A Reappraisal*, p. 10.

8   Ibid., p. 14.

9   Ware, in ibid., pp. 23ff, summarizes the many disagreements among theorists as to the ways and degrees in which parties do these things. Klaus von Beyme (*Political Parties in Western Democracies*, p. 11) argues that the interest-aggregation function of parties is key.

10   On Gramsci and hegemony, see Chantal Mouffe, ed., *Gramsci and Marxist Theory*, especially the contributions by Norberto Bobbio, Jacques Texier, and Mouffe.

11   Stanley Suval, *Electoral Politics in Wilhelmine Germany*, pp. 16, 55ff.

12   See the works by Steinbach and Rohe in the Bibliography, which are discussed later in this chapter and in chapter 2.

13   Harrop and Miller, *Elections and Voters*, p. 9.

14   Ibid., pp. 9–10. The quotation within the quotation is from David Butler, Howard R. Penniman, and Austin Ranney, 'Democratic and Nondemocratic Elections,' in David Butler, Howard R. Penniman, and Austin Ranney, eds., *Democracy at the Polls: A Comparative Study of Competitive National Elections*, p. 9.

15   Harrop and Miller argue, for example, that Ronald Reagan's victory in the 1980 presidential election in the United States helped create the impression of a 'new conservative electorate,' even though opinion polls did not bear out the impression that the voters were endorsing Reagan's conservative agenda. In short, the interpretation of the result affected American politics (*Elections and Voters*, p. 78).

16   Ibid., p. 259.

17   This is a point developed most effectively by David Blackbourn and Geoff Eley (*Peculiarities of German History*).

18   A good example would be Dahrendorf, *Society and Democracy in Germany*.

19   Butler, Penniman, and Ranney, 'Democratic and Nondemocratic Elections,' in Butler, Penniman, and Ranney, eds., *Democracy at the Polls*, p. 1.

20   Ibid., p. 3. This definition is endorsed by Harrop and Miller (*Elections and Voters*, p. 6), who add that the wider environment provided by the media, the judiciary, the administrators of elections, the parties, and the general culture must be supportive of the rules.

21   Axel Hadenius, *Democracy and Development*.

22   Turn-of-the-century Germany would receive high marks for open and correct

elections, low marks for the effectiveness of the elected legislature, a grade of zero for its executive being unelected, moderately high marks for political freedoms and freedom of opinion, and very high marks for lack of violence.

23 Maurice Duverger, *Les Partis politiques*, p. 1.

24 'Une fois nées ces deux cellules-mères, groupes parlementaires et comités électoraux, il suffit qu'une coordination permanente s'établisse entre ceux-ci et que des liens réguliers les unissent à ceux-là pour qu'on se trouve en face d'un véritable parti' (ibid., pp. 7–8). On the enduring influence of the work of Duverger (or incapacity of theorists, at least until recently, to go beyond it) see Panebianco, *Political Parties*, pp. 50ff. On the German case, see Thomas Nipperdey, *Organisation der deutschen Parteien*, chap. 1.

25 Duverger, *Les Partis politiques*, p. 21. (The 'second' revolution came with the organization of Communist parties between 1925 and 1930.)

26 Duverger uses the term 'section' in an attempt to convey that in the new model, the components of the party organization were so tightly integrated that the separation of one unit (a constituency association, a youth auxiliary) from the whole was inconceivable.

27 Although Ostrogorski is less well known than Michels, it was apparently Ostrogorski who pointed out to both Michels and Max Weber that the SPD was, 'outside the anglo-Saxon realm, the only [party] which is technically fully developed.' Michels and Weber apparently accepted Ostrogorski's view that the SPD epitomized the modern trend of political organization. See Seymour Martin Lipset's 'Introduction' to M. Ostrogorski, *Democracy and the Organization of Political Parties*, which was originally published in 1902. Michels's *Political Parties: A Sociological Study of the Oligarchical Tendencies of Modern Democracy* was originally published in 1915.

28 Panebianco, *Political Parties*, p. 37, who prefers the term to Michels's 'oligarchy' or Duverger's 'inner circle' because the group is not always so closed, secretive, uniform, or centralized as the other terms may imply.

29 Beyme, *Political Parties in Western Democracies*, p. 1. Beyme characterizes this kind of disdain for parties as 'a normatively oriented prudery' (ibid.) that dominated well into the twentieth century. Many writers now disagree with Michels's analysis as oversimplified and incorrect. See Beyme, *Political Parties*, p. 164; Ware, *Citizens, Parties and the State*, p. 151; Hans Daalder, 'Parties, Elites, and Political Developments in Western Europe,' in LaPalombara and Weiner, eds., *Political Parties and Political Development*, pp. 69–70. Panebianco (*Political Parties*) finds some of Michels's arguments to be of enduring use while rejecting others (compare pp. 164–5 and pp. 186ff).

30 Panebianco, *Political Parties*, p. 70.

31 Seymour M. Lipset and Stein Rokkan, 'Cleavage Structures, Party Systems, and

Voter Alignments: An Introduction,' in Seymour M. Lipset and Stein Rokkan, eds., *Party Systems and Voter Alignments: Cross-National Perspectives*, pp. 1–64.

32 For an overview of the parties and their social and regional support, see Gerhard A. Ritter, 'The Social Bases of the German Political Parties, 1867–1920,' in Karl Rohe, ed., *Elections, Parties and Political Traditions*, pp. 27–52. It is important to point out that the parties can be grouped in a variety of ways; the scheme used here emphasizes ideology rather than electoral combinations. Ritter (ibid.) uses a similar fourfold grouping. There is also merit to the five-party categorization that splits liberals into National Liberals and left liberals (Karl Rohe, 'German Elections and Party Systems,' p. 9). Beyme (*Political Parties*, pp. 31ff) lists the six great 'spiritual families' of European political parties before the 1920s (in order of their emergence) as liberal and Radical parties; conservatives; socialists and Social Democrats; Christian Democrats; agrarian parties; and others such as regional or ethnic parties.

33 The most systematic statistical examination of the stability hypothesis is surely Stefano Bartolini and Peter Mair, *Identity, Competition, and Electoral Availability: The Stabilisation of European Electorates 1885–1985.*

34 Four of the key international comparative works on elections and party systems in the modern era are Arend Lijphart, Don Aitkin et al., *Electoral Systems and Party Systems: A Study of Twenty-Seven Democracies, 1945–1990* ; Andrew Reeve and Alan Ware, *Electoral Systems: A Comparative and Theoretical Introduction*; Kenneth Janda, *Political Parties : A Cross-National Survey*; and Richard Rose, ed., *Electoral Behavior: A Comparative Handbook.*

35 Mark N. Franklin et al., *Electoral Change: Responses to Evolving Social and Attitudinal Structures in Western Countries*, esp. p. 5.

36 Panebianco, *Political Parties*, p. xiii. On the 'new institutionalism,' see also Ware, *Citizens, Parties and the State*, esp. pp. 74–6.

37 'En définitive, système de partis et système électorale sont deux réalités indissolublement liées, parfois mêmes difficiles à séparer par l'analyse' (Duverger, *Les Partis politiques*, p. 235). More recent support of 'Duverger's Law,' or of a restated version of the same idea, can be found in D.W. Rae, *The Political Consequences of Electoral Laws*; and Rein Taagepera and Matthew Soberg Shugart, *Seats and Votes: The Effects and Determinants of Electoral Systems*, p. 65.

38 Taagepera and Shugart, *Seats and Votes*, p. 2.

39 Beyme, *Political Parties*, p. 265.

40 Harrop and Miller, *Elections and Voters*, p. 69.

41 Volker Berghahn, *Imperial Germany, 1871–1914: Economy, Society, Culture and Politics*, p. 212.

42 There was also the technical requirement that voters be resident at the time of enumeration in the district in which their vote was to be cast; see below con-

cerning the drawing up of voters' lists. On the suffrage and electoral system in general, see H.W. Koch, *A Constitutional History of Germany in the Nineteenth and Twentieth Centuries*; Gerhard A. Ritter and M. Niehuss, *Wahlgeschichtliches Arbeitsbuch*; and, for a contemporary view, Charles Seymour and Donald Paige Frary, *How the World Votes: The Story of Democratic Development in Elections*, vol. 2, pp. 1–40.

43 Suval, *Electoral Politics in Wilhelmine Germany*, pp. 21–2. Poor laws varied, however, by state; estimates for Alsace-Lorraine show 2 to 4 per cent of the total population were on poor relief in small towns, but as much as 14 per cent in the city of Colmar and 22 per cent in Strasbourg (Hermann Hiery, *Reichstagswahlen im Reichsland*, p. 119). Presumably many of those on poor relief were widows and young orphans, hence ineligible to vote in any case.

44 Ritter and Niehuss, *Wahlgeschichtliches Arbeitsbuch*, p. 41.

45 Theodore S. Hamerow, 'The Origins of Mass Politics in Germany 1866–1867,' in Imanuel Geiss and Bernd Jürgen Wendt, eds., *Deutschland in der Weltpolitik des 19. und 20. Jahrhunderts*, pp. 105–20; and, more recently, Peter Steinbach, 'Reichstag Elections in the Kaiserreich,' in Larry E. Jones and James Retallack, eds., *Elections, Mass Politics and Social Change*, pp. 131ff. See, at greater length, Steinbach's *Die Zähmung des politischen Massenmarktes: Wahlen und Wahlkämpfe im Bismarckreich* (3 vols.).

46 The Saxon system was changed in 1896 to one resembling the Prussian model, and changed again in 1909 to a system that provided extra votes for men with greater income or education. The Bavarian suffrage, as well as being somewhat restricted, was indirect.

47 On the Prussian suffrage, see Thomas Kühne, *Dreiklassenwahlrecht und Wahlkultur in Preussen 1867–1914*.

48 The fact that Reichstag campaigns had much stronger guarantees of free speech, press, and campaigning than many state elections also enhanced their comparatively free and egalitarian nature. On the symbolism of the suffrage issue, see chapter 2 below.

49 The 'passive suffrage' – eligibility to *be* elected – was held by all those who had the active suffrage and, in addition, by soldiers.

50 Taagepera and Shugart, *Seats and Votes*, p. 74.

51 Among the few theorists to analyse these dynamics are Lipset and Rokkan ('Cleavage Structures,' p. 30). The Third and Fifth French Republics had a similar electoral system.

52 Manfred Rauh, in *Föderalismus und Parlamentarismus im wilhelminischen Reich*, goes so far as to argue the Wilhelmine constitution was evolving towards a parliamentary system, but most scholars would not go so far. It is true that the importance of the Bundesrat was declining, and that the importance of the

Reichstag was increasing – one example of this occurred shortly before the 1903 elections when Bülow announced a new law in the Reichstag, the amendment of the Jesuit law, before it had been introduced to the Bundesrat (see chap. 2). But there was little sign of fundamental change in the basic powers of initiating bills or forming ministries.

53 See Bernhard Vogel, Dieter Nohlen, and Rainer-Olaf Schultze, *Wahlen in Deutschland: Theorie-Geschichte-Dokumente 1848–1970*, p. 101; and Nipperdey, *Organisation der deutschen Parteien*, pp. 393–4. This 'fragmentation' particularly concerned the government, whose task it was to find majorities in the Reichstag. For a former chancellor's opinion of this aspect of the party system, see Prince von Bülow, *Deutsche Politik*, pp. 57–9.

54 Max Weber, *From Max Weber: Essays in Sociology*, p. 112. Weber dismissed the SPD as a party run by 'the rule of officials,' and all non-socialist parties as mere 'guilds of notables.' Revealingly he dates these characteristics as existing 'since the 1880s,' that is, since the decline of idealistic, national issues, and of liberalism, in German politics.

55 Günther Franz, *Die politischen Wahlen in Niedersachsen 1867 bis 1949*, pp. 11 and 20 (the three parties in the province of Hanover were the NLs, Guelphs, and SPD); Hiery, *Reichstagswahlen im Reichsland*, p. 304, on Alsace-Lorraine (Centre, liberals, SPD); Karl Rohe, 'Political Alignments and Re-alignments in the Ruhr,' pp. 155ff (Centre, National Liberals, SPD).

56 In at least one territory, Alsace-Lorraine, the boundaries were deliberately drawn to give greater representation to those areas most loyal to the German government (Hiery, *Reichstagswahlen im Reichsland*, pp. 106–7).

57 See Vogel et al., *Wahlen in Deutschland*, pp. 98–103, on the effects of these disparities.

58 Otto Büsch, in 'Gedanken und Thesen zur Wählerbewegung in Deutschland,' in Otto Büsch et al., eds., *Wählerbewegung in der deutschen Geschichte*, esp. pp. 128–34, argues that because of this deputies with economically conservative, agrarian, or small-town views dominated the Reichstag throughout the period of Germany's industrialization.

59 Eberhard Schanbacher, *Parlamentarische Wahlen und Wahlsystem in der Weimarer Republik*, p. 30.

60 Ibid.

61 Suval, *Electoral Politics in Wilhelmine Germany*, pp. 26–7.

62 Koch, *A Constitutional History of Germany*, p. 134. See also Nipperdey, *Die Organisation der deutschen Parteien*, and Ritter, 'The Social Bases of the German Political Parties,' on the effects of the constitution on the parties. Dieter Fricke, *Zur Organisation und Tätigkeit der deutschen Arbeiterbewegung (1890–1914)*, pp. 28–30, provides further information and includes the text of the Prussian

law. Hiery, p. 84, notes that the old French association law in effect in Alsace-Lorraine was even stricter than the Prussian one.

63 See Dan S. White, *Splintered Party* (chap. 6, 'The Autonomy of the Provinces'), pp. 159–98.

64 *Großherzog Friedrich I*, p. 40 (Jagemann to Brauer, 7/5/98).

65 On Bavaria, Hartmut Kaelble presents data showing that the Bavarian bureaucracy was recruited much more from the free professions, middle officialdom, smaller agrarians, and business classes than was the Prussian. It was less self-recruiting, had a broader social base, and had greater internal mobility ('Soziale Mobilität in Deutschland, 1900–1960,' in Kaelble et al., *Probleme der Modernisierung in Deutschland*, p. 264. See also John Röhl, 'Higher Civil Servants in Germany, 1890–1900,' in James Sheehan, ed., *Imperial Germany*, pp. 142–3.

66 See Barbara Vogel, 'Beamtenkonservatismus: Sozial- und verfassungsgeschichtliche Voraussetzungen der Parteien in Preußen im frühen 19. Jahrhundert,' and Peter-Christian Witt, 'Konservatismus als "Überparteilichkeit": Die Beamten der Reichskanzlei zwischen Kaiserreich und Weimarer Republik 1900–1933,' both in Dirk Stegmann et al., eds., *Deutscher Konservatismus im 19. und 20. Jahrhundert*, pp. 1–31 and 231–80 respectively.

67 See Margaret Lavinia Anderson and Kenneth Barkin, 'Myth of the Puttkamer Purge,' on political disciplining of officials. Concerning SPD organization in the nationalized railroad industry, see Klaus Saul, 'Konstitutioneller Staat und betriebliche Herrschaft: Zur Arbeiter- und Beamtenpolitik der preußischen Staatseisenbahnverwaltung 1890 bis 1914,' in Dick Stegmann et al., eds., *Industrielle Gesellschaft und politisches System*, pp. 315–36.

68 Ritter identifies governmental influence as an important part of the agenda for further election research ('Entwicklungsprobleme,' in Peter Steinbach, ed., *Probleme politischer Partizipation*, pp. 36–7, note 49). Margaret Lavinia Anderson's 'Voter, Junker, *Landrat*, Priest: The Old Authorities and the New Franchise in Imperial Germany,' *American Historical Review* (Dec. 1993): 1448–74), is a fine contribution; it may apply better to the 1870s than to later decades. My own argument is developed at greater length in in chapter 4 (on complaints about conservative influence) and in Brett Fairbairn, 'Authority vs. Democracy: Prussian Officials in the German Elections of 1898 and 1903.'

69 Hubertus Fischer, 'Konservatismus von unten: Wahlen im ländlichen Preußen 1849/52 – Organisation, Agitation, Manipulation,' in Stegmann et al., eds., *Konservatismus*, p. 127.

70 Margaret Lavinia Anderson ('Voter, Junker, *Landrat*, Priest,' p. 1460) argues convincingly that German ideas of legalism and religion were key features of

traditional German culture that offered 'handholds' by which a new oppositional politics could scale the walls of the authoritarian state. If these had not
been reinforced by the press and the Reichstag, however, they would have
been considerably less effective.

71 *SBVR* 9LP 5S, 1897/1898, p. 286. Margaret Lavinia Anderson ('Voter, Junker,
Landrat, Priest,' p. 1456) quotes this statistic (which I included in my 'Authority vs. Democracy,' pp. 811–38) in support of a contention that 'attempts to
influence and intimidate the electorate did not diminish over the years.' My
point was precisely the opposite: more people getting caught does not mean
the crime rate is going up.

72 Hellmut von Gerlach once referred to the committee as the 'Electoral Verification Delay Commission' ('Die Wahlprüfungsverschleppungskommission,'
Die Nation 23 [1905–6]; I am indebted to Jim Retallack for this reference). Von
Gerlach was not, however, an impartial observer – he characterized his own
political career as a 'War on Junkers' and attributed his own electoral defeats
to the manipulations of aristocrats and priests. See Gerlach, *Von Rechts Nach
Links*, pp. 156–73.

73 HSA Hann Hann 174 Hann II Nr. 11; also Hess SA Marburg Best. 180 Hersfeld
Nr. 943.

74 The pamphlet may be found in HSA Berlin Rep. 30 Nr. 595.

75 With all respect to Anderson, who correctly observes that the political Catholicism came together in the 1860s and 1870s ('The Kulturkampf and the Course
of German History,' *Central European History* 19 [March 1986]: 82–115), and to
others who would point out Social Democracy was created in the 1870s and
anti-Semitism in the 1880s, the issue is not when these institutions were created. The 1890s have been identified as a transitional period by most other historians who have examined popular politics. W. Wölk had referred to the
period around 1890 as a 'turning point in the development of the German
Empire' ('Sozialstruktur, Parteienkorrelation und Wahlentscheidung im
Kaiserreich am Beispiel der Reichstagswahl von 1907,' in Büsch et al., eds.,
Wählerbewegung in der deutschen Geschichte, p. 546, note 35). See also Nipperdey,
Die Organisation der deutschen Parteien vor 1918, pp. 31–7; Hans-Jürgen Puhle,
'Parlament, Parteien und Interessenverbände 1890–1914,' in Michael
Stürmer, ed., *Das kaiserliche Deutschland*, pp. 348–9; David Blackbourn, *Class,
Religion, and Local Politics in Wilhelmine Gerrmany*, pp. 9–10 and 14–15; Geoff
Eley, *Reshaping the German Right*, p. vii, and 'Notable Politics, the Crisis of Ger-
man Liberalism, and the Electoral Transition of the 1890s,' in Konrad H.
Jarausch and Larry E.Jones, eds., *In Search of a Liberal Germany*, pp. 187–216;
and James Retallack, *Notables of the Right*.

76 *Honoratiorenpolitik* and its erosion are analysed in more depth in chapter 2.

77 Ernesto Laclau, *Politics and Ideology in Marxist Theory: Capitalism-Fascism-Populism*, p. 143. On populism, in general, see also Margaret Canovan, *Populism*, esp. pp. 3–10.

78 On the nostalgic side is Richard Hofstadter, *The Age of Reform*, while on the progressive-democratic side are Lawrence Goodwyn, *The Populist Moment*, Norman Pollack, *The Populist Response to Industrial America*; and others such as Gene Clanton, *Populism: The Humane Preference in America*.

79 David Peal, 'The Politics of Populism: Germany and the American South in the 1890s,' *Comparative Studies in Society and History* 31 (April 1989): 340–62; and K.D. Barkin, 'A Case Study in Comparative History: Populism in Germany and America,' in Herbert J. Bass, ed., *The State of American History*, pp. 374–96. Both authors see American-German parallels more easily, perhaps, because they interpret the American movements as reactionary.

80 See Derek Offord, *The Russian Revolutionary Movement in the 1880s*; and Peter Brock, *Polish Revolutionary Populism: A Study in Agrarian Socialist Thought from the 1830s to the 1850s* (apart from the general works noted previously).

81 Peter Fritzsche, *Rehearsals for Fascism: Populism and Political Mobilization in Weimar Germany*, esp. pp. 6–9. Fritzsche also draws comparisons to the United States. For the earlier period, Ian Farr has written about peasant leagues as 'populism' ('Populism in the Countryside,' in Richard J. Evans, ed., *Society and Politics in Wilhelmine Germany*, pp. 136–59); while Wilfried Loth (*Katholiken im Kaiserreich*) applies the word in discussing the Centre's agrarian tendencies and radical south-west German agitators in the 1880s and 1890s, emphasizing that these 'populist' movements mixed anti-liberal with democratic elements (pp. 42–51).

82 Michael L. Conniff ed., *Latin American Populism in Comparative Perspective*, especially Conniff's Introduction, pp. 3–30; Lars Schoultz, *The Populist Challenge: Argentine Electoral Behavior in the Postwar Era*; and Rudiger Dornbusch and Sebastian Edwards, eds., *The Macroeconomics of Populism in Latin America*, especially Robert R. Kaufman and Barbara Stalling's 'The Political Economy of Latin American Populism,' pp. 15–43.

83 Gavin Kitching, *Development and Underdevelopment in Historical Perspective: Populism, Nationalism, and Industrialization*.

84 Jeffrey Bell, *Populism and Elitism: Politics in the Age of Equality*. For an excellent attempt to synthesize the changing meaning of populism in the United States, see Michael Kazin, *The Populist Persuasion: An American History*.

85 Laclau, *Politics and Ideology in Marxist Theory*, p. 146.

86 For details, see chapter 3. The phrase 'the parties that rule the masses,' applied to the Centre and the SPD, is from Chancellor Hohenlohe in a cabinet meeting (Min. State 19/4/98(II), in BAK R43F/1817).

87 See the discussion in chapter 2 and the works by Nipperdey, Eley, and Blackbourn cited there.

88 Laclau, *Politics and Ideology in Marxist Theory*, pp. 172–3.

89 *SBVR* 9LP 5S (1897/1898), no. 63.

90 Quoted in Retallack, *Notables of the Right*, p. 92.

91 Alan Ware, *The Logic of Party Democracy*, p. 7. Ware is working here with the negative, modern American use of the term. It is not clear that populism is incompatible with political parties in the ways Ware argues (pp. 171ff), or that, if true, this must be a bad thing.

92 NL, *Politisches Handbuch* (1897), p. 53; *Reichsbote* 9/1/98 'Zur Lage der konservativen Partei,' BHSA Munich Pr A Slg 144.

93 Quoted by Harrop and Miller, *Elections and Voters*, p. 244.

94 See chapter 4.

95 See chapter 6; on Württemberg, see Blackbourn, *Class, Religion, and Local Politics*.

96 See *KöZ* 18/4/03m2 p. 1, and *BT* 28/5/03m p. 3.

97 E. Knobel, *Die Hessische Rechtspartei*, pp. 153, 194–5.

98 Geoff Eley makes a case for such a polarization between moderates and radicals (or populists) in the German Navy League in 'Reshaping the Right,' p. 337 (one of the radicals gave his credentials as being that he was 'a man from the Volk, who grows his cabbages and sometimes also speaks'). Roger Chickering sees a radicalization in the Pan-German League from about 1900, as younger and more agitational members attacked government policies (*We Men Who Feel Most German*, p. 67; also pp. 69, 80). See also chapter 4 on the BdL.

99 Larry Diamond, ed., *Political Culture and Democracy in Developing Countries*.

100 Larry Diamond, 'Introduction: Political Culture and Democracy,' in ibid., p. 5.

101 Lane and Ersson, *Politics and Society in Western Europe*, p. 37.

102 Ibid., p. 44.

103 Thomas Kühne, 'Wahlrecht – Wahlverhalten – Wahlkultur: Tradition und Innovation in der historischen Wahlforschung,' *Archiv für Sozialgeschichte* 33 (1993): 481; Peter Steinbach, 'Reichstag Elections in the Kaiserreich: The Prospects for Electoral Research in the Interdisciplinary Context,' in Jones and Retallack, eds., *Elections, Mass Politics, and Social Change in Modern Germany: New Perspectives*, pp. 119–46.

104 Suval's *Electoral Politics in Wilhelmine Germany* looks mainly at long-term trends over the whole Wilhelmine period, rather than at particular campaigns. See also the new work by Jürgen Schmädeke, *Wählerbewegung im Wilhelminischen Deutschland*, which appeared too recently to be assimilated into the present

book – it has outstanding maps. The only monograph studies of German election campaigns before 1914 are George Dunlap Crothers, *The German Elections of 1907* (published in 1941); and Jürgen Bertram, *Die Wahlen zum Deutschen Reichstage vom Jahre 1912: Parteien und Verbände in der Innenpolitik des Wilhelminischen Reichs* (1964).

105 Gerhard A. Ritter, 'Politische Parteien in Deutschland vor 1918,' in Ritter, *Arbeiterbewegung, Parteien und Parlamentarismus: Aufsätze zur deutschen Sozial- und Verfassungsgeschichte des 19. und 20. Jahrhunderts*, p. 114.

106 Otto Büsch, Introduction to Büsch et al., eds., *Wählerbewegung in der deutschen Geschichte*, p. 6.

107 Rohe, 'Wahlanalyse im historischen Kontext. Zur Kontinuität und Wandel von Wahlverhalten,' *HZ* 234 (1982): 337–8. On historical-electoral methodology, in general, see Rohe's *Wahlen und Wählertraditionen in Deutschland* and his introduction to Rohe, ed., *Elections, Parties and Political Traditions*; Peter Steinbach's 'Reichstag Elections in the Kaiserreich' and 'Stand und Methode der historischen Wahlforschung,' the latter in Kaelble et al. eds., *Probleme der Modernisierung in Deutschland* (and Steinbach's other works); the older synthesis of Nils Diederich, 'Konzepte der Wahlforschung,' in Büsch et al., eds., *Wahlerbewegung in der deutschen Geschichte*; as well as the useful discussion in Hiery's introduction to *Reichstagswahlen im Reichsland.*

108 Stanley Suval's, *Electoral Politics in Wilhelmine Germany* is an outstanding example of the genre of national-level trend studies, deepened in this case by documentary and contextual information. Ritter and Niehuss's indispensable *Wahlgeschichtliches Arbeitsbuch* provides compilations of statistics useful for trend studies at national and regional levels.

109 An excellent general bibliography on regional and local election studies can be found in Ritter and Niehuss, *Wahlgeschichtliches Arbeitsbuch.* Rohe, ed., *Elections, Parties and Political Traditions* deals extensively with regional factors in German politics; see Rohe's introduction for a discussion of the concept of region. Among the significant regional studies of elections, with conclusions important for the national level and for interpretation of elections as a whole, are Hermann Hiery's *Reichstagswahlen im Reichsland* and Rohe's various works on the Ruhr (see Bibliography). One must also refer to regional studies of political parties such as David Blackbourn's *Class, Religion, and Local Politics in Wilhelmine Germany* on the Centre in Württemberg, and Dan White's *Splintered Party* on National Liberalism in Hessen.

110 National-level statistical results for Reichstag elections in the period 1871–1912 may be found in Thomas T. Mackie and Richard Rose, *The International Almanac of Electoral History*; and in Ritter and Niehuss, *Wahlgeschichtliches Arbeitsbuch.*

111 Volker Berghahn's classic work on the fleet examined the intention of using the fleet to win mass support without much considering the reality of whether it did so (*Der Tirpitz-Plan: Genesis und Verfall einer innenpolitischen Krisenstrategie unter Wilhelm II*, esp. pp. 139–57). Without critical examination and without observing Berghahn's careful formulations, the idea that 'social imperialism' and the fleet *did* win mass support for the regime found itself into such pocketbook histories as Eda Sagarra, *A Social History of Germany, 1648–1914*, p. 427 and Winfried Baumgart, *Deutschland im Zeitalter des Imperialismus (1890–1914)*, pp. 53–4, as well as into important books on imperial politics such as John Röhl *Germany without Bismarck: The Crisis of Government in the Second Reich, 1890–1900*, p. 241, and recent works such as Thomas Kohut, *Wilhelm II and the Germans*, pp. 177–91. On sweeping theories of social imperialism for this period see Hans-Ulrich Wehler, 'Sozialimperialismus,' in Wehler, ed., *Imperialismus*, pp. 83–96; and Wehler, *Das Deutsche Kaiserreich 1871–1918*, pp. 166–7. See chapter 2.

112 Quotations from Kohut's 1991 work, *Wilhelm II*, pp. 184, 177, and 190.

113 Dirk Stegmann, *Die Erben Bismarcks: Parteien und Verbände in der Spätphase des wilhelminischen Deutschlands: Sammlungspolitik 1897–1918*. A similar theme is picked up by others, including Hans-Ulrich Wehler (*Das Deutsche Kaiserreich*) and Hans-Jürgen Puhle (see the works listed in the Bibliography). The associated historiographical debate is far too extensive to discuss here; for a convenient summary, see James Retallack, 'Wilhelmine Germany,' in Gordon Martel, ed., *Modern Germany Reconsidered, 1870–1945*, pp. 33–53.

114 Only Geoff Eley, in '*Sammlungspolitik*, Social Imperialism and the Navy Law of 1898,' *MM* 15 (1974): 29–63 (this is reprinted in his *From Unification to Nazism*), has really explored the electoral contradictions and ambiguities of *Sammlungspolitik* in the elections in which the policy was supposedly initiated.

Chapter 2: The Context of Campaigns: Structures and Issues

1 *KZ* 16/6/98ev p. 2.

2 The *Erfurter Allgemeiner Anzeiger*, 17/6/03, 3. Beiblatt p. 1, shows that the polls in Erfurt were all in restaurants, *Gasthöfe*, or hotels. Many polls in Bremen were also in inns (*Bremischer Courier*, 16/6/93 p. 1). Urban polls apparently saw about 400–800 voters during the day, while rural ones were smaller and more variant (see, for example *Bremischer Courier*, ibid., and the statistics in GStAPK XVI. HA Rep. 30 Nr. 595 for constituencies in the Bromberg district).

3 Forms and instructions were sent from Berlin to the state interior ministries, who passed them to their officials. The technical documentation of the

elections is widely preserved in local, regional, and state archives. See, for example, GStAPK XVI. HA Rep. 30 Nr. 595; Hess. SA Marburg Best. 180 Wolfhagen Nr. 1291; HSA Hanover, Hann. 174 Hannover II Nr. 15; BHSA Munich MA 76273.

4 There were clashes with police in Erfurt in May 1898, and in June that year stones were thrown at the police station in Grünberg (Silesis) in conjunction with the voting results (*BT* 27/5/98ev p. 1, 28/5/98ev p. 1, and 18/6/98 p. 1).

5 HSA Hanover Hann. Des. 122a I Nr. 110, nos. 80–93. The terms *Oberpräsident* and *Regierungspräsident* will be translated as 'provincial governor' and 'district governor' respectively.

6 Stanley Suval, *Electoral Politics in Wilhelmine Germany*, pp. 22–30, offers comparative and theoretical arguments regarding the measurement of 'committed' or 'affirming' voting behaviour. Rising participation curves have been taken as indicative of the development of 'modern' democratic mass politics, but at least one critic has noted that the assumptions about 'modernization' have been accepted too unquestioningly. See Peter McPhee, 'Electoral Democracy and Direct Democracy in France, 1789–1851,' *EHQ* 16.1 (Jan. 1986): 77–96.

7 Prince von Bülow, *Memoirs, 1897–1903*, p. 223. Similarly, *Schulthess' Europäischer Geschichtskalender*, the nationalist annual review of politics, said only that the Reichstag elections, 'which were carried out without particular excitement, produced no substantially different composition of the house' (N.S. vol. 14 (1898): 388). For 1903 Bülow dwelt on the elections only long enough to blame the SPD's 'great gains' on the kaiser's tactlessness, as an introduction to what he called his subsequent 'brilliant victories' against socialism (*Memoirs, 1903–9*, pp. 5–6).

8 June 15 was the anniversary of Wilhelm's reign.

9 Miquel, in Min. State 29/7/97, minutes in GStAPK 90a AVIII 1 M,d Nr. 3, nos. 234–8, and also in GStAPK I. HA Rep. 90 128, nos. 230–2.

10 Regarding the press, the SPD daily *Vorwärts* estimated in 1910 that there were 3,929 newspapers and periodicals in Germany: 1,344 described themselves as non-party-political; 710 as official *Amtsblätter*; 492 as affiliated with the Centre Party; 388 LL; 378 nationalist; 303 conservative; 192 NL; 100 SPD; and 17 Polish, Danish, or Guelph (Alex Hall, *Scandal, Sensation, and Social Democracy*, pp. 29–30).

11 Contrast the comprehensive election coverage of the *Berliner Tageblatt* (LL), the intensely partisan agitation of *Vorwärts* (SPD), or the prominent election discussions of *Kölnische Volkszeitung* (Centre) with the *Kölnische Zeitung* (NL), which gave top billing to the Spanish-American War, or the *Kreuzzeitung* (DKP), which despite its radical and agrarian interests allowed its regular reports of court and military matters to push election news to the inside pages.

12 *Volks-Zeitung*, 30 Aug. 1867, no. 202, quoted in Peter Steinbach, 'Reichstag Elections in the Kaiserreich,' p. 119.

13 Eve Rosenhaft, 'Women, Gender, and the Limits of Political History in the Age of "Mass" Politics,' in Larry E. Jones and James Retallack, eds., *Elections, Mass Politics, and Social Change*, p. 149.

14 Ibid., p. 152.

15 See J. Nettl, *Rosa Luxemburg*. Autobiographical excerpts by Baader, Popp, and Roth are collected in Alfred Kelly, ed., *The German Worker*. Baader's autobiography is entitled *Ein steiniger Weg: Lebenserinnerungen* (Berlin 1931).

16 August Bebel, *Woman in the Past, Present and Future* (orig. published 1879; revised 1883); *Die Sozialdemokratie und das allgemeine Stimmrecht: Mit besonderer Berücksichtigung des Frauen-Stimmrechts und Proportional-Wahlsystems* (1895).

17 Rosenhaft, 'Women, Gender, and the Limits of Political History,' p. 162.

18 Suval, *Electoral Politics in Wilhelmine Germany*, p. 168.

19 Ibid., p. 18

20 On *Honoratiorenpolitik* see Thomas Nipperdey, *Die Organisation der deutschen Parteien*; and on its changing and stressed nature in the 1890s, see the various works by David Blackbourn and Geoff Eley in the Bibliography, notably *Peculiarities of German History* and Eley's 'Notable Politics, the Crisis of German Liberalism, and the Electoral Transition of the 1890s,' in Konrad H. Jarausch and Larry E. Jones, eds., *In Search of a Liberal Germany*, pp. 187–216.

21 On the relation between liberalism and associational life, see Jürgen Habermas, 'Strukturwandel der Öffentlichkeit: Untersuchungen zu einer Kategorie der bürgerlichen Gesellschaft' (excerpt in H.-U. Wehler, ed., *Moderne deutsche Sozialgeschichte*, pp. 197–224); Blackbourn and Eley, *Peculiarities of German History* pp. 190–205; and Michael F. John, 'Liberalism and Society: The Case of Hanover' and 'Associational Life and the Development of Liberalism in Hanover, 1848–66.'

22 For information on the Centre Party's structure, see chapter 6.

23 Nipperdey, *Organisation der deutschen Parteien*, pp. 288–94.

24 For example, 'Reichstagswahl: An die Wähler des Wahlkreises Duisburg-Mülheim-Ruhrort,' in HSA Düss. LA Dinslaken 3, where the list of members of the *Vorstand* is in bolder type and takes up more room than the text.

25 *Brem.Cour.* 16/6/93m p. 1. Consider also Moers-Rees, where the 'national' parties proposed a factory-owner to the voters in 1898, and a land-owning economic official in 1903, on the basis of their special economic competence (*KöZ* 28/4/98m p. 1 and 10/5/03m). In Essen the 'personal candidacy' of Krupp was the natural and most effective strategy of the 'national' parties in the constituency his arms works dominated (*VW* 5/5/03 p. 1). See also *KöZ* 9/5/03n p. 2, concerning the undesirability of 'professional politicians' as candidates.

26 'Bürger, an die Urnen!,' *KöZ* 14/6/03S p. 1 (and the same for the following quotations).

27 On the occupations of Reichstag deputies and the increase in the number of professional politicians, see Peter Molt, *Der Reichstag vor der improvisierten Revolution*, table 4, p. 78, and graph 3, p. 79. Naturally, the most famous commentator on this process is Max Weber; see 'Politics as a Vocation,' in *From Max Weber: Essays in Sociology*, pp. 77–128.

28 *BT* 13/6/98ev p. 3; for similar language, *KöZ* 6/6/03ev p. 1.

29 See the report of Beumer's speech in Duisburg in *KöZ* 5/5/03m1 p. 2.

30 *KöZ* 23/4/03ev p. 2.

31 BAP 90 Ma 1 Nr. 49, nos. 34–9 (Marquardsen collection).

32 HSA Düss. Reg. Aachen Präs. 815, nos. 110 and 158, LR Aachen to RP Aachen 12/11/97 and 20/5/98; HSA Düss. Reg. Düss. Präs. 587, no. 3, OB Düss. to RP Düss. 29/1/03 (and other reports in the same files). See GStAPK XVI. HA Rep. 30 Nr. 596, LR Gnesen to RP Bromberg, for an example where the illnesses and resignations of a few chairmen derailed the whole campaign of the 'German' parties.

33 See chapter 3, especially concerning the secret election platform and instructions of the Prussian Ministry of the Interior from January 1898, which may be found in LASH Abt. 301 [Oberpräsidium], Nr. 805: Die Beteiligung der Beamten bei den Wahlen, 1898–1921.

34 *BT* 24/5/98ev p. 3; *BT* 12/5/98ev p. 3 and 24/5/98 p. 3, and *FZ* 5/6/98m2 p. 1; *FZ* 3/6/98ev p. 2; *KöZ* 3/6/98m p. 2; *KöZ* 23/5/03m1 p. 2; *BT* 13/5/03m p. 3, 10/6/03ev p. 3, and 12/6/03ev p. 3.

35 Consider also constituencies 44, 54, 71, 82, 129, 134, 136, 137, and 141 (see Appendix B for constituency list), which saw similar dramatic vote shifts among conservative and liberal parties. These examples are extreme, but the pattern was typical: on the local level, committees of the 'German' or 'state-supporting' parties frequently united right-wing and often middle tendencies, so that these parties had scarcely any independent existence.

36 See chapter 3. David Blackbourn, 'The Politics of Demagogy in Imperial Germany,' *PP* 113 (Nov. 1986): 152–84, examines the meaning of the term 'demagogy' to contemporaries, as a characterization of how the radical nationalists and anti-Semites differed from moderates. James Retallack, *Notables of the Right*, makes much the same point. See also Weber, 'Politics as a Vocation,' where he argues that the new 'professional politicians' of his time, in contrast to the old parties of notables, were 'demagogues' whose party 'machines' practised a 'plebiscitarian democracy.'

37 Rainer Lepsius uses a version of this approach to explain the exclusiveness of Imperial parties in 'Parteiensystem und Sozialstruktur: Zum Problem der

Demokratisierung der deutschen Gesellschaft,' in G.A. Ritter, ed., *Die deutschen Parteien vor 1918*. See the discussion of Lepsius's idea, notably in James Sheehan, 'Klasse und Partei im Kaiserreich: Einige Gedanken zur Sozialgeschichte der deutschen Politik,' in Otto Pflanze, ed., *Innenpolitische Probleme des Bismarck-Reiches*; in Suval, *Electoral Politics in Wilhelmine Germany*; and in Karl Rohe, 'German Elections and Party Systems,' in Rohe, ed., *Elections, Parties and Political Traditions*, pp. 1–25.

38 Karl Rohe, 'Wahlanalyse,' pp. 351, 356–7; Stefan Immerfall and Peter Steinbach, 'Politisierung und Nationalisierung deutscher Regionen im Kaiserreich,' in Dirk Berg-Schlosser and Jakob Schissler, eds., *Politische Kultur in Deutschland: Bilanz und Perspektive der Forschung*, pp. 68–79; and Peter Steinbach, 'Nationalisierung, soziale Differenzierung und Urbanisierung als Bedingungsfaktoren des Wahlverhaltens im Kaiserreich,' *Quantum* 2 (1990).

39 Suval, pp. 61–3. Rohe follows the alternative approach of redefining the concept of 'milieu' to be 'ultimately a social-culturally defined societal collectivity with community character,' in which common lifestyle and attitudes are key factors, ideology helps to stabilize the whole, and common economic interests are helpful but not essential. This is more flexible than Lepsius's version. ('Wahlanalyse,' p. 351, and 'German Elections and Party Systems,' p. 13).

40 Calculation based on author's constituency-level data for Reichstag elections; see Appendix C.

41 The 1898 election does not belong in this category because the government did not use the 1898 fleet bill as an electoral issue, instead ensuring that the legislation was out of the way before the election occurred; also because the Reichstag was not in this case dissolved by the government; and because the election did not show the distinctive pattern of higher participation rates and better performance for the right-wing parties. These observations may be surprising to historians who assumed that the fleet issue was an effective 'social-imperialist' tool in 1898; see below.

42 Helmut Böhme has referred to 1876–9 as the 'second founding of the Reich,' and other historians, in similar vein, see it as the origin of the constellation of forces that dominated the German Empire until its demise (see, for example, H.-U. Wehler, *Das Deutsche Kaiserreich 1871–1918*, pp. 100–2). The study of the 1898 and 1903 elections, revealing as it does the disunity of the alleged agrarian-industrial constellation (see chapter 3), has to call into question how persistent and how fundamental any such structure could have been.

43 See Dan S. White, *The Splintered Party*, pp. 84–122. The introduction of colonial issues by Bismarck in 1884, even without a dissolution and one-issue campaign, may have given the elections a partly 'national' character. There was a modest increase in turnout, and the 'right' (Conservatives and National Liberals) did

increase from 125 seats to 157. Whether the colonies actually figured much in the elections is uncertain, however, since it was not the colony-minded National Liberals who enjoyed the increase, but the Conservatives.

44 'The government bases itself preferentially on the Conservatives, Free Conservatives, and National Liberals' (1898 Ministry of the Interior election directives in LASH Abt. 301 [Oberpräsidium], Nr. 805: Die Beteiligung der Beamten bei den Wahlen, 1898–1921; see chapter 3).

45 After the early 1890s, repression replaced reform as the advocates of the latter in government were defeated; yet no comprehensive repressive measures would pass the Reichstag (see Karl Erich Born, *Staat und Sozialpolitik seit Bismarcks Sturz*, pp. 92–115, 141; and below).

46 See chapter 3 regarding the divisions engendered by economic issues within the governmental coalition, and chapter 4 regarding anti-Semitism and agrarianism during 1898–1903.

47 Nipperdey writes of the 'authoritarian state' with its 'accentuation of the national, with its self-interpretation as "above the parties,"' as a determining influence on German party development (*Organisation der deutschen Parteien*, p. 393). See also Wehler, *Kaiserreich*, pp. 96–100, on 'negative integration' by means of the *Reichsfeinde/-freunde* distinction.

48 Theodore S. Hamerow, 'The Origins of Mass Politics,' p. 120.

49 See Tom Kemp, *Industrialization in Nineteenth-Century Europe*, p. xi and pp. 9ff.

50 On the 'agriculture vs. industry' debate, see K.D. Barkin, *The Controversy over German Industrialization, 1890–1902*; and on agriculture and modernization generally, Alexander Gerschenkron, *Bread and Democracy in Germany*, H.-J. Puhle, *Politische Agrarbewegungen in kapitalistichen Industriegesellschaften*, pp. 28–76, and Jens Flemming, *Landwirtschaftliche Interessen und Demokratie*. Sarah Rebecca Tirrell, *German Agrarian Politics after Bismarck's Fall*, covers the early period 1890–4.

51 H.-J. Puhle, *Agrarische Interessenpolitik und preußischer Konservatismus im wilhelminischen Reich*, appendix 14. This organizational and agitational bent distinguished the BdL from older agricultural interest groups, such as the Deutscher Landwirtschaftsrat of 1872 and the Vereinigung der Steuer- und Wirtschaftsreformer of 1876, or the federation of chambers of agriculture, the Landesökonomiekollegium. These older bodies were closely tied into the Prussian aristocratic and governmental establishment, and played no significant public role in the 1898 and 1903 campaigns. See ibid., pp. 55, 147–8; and Dirk Stegmann, *Die Erben Bismarcks: Parteien und Verbände in der Spätphase des wilhelminischen Deutschlands: Sammlungspolitik 1897–1918*, pp. 37–8.

52 The BdL and its relationship to the Conservatives and to anti-Semitic populism are discussed more fully in chapter 4.

53 See Ian Farr, '"Tradition" and the Peasantry,' in Richard J. Evans and W.R. Lee, eds., *The German Peasantry*, pp. 1–36.

54 BAP Reichskanzlei Nr. 1794, nos. 172–5. See Dieter Fricke, 'Regierungswahlkampf,' pp. 493–9.

55 On the conflict between heavy and finished-product industries, see Hartmut Pogge von Strandmann, 'Widersprüche im Modernisierungsprozeß Deutschlands: Der Kampf der verarbeitenden Industrie gegen die Schwerindustrie,' in Dirk Stegmann et al., eds., *Industrielle Gesellchaft und politisches System*, pp. 225–40. See also H.-P. Ullmann, *Der Bund der Industriellen: Organisation, Einfluß und Politik klein- und mittelbetrieblicher Industriellen im Deutschen Kaiserreich 1895–1914*; and Stegmann, *Die Erben Bismarcks*, pp. 33–5. Membership figures are from Dieter Fricke, ed., *Die bürgerlichen Parteien in Deutschland*, pp. 117–28.

56 Stegmann, *Erben Bismarcks*, pp. 76–80, 88–9.

57 Carl Schorske, *German Social Democracy 1905–1917: The Development of the Great Schism*, pp. 13–22, though old, brings this point out nicely. See also the works by Groh, Guttsman, Nettl, and Roth in the Bibliography.

58 Heinrich August Winkler, 'Der rückversicherte Mittelstand: Die Interessenverbände von Handwerk und Kleinhandel im deutschen Kaiserreich,' in *Liberalismus und Antiliberalismus: Studien zur politischen Sozialgeschichte des 19. und 20. Jahrhunderts*, pp. 83–98; Stegmann, *Erben Bismarcks*, pp. 40–6, 143–4. On the social characteristics and political attitudes of the *Mittelstand*, see David Blackbourn, 'Between Resignation and Volatility: The German Petite Bourgeoisie in the Nineteenth Century,' in Geoffrey Crossick and Heinz-Gerhard Haupt, eds., *Shopkeepers and Master Artisans in Nineteenth-Century Europe*.

59 See particularly Anthony Joseph O'Donnell, 'National Liberalism and the Mass Politics of the German Right, 1890–1907.' Roger Chickering calls the National Liberals 'the political arm of the German-national public' (*We Men Who Feel Most German: A Cultural Study of the Pan-German League, 1886–1914*, p. 204). This is true enough, except that anti-Semites were surely another arm.

60 But see below on the Society for the Eastern Marches.

61 BAP 61 Ve 1 Nr. 504, nos. 14 and 39.

62 Geoff Eley, 'Reshaping the Right: Radical Nationalism and the German Navy League, 1898–1908,' *HJ* 21 (1978): 338.

63 See Chickering, *We Men Who Feel Most German*, on the ideological environment of the League (pp. 15–17, 75–94); and on its concerns and campaigns during 1897–1903 (pp. 58–68; Chickering does not mention elections). The membership of the League makes clear that it was not an organization of the masses, but of educated, even respectable middle-class activists (pp. 103–17).

64 From 1900 the veterans' associations were organized in the Kyffhäuser-Bund, which was intended as an instrument for the ideological indoctrination of

reservists. See Wilhelm Deist, 'Die Armee in Staat und Gesellschaft,' in Michael Stürmer, ed., *Das kaiserliche Deutschland,* p. 330. See chapter 1 on involvement of veterans' associations in politics and resulting complaints to the Reichstag.

65 R.W. Tims, *Germanizing Prussian Poland: The H-K-T Society and the Struggle for the Eastern Marches in the German Empire, 1894–1919,* pp. 70–1. See Geoff Eley, 'German Politics and Polish Nationality,' in Eley, *From Unification to Nazism: Reinterpreting the German Past,* p. 214, on the process by which the anti-Polish campaign spilled over from a regional Prussian concern to an imperial concern in the later 1890s.

66 Thomas Nipperdey, 'Interessenverbände und Parteien in Deutschland vor dem Ersten Weltkrieg,' in *Gesellschaft,* p. 324; Hartmut Pogge von Strandmann, 'Nationale Verbände zwischen Weltpolitik und Kontinentalpolitik,' in Herbert Schottelius and Wilhelm Deist, eds., *Marine und Marinepolitik,* p. 299; Heinrich August Winkler, 'Pluralismus oder Protektionismus? Verfassungspolitische Probleme des Verbandswesens im Deutschen Kaiserreich,' in Winkler, *Liberalismus und Antiliberalismus,* pp. 172–4; H.-J. Puhle, 'Parlament, Parteien und Interessenverbände,' pp. 342–3.

67 A typical distinction, as noted in chapter 1, is to suggest that while interest groups also articulate interests, political parties *aggregate* interests. Thus one can try to define a party, as Ware does, as bodies whose members 'are not simply the representatives of a single interest' (Alan Ware, *Citizens, Parties and the State,* p. 16). This is not easy to apply in practice. The SPD aimed to represent only the working class: is it then not a party? The BdL claimed to represent all the interests of agriculture in many or all regions: is this a single interest? Beyme's approach is more practical: a party has 'less clear-cut boundaries' than an interest group, is 'more oriented ... towards a competitive political market,' and more often shapes its behaviour in response to opposing parties (*Political Parties in Western Democracies,* p. 6) – in short, the differences are ones of degree, not of kind.

68 Stein Rokkan is quoted as having written that the 'proliferation of sectional and functional organizations' led to 'a narrowing of the alternatives for national politics, a fragmentation of the networks of policy-influencing organizations, and a consequent decline in the importance of the electorate-at-large ... leaving the basic decisions to a bargaining process between interest organizations, parties and agencies and departments of the national bureaucracy.' He was referring to contemporary developments in mid-twentieth-century Western democracies (Hans Daalder, 'Parties, Elites and Political Developments,' p. 76).

69 David Blackbourn, *Class, Religion, and Local Politics in Wilhelmine Germany: The*

Centre Party in Württemberg before 1914, makes this argument more subtly and convincingly than most.

70 'Berliner Erklärung' of 1896, in *Programmatische Kundgebungen der National-liberalen Partei*, pp. 60–3.

71 G.W.C. Schmidt, 'Die freisinnige Volkspartei: Wer sie ist und was sie will' (1895); FVP program as published in *BT* 6/5/98m p. 1.

72 'Wahlaufruf der westfälischen Centrumspartei,' *Germ.* 4/6/98m p. 1.

73 Gordon A. Craig, *The Politics of the Prussian Army*, pp. 243–5. For summaries by the parties of the issues in the 1893–8 Reichstag, see 'Der erste fünfjährige Legislaturperiode im Reich,' *BT* 7/5/98m p. 1; 'Wählerversammlung der Krefelder Zentrumspartei,' *Niederrheinische Volkszeitung* 24/5/98 p. 1 (speech by Karl Bachem); and *Handbuch für Sozialdemokratische Wähler* (1898).

74 John C.G. Röhl, *Germany without Bismarck: The Crisis of Government in the Second Reich, 1890–1900*, pp. 112–17. On the bill and its political repercussions, see the documents in GStAPK Rep. 151 HB (M) Nr. 822, especially the minutes of the Prussian Ministry of State from 18/3/1895 (nos. 6–9). On Hohenlohe's handling of it, see J. David Fraley, 'Government by Procrastination: Chancellor Hohenlohe and Kaiser Wilhelm II, 1894–1900,' *CEH* 7.2 (June 1974): 163–4.

75 Röhl (*Germany without Bismarck*, p. 218) and Deist ('Die Armee,' in Stürmer, ed., *Das kaiserliche Deutschland*, p. 320) disagree concerning the significance of a memo written by General Waldersee in January 1897. The memo urged the provocation of a crisis with the Reichstag leading to revision of the suffrage, but may have been merely an opportunistic political posture.

76 See Hartmut Pogge von Strandmann, 'Staatsstreichpläne, Alldeutsche und Bethmann Hollweg,' in Hartmut Pogge von Strandmann and Imanuel Geiss, eds., *Die Erforderlichkeit des Unmöglichen: Deutschland am Vorabend des ersten Weltkrieges*, pp. 7–10. The Centre deputy Karl Bachem claimed in a memo written during the 1898 run-offs that the threat of a coup had caused him to moderate his opposition to the government and try to minimize SPD gains (Bachem papers, HASK 1006 Nr. 88, memo dated 24/6/98). See chapter 6.

77 *Handbuch* (1898), pp. 9–15.

78 See *BT* 9/6/98ev p. 1; and *Krefelder Zeitung* 29/5/98m p. 1, 2/6/98ev p. 1, and 5/6/98m p. 1. Klaus Saul (*Staat, Industrie, Arbeiterbewegung im Kaiserreich*, p. 17) argues that the party's defensiveness on suffrage questions was a sign of the SPD's 'powerlessness.' The propaganda wars in the 1898–1903 Reichstag campaigns imply that advocacy of the Reichstag suffrage was anything but a defensive electoral strategy; it was one of the SPD's most potent weapons for voter recruitment. Every rumour of *Reaktion* helped the SPD, which is one reason the government tried to avoid associating itself with such rumours (see chapter 4).

79 Pogge von Strandmann, 'Staatsstreichpläne,' p. 10. On Saxony's suffrage reform, see Ritter and Niehuss, *Wahlgeschichtliches Arbeitsbuch*, pp. 163–71; James Retallack, 'Antisocialism and Electoral Politics in Regional Perspective: The Kingdom of Saxony,' in Jones and Retallack, eds., *Elections, Mass Politics, and Social Change*, pp. 49–91; and Retallack, '"What Is to Be Done?" The Red Specter, Franchise Questions, and the Crisis of Conservative Hegemony in Saxony, 1896–1909,' *CEH* 23.4 (Dec. 1990): 271–312.

80 Blackbourn, *Class, Religion, and Local Politics*, pp. 53–7.

81 Michael F. John, '"The Final Unification of Germany": Politics and the Codification of the German Civil Law in the Bürgerliches Gesetzbuch of 1896' (unpubl. doct. diss., Oxford, 1983), pp. 127–79; and 'The Politics of Legal Unity in Germany, 1870–1896,' *HJ* 28.2 (1985): 341–55.

82 See Fraley, 'Government by Procrastination,' p. 175.

83 For evidence of the executive, legislative, diplomatic, and political time spent on the courts-martial question during 1897–8, see Hohenlohe, *Memoirs*, pp. 471–2; and *Großherzog Friedrich I*, Jagemann's letters up to March 1898.

84 Fraley ('Government by Procrastination,' p. 179) suggests that Hohenlohe and Tirpitz cleared the way for the passage of the two bills only by convincing the kaiser that they were linked – that he could have his fleet only if he allowed military courts to be reformed.

85 Röhl, *Germany without Bismarck*, p. 216 (comments by Julius Bachem on Centre strategy); on the National Liberals, *BT* 15/5/98S p. 1.

86 On the Centre's legislative ambitions and Lieber's personal victory in the fleet question, see Eckart Kehr, *Schlachtflottenbau und Parteipolitik 1894–1901*, pp. 375–7 ('wollte man die Macht, so mußte man bewilligen'); John K. Zeender, *The German Center Party 1890–1906*, pp. 63–72; Herbert Gottwald, 'Der Umfall des Zentrums: Die Stellung der Zentrumspartei zur Flottenvorlage von 1897,' in Fritz Klein, ed., *Studien zum deutschen Imperialismus vor 1914*, pp. 186–206; Blackbourn, *Class, Religion, and Local Politics*, pp. 37–40; and Wilfried Loth, *Katholiken im Kaiserreich*, pp. 78–80.

87 'Centrum und Weltpolitik,' *BT* 23/5/03ev p. 1.

88 Leaflet in HSA Düss. Reg. Aachen Präs. 815, no. 194; 'Volksfeinde und Volksfreunde,' in Hess. SA Marburg Best. 180 Hersfeld Nr. 922. See also the FVP program in *BT* 6/5/98m p. 1; and Franz Mehring, *Weltkrach und Weltmarkt*, p. 5.

89 *KöVZ* 7/5/98ev p. 1; *Niederrheinische Volkszeitung* 24/5/98m p. 1.

90 'Wahlaufruf der freikonservativen Partei,' *KöZ* 7/5/98m p. 1.

91 *Programmatische Kundgebungen*, pp. 64–8. In chapter 4 it is argued that many National Liberals saw the fleet as an idealistic issue that might distract their party and its supporters from the divisive economic issues of the 1898 campaign.

92 Ritter and Niehuss, *Wahlgeschichtliches Arbeitsbuch,* pp. 38–42.

93 In his study of Oldenburg, Christoph Reinders comes to a number of conclusions about Reichstag campaigns there that differ from the national-level findings of this study. One such conclusion is that the 1898 campaign was a 'national' one with the fleet the main issue. ('Sozialdemokratie und Immigration,' in Wolfgang Günther, ed., *Parteien und Wahlen in Oldenburg,* pp. 65–116, esp. pp. 79–82 and 95–6). Because of local conditions, the fleet may have been emphasized more than elsewhere, but overall turnout here did not increase, the total NL vote did not change significantly, and the main electoral trend was from the LLs to the SPD.

94 On the wide claims for the 'mass support' won by the fleet, see chapter 1, note 111.

95 Eckart Kehr, who is cited by many historians who write about the fleet and *Sammlungspolitik,* was explicit: the fleet appealed *only* to the middle classes, not to the proletarian masses (Kehr, *Schlachtflottenbau und Parteipolitik 1894–1901,* pp. 113, 437–43). Historians have frequently quoted Bülow's argument that a 'lively foreign policy' was the only true means to defeat Social Democracy without noting that he was *not* talking about winning 'mass popularity,' but rather winning liberal leaders and intellectuals away from any possible parliamentary alliance with the SPD (Prince von Bülow, *Deutsche Politik,* pp. 94–9). On liberal vulnerability to imperialist appeals, see Wolfgang Mommsen, 'Wandlungen der liberalen Idee im Zeitalter des Imperialismus,' in Karl Holl and Günther List, eds., *Liberalismus und imperialistischer Staat,* pp. 109–47, esp. pp. 122–5. But note that the largest left-liberal grouping, Eugen Richter's FVP, was not pro-fleet.

96 The Ministry of the Interior's secret platform of January 1898 (LASH Abt. 301 [Oberpräsidium], Nr. 805: Die Beteiligung der Beamten bei den Wahlen, 1898–1921) indicates officials were to support a compromise among agrarians and industrialists. In practice, statements in favour of *Sammlungspolitik* were taken to be statements in favour of agrarians, and on this basis other ministers opposed Miquel's approach in April 1898. On the disagreement within the government, see Min. State, 19/4/98 (II) in BAK R43F/1817 9–11, and chapter 3 below.

97 *Handbuch für Sozialdemokratische Wähler* (1898), p. 8. See Rolf Weidner, *Wahlen und soziale Strukturen in Ludwigshafen am Rhein 1871–1914: Unter besonderer Berücksichtigung der Reichstagswahlen,* p. 417, on the opening of the SPD campaign in Ludwigshafen with an anti-tariff speech in February 1898. The Ministry of the Interior's secret 1898 election directives, too, went into greatest detail on issues and strategies related to the agricultural question (LASH Abt. 301 [Oberpräsidium], Nr. 805: Die Beteiligung der Beamten bei den Wahlen, 1898–1921).

98 *BT* 15/5/98S p. 1; 16/5/98ev p. 1; 24/5/98ev p. 1; 26/5/98ev p. 1; 1/6/98ev
    p. 1; 21/6/98ev p. 1; and 24/6/98ev p. 1.

99 *Germ.* 3/5/03; Richard Müller-Fulda and H. Sittart, *Der Deutsche Reichstag von
    1898 bis 1903*, pp. 6–7; *VW* 16/3/03 pp. 1–2; and the leaflets 'Reichstag-
    swähler von Barmen-Elberfeld!' and 'Arbeiter! Bürger! Wähler!' in HSA
    Düss. Reg. Düss. Präs. 585, nos. 17 and 25.

100 This had taken several years because of the Saxon system of electing one-
    third of the deputies every two years; in 1898 only a third of the electorate
    had experienced the new system, whereas by 1901 all constituencies had seen
    new elections. Also, Social Democrats had resolved their debates about
    whether to use boycotts or protests to fight the new suffrage, and mounted
    an effective campaign.

101 For state elections in Prussia, Bavaria, and Saxony, and concerning their suf-
    frages, a convenient source is Ritter and Niehuss, *Wahlgeschichtliches Arbeits-
    buch*, pp. 132–89. See also Rohe, ed., *Elections, Parties and Political Traditions:
    Social Foundations of German Parties and Party Systems*. Much more could be
    done concerning state suffrages.

102 On the turn-of-the-century 'parity' campaign, see Ronald J. Ross, *Beleaguered
    Tower*, pp. 18–27 (and chap. 6). On the 'Spahn case,' see Christoph Weber,
    *Der 'Fall Spahn' (1901): Ein Beitrag zur Wissenschafts- und Kulturdiskussion im aus-
    gehenden 19. Jahrhundert.*

103 HSA Stuttgart E73 Verz. 61 Nr. 12e, Varnbüler to v. Soden, 4/2/03, 15/2/03,
    7/3/03; and FVg program in *BT* 23/4/03ev p. 1.

104 Puhle, *Agrarische Interessenpolitik*, pp. 166–7.

105 Much historical analysis of the tariff question has centred on the question of
    how much different groups gained or lost, yet in popular politics the issue
    was to a large extent a symbolic and ideological one. See J.A. Perkins, 'The
    Agricultural Revolution in Germany, 1850–1914,' *JEEH* 10 (1981): 74 ('The
    emphasis that has been placed upon the role of the grain-tariff ... is some-
    what surprising in view of the fact that most studies ... deny that it exercised a
    significant influence'); and Ian Farr, 'Populism in the Countryside: The Peas-
    ant Leagues in Bavaria in the 1890s,' in Richard J. Evans, ed., *Society and Poli-
    tics*, p. 147. In any case, tariffs might have been rational for peasants; see
    Robert G. Moeller, 'Peasants and Tariffs in the *Kaiserreich*: How Backward
    Were the *Bauern*?' *Agric. H.* 55.4 (Oct. 1981): 371–2, 382–3.

106 Gerhard Bry, *Wages in Germany*, tables A-1 and A-2, p. 326; Dieter Groh, *Nega-
    tive Integration*, appendix 2, p. 734; 'Parvus,' *Die Handelskrisis und die Gewerh
    schaften* (1901); Bernhard, *Krach-Krisis und Arbeiterklasse: Agitations-Ausgabe*
    (1902).

107 2/5/03; clipping in HSA Stuttgart E130a Nr. 1426. Early in the 1903 cam-

paign, the leading party newspaper, *Vorwärts*, referred to the most important issues in the campaign as the fleet, the tariff, and the arms race; at the height of the battle, it listed them as the tariff, militarism, and civil liberties (*VW* 1/5/03 p. 1, 3/6/03 p. 1, and 16/6/03 pp. 1–2).

108 The press accounts are collected in GStAPK RLB PA 6060 (M).

109 *Programmatische Kundgebungen*, pp. 75–9.

110 *KZ* 19/4/03m p. 1, 11/5/03ev p. 1, and 20/6/03ev p. 1.

111 Bülow to Kaiserlicher Statthalter in Alsace-Lorraine, 17/5/03, in BAK R43F 1792. In June 1903 the interior ministry's directive was simple: 'everywhere those candidates are to be supported, who stand in opposition to the parties that undermine the established order, such as Social Democrats, Poles, Guelphs [and] Danes' (MdI to OP, 12/6/03, in ibid.).

Chapter 3: The Official Machine and the Failure of *Sammlungspolitik*

1 Regarding other German federal states, it appears that in southern Germany officials played a technical function, overseeing the mechanics of voting. I did not find any records in official documents to indicate that they were involved, as officials were in the north, in reporting to ministers on the progress of election campaigns, or in trying to strike backroom deals among political parties. In the Kingdom of Saxony, it seems officials, after the 1880s, played a role analogous to those in Prussia (see the forthcoming work by James Retallack on elections in Saxony).

2 Presumably it is for this reason that so few copies of this document survive. The only one found by the author was in LASH Abt. 301 Nr. 805. Since the existence of this document was unknown to the author at the time of writing 'Authority vs. Democracy: Prussian Officials in the German Elections of 1898–1903' (*Historical Journal* 33.4 [1990]), that article is incomplete compared to the account here.

3 Ibid.

4 Ibid.; emphasis in original.

5 So named by the Badenese ambassador (see *Großherzog Friedrich I*, no. 1851, Jagemann to Brauer 7/5/98).

6 For reports from officials on the elections, see, for example, in the central ministerial files, GStAPK I. HA Rep. 90 Nr. 128; for the Rhineland, HSA Düss. Reg. Düss. Präs. 572; and for Schleswig-Holstein, those in LASH Abt. 301 Nr. 809 and 6757.

7 See the file on the *Berliner Korrespondenz* in BAP RMdI 15253.

8 Jagemann to Brauer 14/2/98 (and for the following also 19/2/98 and 25/2/98), in *Großherzog Friedrich I* (nos. 1810, 1812, 1815).

9 BAP RMdI 15421, nos. 5–11; GStAPK Rep. 151 HB (M) Nr. 890, nos. 95–101 (and the same for the remainder of the paragraph).

10 HSA Düss. Reg. Aachen Präs. 679, no. 74; see also HSA Hanover Hann. 174 Hann. II Nr. 11 and GStAPK XVI. HA Rep. 30 Nr. 596.

11 See, for example, *BT* 2/5/03ev.

12 GStAPK Rep. 77 CB tit. 867 (M) Nr. 17 Adh. 1; also HSA Düss. Reg. Aachen Präs. 815 and 816 I.

13 For example, in Posen (GStAPK XVI. HA Rep. 30 Nr. 596) and Schleswig-Holstein (LASH Abt. 301 Nr. 6478, Landrat in Tondern to OP 15/4/03).

14 GStAPK Rep. 77 CB tit. 867 (M) Nr. 17 Adh. II, no. 1.

15 *Wen wählen wir?*, like other leaflets in the series (which included *Sind Industrie und Landwirtschaft Gegner?*, *Was will der Ruf zur Sammlung?*, *Freisinn, Sozialdemokratie und Landwirtschaft*, and others) can be found in many of the 'secret' files of Prussian officials. There is a fairly complete collection in HSA Düss. Reg. Aachen Präs. 815.

16 Once again the leaflets are widely available in government 'secret' files. See HSA Düss. Reg. Aachen Präs. 816 I.

17 HSA Hanover Hann. 174 Hann. II Nr. 11; HSA Düss. Reg. Düss. Präs. 583, no. 240 (and the same for the following).

18 HSA Düss. Reg. Aachen Präs. 816 I, nos. 39–46.

19 HSA Düss. Reg. Düss. Präs. 584, nos. 5–6, 14–15, 21, 30, 41.

20 HSA Düss. Reg. Düss. Präs. 585, no. 3.

21 HSA Hanover Hann. 122a i Nr. 108, nos. 98–100.

22 GStAPK XVI. HA Rep. 30 Nr. 576.

23 See the January 1898 guidelines, LASH Abt. 301 [Oberpräsidium], Nr. 805: Die Beteiligung der Beamten bei den Wahlen, 1898–1921. These discouraged *Oberpräsidenten* and *Regierungspräsidenten* generally from running for office, and suggested that a candidacy by a *Landrat* should be a last resort.

24 *KöZ* 11/6/98ev.

25 GStAPK XVI. HA Rep. 30 Nr. 596.

26 Ibid.

27 GStAPK I. HA Rep. 90 Nr. 306; GStAPK Rep. 77 CB tit. 867 (M) Nr. 16a Adh. IX; HSA Hanover Hann. 174 Hann. II Nr. 11.

28 Kenneth Janda, 'Comparative Political Parties,' p. 167.

29 Angelo Panebianco, *Political Parties: Organization and Power*, pp. 54–7.

30 Dirk Stegmann, *Erben Bismarcks*, p. 74. One of the Interior Ministry's pamphlets asked, *Was will der Ruf zur Sammlung?* (What does the call to *Sammlung* mean?), and answered: 'the call to *Sammlung* means the unification of voters for the Reichstag elections ... the agreement on a unified electoral program!'

The full text of the *Sammlung* declaration may be found in *Schulthess' Europäischer Geschichtskalender* for 1898, pp. 78–9.

31 See Stegmann, *Erben Bismarcks*, pp. 75–9. More is said about the responses of the various parties in the appropriate chapters below. See Geoff Eley, '*Sammlungspolitik*, Social Imperialism and the Navy Law of 1898,' *MM* 15 (1974): 29–63, on the general difficulties of the policy.

32 Min. State 19/4/98(II), in BAK R43F/1817.

33 The question of whether the Centre was to be included was a sore point for Miquel's *Sammlungspolitik* (see below), and he stressed its inclusion here undoubtedly to help win support for his policy from moderate ministers and the chancellor.

34 Ibid. Hohenlohe also wrote that he believed the SPD's vote gain if agricultural prices increased (in this case, meat prices) would be greater than the peasant disaffection if higher prices were not brought in, meaning the government could not afford to challenge the SPD on this kind of economic issue (*Memoirs*, entry for 7 March 1900).

35 Udo Count zu Stolberg-Wernigerode, writing to Bülow (quoted by Klaus Saul, *Staat, Industrie, Arbeiterbewegung*, p. 14).

36 In 1897 the kaiser had already declared his support for the 'protection of national labour of all productive estates (*Stände*) and strengthening of the *Mittelstand*.' This was interpreted by conservatives in 1898 as imperial sponsorship for electoral *Sammlungspolitik*. (See 'Die Politik der Sammlung im Lichte der Wahlkampf,' *Staatsbürger Zeitung* 17/5/98, in BAP RLB PA 5076.)

37 Min. State 19/4/98, in BAK R43F/1817.

38 *Großherzog Friedrich I*, no. 1851, Jagemann to Brauer 7/5/98.

39 See the argument in *KöVZ* 26/3/03m, and contrast Miquel's comments to the Min. State on 19/4/98 (above). Chapter 6 examines Centre electoral strategy.

40 Geoff Eley's essay '*Sammlungspolitik*, Social Imperialism and the Navy Law of 1898' (*MM* 15 [1974]: 29–63) is the only published work that critically examines the problems of the concept of *Sammlungspolitik* in 1898. Its analysis is borne out by the findings here.

41 Naturally, the exact pattern was more complex than this because the seats were divided up among the *Kartell* parties, not precisely by region, but according to historical precedents and according to who could win in the particular electoral environment (for which, community structure and nature of opposition were decisive). See the grouping of electoral environments used in Appendix A.

42 Where confessional politics (especially a *balance* between the confessions) predominated, the SPD vote 'lagged behind' the national trend. See Karl Rohe,

"'verspätete" Region' and his other publications on the Ruhr, and the discussion in Appendix A of mixed-confession constituencies.

43 GStAPK I. HA Rep. 90 128, nos. 262–3; *BT* 26/6/98.

44 These cases are discussed further in chapter 5.

45 Min. State 19/3/98, 22/3/98, 12/4/98, in GStAPK RdI (M) 15338.

46 Min. State 29/7/97 in GStAPK 90a AVIII 1,d (M) Nr. 3, nos. 234–8; also in GStAPK I. HA Rep. 90 128, nos. 230–2.

47 Min. State 4/3/98, in BAK R43F/1817.

48 Min. State 19/4/98 (I), in BAK R43F/1817.

49 Memo in BAP RdI 14644, no. 64.

50 Min. State 14/3/03, in BAK R43F/1792.

51 Min. State 18/3/03, in BAK R43F/1792. On the constitutional arguments, see 'Zum Reichstagswahltermin,' *Die Post* 30/3/03.

52 BHSA Munich MA 76274, Berchtenfeld to MdA 16/3/03 and 25/3/03.

53 *VW* 31/3/03, 1/4/03, 4/4/03; *NAZ* 3/4/03; *BT* 27/3/03ev, 3/4/03. Many of these articles are collected in BAP RdI 14644.

54 See Posadowsky's comments, Min. State 4/3/98, in BAK R43F/1817; Berchtenfeld to MdA 25/3/03, in BHSA Munich MA 76274.

55 John C.G. Röhl, *Germany without Bismarck*, esp. pp. 223ff; BHSA Munich MA 95007 (report of Bavarian ambassador 8/3/99, concerning Hohenlohe's health and energy); David J. Fraley, 'Government by Procrastination: Chancellor Hohenlohe and Kaiser Wilhelm II 1894–1900,' *CEH* 7.2 (1974): 159–83.

56 *NZ* 8/6/98; see also *FZ* 8/6/98m3 and *Großherzog Friedrich I*, no. 1856 (Jagemann to Reck 9/6/98), for discussion of the intention of the leak. Many clippings on the subject are collected in BAP RLB PA 5076.

57 BAK R43F/17, telegram from Posadowsky to Hohenlohe 5/6/98. The published form of the statement appeared in virtually every major newspaper on 8/6/98.

58 *KöVZ* 8/6/98; *NAZ* 10/6/98; *KZ* 12/6/98m p. 1.

59 *VW* 8/6/98 p. 1; *FZ* 8/6/98m3 p. 1 (quotes reports of other papers).

60 *Staatsbürger Zeitung* 12/6/98, in BAP RLB PA 5076 (see also *BT* 12/5/98m and 13/5/98 1BB).

61 Bachem papers, HASK 1006 Nr. 197 and Nr. 198, memo of 19/6/03 and related material.

62 Quoted in *BT* 2/5/03ev pp. 1–2 and in RWSA Münster Oberpräs 2681/2–10.

63 Quotations from *KöZ* 24/5/98m and *Krefelder Zeitung* 2/5/98n. See *Großherzog Friedrich I*, nos. 1808ff. for party leaders' opinions about the advantages and disadvantages of the fleet issue.

64 *SBVR* 9LP 5S 1897/1898, III, pp. 1818–27.

65 HSA Hanover Hann. 122a I Nr. 13, nos. 246–51.

66 *KZ* 2/5/03ev p. 1 ('Die Reichstagswahlen in Baiern') and 14/6/03m p. 1 ('Die innere Politik der Woche').

67 The index used is Herfindahl's index, an index of industrial concentration; see Alexis Jacquemann, *The New Industrial Organization: Market Forces and Strategic Behavior*, p. 51. Here I have applied Herfindahl's index to political parties, to measure the degree of concentration of votes within a specified grouping. It is calculated as the sum of the squares of the individual parties' shares of their total vote, each party's share being a ratio from 0 to 1. The theoretical value of the index ranges from $1/n$ where n equals the number of the parties, to 1. (A value of $1/n$ would be obtained only where all parties ran candidates and all the candidates won equal shares of the vote; a value of 1 would be produced if only one candidate from all the parties recorded votes in one seat.) The values in the table are averages among all constituencies.

68 'Type 2' seats, as explained in Appendix A, accounted for most of the mandates won by anti-Semitic candidates. Though certain anti-Semitic parties won votes in cities, they usually did not win a high enough proportion to take the seat.

69 The assumption here is that competition among a group of parties where none of them has a chance of winning should not be regarded as evidence of serious division. 'Some chance of winning' is defined arbitrarily as all the parties of the right receiving, together, at least 20 per cent of the first-ballot votes. If other parties' votes were widely dispersed, a 20 per cent base of support could put a candidate within striking distance of making it into the second-place spot and thereby into a run-off – it could at least be close enough that unity would be important.

70 The coalition is judged to have 'broken down' if there were significant candidacies (5 per cent of the votes or more) from more than one of the parties concerned. 'Agrarians' are counted here as Agrarian League only. Regarding 'winnable' seats, see the previous note. The same definitions ('significant,' 'agrarian') are followed for the remainder of the paragraph.

71 The 1912 elections were fought with substantially different party alignments (united liberals, Conservative-Centre alliance) and are not directly comparable.

72 This unity was in a losing cause – see chapter 7 on the Social Democratic victory of 1903 in Saxony.

73 Arthur Levysohn, 'Politische Wochenschau,' *BT* 29/5/98S p. 1; *DTZ* 24/2/03, in BAP RLB PA 6060, no. 37.

74 *Großherzog Friedrich I*, nos. 1847 and 1859.

75 *Corr. d. BdL* 5/5/1903; *KZ* 14/4/03 ev p. 1 (also 14/6/03 p. 1); *BT* 7/5/03m p. 1. For other press and political reactions to the government's 'passive' bear-

ing, 'lack of courage and energy,' and 'directionlessness' in 1903, see Saul, *Staat, Industrie, Arbeiterbewegung*, pp. 13–15.
76 *VW* 27/6/03.
77 *Großherzog Friedrich I*, no. 2402 (Jagemann to Brauer 14/3/03).
78 *BT* 17/4/03m
79 *RWZ* 17/6/03ev.
80 *DTZ* 13/12/02.

Chapter 4: Mass Politics and the Right

1 Maurice Duverger, *Les Partis politiques*, p. 468.
2 The phrase 'dominant coalition' is taken from Angelo Panebianco, *Political Parties*; see chapter 1.
3 Wolfgang Treue, ed., *Deutsche Parteiprogramme*, pp. 74–6.
4 Among Protestant 'German' seats, in 1890 Conservatives were ahead of left liberals in rural seats where large landownership predominated, behind where it did not (cons. 42 per cent to left lib. 33 per cent, type 1; cons. 23 per cent to left lib. 29 per cent, type 2). The two parties were the largest two in both types of seats in 1890. Conservatives did less well, overall, than left liberals in purely urban seats (9 per cent to 20 per cent, type 4), and mixed rural-urban (cons. 16 per cent to left lib. 24 per cent, type 3a), and also trailed the SPD and National Liberals in these categories of seats. Eastern Prussia was the core of both DKP and left-liberal support: Conservatives won 57 per cent of all votes and 59 per cent of all seats; left liberals 41 per cent and 36 per cent, in the provinces from Brandenburg east, which made up 32 per cent of Reichstag constituencies (these include East and Wess Prussia, Pomerania, Posen, and Silesia, as well as Brandenburg). On constituency typology, see Appendix A.
5 *KZ* 9/6/03m p. 1. The other two leaflets were simply a published version of the national election declaration, and a discussion of the party's general policies.
6 Hess. SA Marburg Best. 180 Frankenberg Nr. 1121.
7 From the 1882 *Wahlaufruf* (Treue, pp. 66–7).
8 *KöZ* 7/5/98m p. 1
9 For example, see chapter 3 on the candidacy of Tiedemann in Bromberg.
10 Hubertus Fischer, 'Konservatismus von unten,' p. 127.
11 Konrad von Zwehl, 'Zum Verhältnis von Regierung und Reichstag im Kaiserreich (1871–1918),' in G.A. Ritter, ed., *Regierung, Bürokratie und Parlament in Preußen und Deutschland von 1848 bis zur Gegenwart*, pp. 108–9.
12 *BT* 24/5/98ev.
13 *SBVR* 10 LP 1S, 1898/1900, no. 126; Min. State 8/2/99 in GStAPK I. HA Rep. 90 Nr. 128, nos. 268–9.

14 *SBVR* 11LP 1S, 1903, no. 269.
15 Ibid., and 10LP 1S, no. 264. See also 10LP 1S, no. 214.
16 Prof. R. Siegfried, *Die verschwiegende Wahlurne* (may be found in GStAPK I. HA Rep. 90 Nr. 128, no. 284). See Margaret Lavinia Anderson, 'Voter, Junker, Landrat, Priest,' p. 1457, who is concerned more to prove that employers *could* violate secrecy than to assess whether many of them *did* do so.
17 Hellmut von Gerlach remained dissatisfied: see 'Die sogenannte Wahlurne,' *Die Nation* 22. 44 (1904–5): 692–4. Von Gerlach was an anti-Semitic and then National-Social politician who ran against a number of Conservative magnates.
18 Willy Brandt, *My Road to Berlin*, p. 30. Von Gerlach (*Von Rechts nach Links*) also tells stories of manipulative devices by rural landowners to control their workers. Without trivializing the situation of dependency in which many labourers lived, historians need to take care in generalizations about 'East Elbian' conditions. The constituencies dominated by large estates and Conservative nobles were not the whole of eastern Germany, but just thirty-four seats, mostly in a belt near the Baltic shore from Holstein to East Prussia (type 1 seats; see Appendix A). Often-quoted stories of electoral manipulation, including Brandt's and Gerlach's, refer to a social-political environment that was decisive in less than 10 per cent of Reichstag seats.
19 *SBVR* 10LP 1S, 1898/1900, no. 208.
20 *SBVR* 10LP 1S, 1898/1900, no. 265; on related cases, see also nos. 141, 142, 175, 192, 214.
21 *SBVR* 10LP 1S, 1898/1900, no. 142 (see also no. 384).
22 Although Tivoli is often seen as a great anti-Semitic victory, the program emphasized, in its specifics, orthodox *Mittelstandspolitik* (attacks on the 'privileges of big financial capital,' guilds and cooperatives to help artisans, tariffs and inheritance law reform for peasants, etc.). Other than a vague statement against 'Jewish influence on the life of our *Volk*,' the program demanded only 'energetic intervention of state power against ... un-German abandonment of honour and faith in commercial business' (Treue, ed., *Deutsche Parteiprogramme*, pp. 74–6). The lack of more content specifically concerning Jews and social reform to help 'Germans' disappointed many anti-Semites (R.S. Levy, *The Downfall of the Anti-Semitic Political Parties in Imperial Germany*, p. 83).
23 On the cresting of the Hammerstein-Stöcker faction in 1892, see James N. Retallack, *Notables of the Right*, pp. 77–99.
24 Levy, *Downfall of the Anti-Semitic Political Parties*, p. 256.
25 Retallack, *Notables of the Right*, p. 95. On the governmental backlash, see ibid., pp. 95ff; and 'Conservatives *contra* Chancellor.'
26 Retallack, *Notables of the Right*, p. 92.

27 'Zur Lage der konservativen Partei,' *Reichsbote* 9/1/98, in BHSA Munich Pr A Slg 144.

28 Stanley Suval, *Electoral Politics in Wilhelmine Germany*, pp. 152–3.

29 Retallack, *Notables of the Right*, p. 98.

30 Peter Pulzer, *The Rise of Political Anti-Semitism*, pp. 126, 189. Levy argues that the 'real strength' of the anti-Semites declined after 1896 and that their morale was broken by 1898 (pp. 195–225). Anti-Semites won twenty-two seats in 1907, but mainly as anti-socialist compromise candidates with support from *Kartell* parties they once criticized.

31 Pulzer interprets the Böckel movement as a second wave of anti-Semitism, this time from below, following the first wave of Conservative-sponsored anti-Semitism in the early 1880s (p. 107).

32 'An die Wähler des Wahlkreises Marburg-Kirchhain-Frankenberg-Vöhl!' and 'Die Antisemiten kommen!,' both in Hess. SA Marburg Best. 180 Frankenberg Nr. 1121; and 'Böckel oder Excellenz General z.D. von Bartenwerffer?' ibid. Best. 165 Nr. 47.

33 See the pamphlets in the same archival sources cited in the previous note. The 1903 campaign was conducted on similar lines, with the National-Social candidate von Gerlach trying to discredit the anti-Semite and the Conservative for being the same (neither a real populist). See Suval, *Electoral Politics in Wilhelmine Germany*, pp. 152–6.

34 Thomas Nipperdey and Reinhard Rürup, 'Antisemitismus – Entstehung, Funktion und Geschichte eines Begriffs,' in Nipperdey, *Gesellschaft, Kultur, Theorie*, p. 125. For an anti-Semitic explanation of their own black-red-gold imagery, see 'Leitziele für eine deutsch-soziale Reformpartei' (Darmstadt, n.d.), in BAK ZSg 1 E24.

35 See 'Gegen die Brot-Vertheurer!,' a German-Social pamphlet (Leipzig, n.d.), and 'Macht die Augen auf!' (Leipzig, n.d.), in BAK ZSg 1 E2; and Dr W. Giese, *Die Judenfrage am Ende des XIX. Jahrhunderts* (Berlin, 1899).

36 On Naumann's role in promoting liberal unity, see B. Heckart, *From Bassermann to Bebel: The Grand Bloc's Quest for Reform in the Kaiserreich, 1900–1914*, pp. 4–34.

37 See 'Entwurf des Programms der christlich-sozialen Partei' and 'Programm der christlich-sozialen Partei,' in BAK ZSg 1 E/73. There are no dates on these programs.

38 See Oberst z.D. von Krause (chairman of the Berlin DKP), 'Zum Austritt Stöckers aus der konservativen Partei,' and 'Rede des Abgeordneten Freiherrn von Stumm-Halberg zu Neunkirchen am 12. April 1896,' *Neue Saarbrücker Zeitung* 16/4/96 p. 1, both in BAP RT 31995, nos. 34–5. On the significance of Stöcker's defeat, see also Retallack, *Notables of the Right*, pp. 116–26.

39 On the other hand, given the small number of serious anti-Semitic candidacies among the Reichstag's 397 seats, it could be interpreted as striking that
any significant coefficients emerge at all.

40 In the 1898 and 1903 elections (combined) anti-Semites won 1 mandate in
type 1 seats, 15 in type 2, 6 in type 3a, and 1 in type 4. They also won 1 type 7b
seat for a total of 24 elected deputies. (On the typology, see Appendix A.)

41 Pulzer comments that key areas of anti-Semitic success were areas of 'passive
and apathetic conservatism' not yet penetrated by modern parliamentary
party politics (pp. 113–16).

42 Of three cases between 1890 and 1903 in which an anti-Semite won in a Protestant urban seat (type 4), two were in Royal Saxony in 1893; the other was in
Kassel in Hesse-Nassau (strongly influenced by the surrounding anti-Semitic
countryside) in 1903.

43 From official election statistics as described in Appendix C. Other seats where
anti-Semites (not including the BdL) replaced earlier Conservative candidacies or appear to have taken votes away from Conservatives during the period
1893–1903 include nos. 29, 30, 37, 47, 51, 58, 67, and 137. Typically, in these
cases, the Conservative vote fell significantly when an anti-Semitic candidate
ran, and rose again in subsequent elections if no such candidate ran.

44 Many anti-Semitic candidates were also sponsored by the BdL, a fact propagandists used to discredit the latter (NL *Politisches Handbuch* [1897], p. 192).
This could, however, cause problems for the anti-Semites as well, because of
the excessively establishmentarian and Conservative associations of the
League; see the example of Böckel above.

45 H.-J. Puhle, *Agrarische Interessenpolitik*, pp. 72–110, documents the militant anti-
Semitism of BdL functionaries.

46 On the gradual split between anti-Semites and Conservatives by 1893–6, see
Levy, pp. 67–90, and Retallack, *Notables of the Right.*

47 Anti-Semites continued to be included in 'national' or 'state-supporting' coalitions, but from 1898 onward had difficulty winning seats without the help of
such coalitions.

48 See Puhle, *Agrarische Interessenpolitik*, pp. 168–75, on the connection between
the DKP and the BdL; cf. Retallack, *Notables of the Right*, chapters 8 and 10.

49 H.-U. Wehler, *Kaiserreich*, p. 85. Clearly the BdL boosted organization and
activism in many rural areas, usually to the Conservatives' benefit, and this
provided some of the advantages to the Conservatives of 'modern' electoral
organization; but it is too much to claim the party was 'transformed' into a
modern type, and the claim that it won 'new classes of the electorate' is
refuted below.

50 P. Molt, *Der Reichstag vor der improvisierten Revolution*, p. 249. The claim is over-

stated, as DKP election committees did oppose the BdL during 1898–1903 in some cases, and in many more only official intervention held the two together, usually by making the BdL rather than the Conservatives give in. It may have mainly been in agrarian seats marginal to the Conservatives (type 2) that the BdL could dominate the party. In type 1 (large-landownership) seats there is no sign of any divergence between the two, indicating that BdL activism flowed within existing DKP channels.

51 Molt, *Der Reichstag vor der improvisierten*, p. 283. See Thomas Nipperdey, *Organisation der deutschen Parteien*, p. 249, and Dirk Stegmann, *Erben Bismarcks*, p. 20, for similar interpretations. Puhle is somewhat more careful in stressing the BdL's autonomy *vis à vis* the party proper, calling it a 'powerful prototype of a new sort of political organization on the boundary between party and interest group' ('Parlament, Parteien und Interessenverbände,' p. 361). He writes elsewhere of the way it (re-) 'shaped' or 'distorted' (*verformt*) the DKP ('Radikalisierung und Wandel des deutschen Konservatismus vor dem ersten Weltkrieg,' in G.A. Ritter, ed., *Die deutschen Parteien*, pp. 164–86).

52 See Retallack, *Notables of the Right*, and 'Conservatives *contra* Chancellor.'

53 Karl Erich Born, 'Structural Changes in German Social and Economic Development at the End of the Nineteenth Century,' in James Sheehan, ed., *Imperial Germany*, p. 34.

54 Puhle ('Radikalisierung') emphasizes the new type of professional politician, campaigning, structure, and ideology the BdL brought to the Conservative Party, helping the latter adapt to new political conditions created by social change.

55 On the phenomenon of peasant populism generally, see David Blackbourn's 'Peasants and Politics in Germany 1871–1914' *EHQ* 14.1 (Jan. 1984): 47–76; and 'The Politics of Demagogy in Imperial Germany,' *PP* 113 (Nov. 1986): 152–84.

56 *KZ* 5/6/98m p. 1; on approaches between the peasants and the south German liberals, see *Fränkischer Kurier* 18/9/96 and other clippings in BHSA Munich Pr A Slg 1475. The People's Party thought 'the kernel of the movement is a thoroughly democratic one' and suggested alliance was possible if the League did not pursue purely agrarian demands.

57 Dietrich Thränhardt, *Wahlen und politische Strukturen in Bayern*, p. 6. The correlation was +24 in 1890 and +22 in 1907, but in the three intervening elections it was only +2, −1, and +10.

58 Quotations from *Badische Landeszeitung* 8/9/96 and *DTZ* 29/5/03 (clippings in BHSA Munich Pr A Slg 1475 and 113 respectively). On the history and regional divisions of the peasants' leagues (a complex story), see Dieter Fricke, ed., *Die bürgerlichen Parteien*, pp. 66–78; and (for a contemporary sum-

mary) 'Die Bauernbewegung in Bayern,' *Münchener Post* 28/7/99, in BHSA Munich Pr A Slg 1475.

59 I. Farr, 'Populism in the Countryside,' in Richard Evans, ed., *Society and Politics*, esp. pp. 144-5.

60 Retallack, *Notables of the Right*, pp. 131ff.

61 See Hannelore Horn, 'Die Rolle des Bundes der Landwirte im Kampf um den Bau des Mittellandkanals,' *Jahrbuch für die Geschichte Mittel- und Ostdeutschlands* 7 (1958): 273-358; also her book *Der Kampf um den Bau des Mittellandkanals*.

62 'Conservatismus,' 6/5/02, in BAK R43F 1391/5.

63 'Deutsche Wähler' in Hess. SA Marburg Best. 180 Hersfeld Nr. 922.

64 'Mahnruf an die Berufsgenossen von einem Rheinischen Bauer,' in HSA Düss. Reg. Aachen Präs. 816 I, nos. 120-1.

65 On the kaiser's resistance to the agrarian wing, which he considered 'a burden to the party,' and on his advocacy of a strong alliance with the National Liberals, see William II, *My Memoirs: 1878-1918*, pp. 31-2.

66 One anti-Semite won a type 1 seat in each of 1898 and 1903.

67 In type 2 seats, the conservative parties declined from 33-4 per cent of the vote and 27-8 seats in 1890 and 1893, to 27-8 per cent and 20 seats in each of 1898 and 1903. In 1903 the anti-Semites and BdL won 11 per cent and 10 of these seats. The agrarian/anti-Semitic gain in these seats from 1890 to 1903 was +9 per cent and +7 seats; the conservative loss was -6 per cent and -7 seats. The net loss was all by the DKP; the RP was steady at 5 seats (see Appendix A).

68 Type 3a. The conservatives parties declined here from 23 per cent in 1890 to 14 per cent in 1903, when anti-Semites and the BdL won 10 per cent and 8 seats. The SPD gains were mainly at the expense of the left liberals, who lost 17 per cent and 11 seats over the same period.

69 See chapter 3 for examples of the attitudes of officials and the government.

70 The right-wing National Liberal *KöZ* openly expressed its contempt for the agrarian extremists by commenting sarcastically on how useless it was to try to turn back the 'current' of 'modern development' in this way ('Zu den Reichstagswahlen. Die Wahlparole des Bundes der Landwirte,' 26/5/03m2 p. 2).

71 HSA Stutt. E73 Verz. 61 Nr. 12e, Varnbüler to v. Soden 1/7/03.

72 On the last point, the success of the Social Democrats in weaving a campaign against tariffs and agrarians into a campaign for popular rights and fair taxation, see chapters 2 and 7.

73 Navalism, *Weltpolitik*, and the colonial issues of 1907 were less effective for the Conservatives as 'national' issues than the military bills of 1887 and 1893 had been.

74 Besides the substantial literature in the Bibliography concerning the SPD's agrarian policy, see also Retallack, *Notables of the Right*, chapter 11.

75 See Rudolf Heberle, *From Democracy to Nazism.*
76 Suval, *Electoral Politics in Wilhelmine Germany*, passim.

Chapter 5: The Low Ebb of Liberalism

1 One Reichstag deputy spoke of the increasing remoteness of the upper echelons of society as a process of 'Ballinization,' referring to Albert Ballin, liberal head of the HAPAG shipping firm (Lamar Cecil, *Albert Ballin*, p. 132).
2 Two excellent overviews of the situation of liberalism are James Sheehan, *German Liberalism in the Nineteenth Century*, and Dieter Langewiesche, 'German Liberalism in the Second Empire, 1871–1914,' in Konrad H. Jarausch and Larry E. Jones, eds., *In Search of a Liberal Germany*, pp. 217–36. The Jarausch/ Jones edition and David Blackbourn and Richard J. Evans, eds., *The German Bourgeoisie*, bring together a variety of essays reassessing liberalism and the middle classes.
3 Hartmut Pogge von Strandmann, 'The Liberal Power Monopoly in the Cities of Imperial Germany,' in Larry E. Jones and James Retallack, eds., *Elections, Mass Politics, and Social Change*, pp. 93–117.
4 Karl Rohe writes: '... the political "meaning" of a vote, especially for liberal parties, which were notorious for presenting different images in different regions, could differ tremendously from region to region – from sometimes being mainly an anti-catholic, an anti-separatist or an anti-socialist vote to being primarily a liberal vote in a proper and narrower sense of the word' ('German Elections and Party Systems in Historical and Regional Perspective: An Introduction,' in Rohe, ed., *Elections, Parties and Political Traditions*, p. 9).
5 In the three elections from 1893 to 1903, liberals won 90, 95, and 87 seats respectively. Until 1890 liberal parties had divided among themselves well over 100 seats. See G.A. Ritter and M. Niehuss, *Wahlgeschichtliches Arbeitsbuch*, pp. 38–42, for an overview of the election results during 1871–1914.
6 The electoral advance of the SPD brought it by 1898 very close to these same levels of support in many liberal constituencies (the SPD's average vote in 1898 was 27 per cent), thus threatening to push the liberals out of the run-offs. By and large, very few seats were won with less than 25–30 per cent of the first-ballot vote, and while the liberals were better at winning run-offs than any other party, their support in many areas was falling below even these low levels.
7 See Sheehan, *German Liberalism*, esp. pp. 1–50, 79–122.
8 *From Max Weber: Essays in Sociology*, p. 111.
9 In 1881 the liberal parties won back most (but not all) of what had been lost in the exceptionally heavy defeat of 1878. Up to the 1890s, National Liberal and

left-liberal votes moved in inverse relation to each other, so that combining the vote totals in the way done here measures the attractive power of all the liberal parties while factoring out movement of votes among them.

10 See chapter 4.

11 The number of run-off contests in these seats declined by 40 per cent. As explained in Appendix A, type 4 constituencies, in addition to being at least 75 per cent Protestant, were those purely urban constituencies where particularist candidates received less than 25 per cent of the vote.

12 The conservative vote also declined in these type 3a seats (from 29 per cent in 1890 to 20 per cent in 1903) but was almost exactly balanced by the growth of anti-Semitic support (from 1 to 9 per cent). As in the previous example, the seats considered here are only Protestant 'German' ones.

13 Types 1, 5, and 2 respectively.

14 See Appendix A.

15 On the dilemma of nationalism and interests, see Geoff Eley, *Reshaping the German Right*, and his essay in Larry Jones and James Retallack, eds., *Between Reform, Reaction and Resistance.*

16 On the National Liberals in Hessen, see Dan White, *The Splintered Party: National Liberalism in Hessen and the Reich.* On Haas, see Rudolf Maxeiner, *Vertrauen in die eigene Kraft: Wilhelm Haas*; and Adalbert Feineisen, *Wilhelm Haas.*

17 The data may be consulted in Ritter and Niehuss, *Wahlgeschichtliches Arbeitsbuch*, pp. 41, 125.

18 The Wilhelmine record for winning the fewest votes on the first ballot and still winning the seat on the second is probably held by the National Liberals in Wolmirstedt-Neuhaldensleben, where they won the run-off against the SPD in 1912 after gaining only 22 per cent of the first-ballot vote.

19 On the conflict between the DVP and the FVP, for example, which frequently drove the latter into alliance with NL candidates in certain areas, see James C. Hunt, *People's Party*, pp. 41–2.

20 'Candidatenrede des Herrn Ernst Bassermann gehalten in der national-liberalen Wählerversammlung am Montag den 13. Juni im Saalbau in Mannheim' (apparently 1903), in BHSA Munich Slg Varia 38.

21 'Interessenvertretung,' *BT* 22/6/98m p. 1.

22 Richter and the FVP, with their stubborn commitment to independence and opposition, prevented any such national-level coordination among the parties. See Ina S. Lorenz, *Eugen Richter*, pp. 62–3. On the DVP, see Hunt, *People's Party.*

23 *Sachsenschau* 25/12/97 p. 1, quoting *Magdeburger Zeitung*, in BAP RLB PA 6131, no. 4.

24 'Politische Wochenschau,' *BT* 1/5/98S p. 1.

25 'Liberale Wahlnotwendigkeiten,' *BT* 15/5/03m p. 1; also 'Das Zünglein an der Wage,' 20/6/03ev p. 1.

26 On the FVg and liberal unity, see Beverley Heckart, *From Bassermann to Bebel*, pp. 29–30.

27 'Die Einigung im freisinnigen Lager,' *BT* 24/5/98ev p. 1.

28 'Zum Verhältnis der Freisinnigen Volkspartei und Freisinnigen Vereinigung,' *FZ* 28/5/98m2 p. 2; 28/5/98ev p. 2; 1/6/98m3 p. 1; 7/6/98m2 p. 1.

29 See Heckart, *Bassermann to Bebel*, pp. 38–40; and G.F. Mundle, 'The German National Liberal Party,' pp. 83–90.

30 Dr Friedrich Goldschmidt and Dr Friedrich Siebert, eds., *Schwarz-Weiß-Rot: Jungliberales Jahrbuch*, vol. 1 (Munich 1904); quotation from the contribution to the volume by Kulemann (p. 16).

31 See Heckart, pp. 3–16, and Sheehan, *German Liberalism*, p. 267.

32 On the ways in which anti-Semites and the SPD absorbed and exploited previously liberal ideas in election campaigns, see chapters 4 and 7.

33 Michael John, 'Liberalism and Society: The Case of Hanover,' *EHR* 102 (1987): 579–98; Lothar Gall, *Der Liberalismus als regierende Partei: Das Großherzogtum Baden zwischen Restauration und Reichsgründung*, pp. 29–40, 494; and Sheehan, *German Liberalism*, pp. 125–6.

34 Sheehan, *German Liberalism*, pp. 165–9, 204, 239–42; Anthony O'Donnell, 'National Liberalism,' chart, pp. 54–5; Hartwig Thieme, 'Die soziale und politische Struktur der nationalliberalen Fraktion,' in G.A. Ritter, ed., *Die deutschen Parteien*, pp. 245–6. As far as industrialists are concerned, the distinction was not so much higher or lower status (Georg von Siemens was a left liberal), but heavy or light industry. Shipping, banking, export, and electrical and chemical magnates tended to be left liberal, while coal, iron, and steel (the kind of industries organized in the CDI rather than the BdI) tended to be National Liberal or Free Conservative. See Hartmut Pogge von Strandmann, 'Kampf der verarbeitenden Industrie.'

35 Armin Steyer, 'Die Entwicklung der liberalen Parteien in Oldenburg: Eine regionalhistorische Untersuchung auf der Grundlage der Reichstagswahlen von 1893 bis 1912,' in Wolfgang Günther, ed., *Parteien und Wahlen in Oldenburg*, pp. 21–63; also see the other essays in the same collection.

36 White, *Splintered Party*, pp. 3–4, 97. O'Donnell ('National Liberalism') sees National Liberals as a 'subsidiary elite' distinguished by their consistent participation in the regime (p. 48); and George Frederick Mundle ('The German National Liberal Party 1900–1914,' pp. 106–13) emphasizes (like White) their regional decentralization. The text of the Heidelberg Declaration is in Wolfgang Treue, ed., *Deutsche Parteiprogramme*, pp. 69–70.

37 The text of the *Kartell* election declaration by the three parties can be found in

Programmatische Kundgebungen der Nationalliberalen Partei 1866–1913 (hereafter *PKdNP*), in BAK ZSg 1 74/4, pp. 37–8. The *Kartell* party that was incumbent or (where an opponent held the seat) was strongest was to name the candidate; where this could not be realized, complete *Kartell* solidarity was in any case to be unconditionally achieved. The party executives were to supervise their press and pamphlets to prevent any statements that might antagonize allies.

38 Thieme notes that in state elections the party's base was (in order) Hanover, the Rhine province, Westphalia, Saxony, and Hesse-Nassau, together providing 82 per cent of the deputies in 1913 ('Die soziale und politische Struktur,' p. 243). In Reichstag elections, with the equal suffrage, National Liberals could elect few deputies from the Rhineland and Westphalia.

39 For an example of the sort of anti-clerical campaign conducted by the National Liberals in the Rhineland, see Hans-Joachim Horn, 'Die politischen Strömungen in der Stadt Bonn, in Bonn-Land und im Kreis Rheinbach von 1879–1900' (dissertation, Bonn, 1968), pp. 305–9, on the 1898 Reichstag campaign.

40 See O'Donnell, 'National Liberalism,' particularly pp. 331–79 concerning the Society for the Eastern Marches, the Evangelical League, and the Navy League. As noted in chapter 2, it is important to emphasize the role of the veterans' associations in anti-socialist campaigns.

41 *PKdNP*, pp. 55–60, 64–8, and 75–9 (for the legislative background to these issues see chap. 2). Bennigsen had said at the party conference in 1898 that 'the danger threatens us that the struggle of economic issues will call forth a division among us' (*BT* 2/5/98m p. 1), but in 1903 the language was much more radical, virtually lumping 'interests' together with socialists as enemies of the state.

42 *Erklärung* of 7/3/98 in response to the 'Economic Declaration,' in *PKdNP*, p. 63; also in *Schulthess' Europäischer Geschichtskalender* (1898), p. 78. The 1898 *Wahlaufruf* repeats the formula nearly word for word; see *PKdNP*, p. 67.

43 1903 *Aufruf*, in *PKdNP*, pp. 75–9.

44 *FZ* 19/4/03m2 p. 1, clipping in HSA Stuttgart E130a Nr. 88.

45 *Augsburger Abendzeitung* 4/5/03, clipping in BAP RLB PA 5084.

46 Quotations from 'Beumers Programm: Rede des Reichstags- und Landtagsabgeordneten Dr. Beumer in der Tonhalle zu Duisburg-Hochfeld am 2. Mai 1903,' in GStAPK 150/3; and *RWZ* 1/6/98m p. 1.

47 The party's real, irremediable decline at the Reich-wide level was spread over the elections from 1890 to 1898. The 1890 loss appears to have been mainly to left liberals and the SPD, and 1893 perhaps to anti-Semites, so that 'agrarianism' is only one factor. The 1890 and 1893 elections merit further study. In 1903 the party recovered somewhat, as a result of the clarifying of

'governmental'-'agrarian' lines and remained roughly stable thereafter.

48 Statistics on FVP and Fvg candidacies from *BT* 28/5/03m p. 3. On the DVP see Klaus Simon, 'Die soziale Struktur der württembergischen Volkspartei,' in Ritter, ed., *Die deutschen Parteien*, and Hunt, *People's Party*.

49 On Richter and his methods, see Lorenz, *Eugen Richter: Der entschiedene Liberalismus in wilhelminischer Zeit*, and on the differences between the FVP and the FVg, Ludwig Elm, *Zwischen Fortschritt und Reaktion*, pp. 3–9. It remains curious that Richter's party has been the least-studied of the three; perhaps this indicates some regional or intellectual bias on the part of historians.

50 See the extensive collection of pamphlets from 1890 in BAK ZSg 1 46/7, notably 'Wähler von Dresden-Altstadt!', 'Was die Deutsche Freisinnige Partei will und was sie nicht will,' 'Arbeiter in Stadt und Land!', 'Frei muß das Brot sein und frei sein das Licht!', 'Wählt keinen Landrath!', 'Gegen die Konservativen!', 'Gegen den Kartellmischmasch!', and 'Kartellkatechismus.'

51 See the 1898 election declaration in *BT* 6/5/98m p. 1. The long-term party program focused on constitutional liberties and moderate social reform conditioned by *laissez-faire* (Eisenach program of 1894 [Treue, pp. 78–81]).

52 *Deutsches Reichsblatt* 16/4/98 p. 1 (BAP RLB PA 5076); and *BT* 11/6/03m p. 1.

53 In 1898, 86 of the 153 seats where left-liberal performance was better than average were in northeastern, southeastern, or central Prussia; in 1903, 75 of 135 were. Of the remainder, 31 (1903: 19) were in Protestant southern Germany; 21 (23) were in the *Kleinstaaten*.

54 The constituency types discussed in this paragraph are types 1, 2, and 3a in the order of introduction.

55 Type 4 seats (Protestant, 'German,' 40 per cent or more of population in cities of more than ten thousand people).

56 With a 74 per cent turnout on the first ballot, the RP won 7,297 votes (33 per cent), the left liberals 8,346 (37 per cent), the SPD 6,053 (27 per cent), and others 669 (Centre and anti-Semite). The SPD clearly had the balance of power. On the second ballot, conservative support went up by 141 votes to 7,438, liberal by 5,711 to 14,057.

57 SPD support increased by 681 in the run-off, FVP support by 5,177, with the RP having held the balance of power with a first-ballot vote of 6,866.

58 In 1907 and 1912 conservative first-ballot support collapsed, going to the left liberals, but even so they could win the seat only by 11 votes in the 1912 run-off.

59 All of the strong FVP seats mentioned here had Catholic minorities of 10–20 per cent, a significant factor which slowed SPD penetration (see chap. 7) and helped left liberals because of the regular electoral ties between the Centre and the FVP (see below).

60 Armin Steyer, 'Die Entwicklung der liberalen Parteien in Oldenburg.'
61 Increases of 15 per cent in run-offs were almost never achieved (given fairly high and fairly steady turnout) except where support from other parties was a factor. The opponents were NL(3), RP(2), and BdL, C, and anti-Semites (1 each). Other third-place parties were particularists, who also sometimes supported the SPD as a protest vote. A disproportionate number of these cases were in southern Germany and involved the DVP as the liberal party concerned.
62 Both publications may be found in BAK ZSg 1 46/5.
63 NAZ quoted in BT 18/6/98ev p. 1; 'Verspätete Einsicht,' BT 23/6/98m. On Richter's role in frustrating liberal unity, see above and Lorenz, Eugen Richter, pp. 62–3; Heckart, Bassermann to Bebel, p. 31.
64 See chapter 6 regarding the 'double majority' strategy. The Centre-FVP arrangements are all the more remarkable because they were mainly Prussian, whereas generally Prussia was more polarized in party alignments and saw less fluidity than southern election battles.
65 Quotes from 'Nationalliberale Phrasen,' Pfälzische Volkszeitung 24/11/97 (in BHSA Munich Pr A Slg 147), and the 1887 pamphlets 'Gegen die National-liberalen!' and 'Wählt deutschfreisinnig!' (BAK ZSg 1 46/7).

Chapter 6: Fortress Mentalities: The Catholic Centre and Particularists

1 Jürgen Kuczynski, 1903, p. 48.
2 L. Bergsträßer, Geschichte der politischen Parteien, pp. 42, 132–3.
3 John K. Zeender, The German Center Party, p. 4; see also David Blackbourn, Class, Religion, and Local Politics, p. 25, and Wilfried Loth, Katholiken im Kaiserreich.
4 Otto Büsch, 'Gedanken und Thesen zur Wählerbewegung in Deutschland,' in Otto Büsch, Wolfgang Wölk, and Monika Wölk, eds., Wählerbewegung in der deutschen Geschichte, chart, p. 129.
5 R.J. Ross, Beleaguered Tower: The Dilemma of Political Catholicism in Wilhelmine Germany, p. xiii, emphasizes the social/electoral significance of the 'tower' symbolism, which applied especially to the Kulturkampf era. The 'decisive position' terminology came, of course, only in the 1890s.
6 Germania quoted 'Fester nach jedem Sturm / Stehet der Centrumsthurm!' twice in two days after the 1903 Reichstag results (17/6/03ev p.1 and 19/6/03m p. 1).
7 J. Sperber, Popular Catholicism in Nineteenth-Century Germany, argues that the Kulturkampf coincided with a 'growing cohesion of the Catholic milieu' and created a state of 'permanent political mobilization' that made elaborate campaigns unnecessary for the Centre Party (p. 253).

8 Controversy was heightened by examples like the 'Spahn case' of 1901; see chapter 2.

9 M. Erzberger, 'Der Stille Kulturkampf' (n.d., c. 1911); M. Erzberger, ed., *Beiträge zur Parität in Württemberg* (1903). These publications may be found in BAK ZSg 2/8 and ZSg 1 108/2 respectively. See also Ross, *Beleaguered Tower*, pp. 18ff. The 'Protestantization' argument, which related to eastern Prussia, was a wilful misconstrual of the Prussian government's anti-Polish policies.

10 Quoted in Kuczynski, *1903*, p. 47.

11 During 1898–1903 this was more true where the party's traditional style and aristocratic leadership prevailed, rather than in areas like southern Germany, which had a more popular style, or the Rhineland, where the party leaders were more middle-class and were concerned more explicitly with programs and strategies.

12 *Germ.* 4/6/98m p. 1.

13 Program in *Westfälischer Merkur* 31/5/03m p. 1; comment in *Münsterischer Anzeiger und Münsterischer Volkszeitung* 7/6/03m p. 1 (both in RWSA Münster Oberpräs 2681/2, nos. 40 and 46).

14 The Poles, rather than the Centre, mobilized many Catholic voters in eastern Prussia; the Guelphs in Hanover and liberals or particularists in Alsace-Lorraine received Centre votes; the Bavarian Peasants' League was strong for a decade in Old Bavaria; and the SPD took a number of Catholic cities.

15 *BT* 19/6/03ev p. 1.

16 Johannes Schauff, *Katholische Wähler und Zentrumspartei* (1928), excerpt in Büsch, Wölk, and Wölk, p. 222. The trend after 1903 implies a failure to maintain such intense loyalty. On the basis of detailed statistics for the Rhineland, Sperber disputes Schauff's findings and concludes from regression analysis that 97–9 per cent of voting Catholics voted Centre there in the 1874–81 Reichstag elections (pp. 254–5, note 5, and table 6.2, p. 256).

17 W. Schulte, 'Die ökologischen Korrelate der Parteien in den württembergischen Wahlen,' in Büsch, Wölk, and Wölk, pp. 468–70. Centre support increased in a similar way in the rural Rhineland (K. Müller, 'Das Rheinland als Gegenstand der historischen Wahlsoziologie,' in ibid. p. 402).

18 This is not the same as saying that 80 or 90 per cent of Catholics across the empire voted for the Centre Party. Rather, it means that the best-fit model for the Centre popular vote is an equation wherein it is assumed that 80 or 90 per cent of Catholics voted for the Centre – this is by far the largest positive coefficient in the table – and then this is modified by the other predictor variables in the regression to produce the actual share of the vote. Since most of the other predictor variables in table 11 have negative coefficients, this likely means the actual proportion of Catholics voting for the Centre was consider-

ably lower. (For example, estimate the Centre vote share at 80 per cent of the Catholic population, but then reduce this predicted vote by 5 per cent in large-landownership districts, by 50 per cent in Posen, etc. There are many variables that reduce the estimated 80–90 per cent vote, and only one other small one that adds to it.) Schulte's figure of 70 per cent remains plausible – certainly it was not much higher.

19 Klaus Müller, 'Zentrumspartei und agrarische Bewegung im Rheinland 1882–1903,' in K. Repgen and S. Skalweit, eds., *Spiegel der Geschichte*, p. 850.

20 *KöZ* 26/5/03m1 p. 2 and 12/6/03m2 p. 1; RP Trier to OP Koblenz 28/7/98, in GStAPK Rep. 77 tit. 253a (M) Nr. 26.

21 *Bayerischer Kurier*, May 1903, clipping in BHSA Munich Pr A Slg 117.

22 See David Blackbourn, 'Political Alignment of the Centre,' p. 823; Müller, 'Das Rheinland als Gegenstand,' pp. 402–3.

23 'Die Wahlen und die Parteien,' *Posener Tageblatt* 24/5/98, clipping in BAP RLB PA 5076.

24 The party's populist style and image is the main theme of Blackbourn's *Class, Religion, and Local Politics*. Its constitutional/electoral strategy, on the other hand, has been given too little attention.

25 M. Erzberger, 'Die Bedeutung des Zentrums für das deutsche Reich,' p. 220, in BAK ZSg 2/8. See also Blackbourn, *Class, Religion, and Local Politics*, pp. 33, 231–2, and 'Political Alignment of the Centre,' pp. 822–3; and Loth, *Katholiken im Kaiserreich*, chapter 1. On the 1898 naval law, see Zeender, *The German Center Party*, pp. 63ff; and Herbert Gottwald, 'Der Umfall des Zentrums.'

26 Angelo Panebianco, *Political Parties*, p. 37.

27 In January 1898 the Bachem press produced a report on anti-Catholic policies in Prussia, detailing cases of bias in official statements, hiring and promotion, granting of subsidies, and appointments to local government commissions. The report noted that the proportion of Catholics in the civil service 'sinks from west to east ... reflecting the ... time that the various provinces have stood under the Prussian sceptre' – taking anti-Polish policies as anti-Catholic ones. See *KöVZ* 8/1/98ev p. 1, 16/1/98m p. 1, and 18/1/98ev p. 1; and other materials in the Bachem papers, HASK 1006–85 and 1006–92 to -96. See also the works by Zeender, Blackbourn, Loth, Ross, and Sperber previously cited, as well as James C. Hunt, '"Die Parität in Preußen" (1899): Hintergrund, Verlauf und Ergebnis eines Aktionsprogramms der Zentrumspartei.'

28 See, for example, Erzberger, 'Bedeutung,' p. 221; Martin Spahn, 'Das Deutsche Zentrum,' in BAK ZSg 2/8. The Centre's treatment of the fleet question in its 1898 propaganda is discussed in chapter 2. One success of the parity campaign was more numerous appointments of Catholics to senior civil service positions in the period 1899–1906, which, however, along with the govern-

ment's other concessions to the party (the Jesuit law), contributed to an anticlerical backlash peaking during 1904–9. See Hunt, '"Parität in Preußen,"' pp. 428–32.

29 Statistics on the growth and development of the peasant associations may be found in Dieter Fricke, ed., *Die bürgerlichen Parteien*, pp. 250–76. See below on the politics of agrarian demands within the Centre Party, and on the rebel agrarians in the Rhineland and Westphalia. On the party's relation to the peasantry, see, again, Blackbourn's works in the Bibliography, and Ian Farr's articles on Bavaria: 'From Anti-Catholicism to Anticlericalism: Catholic Politics and the Peasantry in Bavaria, 1860–1900,' *ESR* 13. 2 (April 1983): 249–69; and 'Populism in the Countryside: The Peasant Leagues in Bavaria in the 1890s,' in Richard J. Evans, ed., *Society and Politics*, pp. 136–59.

30 See Fricke, ed., *Die bürgerlichen Parteien*, pp. 810–34.

31 Siebertz, *ABC-Buch*, pp. 609–13.

32 On the VkD, see *Germ.* 7/6/98m p. 1; leaflets in HSA Düss. Reg. Aachen Präs. 815, nos. 214–17. The voting trends referred to are those in type 6 constituencies.

33 Loth analyses political Catholicism in terms of four component movements that could ally in different ways with each other: the aristocracy, the agrarian and *Mittelstand* 'populists,' the workers, and the bourgeois leaders. The middle-class elements gained control by defeating the aristocracy with the help and legitimation of the 'populists' and workers in the 1890s, then found increasingly after 1900 that they could not satisfy the demands of the masses. The result was a fundamental crisis in the party during 1906–9 (see esp. pp. 382–6).

34 See the discussion above of Schauff's work.

35 *Germ.* 3/5/03m p. 1 and 3/6/03m p. 1.

36 Siebertz, *ABC-Buch*, pp. 23–8; Dr Franz Ser. Pichler, 'Centrum und Landwirtschaft,' in BAP RLB PA 5895.

37 *BT* 12/5/98ev p. 3, *FZ* 18/5/98m2 p. 1. See Blackbourn, *Class, Religion, and Local Politics*, pp. 47–52; and Müller, 'Zentrumspartei und agrarische Bewegung,' pp. 847–50.

38 *Der Westfale* 25/5/98 p. 1 and *Berliner Neueste Nachrichten* 9/6/98 (clippings in BAP RLB PA 5895); *KöZ* 4/6/98ev p. 2. The prominence of Schreiner, a former schoolteacher, in the Rhenish Peasants' Association parallels the incorporation of middle-class activists in the Agrarian League. In 1903 the *RWZ* commented that Loë had given Schreiner so much influence that the latter had become a 'silent co-regent' of the peasant association (Müller, 'Zentrumspartei und agrarische Bewegung,' pp. 848–9).

39 Again, this echoes Blackbourn's work on Württemberg (*Class, Religion, and Local Politics*).

40 *KöZ* 30/4/03m2 p. 2; *BT* 9/4/03m p. 1. See also Müller, 'Zentrumspartei und agrarische Bewegung,' pp. 853–6. On the Bavarian Peasants' League, see chapter 4.

41 See Bachem papers, HASK 1006 194; Rhenanus, *Christliche Gewerkschaften oder Fachabteilungen in kathol. Arbeitervereinen?*, p. 88 (in BAK ZSg 2/321); Zeender, section 6. The urban seats referred to are the type 6 ones; see below for more on Centre-SPD competition for votes.

42 Quoted in Kuczynski, *1903*, p. 48.

43 Police report on meeting in Friedheim, District of Wirsitz, 14/6/03, in GStAPK XVI. HA Rep. 30 Nr. 596; police report on meeting in Czarnikau, 21/6/03, in ibid.

44 Translations from *Wiarus-Polski*, Bochum, esp. 17/5/98, 29/5/98, and 14/6/98, in HSA Düss. Reg. Düss. Präs. 880.

45 On Oppeln and Silesia, see *BT* 8/4/03ev p. 1; *Schlesische Zeitung* (Breslau) 10/11/02ev; and the documents in GStAPK Rep. 77 CB tit. 867 (M) Nr. 17, especially the reports by OP Schlesien to MdI, 19/10/02, and of OP Oppeln to MdI, 27/12/02. One seat in East Prussia, Braunsberg-Heilsberg, was excepted from the Polish demands because its population, though Catholic, was not Polish. See *KöVZ* 12/2/03ev (clipping in HSA Düss. Reg. Düss. Präs. 583); *KöVZ* 4/4/03m p. 1; and the clippings in the Bachem papers, HASK 1006 195–6.

46 Siebertz, *ABC-Buch*, pp. 505–8.

47 *KöVZ* 21/9/97ev p. 1. Bachem's memo of June 1898 concerning the threat of a *Staatsstreich* (HASK 1006 88) suggests that the threat of *Reaktion* influenced the Centre to support the fleet bill and to be more friendly to the National Liberals in the run-offs instead of the left liberals. But the *first*-ballot alliance with the FVP remained; the alliance with the National Liberals was only against the SPD; and party leaders likely wanted to compromise on the fleet anyway. The party's actual behaviour was thus more in line with the 'double majority' than with alliance to the right. See below.

48 See *BT* 9/6/98ev p. 1; *Germ.* 14/5/98ev p. 1, 29/5/98m p. 1, and 8/6/98ev p. 1; *KöVZ* 12/5/98ev p. 1; *Niederrhein. VZ* 12/5/98ev p. 1 (in HASK 8006 86d); Berchtenfeld to MdA, 30/4/03, in BHSA Munich MA 76274.

49 See chapter 7 on the SPD and the suffrage issue; both parties used the issue for all it was worth.

50 Bachem to Porsch, 30/5/03 and 7/6/03, in HASK 1006 194. There were still scattered seats where deals with the conservatives were made. In Dessau-Zerbst, Bachem justified supporting the local conservative because he was a Catholic friendly to small farmers. On Bachem's career and activities, see Rolf Kiefer, *Karl Bachem*, especially (for this period) pp. 90–170.

51 *FZ* 2/6/98m1 p. 1; correspondence and clippings in HASK 1006 86c and 1006 86d.

52 *KöVZ* 25/2/03ev p. 1 and 17/3/03m p. 1.

53 Bachem to Müller, 20/5/98 and 27/5/98, HASK 1006 86d. Müller's efforts to promote second-ballot cooperation between the Centre and the SPD earned him a personal attack in a leaflet entitled 'Reichstagsabgeordneter Richard Müller-Fulda: Mitglied der Zentrumspartei der Vorkämpfer der Sozialdemokratie' (BHSA Munich MA 95484). He was accused of delivering Centre votes to the SPD instead of to the 'national' parties in Wiesbaden.

54 See Merith Niehuss, 'Party Configurations in State and Municipal Elections in Southern Germany, 1871–1914,' in Karl Rohe, ed., *Elections, Parties and Political Traditions*, pp. 83–105.

55 'Das Präs.idium im Reichstage,' dated 21/11/98, in HASK 1006 89. See also Zeender, p. 72, note 77. Schmidt's reasoning implies that he had not thought through the implications of 'double-majority,' for a swing to the left implies that the Centre should balance matters by preventing further leftist gains, rather than offer the left increased help and prestige. See Rolf Weidner, *Wahlen und soziale Strukturen*, pp. 427–31, on Centre-SPD run-off deals in the Palatinate in 1898.

56 Bachem to Müller, 20/5/98 (as previously cited); letter by Bachem, 12/6/03, in HASK 1006 194.

57 See Max Weber, *From Max Weber: Essays in Sociology.*

58 Compare Blackbourn, *Class, Religion, and Local Politics*, pp. 53–7.

59 Siebertz, *ABC-Buch*, excerpt on 'Social Democracy.' On Centre representations of the SPD, see also *KöVZ* 30/3/98m p. 1; Richard Müller-Fulda and H. Sittart, *Der Deutsche Reichstag*, pp. 49–51; 'An die Textilarbeiter Deutschlands!' in HSA Düss. Reg. Düss. Präs. 594; 'An die Wähler der Centrumspartei des Wahlkreises Dortmund-Hörde,' in HSA Düss. Reg. Düss. Präs. 583, no. 250.

60 Klaus Epstein, *Matthias Erzberger*, p. 17.

61 Alois Klöcker, 'Konfession und sozialdemokratische Wählerschaft' (1907) and Rudolf Blank, 'Die soziale Zusammensetzung der sozialdemokratischen Wählerschaft Deutschlands' (1904/05), both reprinted in Büsch, Wölk, and Wölk, pp. 197–207 and 184–96 respectively; G.A. Ritter, 'Strategie und Erfolg,' p. 314, and p. 321, note 12.

Chapter 7: The Rise Of Social Democracy

1 As related in chapter 1.

2 Alex Hall, *Scandal, Sensation, and Social Democracy*, pp. 41–8, as well as 'By Other Means.' The radicalization from 1900 probably has to do with several factors at

the national level: the debate over and defeat of the *Zuchthausvorlage* (1899), which effectively closed the door to any more systematic persecution of Social Democracy; the short recession of 1900–1, which saw bitter strikes and increased polarization; the tariff debates in 1902 in the Reichstag, which emphasized the SPD's *Obstruktion*; and the huge election victory of 1903.

3 *Handbuch für Sozialdemokratische Wähler* (1907), p. 11.

4 Data on social mobility are fragmentary. Kaelble presents general evidence that rates of social mobility were initially low but increasing during 1866–1935, with a particular spurt in the last decade before the First World War ('Soziale Mobilität in Deutschland, 1900–1960,' in Hartmut Kaelble et al., *Probleme der Modernisierung*, pp. 235–327). David Crew's local study of Bochum appears to show little large-scale advancement out of the working class before 1900, with the manual/non-manual distinction a particular barrier ('Definitions of Modernity: Social Mobility in a German Town, 1880–1901,' pp. 53–6).

5 Hall, *Scandal*, pp. 11, 20, 188–9; and chapter 4, passim. D. Groh (*Negative Integration und revolutionärer Attentismus*) also interprets the party's 'verbal radicalism' in similar terms (see below).

6 The MdI warned officials in 1898 and 1903 about these regional campaign organizations and instructed them to keep careful track of their activities. Where other parties had constituency organizations and loose provincial federations, the SPD grouped a small number of related seats together, crossing administrative boundaries where necessary, to construct a rational campaign unit.

7 See D. Fricke, *Zur Organisation und Tätigkeit der deutschen Arbeiterbewegung (1890–1914)*, pp. 197, 211; Groh, *Negative Integration*, appendices 1 and 2, pp. 733–4; Carle E.Schorske, *German Social Democracy*, pp. 13ff.

8 See Vernon Lidtke, *Alternative Culture*; and Lynn Abrams, *Workers' Culture in Imperial Germany: Leisure and Recreation in the Rhineland and Westphalia.*

9 See Dieter Dowe, 'The Workingmen's Choral Movement in Germany,' *Journal of Contemporary History* 13.2 (April 1978): 290; W.L. Guttsman, *German Social Democratic Party*, pp. 167–9, 290.

10 *Political Parties*, pp. 338–9. This quotation is a memorable one considering the SPD's electoral image and appeal (below) – allowing for Michels's typical emotional overstatement.

11 The phrases are Dieter Groh's (*Negative Integration*).

12 *From Max Weber*, p. 112. See Helmut Hirsch, ed., *August Bebel: Sein Leben in Dokumenten, Reden, und Schriften.*

13 Günther Roth pioneered the concept of 'negative integration' in the 1950s, and it has since been adopted with greater systematization by Groh (*Negative Integration*, pp. 75–80) and Wehler, among others.

Notes to pages 213–16 355

14 Richard Evans, 'The Sociological Interpretation of German Labour History,' in Evans, ed., *The German Working Class*, pp 15–53; Vernon Lidtke, *The Alternative Culture*, pp. 6–11. See also the review article by Holger H. Herwig in *CEH* 10.2 (June 1977): 172–7; Richard Breitman, 'Negative Integration and Parliamentary Politics,' esp. p. 185; and Richard Evans, *Proletarians and Politics: Socialism, Protest and the Working Class in Germany before the First World War*, pp. 74ff.

15 The idea that ideologies fight, not for naked power, but for 'hegemony' in society at large – for the status of having one's own assumptions and values taken for granted by others – is of course from Antonio Gramsci. The German SPD had by no means established hegemony, but it had effectively contested the hegemony of others. On Gramsci, see Chantal Mouffe, ed., *Gramsci and Marxist Theory*.

16 Lidtke, *The Alternative Culture*, pp. 4–6. Lidtke's terminology is reminiscent of Lepsius's use of 'social-moral milieu' to describe the Centre's base; see chapter 2. On the uneven development of party affiliates, see Guttsman, p. 200; on the Ruhr, see, besides the relevant works of Karl Rohe listed in the Bibliography, Stephen Hickey, 'The Shaping of the German Labour Movement: Miners in the Ruhr,' in Richard Evans, ed., *Society and Politics*, and his book on the same subject; and Mary Nolan, *Social Democracy and Society: Working Class Radicalism in Düsseldorf 1890–1920*.

17 For the purposes of multiple regression, what is needed are detailed occupational or income statistics broken down by constituency. But the constituency-level statistics, so far as I have been able to determine, distinguish only branches of the economy ('manufacturing,' 'commerce,' 'agriculture'), not social-economic rank within a branch or size of workplace.

18 Of the categories used in the occupational census, 'agriculture' was a distinct sector denoting a relatively narrow range of occupations and statuses, at least if one separates out the large landed estates of the east; whereas the alternative categories, 'industry' or 'commerce,' were vague and contained vast disparities of status, wealth, and separate interests even within a single locality. 'Agriculture' and 'urbanization' are taken in this work as the statistically definable characteristics that best describe real social-economic environments; see Appendix C. Local studies using data from individual polls and local records about employment and wealth offer the only real hope of studying the relationship between 'class' and voting.

19 David Blackbourn, 'Between Resignation and Volatility,' is one of the few accounts of the German *Mittelstand* which attempt to distinguish the wide range of opinions among German artisans and small businessmen, and which recognize the important role played by some segments of these groups within the SPD.

20 Rudolf Blank, 'Die soziale Zusammensetzung der sozialdemokratischen Wählerschaft Deutschlands,' in Otto Büsch, Wolfgang Wölk, and Monika Wölk, eds., *Wählerbewegung*, p. 184. Blank's estimate that the SPD electorate was significantly larger than the total number of Protestant working-class voters is debatable, since it is based on assumptions that workers had the same electoral participation rates and confessional balance as the rest of the electorate; yet it is not to be dismissed out of hand. At any rate, the point here is that even the statistics for 'the working class' do not denote a homogeneous group.

21 Kathleen Canning, 'Gender and the Culture of Work: Ideology and Identity in the World behind the Mill Gate, 1890–1914,' in Larry E. Jones and James Retallack, eds., *Elections, Mass Politics, and Social Change*, p. 199.

22 *Protokoll* for 1897 congress, speech by Bebel, pp. 123–4. (This as well as other party documents cited below may be found in BAK ZSg 1 90.) The final resolution was more specific, expanding Bebel's three points into eight, but followed the same general lines. One speaker in the debate (Bruno Schoenlank, Saxony) raised the fleet issue as an aspect of the constitutional issue.

23 The regional campaign units referred to in note 6 above.

24 *Protokoll* (1898), pp. 12–26.

25 *Protokoll* (1902), pp. 223–45; and 1903, pp. 26, 33. The electoral statistics and the reorientation away from agriculture are discussed in the following section. On the debate in the party about the peasantry in the 1890s, which connected with the revisionism/reformism controversy, the literature is too extensive to mention here. William Harvey Maehl reviews many of the arguments and much of the literature in 'German Social Democratic Agrarian Policy 1890–1895, Reconsidered,' *CEH* 13.2 (June 1980): 121–57.

26 *Handbuch für sozialdemokratische Wähler: Der Reichstag 1893–1898*, and the same for 1898–1903; Karl Kautsky, *Handelspolitik und Sozialdemokratie*; Max Schippel, *Sozialdemokratisches Reichstags-Handbuch*.

27 Gustav Keßler, *Die Ziele der Sozialdemokratischen Partei: Volksthümlich entwickelt*; Karl Kautsky and Bruno Schoenlank, *Grundsätze und Forderungen der Sozialdemokratie: Erläuterung zum Erfurter Programm*.

28 Klaus von Beyme, *Political Parties in Western Democracies*, p. 62, citing A. Kosiol, *Neue Zeit* 24. 2 (1905/06): 65.

29 See (among many others) *VW* 27/4/98 p. 1, 29/4/98 p. 1, 8/5/98 p. 1, 14/5/98 p. 1, and 24/5/98 p. 1.

30 *VW* 19/5/98 p. 2; HSA Düss. Reg. Düss. Präs. 585, no. 18; clipping, *Volkszeitung* 20/4/03, in HSA Düss. Reg. Düss. Präs. 587 no. 13.

31 From Alfred Kelly, ed., *The German Worker*, pp. 170–1. Osterroth later became an SPD organizer and deputy; the autobiography from which this passage was taken was *Vom Beter zum Kämpfer* (Berlin, 1920).

32 'Reichstagswähler! Arbeiter, Bürger, Bauern!' in HSA Düss. Reg. Düss. Präs. 587, no. 11; 'Tausend Millionen Mark!' in HSA Düss. Reg. Aachen Präs. 815, no. 194. See also *Sozialdemokratie und Zentrum: Tatsachen-Material zur Arbeiterversicherung und Zentrumspolitik*, in BAK ZSg 2 321/6. Because of the important concession by the government that no new mass-consumption taxes would be imposed to pay for the 1898 Navy Law, the SPD was unable to accuse the Centre of raising taxes, only of approving measures that 'sooner or later' would require new taxes.

33 See 'Arbeiter und Bürger! Reichstagswähler!' in HSA Düss. Reg. Düss. Präs. 587, no. 11; and 'Was wollen die Sozialdemokraten?' in HSA Düss. Reg. Aachen Präs. 815, no. 192.

34 See 'An die Wähler des Wahlkreises Marburg-Kirchhain-Frankenberg-Vöhl!' in Hess. SA Marburg Best. 180 Frankenberg N2. 1121.

35 *Die Sozialdemokratie und die ländliche Bevölkerung: Eine zeitgemäße Betrachtung* (in BAK ZSg 2/323), esp. pp. 37–40; see also Paul Kampffmeyer, *Junker und Bauer: Zur Entwicklung unserer Agrar-Verhältnisse* (1896), p. 31.

36 Hans Ehrlich, *Gespräche zwischen einem Landmann und einem Sozialdemokraten* (1892), and Paul Kempe, *Christus und die Sozialdemokratie: Für die ländliche Bevölkerung*, both in BAK ZSg 2/323; and Richard Calwer, *Wen wähle ich? Eine Agitationsschrift für die ländliche Bevölkerung für die Reichstagswahlen 1898*, in BAK ZSg 1 90/5.

37 'Volksfeinde und Volksfreunde: Ein Mahnwort an die Reichstagswähler des Wahlkreises Rotenburg-Hersfeld-Hünfeld' (Hess. SA Marburg Best. 180 Hersfeld Nr. 922); 'An die Reichstagswähler des Wahlkreises Elberfeld-Barmen,' 'Reichstagswähler von Barmen-Elberfeld,' and 'Aufruf an die Wähler des Wahlkreises Crefeld!' (in HSA Düss. Reg. Düss. Präs. 585, nos. 9 and 17, and 594, no. 15).

38 'Die Waffen zur Hand!' *VW* 6/4/98 p. 1.

39 'Die Aufstellung der Reichstags-Kandidaten,' *VW* 9/6/03 1. Beilage p. 2.

40 In 1890 there were 54 seats in which no recorded SPD votes were cast; in 1898 only 14 (Dr Adolf Neumann-Hofer, *Die Entwicklung der Sozialdemokratie bei den Wahlen zum Deutschen Reichstag* [1898], p. 52). (Imperial statisticians did not credit to parties vote totals of fewer than 25.)

41 The SPD advance was not by any means sudden; in every election there were seats where its steady progress brought it into the run-offs for the first time. What was special about 1898 was that general SPD support had become high enough for such breakthroughs to occur in many seats at once. In 1898 SPD candidates entered the run-offs for the first time in the Wilhelmine era, and generally stayed there for the rest of it, in constituencies 94, 116, 119, 126, 134, 145, 160, 161, 196, 256, 263, 285, 286, 304, 309,

310, 317, 334, 340, 344, 355, 367, 370, and 396. (On the numbering system, see Appendix B.)

42 *Sächsische Arbeiterzeitung*, 20/6/03 (clipping in HSA Düss. Reg. Düss. Präs. 588).

43 In 1903 the SPD was able to win on the first ballot where it had lost or had to fight a run-off in 1898 in seats 32, 33, 35, 44, 46, 95, 127, 132, 136, 209, 288, 289, 291, 307, 342, 352, 361, 366, and 372 (see Appendix B). The SPD thus gained a stranglehold on these seats, most of which were type 4.

44 When in 1907 the huge SPD victory in Saxony was reversed, the king sent a telegram of congratulations to the MdI, which closed: 'It is a pleasure to be alive now. Friedrich August' (BHSA Munich MA 95484, ambassador in Dresden [Montgelas] to MdA, 12/2/07).

45 On the background to the suffrage revision and regional anti-socialist coalitions, see James Retallack's seminal piece, 'Antisocialism and Electoral Politics in Regional Perspective: The Kingdom of Saxony,' in Jones and Retallack, eds., *Elections, Mass Politics, and Social Change*, pp. 49-91.

46 Other factors in the protest vote included the unpopularity of King Georg of Saxony, scandals in the royal house, and a recent tax increase. See BHSA Munich MA 95484 (ambassador in Dresden [Montgelas] to MdA, 16/1/07). While conceding some of these points and adding many others, Paul Mehnert wrote to Bülow saying the Reichstag result only *justified* the state suffrage change, since without it Saxony would have had, on the basis of 1903 Reichstag results, an SPD majority (BAK R43F/1792, Mehnert to Bülow, 17/6/03). This dubious reasoning was echoed in the Saxon conservative press (see *BT* 20/6/03ev p. 1).

47 Bülow's draft of reply to Mehnert, BAK R43F/1792.

48 Type 4 seats (see Appendix A).

49 Guttsman notes that 'in seven urban constituencies where the Centre Party vote was nearly twice that of the SPD in 1898, the position was almost reversed by 1912,' showing 'a shift of allegiance from denominational to class orientation' (*The German Social Democratic Party*, p. 105). But in type 6 constituencies (Catholic cities), the SPD still lagged 23 per cent behind its performance in type 4 constituencies (Protestant cities) in 1912.

50 G.A. Ritter, 'Strategie und Erfolg,' pp. 317-18.

51 Karl Rohe, 'Die "verspätete" Region.'

52 Another electoral study has commented that 'in reality, the SPD was doing better in rural areas than has been commonly assumed,' though it did not usually *win* in such areas, thus disproving the notion that the SPD became stagnant in its urban strongholds by 1912 (Marvin W. Falk, 'The Reichstag Elections of 1912,' p. 67).

53 See Helmut Hesselbarth, *Revolutionäre Sozialdemokraten, Opportunisten und die*

Bauern am Vorabend des Imperialismus, pp. 246–50; Hans Georg Lehmann, *Die Agrarfrage in der Theorie und Praxis der deutschen und internationalen Sozial-demokratie*, pp. 215–19; and Ritter, 'Strategie und Erfolg,' pp. 316–18.

54 Karl Kautsky, *The Agrarian Question in Two Volumes*, trans. Pete Burgess (orig. publ. Stuttgart, 1899).

55 Quoted by Adam Przeworski and John Sprague, *Paper Stones: A History of Electoral Socialism*, pp. 25–6.

56 'Die drei Millionen und die kleineren Uebel,' *VW* 27/6/03 p. 1. Note the similar pride expressed by Paul Hirsch in making a Berlin seat into a Hochburg for Social Democracy (Hirsch, *Die Sozialdemokratie im Wahlkreise Teltow-Beeskow-Storkow-Charlottenburg*).

57 Quoted in Jürgen Kuczynski, *1903*, p. 163.

58 Kuczynski, *1903*, p. 163. *Heil Dir im Siegerkranz* – hail to thou in the victor's crown – was a tribute to the kaiser, to the tune of *God Save the Queen*.

59 *Bergische Arbeiterstimmen* (Solingen) 19/6/03, clipping in Reg. Düss. Präs. 583, no. 253. Würzburger's 'Die "Partei der Nichtwähler"' of 1907 was an effort to disprove ideas that non-voters were all of one-party persuasion, or would change election results if they voted.

60 'Die Bürger in der Wahlschlacht,' *RWZ* 17/6/03ev. See also Klaus Saul, *Staat, Industrie, Arbeiterbewegung*, pp. 13–17. On the government's lack of an active public strategy and criticism of it from the government's allies, see chapter 3.

61 'Die Reichstagshauptwahl, die bürgerliche Linke und die Polen,' *RWZ* 19/6/03m p. 1 (both this and the previous article can also be found in RWSA Münster Oberpräs 2681/2). The point about SPD gains being at the expense of left liberalism is true as far as seats are concerned and was acknowledged by the party leadership at the congress later in the year.

62 *KZ* 18/6/98 p. 1 and 19/6/98m p. 1; and 'Die innere Politik der Woche,' 21/6/03m p. 1.

63 'Reichstagswahlrecht, Socialistengesetz und Socialdemokratie', *KöZ* 30/4/98m p. 1; see also 'Die innere Politik der Woche,' *KZ* 7/6/03m p. 1.

64 'Die Berliner Reichstagswahlen,' *BT* 17/6/03m p. 1; 'Der Zug nach links!' *BT* 18/6/98ev p. 1; and 'Die Quittung der Imponderabilien,' *BT* 19/6/03m p. 1.

65 Mehnert to Bülow, 17/6/03, and Bülow's draft reply, both in BAK R43F/1792; Varnbüler to v. Soden, 1/7/03, in HSA Stutt. E73 Verz. 61 Nr. 12e.

66 'Die Kruppsche Arbeiterschaft und die Reichstagswahl in Essen' (1903), in BAK R43F/1792.

67 Bülow, *Memoirs*, 1897–1903, p. 223, and 1903–9, pp. 5–7. The Mittler published version is in BHSA Munich MA 76552, as the state governments were asked to encourage its distribution.

68 *Deutsche Politik*, pp. 85–7, 94–5.

69 'Bist Du Sozialdemokrat?' (reprint from *Der Nachbar* [Hamburg]), in BAP RdI Nr. 13577; Otto Müller, 'In der Schenke zur Peterwitz, oder: Was Schulze Großmann von den Sozialdemokraten hält,' in HSA Düss. Reg. Aachen Präs. 815, nos. 142–3.

70 Ernst Fischer, 'Der Werth der Sozialdemokratie für die Arbeiterschaft: Erlebnisse eines in der Partei tätig gewesenes Genossen,' in RWSA Münster Oberpräs 2681/2, nos. 7–11, and in GStAPK XVI. HA Rep. 30 Nr. 595.

71 Theodor Lorentzen, quotations from *Arbeiter-Partei oder Revolutions-Partei: Wer hat Recht, Naumann oder ich?* pp. 4, 10; see also *Die Flotte und der Reichstag* (both published in 1898) and the earlier *Die Ausbeutung der Arbeiter und die Ursachen ihrer Verarmung* (1897).

72 See BAP RdI Nr. 13577, nos. 58–88, including Bueck's letter of 20/2/93. The Austrian finance minister also published a scientific refutation of Marxism; see Eugen von Böhm-Bawerk, *Karl Marx and the Close of His System: A Criticism* (1898), originally published in German in 1896.

73 BAP RdI Nr. 13578, nos. 12–21, esp. no. 18.

74 'Die kommenden Reichstagswahlen,' *RWZ* 7/3/03ev (clipping in RWSA Münster Oberpräs 2681/2); 'Promemoria,' in BHSA Munich MA 76536, a memorandum concerning the SPD by a senior foreign ministry official from about 1894; and on Posadowsky's anti-socialist appeal, see chapter 3.

75 HSA Stutt. E73 Verz. 61 Nr 12e, foreign office letter of 18/4/03 reporting talk given by Posadowsky.

76 See Anthony O'Donnell, 'National Liberalism,' pp. 389–90, on the connections of the League with the parties and other pressure groups; and Dieter Fricke, ed., *Die bürgerlichen Parteien*, for structure and committee membership.

Chapter 8: Conclusion

1 Richard Rose, ed., *Electoral Participation: A Comparative Analysis*, p. 13.

2 Stanley Suval, *Electoral Politics in Wilhelmine Germany*, p. 9.

3 Stefano Bartolini and Peter Mair, *Identity, Competition, and Electoral Availability*, table 4.3, p. 111.

4 If any party got 70 per cent of the votes, the index would be greater than $0.7 \times 0.7 = 0.49$. The value of 0.44 would result if the vote was split among three parties such that one party received 60 per cent and two others 20 per cent each (60–20–20); the value would be 0.42 if the vote was split 50–40–10 or if it was 55–30–15. A result of 40–40–20 would produce an index value of only 0.36.

5 See Lane and Ersson, *Politics and Society in Western Europe*, p. 177.

6 Ibid., p. 184.
7 Klaus von Beyme, *Political Parties in Western Democracies*, p. 261.
8 Giovanni Sartori, 'European Political Parties: The Case of Polarized Pluralism,' in Joseph LaPalombara and Myron Weiner, eds., *Political Parties and Political Development*, pp. 138–9, 153ff; also Beyme, *Political Parties*, pp. 262–3.
9 Angelo Panebianco, *Political Parties*, p. 219, who cites the well-known work of
   Arend Lijphart on the Netherlands. See also Lane and Ersson, *Politics and Society in Western Europe*, pp. 33, 42.
10 See, for example, Volker Berghahn, *Imperial Germany 1871–1914: Economy,
    Society, Culture and Politics*, p. 213, which argues that the institution of run-off
    ballots detracted from democratic egalitarianism by allowing the other parties
    to gang up on the SPD in the run-off.
11 Larry Diamond, 'Introduction: Political Culture and Democracy,' in Larry
    Diamond, ed., *Political Culture and Democracy in Developing Countries*,
    pp. 16–17.

Appendix A: Constituency Typology

1 This scheme is adapted from Brett Fairbairn, 'German Elections,' Appendix 2.
   Social-economic data for this classification and for subsequent graphs, tables,
   regressions, etc., are from the following: *Statistik des Deutschen Reichs*, N.S., vols.
   102–19 (1897–8), occupational census of 1895; vols. 150–1 (1903), census of
   1900; vols. 203–22 (1910), occupational census of 1907; and *Vierteljahrshefte zur
   Statistik des Deutschen Reichs*, vol. 7 (1898), no. 2, and vol. 11 (1902), no. 3
   (rural-urban structure and change). Data on the confessional and rural-urban
   structure of constituencies are also given in the sources previously cited for
   election statistics. The 'large-landownership area' (where holdings of more
   than 100 hectares made up more than one-half of all holdings) is estimated
   from the maps presented in Helmut Hesselbarth, *Revolutionäre Sozialdemokraten, Opportunisten, und die Bauern am Vorabend des Imperialismus* (Berlin,
   1968).
2 For these purposes, a constituency was counted as urban-dominated if it was
   less than one-half rural and if more than 40 per cent of the population resided
   in cities of ten thousand or more inhabitants. Since the economic and social
   impact of cities extended into surrounding communities, a constituency that
   was 40 per cent urban in population was likely urban-dominated.
3 The type 5 seats in the east were Polish ones not contested or only weakly contested by the Polish parties, and represented politically by the Centre.
4 Constituency-level results indicate that about one-third of the vote was frequently the point at which most parties began to make a major impression and

had a chance of reaching a run-off. A party with 33 per cent of the vote was a significant threat. Accordingly, this level was chosen for deciding when a particularist campaign was large enough to shape the campaign as a whole in the constituency in question.

5 See the preceding note. The same rationale was used to determine that a two-thirds majority by one confession was enough to ensure the political domination of the majority.

6 The social-economic statistics used were: percentage of the population that was Catholic; percentage of the population employed in agriculture; large-landownership area or not (dummy variable); percentage of the population in rural areas; and percentage of the population in urban areas. These are the same statistics on which the constituency-type definitions are based, except that the constituency types also involve looking at the percentage of the vote won by particularist parties.

7 Eight dummy variables were used, each representing one constituency type, and with type 5 left out. In the resulting regression, all the types included showed positively and significantly in correlation in every election from 1890 to 1912, except type 7a, which was insignificant. This means that type 5, left out, was strongly negative. R^2 was between .5499 and .6185; F (from the mean) was between 60 and 81 with 8 by 388 degrees of freedom – which is to say, the results are highly significant.

8 See Fairbairn, 'German Elections,' chapters 3 and 5.

Appendix D: Understanding Multiple Regression

1 The note also includes in parentheses the 'degrees of freedom' (DF), a quantity that relates to the number of observations less the number of variables and which is needed by anyone wishing to check these results in a t-table.

2 In some tables, to reduce the length, variables that did not show significant results in at least two or three elections are left out of the table, even though they were part of the regression.

3 In conducting research, large regressions were also run on all the elections together as a single set of observations. These were used in examining variables but are not presented in this book.

4 A t-ratio is obtained by dividing the coefficient by its standard error.

5 The adjusted R^2 takes into account the number of variables used in the regression and is lower than the raw R^2.

6 Note that in the left-hand column the degrees of freedom, DF, for the regression are given in connection with F.

Appendix E: Guide to Abbreviations

1 Debates referenced as *SBVR* #LP #S, where *SBVR* = *Stenographische Berichte über die Verhandlungen des Reichstages*, LP = Legislative Period, S = Session.
2 The holdings of the former Zentrales Staatsarchiv – Merseburg are now at Dahlem and are referenced under GStAPK with an 'M' at the end of the title of the holding in question.

Bibliography

Archival Sources

Bundesarchiv Koblenz (BAK)

The Bundesarchiv's Zeitgeschichtliche Sammlungen (ZSg 1 and ZSg 2) are good sources for political publications by the parties and pressure groups. The following files were particularly relevant for the 1898 and 1903 elections:

ZSg 1, No. 46 – left-liberal parties (extensive collection of FVP documents, especially 1896–1905)

No. 70 – conservative parties

No. 74 – National Liberals (useful handbooks and policy manuals)

No. 85 – Imperial Party

No. 90 – SPD (large and useful collection)

No. 108 – Centre

No. 145 – VkD

Nos. E2, E24, E25, E27, E73 – anti-Semites

ZSg 2, Nos. 12, 323, 324 – socialism (mostly earlier periods)

Nos. 13, 14, 342 – socialism, critics and opponents

Also consulted were ZSg 1, No. 2 (Pan-German League); ZSg 1, No. 195 (Navy League); ZSg 1, No. 211 (Colonial Society); ZSg 1, No. 287 (Evangelical League); ZSg 1, No. E155 (BdL); ZSg 1, No. E130 (HVV). These contained little of relevance to electoral politics. The microfiches of the Reich Chancellory files in collection R43F (duplicates of the originals at Potsdam) contain important letters and minutes of Ministry of State meetings.

Bundesarchiv – Abteilung Potsdam (BAP; formerly DDR Zentrales Staatsarchiv I)

Aside from the Chancellory documents, the most important government documents at Potsdam concerning electoral politics are in the files of the Reich Ministry of the Interior (RdI). These are generally more technical and less political than the documents of the Prussian Ministry of the Interior in Merseburg:

RdI, Nos. 13574–9 – measures against SPD (most mid-1890s)

Nos. 14454ff – election law and its implementation (part of a large collection of material on technical matters, including for example No. 14474 on ballot boxes)

No. 14638 – throne speeches 1900–14 (part of a collection of files concerning Reichstag openings, closings, and dissolutions)

No. 14644 – electoral matters in general, 1898–1906

No. 14671 – election violations in Prussia, 1895–9 (other holdings concern other federal states)

Nos. 14726–7 – election statistics covering 1898–1903

No. 15253 – the *Berliner Korrespondenz* and the official press, 1894–1914 (also No. 15421 for the reorganization of the official press network during 1898–9)

Nos. 15338–40 – the Polish question (covers 1898–1903)

No. 15493 – measures against the Guelph Party, 1899–1904

The Reichslandbund Pressearchiv (i.e., the Agrarian League's clipping archive) provides a very good collection of newspaper articles organized thematically. For the present subject, the following were especially useful:

RLB PA, Nos. 6055, 6056, 6060 – Reichstag, 1895–1903

Nos. 5075–6 – 1898 Reichstag election campaign

Nos. 5083–5 – 1903 Reichstag election campaign

No. 6131 – party politics, 1897–8

No. 5895 – Centre Party and agriculture, 1898–1902

Also consulted were the Marquardsen papers (90 Ma 1), which are useful concerning the National Liberal Party in Bavaria up to 1897.

Geheimes Staatsarchiv Preußischer Kulturbesitz, Berlin-Dahlem (GStAPK)

I. Hauptabteilung contains central papers from the files of the Prussian Ministry of the Interior (Rep. 77) as well as the Ministry of State (Rep. 90). Useful files in the latter include:

Rep. 90, Nos. 128, 306 – governmental campaigns (scanty)

Nos. 112, 124 – technical arrangements for elections

No. 133 – reports and summaries on elections (fragmentary)

XVI. Hauptabteilung contains material from the local and regional governments in Brandenburg (*Landratsämter* in 6B), West Prussia (Districts of Danzig, Rep. 180; and of Marienwerder, Rep. 181), and Posen (District of Bromberg, Rep. 30). Much of this is very useful, especially concerning anti-Polish efforts:

Rep. 30, No. 592 – official funding for campaigns, 1898

Nos. 593–6 – Reichstag elections, 1898–1906 (including technical documents, clippings, letters, and reports from *Landräte*)
Finally, the XII. Hauptabteilung contains a collection of leaflets and posters:
Nos. 45–7 – SPD, 1893–1907
Nos. 104–5 – Centre, 1893 and 1907
Nos. 148–52 – liberals (much on 1907)
Nos. 154–5 – left liberals
Nos. 171–2 – conservatives (mainly 1893 and 1907)
No. 174 – Imperial Party (good collection for 1907)
Like most such collections, other than the one at the Bundesarchiv in Koblenz, this one is weaker on 1898–1903 than on later elections or on some earlier ones; 'national' campaigns appear to have deposited more leaflets in governmental files.

The following documents were consulted at the DDR Zentrales Staatsarchiv II – Merseburg. They are now held at the GStAPK, Berlin-Dahlem.

The files of the Prussian Ministry of the Interior (MdI, Rep. 77) contain a great deal of internal government correspondence concerning Reichstag elections. A substantial part of the MdI material concerning elections, however, was previously moved to GStAPK, Berlin-Dahlem, and is available in the regular holdings there. Rep. 77 tit. 253a (Reichsverfassung) contains some relevant files including the following:

Rep. 77 tit. 253a No. 26 – election leaflets, 1903–4
No. 29 – technical documents on elections (many bundles of files, including complaints of official influence on elections in Prussian provinces: Fasz. 4 is Pomerania, Fasz. 8 is Hanover, etc.)
Even more useful than the main ministry files are the files of the ministerial *Zentralbüro* (Rep. 77 CB), once again especially the holdings concerning 'Reichsverfassung' (tit. 867):

Rep. 77 CB No. 16a – documents concerning the 1898 elections (bundles organized according to province)
No. 17 – the same for 1903 (including the arrangements for funding and distributing anti-SPD leaflets)
The files of the Finance Ministry *Hauptbüro* (Rep. 151 HB) also contain some relevant ministerial discussions of Social Democracy and the press.

Hauptstaatsarchiv Düsseldorf (HSA Düss.)

Abteilung II (Rheinisches Behördenarchiv) contains a great deal of local and regional government material. Unlike many such collections, this one is fairly complete for 1898–1903, including many of the confidential documents. The two most useful collections for these years are those of Regierung Aachen and Regierung Düsseldorf, and especially in each case the *Präsidialbüro* of the district government:

Reg. Düss. Präs. Nos. 572–3 – 1898 elections
Nos. 582–95 – Reichstag elections, 1893–1906
Reg. Aachen Präs. Nos. 815–16 – Reichstag elections, 1893–1912

Besides these there are further files on elections, the press, public order, supervision of associations, and the Polish movement. There is also an extensive collection of documents from *Landratsämter* (for example, LRA Dinslaken and LRA Euskirchen), which contains documents on the 1898 and 1903 Reichstag campaigns. Most correspondence is duplicated, however, in the files of the *Regierung*.

Hauptstaatsarchiv Hannover (HSA Hann.)

Politics in the large Prussian province of Hanover, interesting for its mixture of National Liberal, agrarian, particularist, and Social Democratic elements, is well documented in government files. The files of the *Oberpräsident* (Hann. 122a) contain relevant items under 'Hoheitssachen' (Abt. I), including:

Hann. 122a I No. 13 – Reichstag elections, 1898–1904
Nos. 108–10 – *Zeitungsberichte,* 1897–1905

Also useful are the holdings of Regierung Hildesheim, including Hann. 180 Hildesheim No. 31 (Reichstag elections, 1898).

The documents for the District of Hanover are in Hann. 80 Hann. II and include many personal documents of the president and officials of the district administration. Hann. 80 Lüneburg II contains (in the *Präsidialbüro* files) documents on the political duties and dispositions of officials:

Hann. 174 Hann. II No. 11 – confidential documents, 1898–1919
No. 15 – Reichstag elections, 1903
No. 16 – Reichstag elections, 1898–1903

Other useful holdings are Hann. 310 III (official measures against the Guelph movement) and the *Nachlaß* of Hans Freiherr von Hammerstein-Loxten, who was minister of the interior from 1901 to 1905.

Bayerisches Hauptstaatsarchiv (BHSA Munich)

The Geheimes Staatsarchiv (Abt. II) contains some useful material in the files of the Ministry of External Affairs:

MA Nos. 76273–4 – Reichstag elections, 1893–1905 (mainly technical and statistical information)
Nos. 76533–7 – measures against the SPD (1890s)

Nos. 76544–5 – the same, 1896–7

No. 95484 – Reichstag elections, 1906 (useful reports from Berlin, Dresden, Stuttgart)

No. 95007 – general ambassadorial reports

Nos. 1068–75 – political reports from Berlin, 1897–1903

Berlin 2676–81 – the same

The files of the Bavarian justice ministry (MJu) contain documents on contested elections, but essentially only the printed Reichstag documents.

Abt. IV contains three large collections of leaflets, press clippings, and miscellaneous materials. Most are from the Weimar period, but the Presse-Ausschnitt Sammlung does contain material from the 1890s onward concerning parties and elections.

Hauptstaatsarchiv Stuttgart (HSA Stutt.)

The documents of the Württemberg Ministry of State are Bestand E 130a:

E 130a No. 729 – contested elections

No. 88 – constitutional reform

No. 1018 – measures against Social Democracy, 1903–14

No. 1426 – newspaper clippings on Reichstag elections

The files of the Ministry of the Interior contain little of relevance. The reports of the Berlin ambassadors are in Best. E 73 Verz. 61.

Hessisches Staatsarchiv Marburg (Hess. SA Marburg)

In general, many of the documents from the 1890s are missing. This includes the documents from the *Oberpräsidium* concerning Reichstag elections from 1890 to 1923. Likewise, the files of Regierung Kassel (Bestand 165) are lacking Reichstag election documents during 1886–1913. However, some good pamphlet collections from individual constituencies survive:

Best. 165 No. 46 – Hersfeld-Hünfeld-Rotenburg, 1898

No. 47 – Marburg-Kirchhain-Frankenburg, 1898

The archive also contains documents from *Landratsämter* in Bestand 180:

Best. 180 Hersfeld No. 922 – Reichstag elections, 1898

No. 943 – the same, 1903

Best. 180 Frankenberg No. 1120 – Reichstag elections, 1898

No. 1121 – the same, 1903

Best. 180 Hofgeismar No. 740 – Reichstag elections, 1898

Nos. 741, 754 – the same, 1901–4

370   Bibliography

Nordrhein-Westfälisches Staatsarchiv Münster (SA Münster)

Some documents can be found in the files of the *Oberpräsidium*, of Regierung Arnsberg, and of Regierung Münster. However, there seems to be less material concerning elections for the 1890s than those earlier or later.

Landesarchiv Schleswig-Holstein (LASH)

Abt. 301, Oberpräsident (und Provinzialrat) der Provinz Schleswig-Holstein, contains useful material:

No. 799 – Reichstag elections, 1897–1917
No. 809 – Reichstag elections, general, 1898–1902
No. 6757 – the same, 1903–6
No. 807 – Reichstag election campaigns, 1878–93
No. 6478 – the same, 1893–1911 (mostly 1893)
No. 805 – participation of officials in elections, 1903–21 (contains a copy of the government's secret 1898 election program and directives – the only copy found by the author. See chapter 3 for a discussion of its importance)
No. 808, Nos. 6480–6, Nos. 6502–3 – Schleswig-Holstein constituencies, 1897–1911

Staatsarchiv der Freien Hansestadt Bremen (SA Bremen)

The documents (mainly technical) are in the files of the *Ratsarchiv* and *Senatsregistratur* for foreign affairs, and of the *Behörden* archive for internal affairs.

Hauptarchiv der Stadt Köln (HASK)

The Cologne city archive contains the Karl Bachem papers, which are important for Centre election strategy in 1898 and 1903:

HASK 1006 Nos. 86a and 193–4 – 1898 and 1903 Centre national election declarations (Bachem's draft as well as final versions)
Nos. 86c, 86d – correspondence with Richter and Müller-Fulda, 1898
Nos. 88–90 – on the political situation during 1898–99 (including possibility of a *Staatsstreich*)
Nos. 193–6 – relations with Poles and Guelphs, 1903
Nos. 197–8 – run-off deal with National Liberals, 1903

Printed Sources

PRIMARY SOURCES

Reference Works and Document or Statistical Collections

Bry, Gerhard. *Wages in Germany, 1871–1945*. Princeton, 1960.
Büsch, Otto, Wolfgang Wölk, and Monika Wölk, eds. *Wählerbewegung in der deutschen Geschichte: Analysen und Berichte zu den Reichstagswahlen 1871–1933*. Berlin, 1978.
Deutsches Zeitgenossen-Lexikon. Leipzig, 1905.
Fricke, Dieter, ed. *Die bürgerlichen Parteien in Deutschland: Handbuch der Geschichte der bürgerlichen Parteien und anderer bürgerlicher Interessenorganisationen vom Vormärz bis zum Jahre 1945*. Leipzig, 1968.
– *Zur Organisation und Tätigkeit der deutschen Arbeiterbewegung (1890–1914): Dokumente und Materialen*. Leipzig, 1962.
Fuchs, Walther Peter, ed. *Großherzog Friedrich I. von Baden und die Reichspolitik 1871–1907*. Vol. 4: 1898–1907. Stuttgart, 1980.
Hirsch, Helmut, ed. *August Bebel: Sein Leben in Dokumenten, Reden, und Schriften*. Cologne/Berlin, 1968.
Hohorst, G., J. Kocka, and G.A. Ritter. *Sozialgeschichtliches Arbeitsbuch II: Materialen zur Statistik des Kaiserreichs 1870–1914*. 2d ed. Munich, 1978.
Mackie, Thomas T., and Richard Rose. *The International Almanac of Electoral History*. 3d ed. Washington, D.C., 1991, pp. 156–83.
Matthias, Erich, and Eberhard Pikart. *Die Reichstagsfraktion der deutschen Sozialdemokratie 1898 bis 1918*. Vol. 3. Part 1. Düsseldorf, 1966.
Mommsen, Wilhelm. *Deutsche Parteiprogramme: Eine Auswahl vom Vormärz bis zur Gegenwart*. Munich, 1952.
Ritter, G.A., and M. Niehuss. *Wahlgeschichtliches Arbeitsbuch: Materialen zur Statistik der Kaiserreichs 1871–1918*. Munich, 1980.
Treue, Wolfgang, ed. *Deutsche Parteiprogramme, 1861–1954*. Frankfurt a.M./Berlin, 1954.

Government Publications

Kaiserliches Statistisches Amt. *Statistik des Deutschen Reichs*. New Series. Berlin, v.d. The following were especially useful: vols. 102–19 (1897–8) for the occupational census of 1895; vols. 150–1 (1903) for the census of 1900; vols. 203–22 (1910) for the occupational census of 1907; and vol. 250, no. 1 (1912) for the 1907 and 1912 Reichstag election results.

– *Statistisches Jahrbuch für das Deutsche Reich.* Berlin, v.d.
  Good for general province-level statistical overviews. See vol. 20 (1899) for
  information regarding occupational breakdown as well as the 1898 election
  results; and vol. 24 (1903) for confessional breakdown.
– *Vierteljahrshefte zur Statistik des Deutschen Reichs.* Berlin, v.d.
  Vol. 2, no. 4 (1893): 1893 Reichstag election results; vol. 7, no. 2 (1898) and
  vol. 11, no. 3 (1902): rural-urban structure and change; vol. 9, no. 4 (1900) and
  vol. 12, no. 2 (1903): supplements to the 1898 Reichstag election results; vol. 12,
  no. 3 (1903): 1898 and 1903 election results; and vol. 14, no. 4 (1905) and
  vol. 16, no. 1 (1907): supplements to the 1903 results.
Reichstag. *Stenographische Berichte über die Verhandlungen des Deutschen Reichstages*
  (*SBVR*). Berlin, v.d.
  The *Anlagebände* to *SBVR* also provide Reichstag election statistics. See *SBVR*
  8LP, Anlageband I, for the 1890 election results used in this study (because of
  unavailability of the corresponding Statistisches Amt publications where the
  author was located).

Newspapers

The newspapers listed here are those studied systematically at the Institut für
Zeitungsforschung in Dortmund for the periods of the 1898 and 1903 campaigns.
References to other papers are mainly derived from archival files.

Berliner Tageblatt (*BT*). This broadly left-liberal paper, closer to the FVg than to
  the FVP, had the best national election coverage of any paper, including
  reports of campaign news from correspondents across the Reich.
Frankfurter Zeitung (*FZ*). Another left-liberal paper, important especially for the
  southwest region.
Germania (*Germ*). Lead paper of the national Centre press.
Kölnische Volkszeitung (*KöVZ*). Regional Centre paper for the Rhineland, especially
  attentive to questions of election strategy.
Kölnische Zeitung (*KöZ*). A right-wing, anti-clerical, regional National Liberal
  paper.
Neue Preußische Zeitung (Kreuzzeitung) (*KZ*). German Conservative paper with a dis-
  tinctive radical slant.
Vorwärts (*VW*). Leader of the SPD national press; much election coverage of an
  agitational sort (Berlin edition unless otherwise noted).

Memoirs, Autobiographies, Diaries, Collected Works

Bismarck, Otto von. *Werke in Auswahl.* Vol. 8, part B (Rückblick und Ausblick,
  1890–8). Ed. Rudolf Buchner and Georg Engel. Darmstadt, 1983.

Brandt, Willy. *My Road to Berlin*. Garden City, N.Y., 1960.

Bülow, Prince von. *Deutsche Politik*. Reprinted from *Deutschland unter Kaiser Wilhelm II*. Berlin, 1914.

– *Memoirs*. 1897–1903 and 1903–9. London, 1931.

Gerlach, Hellmut von. *Von Rechts nach Links*. Zurich, 1937 / Hildesheim, 1978.

Hohenlohe-Schillingsfürst, Prince Chlodwig of. *Denkwürdigkeiten der Reichskanzleizeit*. Ed. Karl Alexander von Müller. Stuttgart/Berlin, 1931.

– *Memoirs*. Ed. Friedrich Curtius. London, 1906.

Kelly, Alfred, ed. *The German Worker: Working-Class Autobiographies from the Age of Industrialization*. Berkeley, 1987.

Mehring, Franz. *Politische Publizistik: 1891 bis 1904*. 4th ed. Vol. 14 of *Gesammelte Werke*. Berlin, 1978.

– *Zur deutschen Geschichte von der Revolution 1848/49 bis zum Ende des 19. Jahrhunderts*. 5th ed. Vol. 7 of *Gesammelte Werke*. Berlin, 1980.

Naumann, Friedrich. *Schriften zur Verfassungspolitik*. Vol. 2 of *Werke*. Cologne/Opladen, 1964.

Oldenburg-Januschau, Elard von. *Erinnerungen*. Leipzig, 1936.

Spitzemberg, Baroness. *Das Tagebuch der Baronin Spitzemberg: Aufzeichnungen aus der Hofgesellschaft des Hohenzollernreiches*. Göttingen, 1961.

Weber, Max. *From Max Weber: Essays in Sociology*. Ed. H.H. Gerth and C. Wright Mills. London, 1948.

Westarp, Kuno von. *Konservative Politik im letzten Jahrzehnt des Kaiserreiches*. 2 vols. Berlin, 1935.

William II. *My Memoirs: 1878–1918*. London, 1922.

Miscellaneous Contemporary Publications (Excluding Election Leaflets)

Albert, Robert. *Kaiser-Adressen! Nebst einem Anhang: Krupp'scher Wohltätigkeits-Schwindel. Ein Beitrag zum Fall Krupp*. Munich, 1903.

Astfalck, Cäsar. *Die Besiegung der Sozialdemokratie durch Betätigung des sozialen Empfindens: Vierter Beitrag zur Lösung der sozialen Frage*. Charlottenburg, 1899.

Auer, Ignaz. *Von Gotha bis Wyden*. Berlin, 1901.

Backhaus, R. *Wer sind die Conservativen Hannovers? Rede des Herrn R. Backhaus in der V. Landesversammlung der deutsch-hannoverschen Partei am 28. Mai 1899 in Werden*. Hanover, 1899.

Bebel, August. *Nicht stehendes Heer sondern Volkswehr!* Stuttgart, 1898.

– *Die Sozialdemokratie und das allgemeine Stimmrecht: Mit besonderer Berücksichtigung des Frauen-Stimmrechts und Proportional-Wahlsystems*. Berlin, 1895.

– *Woman in the Past, Present and Future*. Trans. H.B. Adams Walther. Introd. Moira Donald. London, 1988 (orig. publ. 1879, revised 1883).

Bernhard. *Krach-Krisis und Arbeiterklasse: Agitations-Ausgabe.* Berlin, 1902.

Blank, Rudolf. 'Die soziale Zusammensetzung der sozialdemokratischen Wähler-schaft Deutschlands.' In Büsch, Wölk, and Wölk, eds., *Wählerbewegung,* pp. 184–96. Originally published in *Archiv für Sozialwissenschaft und Sozialpolitik* 20 (1904/05): 507–50.

Böhm-Bawerk, Eugen von. *Karl Marx and the Close of His System: A Criticism.* New York, 1898.

Bund der Landwirte. *Agrarisches Handbuch.* Berlin, 1898.

Der Bund der Landwirte: Seine Forderungen und seine Erfolge. Danzig, 1898.

Bürger, H.F. *Soziale Thatsachen und sozialdemokratische Lehren: Ein Büchlein für denkende Menschen, besonders für denkende Arbeiter.* Berlin, 1900.

Cahn, Ernst. 'Die Motive des politischen Wählens.' In Büsch, Wölk, and Wölk, eds., *Wählerbewegung,* pp. 171–83. Originally published in *Patria: Jahrbuch der 'Hilfe,'* ed. Friedrich Naumann, vol. 7 (1907), pp. 1–28.

Calwer, Richard. *Arbeiter-Katechismus: Eine Sozialdemokratische Antwort auf das Preis-Ausschreiben des Pfarrers Weber zur Anfertigung eines Arbeiter-Katechismus für evangelische Arbeiter.* Berlin, 1896.

– *Wen wähle ich? Eine Agitationsschrift für die ländliche Bevölkerung für die Reichstagswahl 1898.* Berlin, 1898.

Caron-Rauenthal, von. *Die Zukunft der Sozialdemokratie.* Elberfeld, 1903.

Ehrlich, Hans. *Gespräche zwischen einem Landmann und einem Sozialdemokraten.* Hamburg, 1892.

Eigenbrodt, August. *Berliner Tageblatt und Frankfurter Zeitung in ihrem Verhalten zu den nationalen Fragen 1887–1914.* Berlin/Schöneberg, 1917.

Endmann, Gustav Adolf. *Nothwendigkeit einer Vermehrung unserer Kriegsflotte zur Wahrung deutscher Ehre und zum Schutze von Deutschlands Handel und Industrie.* Berlin/Leipzig, 1897.

Erzberger, M. *Der stille Kulturkampf.* Hamm (Westf.), n.d. [c. 1911].

– *Beiträge zur Parität in Württemberg.* Stuttgart, 1903.

Eugen Richters Sozialistenspiegel: Die Wahlfälschungen der Aktiengesellschaft Fortschritt. Berlin, 1903.

Falk, Kurt. *Die Bestrebungen der Socialdemokratie beleuchtet vom Irrsinn Eugen Richters.* Nuremberg, 1891.

– *Die christliche Kirche und der Socialismus: Eine socialdemokratische Antwort auf die Encyklika Leo XIII.* Nuremberg, 1891.

Fechenbach-Laudenbach, Reichsfreiherr von. *Die Bedeutung der heutigen Social-demokratie für Staat und Gesellschaft, oder: Was will, kann und soll man?* Frankfurt a.M., 1895.

– *Der Kaiser ruft!* 5th ed. Berlin/Leipzig, 1896.

– *Soll man die Sozialdemokratie zur akuten Revolution, zu Straßenkämpfen, zwingen?* Berlin/Leipzig, 1896.

Fischer, Ernst. *Der Werth der Sozialdemokratie für die Arbeiterschaft: Erlebnisse eines in der Partei thätig gewesenen Genossen.* Berlin, 1897.

Fort mit unserer Marine? Von einem Reichsfreunde. Berlin, 1895.

Fricke, Ferdinand. *Schwarz oder Roth? Socialdemokratisches Bekenntnis eines ehemaligen Ultramontanen: Zugleich ein Beitrag zur Naturgeschichte der Centrumspartei.* Nuremberg, 1894.

Gaulke, Johannes. *Über die Grenzen des Nationalismus und Internationalismus.* Berlin, 1898.

Georg. *Sind die mancherlei unrichtigen statistischen Angaben Bebels in seinem Hauptwerk Fälschungen oder Dummheiten?* Ribnitz, 1892.

Gerlach, Hellmut von. *Das Parlament.* Frankfurt a.M., 1907.

– 'Die sogenannte Wahlurne.' *Die Nation: Berliner Wochenschrift für Politik, Volkswirtschaft und Literatur* 22. 44 (1904–5).

Giese, Dr W. *Die Judenfrage am Ende des XIX. Jahrhunderts: Nach den Verhandlungen des V. allgemeinen Parteitages der Deutsch-sozialen Reformpartei zu Hamburg am 11. September 1899.* Berlin, 1899.

Goldschmidt, Dr Friedrich, and Dr Friedrich Siebert. *Schwarz-Weiß-Rot: Jungliberales Jahrbuch.* Vol. 1. Munich, 1904.

Goldschmidt, Dr P. *Zur Reichstagswahl vom 21. Februar und 2. März 1887.* Berlin, 1887.

Gradnauer, Georg. *Wahlkampf! Die Sozialdemokratie und ihre Gegner.* Dresden, 1911.

Der Handelsvertragsverein, sein Wesen und seine Ziele. Berlin, n.d.

Hartung, Fritz. *Deutsche Verfassungsgeschichte vom 15. Jahrhundert bis zur Gegenwart.* Leipzig/Berlin, 1914.

Heine, Wolfgang. *Wählen oder Nichtwählen? Ein Wort zur Frage der Betheiligung der Sozialdemokratie and den preußischen Landtagswahlen.* Berlin, 1898.

Hirsch, Paul. *Die Sozialdemokratie im Wahlkreise Teltow-Beeskow-Storkow-Charlottenburg: Auf Grund der amtlichen Statistik der Reichstagswahlen von 1890, 93, und 98.* Charlottenburg, 1899.

Hirsch, Paul, and Bruno Borchardt. *Die Sozialdemokratie und die Wahlen zum Deutschen Reichstage.* Berlin, 1907.

Kampffmeyer, Paul. *Junker und Bauer: Zur Entwicklung unserer Agrar-Verhältnisse.* Berlin, 1896.

– *Sozialdemokratie und Kirchentum.* Munich, 1912.

– *Wandlungen in der Theorie und Taktik des Sozialismus.* Munich, 1904.

Kautsky, Karl. *The Agrarian Question in Two Volumes.* Trans. Pete Burgess. London, 1988 (orig. publ. Stuttgart, 1899).

– *Handelspolitik und Sozialdemokratie: Populare Darstellung der handelspolitischen Streitfragen: Agitations-Ausgabe.* Berlin, 1901.

Kautsky, Karl, and Bruno Schoenlank. *Grundsätze und Forderungen der Sozialdemokratie: Erläuterung zum Erfurter Programm.* 3d ed. [?]. Berlin, 1902.

Kempe, Paul. *Christus und die Sozialdemokratie: Für die ländliche Bevölkerung.* 12th ed., Brunswick, 1906.

Keßler, Gustav. *Die Ziele der Sozialdemokratischen Partei: Volksthümlich entwickelt.* Berlin, 1895.

Klöcker, Alois. 'Konfession und sozialdemokratische Wählerschaft.' In Büsch, Wölk, and Wölk, eds., *Wählerbewegung,* pp. 197–207. Excerpt from Klöcker, *Konfession und sozialdemokratische Wählerschaft: Statistische Untersuchung der allgemeinen Reichstagswahlen des Jahres 1907* (Mönchen-Gladbach, 1913).

Kürschner, Joseph. *Deutscher Reichstag: Biographisch-statistisches Handbuch.* 3d ed. (10. L.P. 1898–1903), Berlin/Leipzig, 1898; 4th ed. (11. L.P. 1903–8 [*sic*]), Berlin/Leipzig, 1903.

Liebknecht, Wilhelm. *Kein Kompromiß–Kein Wahlbündnis.* Berlin, 1899.

Lorentzen, Theodor. *Arbeiter-Partei oder Revolutions-Partei: Wer hat Recht, Naumann oder ich?* Leipzig, 1898.

– *Die Ausbeutung der Arbeiter und die Ursachen ihrer Verarmung: Ein Beitrag zur sozialen Frage.* Leipzig, 1898.

– *Die Flotte und der Reichstag: Eine Volkstümliche Erläuterung der Marine-Frage im Anschluß an die Tabellen des Kaisers!* Leipzig, 1897.

Lorenz, Max. *Der nationale Kampf gegen die Sozialdemokratie.* Leipzig, 1897.

Mai, August. *Partei und Gewerkschaft in vergleichender Statistik.* Dresden, 1912.

Maurenbrecher, Max. *Die Gebildeten und die Sozialdemokratie.* Leipzig, 1904.

Mehring, Franz. *Weltkrach und Weltmarkt: Eine weltpolitische Skizze.* Berlin, 1900.

Michels, Robert. *Political Parties: A Sociological Study of the Oligarchical Tendencies of Modern Democracy.* Trans. Eden and Cedar Paul. Introd. Seymour Martin Lipset. New York, 1962 (orig. publ. 1915).

Müller-Fulda, Richard, and H. Sittart. *Der Deutsche Reichstag von 1898 bis 1903: Ein Bericht über die Tätigkeit der Centrumspartei in der abgelaufenen Legislaturperiode.* Cologne, 1903.

Nationalliberale Partei. *Politisches Handbuch der Nationalliberalen Partei.* Berlin, 1907.

– *Politisches Handbuch für nationalliberale Wähler.* 2d ed. Berlin, 1897.

Neumann-Hofer, Dr Adolf. *Die Entwicklung der Sozialdemokratie bei den Wahlen zum Deutschen Reichstag.* 2d ed. Berlin, 1898.

Ostrogorski, M. *Democracy and the Organization of Political Parties.* 2 vols. Ed. and abridged Seymour Martin Lipset. Chicago, 1964 (orig. publ. 1902).

'Parvus.' *Die Handelskrisis und die Gewerkschaften.* Munich, 1901.

– *Die Reichstagswahlen und die Arbeiterschaft.* Leipzig, 1907.

– *Wohin führt die politische Maßregelung der Sozialdemokratie? Kritik der politischen Reaktion in Deutschland.* Dresden, 1897.

Programmatische Kundgebungen der Nationalliberalen Partei 1866–1913. Berlin, 1913.

Quidde, L. *Caligula. Eine Studie über römischen Cäsarwahnsinn.* 31st ed. Berlin, 1926 (written in 1894).

Reichs- und freikonservative Partei. *Materialen zur Reichspolitik: Im Hinblick auf die bevorstehenden Reichstagswahlen.* Berlin, 1890.

Reichsverband gegen die Sozialdemokratie. *Sozialdemokratischer Terrorismus: Kritische Betrachtung nebst einer Auswahl gerichtlich abgeurteilter Terrorismusfälle.* Berlin, 1909.

– *Volkskalender für das Jahr 1910.* Berlin, 1910.

Rhenanus. *Christliche Gewerkschaften oder Fachabteilungen in kathol: Arbeitervereinen? Ein Wort zur Aufklärung.* Cologne, 1904.

– *Der Himmel der Sozialdemokratie in Traum und Wirklichkeit.* Stuttgart, 1893.

Richter, Eugen. *Gegen die Sozialdemokratie.* Berlin, 1896.

– *Politisches ABC-Buch: Ein Lexikon parlamentarischer Zeit- und Streitfragen.* 8th ed. Berlin, 1896; and 10th ed. Berlin, 1903.

– *Sozialistenspiegel.* Berlin, 1903.

Schippel, Max. *Sozialdemokratisches Reichstags-Handbuch: Ein Führer durch die Zeit- und Streitfragen der Reichsgesetzgebung.* Berlin, 1902.

– *Die Währungs-Frage und die Sozialdemokratie: Eine gemeinfaßliche Darstellung der währungspolitische Zustände und Kämpfe.* Berlin, 1896.

Schmidt, G.W.C. *Die freisinnige Volkspartei: Wer sie ist und was sie will.* Dresden, 1895.

Schulthess' Europäischer Geschichtskalender. N.S. vols. 14–18 (1898–1902).

Servocarus. *Die Nothwendigkeit gesetzlichen Schutzes gegen die socialdemokratische Aufreizung wider Kapital und Besitz: Aufruf zu einer Petition and die Reichsbehörden.* Berlin, 1894.

– *Schreiben aus dem Jahre 2000.* Berlin, 1894.

Siebertz. *Politisch-Soziales ABC-Buch: Ein Handbuch für die Mitglieder und Freunde der Zentrumspartei: Auf Grund authentischen Quellenmaterials bearbeitet.* Stuttgart, 1900.

Die Sozialdemokratie und der deutsche Reichstag: Materialen zum Gebrauch für sozialdemokratische Wähler. Berlin, 1889.

Die Sozialdemokratie und die ländliche Bevölkerung: Eine zeitgemäße Betrachtung. Hamburg, 1891.

Sozialdemokratische Partei Deutschlands. *Handbuch für Sozialdemokratische Wähler: Der Reichstag 1893–1898.* Berlin, 1898.

– *Handbuch für Sozialdemokratische Wähler: Der Reichstag 1898–1903.* Berlin, 1903.

– *Handbuch für Sozialdemokratische Wähler anläßlich der Reichstagsauflösung 1906.* Berlin, 1907.

– *Protokoll über die Verhandlungen des Parteitages der Sozialdemokratischen Partei Deutschlands abgehalten zu Hamburg vom 3. bis 9. Oktober 1897.* Berlin, 1897.

– *Protokoll über die Verhandlungen des Parteitages der Sozialdemokratischen Partei Deutschlands abgehalten zu Stuttgart vom 3. bis 8. Oktober 1898.* Berlin, 1898.

– *Protokoll über die Verhandlungen des Parteitages der Sozialdemokratischen Partei Deutschlands abgehalten zu München vom 14. bis 20. September 1902.* Berlin, 1902.
– *Protokoll über die Verhandlungen des Parteitages der Sozialdemokratischen Partei Deutschlands abgehalten zu Dresden vom 13. bis 20. September 1903.* Berlin, 1903.

Spahn, Martin. *Das Deutsche Zentrum.* 2d ed. Mainz/Munich, 1906.

Stumpf-Brentano, Cl. von. *Ravensteins Reichstags-Wahlkarte des Deutschen Reichs, nach dem Ergebnis der Hauptwahlen vom 12. Januar 1912 und der Stichwahlen, mit erstmaliger genauer Abgrenzung der Wahlkreise, auf Grund amtlicher Materialen bearbeitet.* Frankfurt a.M., 1912.

Sunkel, Ernst. *Das Volksblatt für Hessen und Waldeck vom Sommer 1898 zum Sommer 1899: Ein Beitrag zur Kenntnis der deutschen Sozialdemokratie.* Kassel, 1899.

Timm, Johannes. *Sozialdemokratie und Zentrum: Tatsachen-Material zur Arbeiterversicherung und Zentrumspolitik.* Munich, 1902.

Der Umsturz im Reichstag: Eine Darstellung der Kämpfe um den Zolltarif nach dem amtlichen Stenogramm: Mit einer tabellarischen Übersicht der wichtigsten Abstimmungen. Berlin, 1903.

Vollmar, Georg von. *Lehren und Folgen der letzten Reichstagswahlen.* Munich, 1903.
– *Ueber die nächsten Aufgaben der deutschen Sozialdemokratie.* 2d ed. Munich, 1899.
– *Über Staatssozialismus.* Nuremberg, 1892.

Vorster, Julius. *Der Socialismus der Gebildeten Stände: Vortrag gehalten in der General-Versammlung des Vereins der Industriellen des Regierungsbezirks Köln am 20. April 1894.* Cologne, 1894.

Wurm, Emanuel. *Sozialdemokratie und Reichstag: Ein Werkbüchlein zur Reichstagswahl.* Hamburg, 1898.

Würzburger, Eugen. 'Die "Partei der Nichtwähler."' In Büsch, Wölk, and Wölk, eds., *Wählerbewegung,* pp. 207–16. Originally published in *Jahrbuch für Nationalökonomie und Statistik,* 3d ser., 33 (1907): 381–9.

Zu den Reichstagswahlen: Ein freisinniges Werkbüchlein. Berlin, 1898.

SECONDARY SOURCES

Abendroth, Wolfgang. 'The Absolutism of the Hohenzollern State and the Rise of the Social Democratic Party.' In Feuchtwanger, ed., *Upheaval and Continuity,* pp. 47–66.
– 'Aufgaben und Methoden einer deutschen historischen Wahlsoziologie.' In Büsch, Wölk, and Wölk, eds., *Wählerbewegung,* pp. 119–24.

Abrams, Lynn. *Workers' Culture in Imperial Germany: Leisure and Recreation in the Rhineland and Westphalia.* London/New York, 1992.

Albertin, Lothar. 'Der unzeitige Parlamentarismus der Liberalen: Versäumnisse seiner parteiendemokratischen Fundierung.' In Albertin and Link, eds., *Politische Parteien*, pp. 31–62.

Albertin, Lothar, and Werner Link, eds. *Politische Parteien auf dem Weg zur parlamentarischen Demokratie in Deutschland: Entwicklungslininen bis zur Gegenwart.* Düsseldorf, 1981.

Alemann, Ulrich von, ed. *Parteien und Wahlen in Nordrhein-Westfalen.* Cologne/ Stuttgart/Berlin/Mainz, 1985.

Anderson, Margaret Lavinia. 'The Kulturkampf and the Course of German History.' *CEH* 19 (March 1986): 82–115.

– 'Voter, Junker, *Landrat,* Priest: The Old Authorities and the New Franchise in Imperial Germany.' *American Historical Review* (Dec. 1993): 1448–74.

– *Windhorst: A Political Biography.* Oxford/New York, 1981.

Anderson, Margaret Lavinia, and Kenneth Barkin. 'The Myth of the Puttkamer Purge and the Reality of the *Kulturkampf:* Some Reflections on the Historiography of Imperial Germany.' *JMH* 54.4 (Dec. 1982): 647–86.

Bachem, Karl. *Vorgeschichte, Geschichte und Politik der Deutschen Zentrumspartei: Zugleich ein Beitrag zur Geschichte der katholischen Bewegung, sowie zur allgemeinen Ges-chichte des neueren und neuesten Deutschland 1815–1914.* 9 vols. Cologne, 1927–32.

Barkin, Kenneth. 'A Case Study in Comparative History: Populism in Germany and America.' In *The State of American History.* Ed. Herbert J. Bass. Chicago, 1970, pp. 374–96.

– *The Controversy over German Industrialization 1890–1902.* Chicago/London, 1970.

Bartolini, Stefano, and Peter Mair. *Identity, Competition, and Electoral Availability: The Stabilisation of European Electorates 1885–1985.* Cambridge, 1990.

Baumgart, Winfried. *Deutschland im Zeitalter des Imperialismus (1890–1914): Grundkräfte, Thesen und Strukturen.* Frankfurt a.M., 1972.

Bell, Jeffrey. *Populism and Elitism: Politics in the Age of Equality.* Washington, D.C., 1992.

Berghahn, V.R. *Germany and the Approach of War in 1914.* London, 1973.

– *Imperial Germany, 1871–1914: Economy, Society, Culture and Politics.* Providence, R.I., 1994.

– *Der Tirpitz-Plan: Genesis und Verfall einer innenpolitischen Krisenstrategie unter Wilhelm II.* Düsseldorf, 1971.

– 'Der Tirpitz-Plan und die Krisis des preußisch-deutschen Herrschaftssystems.' In Schottelius and Deist, eds., *Marine und Marinepolitik,* pp. 89–115.

Berg-Schlosser, Dirk, and Jakob Schissler, eds. *Politische Kultur in Deutschland: Bilanz und Perspektive der Forschung.* Opladen, 1987.

Bergsträßer, L. *Geschichte der politischen Parteien in Deutschland.* 5th ed. Mannheim/ Berlin/Leipzig, 1928.

Bertram, Jürgen. *Die Wahlen zum Deutschen Reichstage vom Jahre 1912: Parteien und Verbände in der Innenpolitik des Wilhelminischen Reichs.* Bonn, 1964.

- 'Zum Reichstagswahlkampf für die Wahl des Jahres 1912.' In Büsch, Wölk, and Wölk, eds., *Wählerbewegung*, pp. 167–90.

Beyme, Klaus von. *Political Parties in Western Democracies.* Trans. Eileen Martin. Aldershot, Hants., 1985.

Blackbourn, David. 'Between Resignation and Volatility: The German Petite Bourgeoisie in the Nineteenth Century.' In Crossick and Haupt, eds., *Shopkeepers and Master Artisans*, pp. 35–61.

- 'Class and Politics in Wilhelmine Germany: The Center Party and the Social Democrats in Württemberg.' In *CEH* 9.3 (Sept. 1976): 220–49.

- *Class, Religion, and Local Politics in Wilhelmine Germany: The Centre Party in Württemberg before 1914.* New Haven/London, 1980.

- 'Peasants and Politics in Germany 1871–1914.' *EHQ* 14.1 (Jan. 1984): 47–76.

- 'The Political Alignment of the Centre Party in Wilhelmine Germany: A Study of the Party's Emergence in Nineteenth-Century Württemberg.' *HJ* 18.4 (1975): 821–50.

- 'The Politics of Demagogy in Imperial Germany.' *PP* 113 (Nov. 1986): 152–84.

- 'The Problem of Democratisation: German Catholics and the Role of the Centre Party.' In Evans, ed., *Society and Politics*, pp. 160–85.

Blackbourn, David, and Geoff Eley. *The Peculiarities of German History: Bourgeois Society and Politics in Nineteenth-Century Germany.* Oxford/New York, 1984.

Blackbourn, David, and Richard J. Evans. *The German Bourgeoisie: Essays on the Social History of the German Middle Class from the Late Eighteenth to the Early Twentieth Century.* London/New York, 1991.

Böhme, Helmut. *An Introduction to the Social and Economic History of Germany: Politics and Economic Change in the Nineteenth and Twentieth Centuries.* Trans. and Introd. W.R. Lee. Oxford, 1978.

Boldt, Hans. 'Stein Rokkans Parteitheorie und die vergleichende Verfassungsgeschichte.' In Albertin and Link, eds., *Politische Parteien*, pp. 91–107.

Bonham, Gary. 'State Autonomy or Class Domination: Approaches to Administrative Politics in Wilhelmine Germany.' *World Politics* 35.4 (July 1983): 631–51.

Born, Karl Erich. *Staat und Sozialpolitik seit Bismarcks Sturz: Ein Beitrag zur Geschichte der innenpolitischen Entwicklung des Deutschen Reiches 1890–1914.* Wiesbaden, 1957.

- 'Structural Changes in German Social and Economic Development at the end of the Nineteenth Century.' In Sheehan, ed., *Imperial Germany*, pp. 16–38.

Breitman, Richard. 'Negative Integration and Parliamentary Politics: Literature on German Social Democracy 1890–1933.' *CEH* 13.2 (June 1980): 175–97.

Brock, Peter. *Polish Revolutionary Populism: A Study in Agrarian Socialist Thought from the 1830s to the 1850s.* Toronto, 1977.

Büsch, Otto. 'Gedanken und Thesen zur Wählerbewegung in Deutschland.' In Büsch, Wölk, and Wölk, eds., *Wählerbewegung*, pp. 125–67.

Büsch, Otto, Wolfgang Wölk, and Monika Wölk, eds. *Wählerbewegung in der deutschen Geschichte: Analysen und Berichte zu den Reichstagswahlen 1871–1933*. Berlin, 1978.

Butler, David, Howard R. Penniman, and Austin Ranney, eds. *Democracy at the Polls: A Comparative Study of Competitive National Elections*. Washington/London, 1981.

Calhoun, C.J. 'Community: Toward a Variable Conceptualization for Comparative Research.' *SH* 5 (1980): 105–29.

Calkins, Kenneth R. *Hugo Haase: Democrat and Revolutionary*. Durham, North Carolina, 1979.

Canning, Kathleen. 'Gender and the Culture of Work: Ideology and Identity in the World behind the Mill Gate, 1890–1914.' In Jones and Retallack, eds., *Elections, Mass Politics, and Social Change*, pp. 175–99.

Canovan, Margaret. *Populism*. New York/London, 1981.

Castles, Francis G. *Pressure Groups and Political Culture: A Comparative Study*. London/New York, 1967.

Cecil, Lamar. *Albert Ballin: Business and Politics in Imperial Germany, 1888–1918*. Princeton, 1967.

Chickering, Roger. *We Men Who Feel Most German: A Cultural Study of the Pan-German League. 1886–1914*. Boston/London, 1984.

– ed. *Imperial Germany: A Historiographical Companion*. Westport, Conn., 1996.

Childers, Thomas. *The Nazi Voter: The Social Foundations of Fascism in Germany, 1919–1933*. Chapel Hill/London, 1983.

Claggett, William. 'Political Leadership and the Development of Political Cleavages: Imperial Germany, 1871–1912.' *American Journal of Political Science* 26.4 (Nov. 1982): 643–63.

Clanton, Gene. *Populism: The Humane Preference in America: 1890–1900*. Boston, 1991.

Coetzee, Marilyn Shevin. 'The Mobilization of the Right? The Deutscher Wehrverein and Political Activism in Württemberg, 1912–14.' *EHQ* 15.4 (Oct. 1985): 407–30.

Conniff, Michael L., ed. *Latin American Populism in Comparative Perspective*. Albuquerque, 1982.

Conze, Werner. 'Wahlsoziologie und Parteigeschichte.' In Büsch, Wölk, and Wölk, eds., *Wählerbewegung*, pp. 111–18.

Craig, Gordon A. *Germany 1866–1945*. New York/Oxford, 1980.

– *The Politics of the Prussian Army, 1640–1945*. London/Oxford/New York, 1964.

Crew, David F. 'Class and Community: Local Research on Working-Class History in Four Countries.' *HZ* Sonderheft 15 (1986).

- 'Definitions of Modernity: Social Mobility in a German Town, 1880–1901.' *Journal of Social History* 7.1 (Fall 1973): 51–74.

Crossick, Geoffrey, and Heinz-Gerhard Haupt, eds. *Shopkeepers and Master Artisans in Nineteenth-Century Europe.* London/New York, 1984.

Crothers, George Dunlap. *The German Elections of 1907.* New York, 1941.

Daalder, Hans. 'Parties, Elites, and Political Developments in Western Europe.' In LaPalombara and Weiner, eds., *Political Parties,* pp. 43–7.

Dahrendorf, Ralf. *Society and Democracy in Germany.* London, 1968.

Deist, Wilhelm. 'Die Armee in Staat und Gesellschaft.' In Stürmer, ed., *Das kaiserliche Deutschland,* pp. 312–39.

- *Flottenpolitik und Flottenpropaganda.* Stuttgart, 1976.

- 'Reichsmarineamt und Flottenverein 1903–1906.' In Schottelius and Deist, eds., *Marine und Marinepolitik,* pp. 116–45.

Deuerlein, Ernst. *Der Reichstag: Aufsätze, Protokolle und Darstellungen zur Geschichte der parlamentarischen Vertretung des deutschen Volkes, 1871–1933.* Bonn, 1963.

Diamond, Larry, ed. *Political Culture and Democracy in Developing Countries.* Boulder, Colo. and London, 1993.

Diederich, Nils. 'Konzepte der Wahlforschung.' In Büsch, Wölk, and Wölk, eds., *Wählerbewegung,* pp. 169–206.

Dillwitz, Sigrid. 'Die Struktur der Bauernschaft von 1871 bis 1914: Dargelegt auf Grund der deutschen Reichsstatistik.' *Jahrbuch für Geschichte* 9 (1973): 47–128.

Dominick, Raymond. 'Democracy or Socialism? A Case Study of *Vorwärts* in the 1890s.' *CEH* 10.4 (Dec. 1977): 286–311.

Dornbusch, Rudiger, and Sebastian Edwards, eds. *The Macroeconomics of Populism in Latin America.* Chicago, 1991.

Dowe, Dieter. 'The Workingmen's Choral Movement in Germany before the First World War.' *Journal of Contemporary History* 13.2 (April 1978): 269–96.

Duverger, Maurice. *Les Partis politiques.* 8th ed. Paris, 1973.

- *Party Politics and Pressure Groups: A Comparative Introduction.* London, 1972.

Eley, Geoff. 'Capitalism and the Wilhelmine State: Industrial Growth and Political Backwardness in Recent German Historiography, 1890–1918.' *HJ* 21.3 (1978): 737–50.

- 'Defining Social Imperialism: Use and Abuse of an Idea.' *SH* 1.3 (Oct. 1976): 265–90.

- *From Unification to Nazism: Reinterpreting the German Past.* Boston/London/ Sydney, 1986.

- 'Notable Politics, the Crisis of German Liberalism, and the Electoral Transition of the 1890s.' In Jarausch and Jones, eds., *In Search of a Liberal Germany,* pp. 187–216.

- *Reshaping the German Right: Radical Nationalism and Political Change after Bismarck.* London, 1980.
- 'Reshaping the Right: Radical Nationalism and the German Navy League, 1898–1908.' *HJ* 21.2 (1978): 327–54.
- '*Sammlungspolitik*, Social Imperialism and the Navy Law of 1898.' *MM* 15 (1974): 29–63.
- 'Some Thoughts on the Nationalist Pressure Groups in Imperial Germany.' In Kennedy and Nicholls, eds., *Nationalist and Racialist Movements*, pp. 40–67.
- 'The Wilhelmine Right: How It Changed.' In Evans, ed., *Society and Politics*, pp. 112–35.

Elm, Ludwig. *Zwischen Fortschritt und Reaktion: Geschichte der Parteien der liberalen Bourgeoisie in Deutschland 1893–1918.* Berlin, 1968.

Epstein, Klaus. *Matthias Erzberger and the Dilemma of German Democracy.* Princeton, 1959.

Evans, Richard J. *Proletarians and Politics: Socialism, Protest and the Working Class in Germany before the First World War.* New York, 1990.
- *Rethinking German History: Nineteenth-Century Germany and the Origins of the Third Reich.* London, 1987.
- 'The Sociological Interpretation of German Labour History.' In Evans, ed., *The German Working Class*, pp. 15–53.
- 'Wilhelm II's Germany and the Historians.' In Evans, ed., *Society and Politics*, pp. 11–39.
- ed. *The German Working Class 1888–1933: The Politics of Everyday Life.* London, 1982.
- ed. *Society and Politics in Wilhelmine Germany.* London, 1978.

Evans, Richard J., and W.R. Lee, eds. *The German Peasantry: Conflict and Community in Rural Society from the Eighteenth to the Twentieth Centuries.* London/Sydney, 1986.

Fairbairn, Brett. 'Authority vs. Democracy: Prussian Officials in the German Elections of 1898 and 1903.' *HJ*, 33.4 (1990): 811–38.
- 'The German Elections of 1898 and 1903.' Ph.d. diss., University of Oxford, 1987.
- 'Interpreting Wilhelmine Elections: National Issues, Fairness Issues, and Electoral Mobilization.' In Jones and Retallack, eds., *Elections, Mass Politics and Social Change in Modern Germany*, pp. 17–48.
- 'The Limits of Nationalist Politics: Electoral Culture and Mobilization in Germany, 1898–1903.' *Journal of the Canadian Historical Association* (formerly *Historical Papers*) N.S. 1 (1990): 145 70.
- 'Political Mobilization.' In Chickering, ed., *Imperial Germany*, pp. 303–42.

Falk, Marvin William. 'The Reichstag Elections of 1912: A Statistical Study.' Diss. Iowa 1976.

Falter, Jürgen. 'The First German *Volkspartei*: The Social Foundations of the NSDAP.' In Rohe, ed., *Elections, Parties and Political Traditions*, pp. 53–82.

Farr, Ian. 'From Anti-Catholicism to Anticlericalism: Catholic Politics and the Peasantry in Bavaria, 1860–1900.' *ESR* 13.2 (April 1983): 249–69.

– 'Populism in the Countryside: The Peasant Leagues in Bavaria in the 1890s.' In Evans, ed., *Society and Politics*, pp. 136–59.

– '"Tradition" and the Peasantry: On the Modern Historiography of Rural Germany.' In Evans and Lee, eds., *The German Peasantry*, pp. 1–36.

Feineisen, Adalbert. *Wilhelm Haas: Gestalter einer großen Idee.* Neuwied, 1956.

Feuchtwanger, E.J., ed. *Upheaval and Continuity: A Century of German History.* London, 1973.

Finifter, Ada W., ed. *Political Science: The State of the Discipline II.* Washington, D.C., 1993.

Fischer, Hubertus. 'Konservatismus von unten: Wahlen im ländlichen Preußen 1849/52 – Organisation, Agitation, Manipulation.' In Stegmann et al., eds., *Konservatismus*, pp. 69–127.

Flemming, Jens. *Landwirtschaftliche Interessen und Demokratie: Ländliche Gesellschaft, Agrarverbände und Staat 1890–1925.* Bonn, 1978.

– 'Die vergessene Klasse: Literatur zur Geschichte der Landarbeiter in Deutschland.' *HZ* Sonderheft 15 (1986).

Fletcher, Roger. *Revisionism and Empire: Socialist Imperialism in Germany, 1897–1914.* London, 1984.

Forstheimer, Friedrich. 'Der Tirpitzsche Flottenbau im Urteil der Historiker.' In Schottelius and Deist, eds., *Marine und Marinepolitik*, pp. 34–53.

Fraley, J. David. 'Government by Procrastination: Chancellor Hohenlohe and Kaiser Wilhelm II, 1894–1900.' *CEH* 7.2 (June 1974): 159–83.

Franklin, Mark N., et al. *Electoral Change: Responses to Evolving Social and Attitudinal Structures in Western Countries.* Cambridge, 1992.

Franz, Günther. *Die politischen Wahlen in Niedersachsen 1867 bis 1949.* 3d ed. Bremen-Horn, 1957.

Fricke, Dieter. 'Der Regierungswahlkampf von 1907.' In Büsch, Wölk, and Wölk, eds., *Wählerbewegung*, pp. 485–504.

Fritzsche, Peter. *Rehearsals for Fascism: Populism and Political Mobilization in Weimar Germany.* Oxford, 1990.

Gall, Lothar. *Der Liberalismus als regierende Partei: Das Großherzogtum Baden zwischen Restauration und Reichsgründung.* Wiesbaden, 1968.

– 'Liberalismus und "bürgerliche Gesellschaft": Zu Charakter und Entwicklung der liberalen Bewegung in Deutschland.' *HZ* 220 (1975): 324–56.

Geiss, Imanuel. 'Sozialstruktur und imperialistische Dispositionen im zweiten Deutschen Kaiserreich.' In Holl and List, eds., *Liberalismus*, pp. 40–61.

Geiss, Imanuel, and Bernd Jürgen Wendt, eds. *Deutschland in der Weltpolitik des 19. und 20. Jahrhunderts: Fritz Fischer zum 65. Geburtstag.* Düsseldorf, 1973.

Gellately, Robert. *The Politics of Economic Despair: Shopkeepers and German Politics 1890–1914.* London/Beverly Hills, 1974.

Gerschenkron, Alexander. *Bread and Democracy in Germany.* Berkeley/Los Angeles, 1943.

Goodwyn, Lawrence. *The Populist Moment: A Short History of the Agrarian Revolt in America.* Oxford, 1978.

Gottwald, Herbert. 'Der Umfall des Zentrums: Die Stellung der Zentrumspartei zur Flottenvorlage von 1897.' In Klein, ed., *Studien zum deutschen Imperialismus,* pp. 181–224.

Grebing, Helga. *Arbeiterbewegung: Sozialer Protest und kollektive Interessenvertretung bis 1914.* Munich, 1985.

Greive, Hermann. *Geschichte des modernen Antisemitismus in Deutschland.* Darmstadt, 1983.

Groh, Dieter. *Negative Integration und revolutionärer Attentismus: Die deutsche Sozialdemokratie am Vorabend des Ersten Weltkrieges.* Frankfurt a.M./Berlin, 1975.

Günther, Wolfgang, ed. *Parteien und Wahlen in Oldenburg: Beiträge zur Landesgeschichte im 19. und 20. Jahrhundert.* Oldenburg, 1983.

Guttsman, W.L. *The German Social Democratic Party, 1875–1933: From Ghetto to Government.* London, 1981.

Habermas, Jürgen. 'Strukturwandel der Öffentlichkeit: Untersuchungen zu einer Kategorie der bürgerlichen Gesellschaft.' In Wehler, ed., *Sozialgeschichte,* pp. 197–224.

Hadenius, Axel. *Democracy and Development.* Cambridge, 1992.

Hall, Alex. 'By Other Means: The Legal Struggle versus the SPD in Wilhelmine Germany, 1890–1900.' *HJ* 17.2 (1974): 365–86.

– *Scandal, Sensation, and Social Democracy: The SPD Press and Wilhelmine Germany, 1890–1914.* Cambridge, 1977.

Hamerow, Theodore S. 'The Origins of Mass Politics in Germany 1866–1867.' In Geiss and Wendt, eds., *Deutschland in der Weltpolitik,* pp. 105–20.

Hardtwig, W. 'Von Preußens Aufgabe in Deutschland zu Deutschlands Aufgabe in der Welt.' *HZ* 231.2 (Oct. 1980): 265–324.

Harrop, Martin, and William L. Miller. *Elections and Voters: A Comparative Introduction.* London, 1987

Heberle, Rudolf. *From Democracy to Nazism: A Regional Case Study on Political Parties in Germany.* Baton Rouge, 1945.

– 'Wahlökologie und Wahlgeographie.' In Büsch, Wölk, and Wölk, eds., *Wählerbewegung,* pp. 73–84.

Heckart, Beverley. *From Bassermann to Bebel: The Grand Bloc's Quest for Reform in the Kaiserreich, 1900–1914.* New Haven, 1974.

Hesselbarth, Helmut. *Revolutionäre Sozialdemokraten, Opportunisten, und die Bauern am Vorabend des Imperialismus.* Berlin, 1968.

Hickey, Stephen. 'The Shaping of the German Labour Movement: Miners in the Ruhr.' In Evans, ed., *Society and Politics,* pp. 215–40.

– *Workers in Imperial Germany: The Miners of the Ruhr.* Oxford, 1985.

Hiery, Hermann. *Reichstagswahlen im Reichsland: Ein Beitrag zur Landesgeschichte von Elsaß-Lothringen und zur Wahlgeschichte des Deutschen Reiches 1871–1918.* Düsseldorf, 1986.

Hofstadter, Richard. *The Age of Reform: From Bryan to F.D.R.* New York, 1955.

Holl, Karl, and Günter List, eds. *Liberalismus und imperialistischer Staat: Der Imperialismus als Problem liberaler Parteien in Deutschland 1890–1914.* Göttingen, 1975.

Horn, Hannelore. *Der Kampf um den Bau des Mittellandkanals: Eine politologische Untersuchung über die Rolle eines wirtschaftlichen Interessenverbandes im Preußen Wilhelms II.* Cologne/Opladen, 1964.

– 'Die Rolle des Bundes der Landwirte im Kampf um den Bau des Mittellandkanals.' *Jahrbuch für die Geschichte Mittel- und Ostdeutschlands* 7 (1958): 273–358.

Horn, Hans-Joachim. 'Die politischen Strömungen in der Stadt Bonn, in Bonn-Land und im Kreis Rheinbach von 1879–1900.' Diss. Bonn 1968.

Hull, Isabel V. *The Entourage of Kaiser Wilhelm II, 1888–1918.* Cambridge, 1982.

Hunt, James C. 'The Bourgeois Middle in German Politics, 1871–1933: Recent Literature.' *CEH* 9.1 (March 1978): 83–116.

– 'The "Egalitarianism" of the Right: The Agrarian League in Southwest Germany, 1893–1914.' *Journal of Contemporary History* 10 (July 1975): 513–30.

– '"Die Parität in Preußen" (1899): Hintergrund, Verlauf und Ergebnis eines Aktionsprogramms der Zentrumspartei.' *Historisches Jahrbuch* 102 (1982): 418–34.

– *The People's Party in Württemberg and Southern Germany, 1890–1914: The Possibilities of Democratic Politics.* Stuttgart, 1975.

Immerfall, Stefan, and Peter Steinbach. 'Politisierung und Nationalisierung deutscher Regionen im Kaiserreich.' In Berg-Schlosser and Schissler, eds., *Politische Kultur in Deutschland,* pp. 68–79.

Jaeger, Hans. *Unternehmer in der deutschen Politik (1890–1918).* Bonn, 1967.

Janda, Kenneth. 'Comparative Political Parties.' In Finifter, ed., *Political Science: The State of the Discipline II,* pp. 163–91.

– *Political Parties: A Cross-National Survey.* New York, 1980.

Jacquemann, Alexis. *The New Industrial Organization: Market Forces and Strategic Behavior.* Trans. Fatemeh Mehta. Cambridge, Mass., 1987.

Jarausch, Konrad H., and Larry Eugene Jone, eds. *In Search of a Liberal Germany: Studies in the History of German Liberalism from 1789 to the Present.* New York, 1990.

John, Michael F. 'Associational Life and the Development of Liberalism in Hanover, 1848–66.' In Jarausch and Jones, eds., *In Search of a Liberal Germany*, pp. 161–85.

– '"The Final Unification of Germany": Politics and the Codification of the German Civil Law in the Bürgerliches Gesetzbuch of 1896.' Diss. Oxford 1983.

– 'Liberalism and Society: The Case of Hanover.' *English Historical Review* 102 (1987): 579–98.

– 'The Politics of Legal Unity in Germany, 1870–1896.' *HJ* 28.2 (1985): 341–55.

Jones, Larry Eugene, and James Retallack eds. *Between Reform, Reaction and Resistance: Studies in the History of German Conservatism from 1789 to 1945.* Providence, R.I., 1993.

– *Elections, Mass Politics, and Social Change in Modern Germany: New Perspectives.* Cambridge/Washington, D.C., 1992.

Kaelble, Hartmut. *Industrielle Interessenpolitik in der wilhelminischen Gesellschaft: Centralverband Deutscher Industriellen 1895–1914.* Berlin, 1967.

– 'Soziale Mobilität in Deutschland, 1900–1960.' In Kaelble et al., *Probleme der Modernisierung*, pp. 235–327.

Kaelble, Hartmut, et al. *Probleme der Modernisierung in Deutschland: Sozialhistorische Studien zum 19. und 20. Jahrhunderts.* Opladen, 1978.

Kazin, Michael. *The Populist Persuasion: An American History.* New York, 1995.

Kehr, Eckart. 'Imperialismus und Schlachtflottenbau.' In Wehler, ed., *Sozialgeschichte*, pp. 289–308.

– *Schlachtflottenbau und Parteipolitik 1894–1901: Versuch eines Querschnitts durch die innenpolitischen, sozialen und ideologischen Voraussetzungen des deutschen Imperialismus.* Berlin, 1930.

Kemp, Tom. *Industrialization in Nineteenth-Century Europe.* 2d ed. London, 1985.

Kennedy, Paul M. 'German Colonial Expansion: Has the "Manipulated Social Imperialism" Been Antedated?' *PP* 54 (1972): 134–41.

– 'Tirpitz and the Second Navy Law of 1900: A Strategical Critique.' *MM* 2 (1970): 33–57.

Kennedy, Paul, and Anthony Nicholls, eds. *Nationalist and Racialist Movements in Britain and Germany before 1914.* London, 1981.

Kiefer, Rolf. *Karl Bachem 1858–1945: Politiker und Historiker des Zentrums.* Mainz, 1989.

Kirchheimer, Otto. 'The Transformation of the West European Party Systems.' In LaPalombara and Weiner, eds., *Political Parties*, pp. 177–214.

Kitching, Gavin. *Development and Underdevelopment in Historical Perspective: Populism, Nationalism, and Industrialization.* Rev. ed. London, 1989.

Klein, Fritz, ed. *Studien zum deutschen Imperialismus vor 1914.* Berlin, 1976.

Knobel, Enno. *Die Hessische Rechtspartei: Konservative Opposition gegen das Bismarckreich.* Marburg, 1975.

Koch, H.W. *A Constitutional History of Germany in the Nineteenth and Twentieth Centuries.* London/New York, 1984.

Kohut, Thomas A. *Wilhelm II and the Germans: A Study in Leadership.* Oxford, 1991.

Kruck, Alfred. *Geschichte des Alldeutschen Verbandes, 1890–1939.* Wiesbaden, 1954.

Kuczynski, Jürgen. *1903: Ein normales Jahr im imperialistischen Deutschland.* Cologne, 1988.

Kühne, Thomas. *Dreiklassenwahlrecht und Wahlkultur in Preussen 1867–1914: Landtagswahlen zwischen korporativer Tradition und politischem Massenmarkt.* Düsseldorf, 1994.

– 'Wahlrecht – Wahlverhalten – Wahlkultur: Tradition und Innovation in der historischen Wahlforschung.' *Archiv für Sozialgeschichte* 33 (1993): 481–547.

Laclau, Ernesto. *Politics and Ideology in Marxist Theory: Capitalism-Fascism-Populism.* London, 1977.

Lambi, Ivo Nikolai. *Free Trade and Protection in Germany, 1868–1879.* Wiesbaden, 1963.

– *The Navy and German Power Politics, 1862–1914.* Boston, 1984.

Lane, Jan-Erik, and Svante O. Ersson. *Politics and Society in Western Europe.* 2d ed. London, 1991.

Langewiesche, Dieter. 'German Liberalism in the Second Empire, 1871–1914.' In Jarausch and Jones, eds., *In Search of a Liberal Germany*, pp. 217–36.

LaPalombara, Joseph, and Myron Weiner, eds. *Political Parties and Political Development.* Princeton, 1966.

Lederer, Emil. 'Das ökonomische Element und die politische Idee im modernen Parteiwesen.' In Ritter, ed., *Die deutschen Parteien*, pp. 120–36.

Lehmann, Hans Georg. *Die Agrarfrage in der Theorie und Praxis der deutschen und internationalen Sozialdemokratie: Vom Marxismus zum Revisionismus und Bolshewismus.* Tübingen, 1970.

Lepsius, M. Rainer. 'Parteiensystem und Sozialstruktur: Zum Problem der Demokratisierung der deutschen Gesellschaft.' In Ritter, ed., *Die deutschen Parteien*, pp. 56–80.

Levy, Richard S. *The Downfall of the Anti-Semitic Political Parties in Imperial Germany.* New Haven/London, 1975.

Lidtke, Vernon L. *The Alternative Culture: Socialist Labour in Imperial Germany.* New York/Oxford, 1985.

– 'Recent Literature on Workers' Culture in Germany and England.' *HZ* Sonderheft 15 (1986).

Lijphart, Arend, Don Aitkin, et al. *Electoral Systems and Party Systems: A Study of Twenty-Seven Democracies, 1945–1990.* Oxford, 1994.

Lipset, Seymour Martin. *Political Man: The Social Bases of Politics.* 2d ed. London, 1983.

Lipset, Seymour M., and Stein Rokkan. 'Cleavage Structures, Party Systems, and Voter Alignments: An Introduction.' In Lipset and Rokkan, eds., *Party Systems and Voter Alignments*, pp. 1–64.

– eds. *Party Systems and Voter Alignments: Cross-National Perspectives.* New York, 1967.

Loock, H.-D., and H. Schulze, eds. *Parlamentarismus und Demokratie im Europa des 19. Jahrhunderts.* Munich, 1982.

Lorenz, Ina Susanne. *Eugen Richter: Der entschiedene Liberalismus in wilhelminischer Zeit 1871 bis 1906.* Husum, 1981.

Loth, Wilfried. *Katholiken im Kaiserreich: Der politische Katholizismus in der Krise des wilhelminischen Deutschlands.* Düsseldorf, 1984.

Maehl, William Harvey. 'German Social Democratic Agrarian Policy 1890–1895, Reconsidered.' *CEH* 13.2 (June 1980): 121–57.

Mann, Bernhard. 'Zwischen Hegemonie und Partikularismus: Bemerkungen zum Verhältnis von Regierung, Bürokratie und Parlament in Preußen 1867–1918.' In Ritter, ed., *Die deutschen Parteien*, pp. 76–89.

Mann, Golo. 'The Second German Empire: The Reich That Never Was.' In Feuchtwanger, ed., *Upheaval and Continuity*, pp. 29–46.

Martel, Gordon, ed. *Modern Germany Reconsidered, 1870–1945.* London/New York, 1992.

Maxeiner, Rudolf. *Vertrauen in die eigene Kraft: Wilhelm Haas, Sein Leben und Wirken.* Wiesbaden, 1976

McPhee, Peter. 'Electoral Democracy and Direct Democracy in France, 1789–1851.' *EHQ* 16.1 (Jan. 1986): 77–96.

Menke-Glückert, Peter. 'Wilhelminischer Liberalismus aus aktueller Sicht.' In Holl and List, eds., *Liberalismus und imperialistischer Staat*, pp. 35–9.

Messerschmidt, Manfred. 'Reich und Nation im Bewußtsein der wilhelminischen Gesellschaft.' In Schottelius and Deist, eds., *Marine und Marinepolitik*, pp. 11–33.

Milatz, Alfred. 'Die linksliberalen Parteien und Gruppen in den Reichstagswahlen 1871 bis 1912.' In Büsch, Wölk, and Wölk, eds., *Wählerbewegung*, pp. 325–44.

Möckl, Karl. *Die Prinzregentenzeit: Gesellschaft und Politik während der Ära des Prinzregenten Luitpold in Bayern.* Munich/Vienna, 1972.

Moeller, Robert G. 'Peasants and Tariffs in the *Kaiserreich*: How Backward were the *Bauern*?' *Agricultural History* 55.4 (Oct. 1981): 370–84.

Molt, Peter. *Der Reichstag vor der improvisierten Revolution.* Cologne/Opladen, 1963.

Mommsen, Wolfgang J. 'Domestic Factors in German Foreign Policy before 1914.' *CEH* 6.1 (March 1973): 223–68.

– 'Wandlungen der liberalen Idee im Zeitalter des Imperialismus.' In Holl and List, eds., *Liberalismus und imperialistischer Staat*, pp. 109–47.

Monshausen, Theo. 'Politische Wahlen im Regierungsbezirk Koblenz 1880 bis 1897.' Diss. Bonn 1969.

Mosse, G.L. *The Crisis of German Ideology: Intellectual Origins of the Third Reich.* New York, 1964.

Mouffe, Chantal, ed. *Gramsci and Marxist Theory.* London, 1979.

Müller, Klaus. 'Das Rheinland als Gegenstand der historischen Wahlsoziologie.' In Büsch, Wölk, and Wölk, eds., *Wählerbewegung*, pp. 393–408.

– 'Zentrumspartei und agrarische Bewegung im Rheinland 1882–1903.' In Repgen and Skalweit, eds., *Spiegel der Geschichte*, pp. 828–57.

Mundle, George Frederick. 'The German National Liberal Party, 1900–1914: Political Revival and Resistance to Change.' Diss. University of Illinois at Urbana-Champagne 1975.

Nettl, J. *Rosa Luxemburg.* Oxford, 1966.

Niehuss, Merith. 'Party Configurations in State and Municipal Elections in Southern Germany, 1871–1914.' In Rohe, ed., *Elections, Parties and Political Traditions*, pp. 83–106.

Nipperdey, Thomas. *Gesellschaft, Kultur, Theorie: Gesammelte Aufsatze zur neueren Geschichte.* Göttingen, 1976.

– 'Grundprobleme der deutschen Parteigeschichte im 19. Jahrhundert.' In Ritter, ed., *Die deutschen Parteien*, pp. 32–54.

– *Die Organisation der deutschen Parteien vor 1918.* Düsseldorf, 1961.

Nocken, Ulrich. 'Corporatism and Pluralism in Modern German History.' In Stegmann et al., eds., *Industrielle Gesellschaft*, pp. 37–56.

Nolan, Mary. *Social Democracy and Society: Working Class Radicalism in Düsseldorf 1890–1920.* New York/London, 1981.

Nolte, E. 'Deutscher Scheinkonstitutionalismus?' HZ 228 (1979): 529–50.

O'Donnell, Anthony Joseph. 'National Liberalism and the Mass Politics of the German Right, 1890–1907.' Diss. Princeton 1974.

Offord, Derek. *The Russian Revolutionary Movement in the 1880s.* Cambridge, 1986.

Panebianco, Angelo. *Political Parties: Organization and Power.* Trans. Marc Silver. Cambridge, 1988 (orig. Italian edition 1982).

Peal, David. 'The Politics of Populism: Germany and the American South in the 1890s.' *Comparative Studies in Society and History* 31 (April 1989): 340–62.

Perkins, J.A. 'The Agricultural Revolution in Germany, 1850–1914.' *JEEH* 10 (1981): 71–118.

Pflanze, Otto, ed. *Innenpolitische Probleme des Bismarck-Reiches.* Munich/Vienna, 1983.

Pogge von Strandmann, Hartmut. 'The Domestic Origins of Germany's Colonial Expansion under Bismarck.' PP 42 (1969): 140–59.

– 'The Liberal Power Monopoly in the Cities of Imperial Germany.' In Jones and Retallack, eds., *Elections, Mass Politics and Social Change*, pp. 93–117.

– 'Nationale Verbände zwischen Weltpolitik und Kontinentalpolitik.' In Schottelius and Deist, eds., *Marine und Marinepolitik*, pp. 296–317.

- 'Staatsstreichpläne, Alldeutsche und Bethmann Hollweg.' In Pogge and Geiss, eds., *Die Erforderlichkeit des Unmöglichen*, pp. 7–45.
- 'Widersprüche im Modernisierungsprozeß Deutschlands: Der Kampf der verarbeitenden Industrie gegen die Schwerindustrie.' In Stegmann et al., eds., *Industrielle Gesellschaft*, pp. 225–40.

Pogge von Strandmann, Hartmut, and Imanuel Geiss, eds. *Die Erforderlichkeit des Unmöglichen: Deutschland am Vorabend des ersten Weltkrieges*. Frankfurt a.M., 1965.

Pollack, Norman. *The Populist Response to Industrial America: Midwestern Populist Thought*. Cambridge, Mass., 1962.

Przeworski, Adam, and John Sprague. *Paper Stones: A History of Electoral Socialism*. Chicago, 1986.

Puhle, Hans-Jürgen. *Agrarische Interessenpolitik und preußischer Konservatismus im wilhelminischen Reich (1893–1914): Ein Beitrag zur Analyse des Nationalismus in Deutschland am Beispiel des Bundes der Landwirte und der Deutsch-Konservativen Partei*. Hanover, 1966.
- 'Parlament, Parteien und Interessenverbände 1890–1914.' In Stürmer, ed., *Das kaiserliche Deutschland*, pp. 340–77.
- *Politische Agrarbewegungen in kapitalistischen Industriegesellschaften: Deutschland, USA und Frankreich im 20. Jahrhundert*. Göttingen, 1975.
- 'Radikalisierung und Wandel des deutschen Konservatismus vor dem ersten Weltkrieg.' In Ritter, ed., *Die deutschen Parteien*, pp. 165–86.

Pulzer, Peter. *The Rise of Political Anti-Semitism in Germany and Austria*. New York/London/Sydney, 1964.

Rae, Douglas W. *The Political Consequences of Electoral Laws*. New Haven, 1967.

Rauh, Manfred. *Föderalismus und Parlamentarismus im wilhelminischen Reich*. Düsseldorf, 1973.
- *Die Parlamentarisierung des Deutschen Reiches*. Düsseldorf, 1977.

Reeve, Andrew, and Alan Ware. *Electoral Systems: A Comparative and Theoretical Introduction*. London, 1992.

Reinders, Christoph. 'Sozialdemokratie und Immigration: Eine Untersuchung der Entwicklungsmöglichkeiten der SPD in einem überwiegend ländlich geprägten Reichstagswahlkreis auf der Grundlage der Wahlbewegung von 1893 bis 1912.' In Günther, ed., *Parteien und Wahlen in Oldenburg*, pp. 65–116.

Repgen, Konrad, and Stephan Skalweit, eds. *Spiegel der Geschichte: Festgabe für Max Braubach zum 10. April 1964*. Münster, 1964.

Retallack, James N. 'Antisocialism and Electoral Politics in Regional Perspective: The Kingdom of Saxony.' In Jones and Retallack, eds., *Elections, Mass Politics, and Social Change*, pp. 49–91.
- 'Conservatives *contra* Chancellor: Official Responses to the Spectre of Conservative Demagoguery from Bismarck to Bülow.' *CJH* 20.2 (Aug. 1985): 203–36.

– *Notables of the Right: The Conservative Party and Political Mobilization in Germany, 1876–1918.* Boston, 1988.
– 'Social History with a Vengeance? Some Reactions to H.-U. Wehler's "Das Deutsche Kaiserreich."' *German Studies Review* 7.3 (Oct. 1984): 423–50.
– '"What Is to Be Done?" The Red Specter, Franchise Questions, and the Crisis of Conservative Hegemony in Saxony, 1896–1909.' *CEH* 23.4 (Dec. 1990): 271–312.
– 'Wilhelmine Germany.' In Martel, ed., *Modern Germany Reconsidered*, pp. 33–53.
Ringer, Fritz K. *The Decline of the German Mandarins: The German Academic Community, 1890–1933.* Cambridge, Mass., 1969.
Ritter, G.A. *Arbeiterbewegung, Parteien und Parlamentarismus: Aufsätze zur deutschen Sozial- und Verfassungsgeschichte des 19. und 20. Jahrhunderts.* Göttingen, 1976.
– 'The Social Bases of the German Political Parties, 1867–1920.' In Rohe, ed., *Elections, Parties and Political Traditions*, pp. 27–52.
– *Staat, Arbeiterschaft und Arbeiterbewegung in Deutschland: Vom Vormärz bis zum Ende der Weimarer Republik.* Berlin/Bonn, 1980.
– 'Staat und Arbeiterschaft in Deutschland von der Revolution 1848/49 bis zur nationalsozialistischer Mactergreifung.' *HZ* 231.2 (Oct. 1980): 325–68.
– 'Zur Strategie und Erfolg der sozialdemokratischen Wählerrekrutierung im Kaiserreich.' In Büsch, Wölk, and Wölk, eds., *Wählerbewegung*, pp. 313–24.
– ed. *Die deutschen Parteien vor 1918.* Cologne, 1973.
– ed. *Regierung, Bürokratie und Parlament in Preußen und Deutschland von 1848 bis zur Gegenwart.* Düsseldorf, 1983.
Rohe, Karl. 'German Elections and Party Systems in Historical and Regional Perspective: An Introduction.' In Rohe, ed., *Elections, Parties and Political Traditions*, pp. 1–26.
– 'Konfession, Klasse und lokale Gesellschaft als Bestimmungsfaktoren des Wahlverhaltens: Überlegungen und Problematisierungen am Beispiel des historischen Ruhrgebiets.' In Albertin and Link, eds., *Politische Parteien*, pp. 109–26.
– 'Political Alignments and Re-alignments in the Ruhr, 1867–1987: Continuity and Change of Political Traditions in an Industrial Region.' In Rohe, ed., *Elections, Parties and Political Traditions*, pp. 107–44.
– 'Die "verspätete" Region: Thesen und Hypothesen zur Wahlentwicklung im Ruhrgebiet vor 1914.' In Steinbach, ed., *Probleme politischer Partizipation*, pp. 231–52.
– 'Die Vorgeschichte: Das Parteiensystem in den preußischen Westprovinzen und in Lippe-Detmold 1871–1933.' In Alemann, ed., *Parteien und Wahlen in Nordrhein-Westfalen*, 22–47.
– 'Wahlanalyse im historischen Kontext: Zur Kontinuität und Wandel von Wahlverhalten.' *HZ* 234 (1982): 337–57.

– *Wahlen und Wählertraditionen in Deutschland.* Frankfurt, 1992.
– ed. *Elections, Parties and Political Traditions: Social Foundations of German Parties and Party Systems, 1867–1987.* New York, 1990.
Röhl, John C.G. 'Beamtenpolitik im wilhelminischen Deutschland.' In Stürmer, ed., *Das kaiserliche Deutschland,* pp. 287–311.
– *Germany without Bismarck: The Crisis of Government in the Second Reich, 1890–1900.* London, 1967.
– 'Higher Civil Servants in Germany, 1890–1900.' In Sheehan, ed., *Imperial Germany,* pp. 129–51.
Röhl, John C.G., and Sombart, Nicolaus, eds. *Kaiser Wilhelm II: New Interpretations.* Cambridge/London/New York, 1982.
Rokkan, Stein. *Citizens, Elections, Parties: Approaches to the Comparative Study of the Processes of Development.* New York/Oslo, 1970.
– 'Electoral Mobilization, Party Competition and National Integration.' In LaPalombara and Weiner, eds., *Political Parties,* pp. 241–61.
– 'Wahlrecht und Wahlentscheidung.' In Büsch, Wölk, and Wölk, eds., *Wählerbewegung,* pp. 85–96.
Romeyk, Horst. 'Die politischen Wahlen im Regierungsbezirk Koblenz 1898 bis 1918.' Diss. Bonn 1969.
Rose, Richard, ed. *Electoral Behavior: A Comparative Handbook.* New York, 1973.
– ed. *Electoral Participation: A Comparative Analysis.* Beverly Hills, 1980.
Rosenberg, Hans. 'Political and Social Consequences of the Great Depression of 1873–1896 in Central Europe.' In Sheehan, ed., *Imperial Germany,* pp. 39–60.
Rosenhaft, Eve. 'Women, Gender, and the Limits of Political History in the Age of "Mass" Politics.' In Jones and Retallack, eds., *Elections, Mass Politics, and Social Change,* pp. 149–73.
Ross, Ronald J. *Beleaguered Tower: The Dilemma of Political Catholicism in Wilhelmine Germany.* Notre Dame/London, 1976.
Roth, Anni. 'Politische Strömungen in den rechtsrheinischen Kreisen Mülheim, Wipperfürth, Gummersbach, Waldbröl und Sieg des Regierungsbezirks Köln 1900–1919.' Diss. Bonn 1968.
Roth, Günther. *The Social Democrats in Imperial Germany: A Study in Working Class Isolation and National Integration.* Totowa, New Jersey, 1963.
Sagarra, Eda. *A Social History of Germany, 1648–1914.* New York, 1977.
Sartori, Giovanni. 'European Political Parties: The Case of Polarized Pluralism.' In LaPalombara and Weiner, eds., *Political Parties,* pp. 137–76.
Saul, Klaus. *Staat, Industrie, Arbeiterbewegung im Kaiserreich: Zur Innen- und Außenpolitik des wilhelminischen Deutschlands, 1903–1914.* Düsseldorf, 1974.
– 'Um die konservative Struktur Ostelbiens: Agrarische interessen, Staatsver-

waltung und ländliche "Arbeiternot." Zur konservativen Landarbeiterpolitik in Preußen-Deutschland, 1889–1914.' In Stegmann, et al., eds., *Konservatismus*, pp. 129–98.

Saul, Klaus, Jens Flemming, Dirk Stegmann, and Peter-Christian Witt, eds. *Arbeiterfamilien im Kaiserreich: Materialen zur Sozialgeschichte in Deutschland, 1871–1914.* Düsseldorf, 1982.

Schanbacher, Eberhard. *Parlamentarische Wahlen und Wahlsystem in der Weimarer Republik: Wahlgesetzgebung und Wahlreform im Reich und in den Ländern.* Düsseldorf, 1982.

Schauff, Johannes. 'Katholische Wähler und Zentrumspartei.' In Büsch, Wölk, and Wölk, eds., *Wählerbewegung*, pp. 219–24.

Schmädeke, Jürgen. *Wählerbewegung im Wilhelminischen Deutschland.* 2 vols. Berlin, 1995.

Schorske, Carl E. *German Social Democracy 1905–1917: The Development of the Great Schism.* Cambridge, Mass., 1955.

Schottelius, Herbert, and Wilhelm Deist, eds. *Marine und Marinepolitik im kaiserlichen Deutschland 1871–1914.* Düsseldorf, 1972.

Schoultz, Lars. *The Populist Challenge: Argentine Electoral Behavior in the Postwar Era.* Chapel Hill, N.C., 1983.

Schulte, Wolfgang. 'Die ökologischen Korrelate der Parteien in den württembergischen Wahlen zur Zeit des Kaiserreichs.' In Büsch, Wölk, and Wölk, eds., *Wählerbewegung*, pp. 454–81.

Schulze, Hagen. 'Preußen und das Reich.' In Loock and Schulze, eds., *Parlamentarismus und Demokratie*, pp. 156–72.

Schumpeter, Joseph A. *Capitalism, Socialism, and Democracy*, 3d ed. New York, 1975 (1st ed. publ. 1942).

Schwarz, Max, ed. *MdR: Biographisches Handbuch der Reichstage.* Hanover, 1965.

Seymour, Charles, and Donald Paige Frary. *How the World Votes: The Story of Democratic Development in Elections.* 2 vols. Springfield, Mass., 1918.

Sheehan, James J. 'Conflict and Cohesion among German Elites in the Nineteenth Century.' In Sheehan, ed., *Imperial Germany*, pp. 62–92.

– *German Liberalism in the Nineteenth Century.* Chicago, 1978.

– 'Klasse und Partei im Kaiserreich: Einige Gedanken zur Sozialgeschichte der deutschen Politik.' In Pflanze, ed., *Innenpolitische Probleme*, pp. 1–24.

– 'Politische Führung im Deutschen Reichstag, 1871–1918.' In Ritter, ed., *Die deutschen Parteien*, pp. 81–99.

– ed. *Imperial Germany.* New York / London, 1976.

Simon, Klaus. 'Die soziale Struktur der württembergischen Volkspartei und ihre Auswirkung auf Programm und Politik der Partei (1882–1914).' In Ritter, ed., *Die deutschen Parteien*, pp. 224–42.

Smith, Woodruff, and Sharon A. Turner. 'Legislative Behaviour in the German Reichstag, 1898–1906.' *CEH* 14.1 (March 1981): 3–29.

Sperber, Jonathan. *Popular Catholicism in Nineteenth-Century Germany.* Princeton, 1984.

Stegmann, Dirk. *Die Erben Bismarcks: Parteien und Verbände in der Spätphase des wilhelminischen Deutschlands: Sammlungspolitik 1897–1918.* Cologne/Berlin, 1970.

– 'Wirtschaft und Politik nach Bismarcks Sturz: Zur Genesis der Miquelschen Sammlungspolitik 1890–1897.' In Geiss and Wendt, eds., *Deutschland in der Weltpolitik,* pp. 161–84.

Stegmann, Dirk, Bernd-Jürgen Wendt, and Peter-Christian Witt, eds. *Deutscher Konservatismus im 19. und 20. Jahrhundert: Festschrift für Fritz Fischer zum 75. Geburtstag und zum 50. Doktorjubiläum.* Bonn, 1983.

– eds. *Industrielle Gesellschaft und politisches System: Beiträge zur politischen Sozialgeschichte: Festschrift für Fritz Fischer zum siebzigsten Geburtstag.* Bonn, 1978.

Steinbach, Peter. 'Nationalisierung, soziale Differenzierung und Urbanisierung als Bedingungsfaktoren des Wahlverhaltens im Kaiserreich.' *Quantum* 2 (1990).

– 'Reichstag Elections in the Kaiserreich: The Prospects for Electoral Research in the Interdisciplinary Context.' In Jones and Retallack, eds., *Elections, Mass Politics, and Social Change,* pp. 119–46.

– 'Stand und Methode der historischen Wahlforschung: Bemerkungen zur interdisziplinären Kooperation von moderner Sozialgeschichte und den politisch-historischen Sozialwissenschaften.' In Kaelble et al., eds., *Probleme der Modernisierung,* pp. 171–234.

– *Die Zähmung des politischen Massenmarktes: Wahlen und Wahlkämpfe im Bismarckreich im Spiegel der Hauptstadt- und Gesinnungspresse.* 3 vols. Passau, 1990.

– ed. *Probleme politischer Partizipation im Modernisierungsprozeß.* Stuttgart, 1982.

Steinberg, Jonathan. *Yesterday's Deterrent: Tirpitz and the Birth of the German Battle Fleet.* London, 1965.

Stern, Fritz. 'Die politische Folgen des unpolitischen Deutschen.' In Stürmer, ed., *Das kaiserliche Deutschland,* pp. 168–86.

– *The Politics of Cultural Despair: A Study in the Rise of the Germanic Ideology.* Berkeley, 1961.

Steyer, Armin. 'Die Entwicklung der liberalen Parteien in Oldenburg: Eine regionalhistorische Untersuchung auf der Grundlage der Reichstagswahlen von 1893 bis 1912.' In Günther, ed., *Parteien und Wahlen in Oldenburg,* pp. 21–63.

Stürmer, Michael, ed. *Das kaiserliche Deutschland: Politik und Gesellschaft 1870–1918.* Düsseldorf, 1970.

Suval, Stanley. *Electoral Politics in Wilhelmine Germany.* Chapel Hill/London, 1985.

Taagepera, Rein, and Matthew Soberg Shugart. *Seats and Votes: The Effects and Determinants of Electoral Systems.* New Haven, 1989

Tenfelde, Klaus, ed. *Historische Zeitschrift.* Sonderheft 15: *Arbeiter und Arbeiterbewegung im Vergleich.* Munich, 1986.

Thieme, Hartwig. 'Die soziale und politische Struktur der nationalliberallen Fraktion des Preußischen Abgeordnetenhauses und ihre Stellung in der Gesamtpartei 1914–1918.' In Ritter, ed., *Die deutschen Parteien,* pp. 243–69.

Thränhardt, Dietrich. *Wahlen und politische Strukturen in Bayern 1848–1953: Historisch-soziologische Untersuchungen zum Entstehung und zur Neuerrichtung eines Parteiensystems.* Düsseldorf, 1973.

Tims, Richard Wonser. *Germanizing Prussian Poland: The H-K-T Society and the Struggle for the Eastern Marches in the German Empire, 1894–1919.* New York, 1966.

Tirrell, Sarah Rebecca. *German Agrarian Politics after Bismarck's Fall: The Formation of the Farmers' League.* New York, 1951.

Tormin, Walter. 'Der Reichstag im Kaiserreich.' In Schwarz, ed., *Biographisches Handbuch der Reichstage,* pp. 115–36.

Ullmann, Hans-Peter. *Der Bund der Industriellen: Organisation, Einfluß und Politik klein- und mittelbetrieblicher Industriellen im Deutschen Kaiserreich 1895–1914.* Göttingen, 1976.

Vogel, Bernhard, Dieter Nohlen, and Rainer-Olaf Schultze. *Wahlen in Deutschland: Theorie-Geschichte-Dokumente 1848–1970.* New York/Berlin, 1971.

Volkov, Shulamit. *The Rise of Popular Anti-Modernism in Germany: The Urban Master Artisans, 1873–1896.* Princeton, 1978.

Ward, Frank Joseph. 'The Center Party and the German Election of 1907.' Diss. University of California at Los Angeles 1984.

Ware, Alan. *Citizens, Parties and the State: A Reappraisal.* Princeton, 1987.
– *The Logic of Party Democracy.* New York, 1979.

Weber, Christoph. *Der 'Fall Spahn' (1901): Ein Beitrag zur Wissenschafts- und Kulturdiskussion im ausgehenden 19. Jahrhundert.* Rome, 1980.

Wehler, Hans-Ulrich. 'Bismarck's Imperialism 1862–1880.' *PP* 48 (1970): 119–55.
– *Das Deutsche Kaiserreich 1871–1918.* Göttingen, 1977.
– *Krisenherde des Kaiserreichs 1871–1918: Studien zur deutschen Sozial- und Verfassungsgeschichte.* Göttingen, 1970.
– ed. *Imperialismus.* Cologne/Berlin, 1970.
– ed. *Moderne deutsche Sozialgeschichte.* Düsseldorf, 1981.

Weidner, Rolf. *Wahlen und soziale Strukturen in Ludwigshafen am Rhein 1871–1914: Unter besonderer Berücksichtigung der Reichstagswahlen.* Ludwigshafen, 1984.

White, Dan S. *The Splintered Party: National Liberalism in Hessen and the Reich, 1867–1918.* Cambridge, Mass. / London, 1976.

Wichard, Rudolf. *Wahlen in Hildesheim 1867 bis 1972.* Hildesheim/New York, 1975.

Wilke, Ekkehard-Teja P.W. *Political Decadence in Imperial Germany: Personnel-Political Aspects of the German Government Crisis 1894–1897.* Urbana/Chicago/London, 1976.

Winkler, Heinrich August. *Liberalismus und Antiliberalismus: Studien zur politischen Sozialgeschichte des 19. und 20. Jahrhunderts.* Göttingen, 1979.

– ed. *Organisierter Kapitalismus: Voraussetzungen und Anfänge.* Göttingen, 1974.

Winzen, Peter. *Bülows Weltmachtkonzept: Untersuchungen zur Frühphase seiner Außenpolitik 1897–1901.* Boppard am Rhein, 1977.

Witt, Peter-Christian. 'Innenpolitik und Imperialismus in der Vorgeschichte des 1. Weltkrieges.' In Holl and List, eds., *Liberalismus und imperialistischer Staat,* pp. 7–34.

– 'Konservatismus als "Ueberparteilichkeit": Die Beamten der Reichskanzlei zwischen Kaiserreich und Weimarer Republik 1900–1933.' In Stegmann et al., eds., *Konservatismus,* pp. 231–80.

Wölk, Wolfgang. 'Sozialstruktur, Parteienkorrelation und Wahlentscheidung im Kaiserreich am Beispiel der Reichstagswahl von 1907.' In Büsch, Wölk, and Wölk, eds., *Wählerbewegung,* pp. 505–48.

Zang, Gert, ed. *Provinzialisierung einer Region: Regionale Unterentwicklung und liberale Politik in der Stadt und im Kreis Konstanz im 19. Jahrhundert: Untersuchungen zur Entstehung der bürgerlichen Gesellschaft in der Provinz.* Frankfurt a.M., 1978.

Zangerl, Carl H.E. 'Courting the Catholic Vote: The Center Party in Baden, 1903–13.' *CEH* 10.3 (Sept. 1977): 220–40.

Zeender, John K. *The German Center Party 1890–1906. (Transactions of the American Philosophical Society* N.S. 66.1 [1976].)

Zmarzlik, Hans-Günther. 'Das Kaiserreich als Einbahnstraße?' In Holl and List, eds., *Liberalismus und imperialistischer Staat,* pp. 62–71.

Zwehl, Konrad von. 'Zum Verhältnis von Regierung und Reichstag im Kaiserreich (1871–1918).' In Ritter, ed., *Regierung, Bürokratie und Parlament,* pp. 90–116.

Index